Accounting for the banker

Second Edition

Don A. Egginton

Longman
London and New York

Longman Group Limited
Longman House, Burnt Mill, Harlow
Essex CM20 2JE, England
Associated companies throughout the world

Published in the United States of America
by Longman Inc., New York

First published 1977
Fourth impression 1980
Second edition 1982

British Library Cataloguing in Publication Data

Egginton, Don A.
Accounting for the banker.—2nd ed.
1. Accounting 2. Banks and banking—Accounting
I. Title
657'.024332 HF5635
ISBN 0-582-29633-1

Library of Congress Cataloguing in Publication Data

Egginton, Don A.
Accounting for the banker.
Includes bibliographical references and index.
1. Banks and banking—Accounting. I. Title.
HG1706.E5 1982 657'.833 82-13018
ISBN 0-582-29633-1

Set in IBM Journal Roman
Printed in Great Britain by
The Pitman Press Ltd., Bath

Contents

Preface

The purpose of this book is implicit in its title: to offer an exposition of the subject of accounting which is directed towards the needs of the banker.

The banker's interest in accounting information is particularly concerned with lending. As a lender he has more opportunity to explore behind the customer's annual financial reports than the 'arm's-length' user for whom those reports are primarily prepared. On the other hand the banker's stance is different from that of the preparer of accounts, to whom many accounting textbooks are directed.

The approach I have attempted to follow has been to explain the basic material in the area of accounting which a banker needs to understand if he is equipped to appreciate a business customer's finances. That has led me to examine many issues which are necessary for a background knowledge, but which do not supply the banker with ready-made techniques for practising on the next customer he meets. It has also led me to curtail the consideration of a variety of topics which are interesting and controversial for accountants but whose pursuit would not serve the purpose in hand.

Many readers of this book are likely to be preparing for the second stage of their banking examinations, although I hope that its contents will also prove useful to experienced bankers. Consequently the majority of readers will have at least an introductory knowledge of accounts. Despite that, Chapter 2 provides a simple explanation of the double-entry recording process and Chapter 3 examines the principles of the three main accounting summaries. The reason for this apparent contradiction is that these chapters offer revision for students and provide the means of expressing certain basic ideas which are important to later understanding. These are, in particular, the notion of *movement* in the operating and accounting structure of the living enterprise as an antidote to the traditional static balance sheet view, and the distinctions between flows of cash, working capital and profits. In my experience the confusion of banking students on such basic issues is often a hindrance to their understanding of more advanced aspects of the interpretation of accounting information.

The subsequent sequence of chapters is largely dictated by the need to give the reader certain pieces of information before going on to a fresh topic. Chapter 4 develops from the preceding chapters in presenting a largely 'insider' view of costs, profits and cash flows. Chapters 5, 6 and 7 examine tax, project appraisal and financial structure – all of which have substantial implications for the business customer's finances. Chapters 8 and 9 cover financial reporting in company accounts and accounting for price changes – popularly known as 'inflation accounting'. Aspects relating to interpretation of accounting information occupy

Chapters 10 and 11. Finally, in recognition that risk-taking cannot always be successful, Chapter 12 considers financial failure.

It is sometimes said that accountants are rarely happy about any mathematical process which goes beyond addition and subtraction, and in preparing this book I have tried to bear in mind that bankers are not on average more numerate than accountants. It has, however, proved necessary to go as far as multiplication and division and to use some equations with algebraic symbols. I hope that these features will not prove unduly daunting.

Some calculations which may strike many bankers as outlandish are those involving probabilities in the consideration of risk – although any readers familiar with the finance literature or decision theory may object that the treatments adopted are oversimplified. My response to both groups would be that a simple framework for ideas on risk can swiftly convey a basic appreciation which could not be achieved from pages of discussion.

Another aspect on which I have tried to strike a balance concerns the references. These references, which are given at the end of each chapter together with the notes, can serve as signposts for further reading; some are specifically expressed in those terms, although others appear purely as acknowledgements of material in the text. However, the references have been kept to a minimum to avoid intimidating the reader, and in certain cases material which has influenced the arguments has not been referenced, although 'leads' have been supplied (for example, in Chapters 6 and 7).

It has been suggested to me that the book which has emerged may be of interest to many non-bankers. Such individuals to whom it seems most likely to appeal would be non-accounting executives in industry who are seeking a broad understanding of the accounting process and its implication for financing.

In the preparation of this volume I have received help and encouragement from many people. First mention must go to Eric Glover, Director of Studies at the Institute of Bankers, who has provided both information and introductions. It is Eric Glover who must share responsibility with Peter Spiro, Librarian of the Institute, for giving encouragement to the original idea for this textbook – longer ago than I care to admit. I am also grateful to the Institute of Bankers for permission to adapt material which I wrote for the *Journal of the Institute of Bankers* in 1974 and 1975, and to the Institute of Bankers in Scotland for advice received.

The bankers from whom I have received assistance and advice are very numerous. Much of this help related to the survey of information for company lending which appears in Appendix F and is the subject of comment in Chapter 11. But, in addition, I benefited from background discussions which influenced my general approach. I appreciated the courtesy and frankness with which my enquiries were answered. Since the list of individual participants in the survey would be very long, and in any case some bankers would prefer not to be named, I hope I will be forgiven for conveying thanks to the institutions involved: the Bank of Ireland, Barclays Bank, the Industrial and Commercial Finance Corporation, Lloyds Bank, the Midland Bank, the National Westminster Bank, the Northern Bank and the Bank of Scotland.

My thanks are also due to several people who read sections of the typescript: Pete Elliott, John Farrar, Steve Garner, Geoff Whittington and particularly Richard Morris who bravely read it all. Their comments were invaluable but the errors that remain are undoubtedly the result of overlooking some of their advice. Val Harvey and Mary Harthan, who did most of the typing, cheerfully transformed my handwriting and some very messy tables of figures into a legible form. Finally, I must acknowledge the patience of two groups of people: the editorial staff of Longman who were extraordinarily tactful over a long-delayed typescript and the members of my family, whose support was unfailing.

Don Egginton

June 1976

Preface to the Second Edition

A number of developments have led to this new edition. The Companies Act 1981 has greatly changed the rules for the presentation of company accounts, although the effect on content is more modest. Accounting standards have been pouring forth from the Accounting Standards Committee, bringing mixed blessings and changes which affect the accounting reports of bank customers.

The chapters most concerned with these changes are Chapters 8 and 9, on company accounts and accounting for price changes. Chapter 8 has been reorganized, and introduces the 1981 Companies Act, several new standards and the prospective leasing standard. A full example of a company's accounts under the 1981 Act is provided in Appendix B, which has comments giving reasons for the treatment of each item. Also connected with Chapter 8 is Appendix C, which provides most of the text of Schedule 1 of the 1981 Act, including the new formats required for accounts.

Chapter 9 has been largely rewritten to include the standard on current cost accounting, SSAP 16. However, as I am critical of certain aspects of SSAP 16 I have retained the approach of comparing 'simple' profit concepts, before launching into the standard itself. I hope this will give the reader some understanding of the important issues in price change accounting.

Smaller changes involve Chapter 5, which now includes the new method of stock relief for taxable profits, and Chapter 7, where alterations involve both the 1980 and 1981 Companies Acts.

I have been very conscious of the dangers of adding extra material to burden the reader. Consequently I have also done some pruning. In places this has involved simpler wording, but I have also deleted some tables of ratios which no longer seem essential. As a result the overall length of the book has hardly changed.

Unlike the first edition, this revision was written in a very short time. My thanks go to Val Harvey and Janet Wright who did the typing in even shorter time, in addition to their other duties.

Don Egginton

February 1982

Acknowledgements

We are grateful to the following for permission to reproduce copyright material:

Arthur Young McClelland Moores & Co for the Report and Accounts of Good Practice Limited from *The Companies Act 1981: Model Accounts*; British Leyland Motor Corporation Limited for summary of results 1973 and 1974 derived from *1974 Report*; The Director Publications Limited for a Table from 'The Why and How of Company Investment' from *The Director*, November 1970; Her Majesty's Stationery Office for reproduction of Schedule 1 from the *Companies Act 1981*; Institute of Bankers for adapted material from Question 7 of the Accountancy (Stage 2) examination April 1981 and from articles by D. A. Egginton, 'The Inflation Accounting Bandwagon, Oct. 1974', 'Taxes and Cash Flows, April 1975 and June 1975' in *Journal of the Institute of Bankers*.

Chapter 1

Aims and cautions

A bank that is so conducted as never to make a loss, will seldom make much profit.
J. W. Gilbart: *A Practical Treatise on Banking*

1.1 The banker and accounting information

The banker's need for some understanding of accounting statements is easily explained: the competent banker must be capable of appreciating the financial affairs of his business customers and accounts provide a fundamental source of financial information. How much the banker should know about the subject of accounting, and how much of this knowledge may contribute to his activities, are less readily determined. In approaching these questions it is necessary to commence with something about accounting.

Accounting is concerned with the quantification and interpretation of past and prospective economic transactions. The figures involved are commonly referred to as *data,* giving rise to the term 'data processing' to describe the mechanics of recording and summarizing, particularly when electronic equipment is used – equivalent, in non-electronic jargon, to double-entry bookkeeping. The dictionary definition of data as 'facts' should not mislead us into assuming that accounting deals in certainties, even when the accounting data relate to the past. Nowadays 6-year-old school-children learn that all forms of measurement involve estimation, and users of accounts should never forget that accounting is far from being an exception to that rule. Nor do accounting data invariably provide information in the sense of being *relevant* to a particular user's purpose, although it is convenient to refer to 'accounting information' when we are optimistically assuming that some parts of the data have relevance.

Any person or organization which indulges in economic transactions is a potential object of the accountant's attentions, but this book is essentially concerned with the profit-seeking enterprise. Such an enterprise, whether sole trader, partnership or company, will be described as a *business* or *firm* when legal status is not at issue; readers accustomed to assuming that a firm is a partnership are forewarned. Although many aspects of accounting can be applied to non-profit activities it is in the business sector that accounting can be most helpful to the banker – and it is that sector which provides by far the largest part of UK bank lending. Within the business sector companies are dominant, and they also prepare most accounting information; consequently, an emphasis on companies is appropriate.

The banker's primary concern with accounting information for lending purposes is set in the context of a continuing banker–customer relationship. The familiar annual accounts (balance sheet, profit and loss account and, increasingly, funds flow statement) are widely used by lenders, but they represent the externally visible tip of the iceberg of accounting activity. A great deal of control and decision information is prepared for internal use, particularly within the larger firm. The quality of such information is a key to the firm's conduct of its financial affairs.

Elements of the internal data, such as budgets, can contribute to lending decisions not simply in terms of figures but in providing clues to general competence in financial management. Small businesses often manage to survive with what Americans call a 'seat of the pants approach' – a mixture of intuition, luck, bravado and prayer, according to the temperament of the individual entrepreneur. Successful larger enterprises require planning, co-ordination, delegation and control, which demand (among other things) the underpinning of a viable accounting system. A transition to a larger scale of operations usually needs to be backed by corresponding developments in management approach if the experience is not to be painful for both the firm and its bankers. Moreover, the stable small firm can often benefit from relatively simple improvements in its techniques – in this respect the Bolton Report on Small Firms[1] is worth quoting at length:

The role of the bank manager as a business adviser is necessarily . . . limited. This is not true of the specialised investment houses like ICFC or the merchant banks, whose interest in the management of their client companies is very close, but the majority of small firms do not seek advice from them. Branch managers of the Clearing Banks naturally vary a great deal in their ability and readiness to give management advice of a general nature and it would clearly be unrealistic to expect them to spend much time in doing so: the cost of a day spent on the affairs of a small customer could easily exceed the annual profit of the bank on that customer's account. Even if management advice were charged for, the bank manager might merely be operating, insofar as he strayed outside financial matters, as a relatively inexpert management consultant to the detriment of his main function. We hope, however, that the Clearing Banks will consider whether they could further improve their services to the small businessman in two particular respects. *[Only the first is relevant here.] First, if it were possible for the banks to impose as a normal condition for the grant of an overdraft to a firm the production of regular cash-flow statements, or the employment of adequate estimating and budgetary systems, and if such disciplines, valuable in their own right, came to be recognised as being helpful for obtaining bank finance, the efficiency of small firms might be much increased. We do not suggest that a control system should be insisted on as a kind of bureaucratic formality, but rather that the bank manager might be able to improve the efficiency of his customers, in their interests and his own. He could also help them by pointing out the benefits of certain simple indices of the health of a business. . . . In this way he would give powerful support to the efforts of the accountant in improving the performance and hence the overall viability of the small firm sector.*

The extent to which bankers seek detailed accounting information beyond the annual accounts tends to depend on the circumstances of the lending; in general the larger the lending in relation to the customer's resources and the longer the contemplated lending period the greater are the banker's information requirements, in accounting and other forms, before and during lending. As the Bolton Report suggests, concern with such aspects is greatest in financial institutions which lend for long periods or contemplate equity participation – but the preference of clearing banks for short-term lending does not preclude an enduring interest in their customers' activities. Overdraft lending, although nominally repayable on demand, may in practice be tied up for several years, intentionally and otherwise. Moreover, UK banks have extended their involvement with term lending to a very considerable extent in recent years. The clearers are now providing finance over a wide time range, from the traditional short-run advance to the long-term loan. The banker needs a corresponding breadth of understanding of the customer's finances.

The above discussion explains why this book aims to provide a much wider view of financial information than 'how to read a balance sheet'. Chapters 4–7 in particular contain elements which, it is hoped, will contribute to this wider view. The treatment is intended to lend perspective and bring out some interrelationships between different aspects of potential interest to the banker – while avoiding excessive depth. From this background later chapters proceed to examine the content, limitations and implications of annual accounts.

1.2 The risk element

Risk is the so far unmentioned element which is central to bank lending decisions, and indeed all business decisions. Accounts can provide some clues to risk, but the banker's overall assessment must determine whether risk is within an acceptable margin. Since the risk context is so important, and yet apparently so difficult for banking students to understand, some attempt at definition is desirable. Definition does not solve the problem, but it helps to clarify the search.

A dictionary definition of risk is 'the chance of loss or unfavourable consequences'. Loss in lending may occur through financial failure of the customer or less dramatically through additional costs incurred in 'nursing' shaky lending. As Gilbart recognized in the opening quotation to this chapter, the efficient banker does not seek to eliminate risk but attempts to *balance* risk against prospective return from lending. This is implied when a lending proposition is described as a 'fair risk' – but that phrase needs closer examination.

Risk in its finance usage involves unknown outcomes to which objective or subjective probabilities can be attached. A simple example of an objective probability can be provided by the tossing of an unbiased coin. Sceptics can establish objective probabilities for the outcomes by a large number of trials, but to most of us it is obvious that 'heads' and 'tails' are equally probable – each has a 50 per cent chance of success, or a probability of 0.5 (where certainty = 1). A 'fair risk' for someone who staked £1 on the toss of a coin would imply payment of £2 for a successful outcome; over a very large number of throws gains should equal losses. Ignoring the possibilities of interest payments for the moment, this can be generalized in a simple formula as

$$\underset{\pounds 1}{\text{required return}} = \underset{\pounds 2}{\text{contractual return}} \times \underset{0{\cdot}5}{\text{probability of success}}$$

This example is a far cry from banking, but it has one important parallel. The returns required from different categories of lending are evident in the scale of interest rates charged by banks. A typical range of rates would be between 1 and 5 per cent per year above base rate. The base rate can be regarded as an absolutely risk-free lending rate, with the premiums above that level compensating for risk. There is a complication in the proportionately greater costs of dealing with small advances: the administrative costs of a £500 advance are likely to be more than one-hundredth of those of a £50,000 advance. The difference may be covered by the commission element in bank charges, but some of the premium charged to the small borrower (who is typically a greater risk) may also partially compensate for such costs. This complication is least relevant at the lower end of the premium scale, where companies tend to borrow at between 1 and 2 per cent above base rate. For a solidly dependable company borrowing at 1½ per cent above a base rate of, say, 12 per cent, the contractual interest rate is 13½ per cent per year. In effect the customer contracts to repay £1·135 at the end of a year for each £1 borrowed; assuming that the bank seeks a risk-free return of £1·12, the implied probability of successful repayment can be derived by adapting the previous equation as follows:

$$\underset{\text{£1·12}}{\text{required return}} = \underset{\text{£1·135}}{\text{contractual return}} \times \underset{\text{P}}{\text{probability of success}}$$

$$\text{Thus P} = \frac{\text{£1·12}}{\text{£1·135}} = 0{\cdot}987$$

This probability of almost 0·99 implies that the premium element in the contractual interest rate would compensate only for lending propositions in which the chance of failure to repay at the end of the year was 1 in 100 or less. Other premiums would, of course, suggest different probability levels. For example, 4 per cent above a base rate of 12 per cent (which is as high as many bankers might wish to go) suggests a success probability of 0·965. These are fine margins compared with those which often apply in business decisions, although lending on the overall activities of a firm is inherently less risky than any individual business project.

A number of qualifications must be made about this analysis, which in themselves reveal something of the banker's decision problems. First, there are the differences between lending and coin-tossing. Clearly, lending involves subjective, not objective probabilities; the banker does not go to the length of quantifying probabilities on individual propositions, but the probabilities are implicit in his decisions. Moreover, there is an important distinction between the gambling objective of coin-tossing and productive risk-taking; the distinction is less a matter of the risk involved than of the purpose of the venture. Gambling merely involves prospective transfer of wealth between individuals; productive risk-taking, such as a pharmaceutical company's research for a new drug, might involve greater risks but offers the prospect of a net addition to economic welfare. Bankers traditionally concern themselves with such distinctions as part of their examination of the purpose of borrowing.

It must also be recognized that this analysis tends to overstate loss experience, at least in recent years by major British banks. One estimate of loss experience is given by the specific provisions for bad debts which are disclosed by the UK clearing banks. These may typically range from well under 0.1 per cent to some 0.7 per cent. The figures are cautious compared with debts actually written off, which give much lower results. So the chances of loss may well be nearer to 1 in 1,000 than to the 1 in 100 probability suggested earlier.

At least four reasons can be suggested for the discrepancy between the analysis and the bad debt experience:

1. All costs of 'unsuccessful' lending do not show up as bad debts; the administrative costs of salvaging some or all of a weak advance can be substantial.
2. The analysis is more likely to be suggestive of the limits of acceptable risk than of average experience. Many lending propositions which come within the risk limits are unlikely to be given a fine adjustment of interest rates.
3. Risk-takers in financial markets tend to require compensation for their risk above that which would be implied by a simple calculation of implied probabilities. Thus a calculation from interest-rate premiums to implied probabilities is likely to err in overestimating acceptable risk.
4. In lending, bankers are not merely concerned with the risks which occur in a reasonably stable economic environment; they have also to bear in mind that their lending may be put to the test in conditions of considerable economic adversity.

This discussion has attempted to provide a general framework for understanding the nature of the banker's risk-taking in lending. It is clear that although bankers require a high degree of confidence in the outcome of their lending, it must be some way short of certainty. The function of accounts in all this is not to provide a substitute for a crystal ball, but to make a significant contribution to the information on which the banker bases his risk assessment.

1.3 Accounting aims

Accounting reports on the resources and past transactions of firms are not specifically designed for bankers making lending decisions, but are multipurpose. The accountant's solution to different information needs is to attempt to act neutrally.

The overall aims which influence accounting reports, particularly those going to users outside the firm's management, are summarized below.

1. *Continuity:* a firm is to be treated as a continuing, ongoing operation for accounting purposes; this is commonly called the *going-concern* approach.
2. *Consistency:* accounting methods should be adopted consistently from one period to another.
3. *Conservatism:* nowadays coyly called *prudence,* this requires that profits should not be recognized in accounts until their realization is 'reasonably certain', but that all losses and liabilities should be provided for.
4. *Objectivity:* the amounts attached to items in accounts should not be biased. One suggested definition of objectivity is that the amount assigned to a particular item in a set of accounts will be objective if two independent observers would be likely to assign the same amount to the item.
5. *Money measurement:* accounts are to be expressed in money terms to permit comparison between firms and time periods.
6. *Disclosure:* information should be disclosed which is needed by the user of the accounts.

The reader may notice that these aims are not necessarily consistent or easy to implement: the seller of a business might consider that 'prudent' accounts lacked objectivity for his purposes; some users of accounts might be interested in disclosure of information on the firm's position if it ceased operating rather than on a going-concern basis, and so on. The extent to which the different aims are implemented therefore depends on more detailed rules. For the implementation of the accounting aims there have grown up generally accepted accounting rules which are termed *conventions.* The British professional bodies prefer, however, to employ a more elaborate range of titles[2]:

Fundamental accounting concepts – essentially the first three aims mentioned above;

Accounting bases – acceptable methods of treatment in accounts, of which there may be more than one in any given situation;

Accounting standards – those conventions which have been specifically agreed and published by the British professional accountancy bodies (through the Accounting Standards Committee, a joint committee of the UK and Irish accountancy institutes [3]).

In this book the terms most frequently used will be *convention* and *accounting standard*. 'Convention' will be used in the widest sense of a generally accepted accounting rule, whether or not it is the subject of a standard.

One basic convention which is in the course of being eroded, but which will be adhered to in considering accounting records in Chapters 2 and 3, is that of recording amounts at *historical cost*, the original cost at which a transaction took place. The long use of historical cost stems partly from objectivity and conservatism (aims 4 and 3), but price changes raise doubts about the relevance of figures and also the comparability of money amounts of different time periods (under aim 5). The issue of reflecting price changes in accounts will be deferred until Chapter 9.

The sixth aim, that of disclosure, is the area where legislative rules rather than professional conventions are dominant – at least so far as companies are concerned. The Companies Acts 1948 to 1981 set out requirements for disclosure which will be considered in Chapter 8.

Notes and references

1. *Report of the Committee of Inquiry on Small Firms*, Cmnd 4811, HMSO (1971), p. 119.
2. *Statement of Standard Accounting Practice 2 (SSAP 2): Disclosure of Accounting Policies*, Institute of Chartered Accountants in England and Wales (1971).
3. These are:
   Institute of Chartered Accountants in England and Wales
   Institute of Chartered Accountants of Scotland
   Institute of Chartered Accountants in Ireland
   Association of Certified Accountants
   Institute of Cost and Management Accountants
   Chartered Institute of Public Finance and Accountancy

   Standards issued by the ASC are published by all of these institutes. However, throughout this book the Institute of Chartered Accountants in England and Wales is shown as the publisher of individual standards, purely for brevity.

Chapter 2

Accounting structure

2.1 The operating cycle

Time is central to many of the purposes and problems of accounting. The buying and selling of goods by businesses do not occur in conveniently matched simultaneous transactions: there are time lags between purchases and payments and between sales and receipts. Some purchased resources, such as machinery, are used up over many years, while others such as electricity yield their benefits instantaneously. As a consequence accounting records are needed, not only to keep track of diverse transactions with outsiders but also to provide the basis for summarizing the financial situation of the firm over time.

Accounting summaries are prepared annually for virtually all business enterprises of any significance, in order to present information on the effects of transactions during the year and the financial position at the end of the year. Of the many compelling reasons for this practice, not the least are the need to supply tax authorities with a starting-point for the calculation of taxable profit and, in the case of companies, the Companies Act requirement for presentation of accounts to shareholders once a year. In most enterprises, of course, further accounting summaries are prepared for management use throughout the year. However, the usual distinguishing features of the annual accounts are that they are audited by independent accountants and they are primarily intended for non-management use by such 'external' users as shareholders and creditors – including bankers.

The widespread adoption of an annual accounting period for external financial reports may tempt the reader to assume that a year has some mysterious and fundamental financial significance. It is true that activities governed by the seasons have an annual pattern: a farmer who buys seed, grows, harvests and sells his crop will encompass one full cycle of his financial activities in a year's accounts. Similarly, there are many products, from Christmas cards to swimsuits, that are subject to annual cycles of demand. But for a host of other activities a year is merely a necessarily arbitrary financial period: it has as little relevance to the operations of a construction company which takes 3 years to complete a bridge as it has to the activities of a greengrocer who clears his stocks on average three times a week.

The period of time which does have some genuine financial significance for a firm is the time taken to complete a sequence of operating and trading activities, since that determines financing requirements. Business activity is, of course, continuous, and in most enterprises a variety of different transactions at different stages of completion would be in progress simultaneously. Nevertheless, the *average* period taken to convert cash into goods and back again provides a useful notion for introducing certain accounting and financial relationships.

The circular process of conversion from cash to goods and back to cash, for the purpose of achieving a profit on the way, is often termed the 'operating cycle'. An exceedingly simple operating cycle for someone buying and selling goods for cash only, such as a street newspaper seller, could be represented as

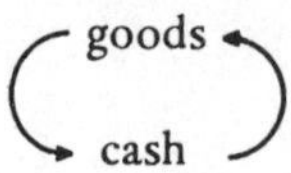

Since the newspaper seller operates on a street pitch he has no problems of rent or of any business costs other than the purchase of newspapers. His operating cycle would be a single day, assuming for simplicity that he purchased for cash at the beginning of the day and that the newspaper publishers repurchased any unsold papers for cash at the end of the day. The financial implications suggested by this short operating cycle are two-fold:

1. Financial resources tied up in the enterprise would be small relative to sales. If the newspaper seller worked for, say, a 300-day year he would need only sufficient resources to finance one-three-hundredth of the annual cost of sales. Compare this with the finance needed if he were selling magazines which took, on average, a week to sell: seven times as much would be required to support the same volume of annual sales. The message is clear: the longer the operating cycle the greater the finance required by a firm to support any given amount of annual sales.
2. There would be no doubt about the valuation to be placed on the newspaper seller's *assets* (business possessions) when his accounts were prepared at the end of the year, because he converts his goods into cash by the end of each day. But if he were selling magazines the problem of valuing the 7-day average stockholding would arise. The value of the stocks would depend on the saleability of the magazines or on 'sale or return' agreements with the publishers: a loss in value on unsaleable magazines would reduce profit. The second generalization which can be hazarded is: the longer the operating cycle the more will profit tend to depend on values assigned in the accounts to non-cash holdings.

Although the newspaper-seller example is excessively simple it validly emphasizes that the essence of business activity is *movement*. Accounts, in recording each financial facet of an enterprise's progress, reflect such movement: the operating cycle is therefore reflected in an accounting cycle. The analogy will be used to provide a bird's-eye view of the working of a simple accounting system in section 2.2.

2.2 The accounting cycle

For the benefit of any reader whose existence has so far been untroubled by double-entry bookkeeping[1], it must first be explained that every financial transaction involves two aspects: each monetary amount must go to somewhere or somebody and come from somewhere or somebody. Correspondingly, every account has two sides: the *debit* (traditionally always the left) side of the account can be considered as the side receiving benefit, while an entry on the *credit* (right) side of the account records the providing of benefit. To record its dual aspects every transaction must be entered in one account as a debit and in some other account as a credit. Thus the receipt of £100 cash by a business from one of its debtors named Bloggs would be recorded in the two separate accounts below:

Bloggs

	5 Nov. 19–0 Cash £100

Cash

5 Nov. 19–0 Bloggs £100	

Double-entry procedures are illustrated more fully in Fig. 2.1, which shows simple accounting records for the first 5 *weeks* of a newly established business, up to 31 December 19–0. It need hardly be said that the circular layout is adopted for its visual representation of accounting movements, and that in reality accounts reside more mundanely and sequentially in ledgers or in computer data stores. In Fig. 2.1 the double-entry process is shown by arrows from the credit side of one account to the debit side of the next. The circled numbers on the arrows correspond to the transactions which will be explained in sequence below.

1. Weaver started a basket-weaving business with £500 cash. Clearly a debit entry is appropriate in the cash account ('receiving' account) of the newly established enterprise.

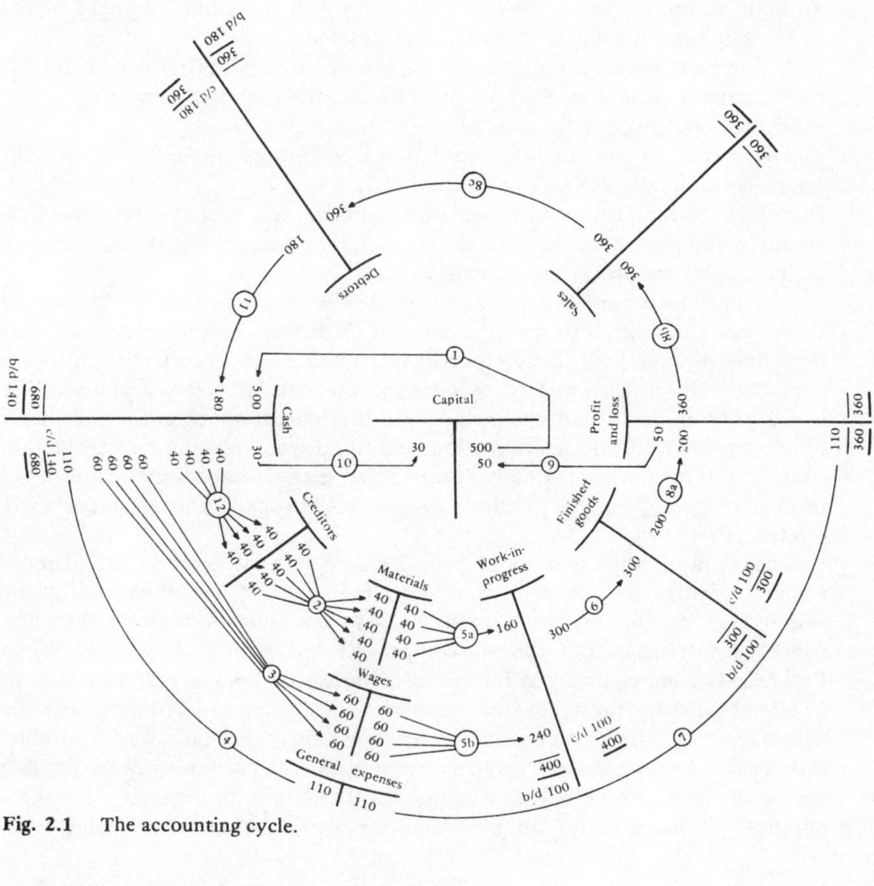

Fig. 2.1 The accounting cycle.

Weaver, who provided the money, has a claim against the business which is shown by a credit to capital account. Thus the firm started with an asset of £500 and a claim of £500.

The word 'capital' can have some subtly different meanings; here it means simply Weaver's ownership claim against the business. In the accounts of a sole trader like Weaver, or of a partnership, it is usual to add to capital any profit remaining in the business at the end of the accounting year, or to deduct residual losses. Companies, however, are legally required to maintain a separate account for share capital, representing shares issued to shareholders; retained profits would be left as a balance on a profit and loss account or a separate 'reserves' account.

The capital account representing Weaver's ownership claim appears in the centre of Fig. 2.1, which accords with the traditional view of ownership as the focus of the control, risks and rewards of the enterprise.

2. Materials were purchased on credit for £40 in each of the first 5 weeks of the firm's operations. These transactions are recorded by credits to creditors and debits to materials.

   In practice, of course, credits would be made to accounts in the name of suppliers. These accounts would normally be contained in a separate creditors (or 'purchases') ledger, and the creditors' account adopted here really represents a summary of that ledger. A variety of accounts would also normally be maintained for different materials, commonly in a separate segment of the accounting system concerned with 'cost accounts'.

3. Only 4 weeks' wages, at £60 per week, are recorded because weaving did not start until the second week of the firm's existence – using the materials which were purchased the previous week.

   The wages account can be regarded as a temporary home for the benefits arising from the services of employees.

4. During the 5-week period £110 was incurred in general expenses, recorded by a credit to cash and debit to general expenses. The amount might have included such items as rent and selling expenses.

5. For a firm which purchases goods for resale the determination of the costs of these goods is a straightforward matter of recording from invoices. But for a firm like this one, which uses purchased resources to manufacture into the goods it sells, it is necessary to calculate the cost of goods produced. The appropriate choice of costs to include in this calculation is a controversial issue of importance to profit determination, and full discussion will be deferred until later. In this example it is simply assumed that materials and wages contributed to cost of goods, so that sundry expenses are ineligible and are accordingly treated differently.

The work-in-progress account provides a repository for the costs of those resources which are consumed in production. Four weeks' work by the employees, represented by 4 weeks' wages, has gone into production; the consequent transfer into the work-in-progress account is shown as (5b) in Fig. 2.1. The materials taken into production would be a question of fact, to be determined by the record of materials issued from stores in any sizeable manufacturing establishment, but here it is assumed that each week's production used the previous week's purchase materials. The conveniently regular £40 per week gives the transfer totalling £160 (marked 5a), leaving 1 week's purchase of materials in stock – thus average materials take 1 week from purchase to absorption into work-in-progress.

A firm would normally need a more complex recording system than is illustrated here in order to keep track of materials which are used and those which are left in stock: specifically a 'perpetual inventory system'. Moreover, most firms manufacturing a variety of products would maintain a large number of 'job' or 'process' accounts to serve a similar function to our single work-in-progress account, but that difference is more a matter of volume than of principle.

6. Work-in-progress was charged with costs which represented the inputs to the manufacturing process; when outputs are completed their costs are correspondingly transferred out of work-in-progress and into the finished goods account. In this case £300 has been transferred, representing 3 of the 4 weeks' inputs which have been completed. Consequently 1 week's inputs are still in a partially completed state; this is represented by the £100 marked c/d (carried down) in Fig. 2.1. The amount appears as a debit balance brought down (b/d) into the next accounting period.

   In practice it is not a simple matter to determine how much cost to assign to finished goods and how much to assign to the partially completed items remaining in work-in-progress. Where the firm keeps appropriate subsidiary records there is relatively little difficulty in identifying material and wage costs for specific items of work-in-progress – for example, materials costs could be recorded for each batch of baskets commenced, and the hours spent by employees on those batches could be similarly recorded to give wage costs. In that case, as every batch is completed, actual costs could be transferred to finished goods; the balance remaining would represent work-in-progress. But when it is not possible to identify costs associated with specific batches of production it is necessary to examine the physical work-in-progress at the end of an accounting period, and to estimate what has gone into the partially completed work on the basis of average costs. In this way a figure for the balance of work-in-progress at cost is obtained, the remaining cost of inputs being transferred out to finished goods.

   A further, more fundamental, problem involves 'overhead' costs which are difficult to identify with particular outputs. For example, how could costs of rent possibly be divided between batches of shopping baskets and batches of basket chairs? The methods which would usually be adopted involve allocating overhead costs on some basis related to those costs directly identifiable with individual batches – such as a percentage addition to wage costs, or so much overhead cost allocated for each hour worked. This issue has profit-measurement implications which will be considered in Chapter 4.

7. General expenses of £110 have been treated as costs to be written off against the profit calculation, rather than as items leading specifically to production of goods. The reader may observe that some of these expenses might have been treated as overhead costs, and might therefore have been charged into work-in-progress. However, not all such items would be eligible, and to avoid going into details at this stage the entire amount has been treated as an expense of the current period and charged to the profit and loss account.

8. Finished goods which cost £200 were sold on credit for £360. This event, an objective of the earlier business operations, yields a gain which must go into the profit calculation. Recording in the accounts of the business takes place in three separate steps, shown in Fig. 2.1 as 8a, 8b and 8c:

(a) £200 credit to finished goods and debit to profit and loss account;
(b) £360 credit to profit and loss account, debit to sales;
(c) £360 credit to sales, debit to debtors; in fact the debit(s) would go to individual accounts of customers.

The usual procedure would involve entering transaction (c) before the other two shown in Fig. 2.1 as 8a and 8b. When a sale is made the firm needs to update its records swiftly to keep track of who owes money: thus entries like 8c are made frequently. Profit calculations, however, take place less often – at the end of a year for the audited accounts intended for external users, although more frequently for internal management purposes. Thus entries 8a and 8b would take place only at the end of an accounting period when the effects of transactions over the whole period were being taken into the profit calculation: the £200 cost of goods sold and the £360 sales revenue for 5 weeks would be added into the total figures transferred at the end of an accounting period of 1 year.

The reader may notice that the transfer of £200 out of the finished goods account leaves £100 stock at the period – which happens to be 1 week's production of goods.

How would the figure of £200 have been obtained? Perhaps it represents 100 units at an average cost of £2 per unit, the average cost having been derived from 150 units transferred into finished goods at a total amount of £300. Usually the determination of cost of goods sold and the cost of stocks is far less straightforward than that, but simplicity will suffice here.

9. As a result of the transactions which have taken place during the 5 weeks of trading Weaver has made a profit of £50. This is often called *net profit* because not only the £200 cost of goods but also other forms of expense (£110) have been deducted (or 'netted') from the £360 revenue.

   The net profit has been transferred to Weaver's capital account, which is the usual procedure in the case of a sole trader – except that transfer would only be made at the end of the accounting year. Weaver would, of course, be liable for tax, but that aspect is not being considered here.

10. Weaver made a withdrawal of £30 for his own use; the transaction is recorded as a credit to cash and debit to capital account. From the ownership viewpoint this demonstrates the last stage in the process of providing capital, earning profits and withdrawing part of the rewards of operating activities. The accounting cycle in the illustration is not quite complete however; two transactions remain.
11. Debtors paid £180, which is recorded by a credit to debtors (in reality their individual accounts) and a debit to cash. That represents 1 week's sales; payment for a further week's sales remain outstanding.
12. Cash was paid to creditors for 4 weeks' purchases totalling £160, leaving a balance of £40 outstanding for 1 week's purchases.

Transactions have come full circle with the payments by debtors and to creditors – although it should be appreciated that the cycle is not 'finished' but will continue to move through the diverse transactions of the ongoing firm. In one sense, however, cash receipts provide the culmination of the operating cycle: they return the firm's resources to an all-purpose form. The firm can divert cash very easily into any economic activity, but options are limited elsewhere in the operating cycle: for example, little can be done with work-in-progress except complete it.

If the operating cycle culminates in cash transactions why was the profit recorded earlier in item 9? After all, the profit calculation is usually regarded as a major end result of the accounting process; certainly Weaver, as owner, would be likely to adopt that view. The reason is that profit represents an increase in owners' command over resources, including non-cash resources. Thus the profit calculation is not dependent on the receipt of cash from debtors, provided they are expected to pay eventually; Weaver's profit would have been £50 even if cash receipts had been £1 or £360 instead of £180.

The fundamental point being made here may seem glaringly obvious, but it is one which is prone to ensnare the innocent user of accounts: profit is not cash, so that the earning of profit need not produce a corresponding *cash* flow in the current period. Profit is the difference between revenues and costs, neither of which is limited to current period cash transactions. On the revenue side the usual rule is that revenue is recognized when goods or services are supplied and a legally enforceable right to receive payment from the customer is obtained; whether cash is to be received immediately or at some future date is irrelevant to the current calculation of profit.

Profit measurement is a much more elaborate ritual than may appear from the Weaver example. Calculation is preceded by a *trial balance,* which records the balances in the ledger accounts prior to final adjustment at the end of the accounting period, an approach developed in section 2.3. A trial balance is merely a list of balances in the ledger accounts at any point of time – for which, of course, the rule of double entry demands that totals of debit balances must always equal credit balances. After the calculation of profit the remaining balances are 'classified' or grouped in a *balance sheet*; the title is over-generous for Weaver's list of balances at 31 December 19–0 shown in Fig. 2.2, but that presentation is enough for the time being.

Fig. 2.2 Weaver's 'balance sheet' at 31 December 19–0.

	£	£
Capital		520
Creditors		40
Materials	40	
Work-in-progress	100	
Finished goods	100	
Debtors	180	
Cash	140	
	£560	£560

The nature of Weaver's operating cycle is reflected in the balances remaining on the accounts in Fig. 2.1, which have been transferred to Fig. 2.2. At the end of the accounting period 1 week's credit, for £40, is still being provided by creditors – which conveniently offsets 1 week's holding of materials. A week's time lag in the production process arises from the work-in-progress balance of £100 (one-quarter of the 4 weeks' inputs). A second week's time lag is added by the £100 in finished goods. Finally, a third week's time lag is added by debtors, since one-half of the 2 weeks' production sold for £360 remains unpaid for. Thus Weaver's *3-week operating cycle* has determined the composition of most of the items in his balance sheet.

Apart from Weaver's capital, the items in his balance sheet all 'circulate' in the sense that they are largely consumed and replenished during an operating cycle. The net amount of such items is therefore sometimes called *circulating capital,* although the term usually adopted nowadays is *working capital.* The essential character of these items is that they are short-term, or current, and they are consequently called *current assets* and *current liabilities.* It is the excess of current assets over current liabilities (in other words, net current assets) which is called working capital. In Weaver's case all his resources of £520 are in working capital.

2.3 Profit measurement and final adjustments

Profit is an increase (and loss a decrease) in the owners' command over resources arising from a firm's transactions during an accounting period – excluding, of course, any changes through the introduction or withdrawal of resources by the owners. Consequently, it is impossible to examine profit without saying something about the balance sheet which records the resources held by the firm at the end of the accounting period; the two, which are commonly termed the *final accounts,* are inevitably interrelated. However, it will be convenient to emphasize profit aspects before turning later to more detailed consideration of the balance sheet.

In profit measurement all resources that are considered to have yielded up their benefits in the accounting period, called costs or expenses, are offset against revenue – which is composed of all benefits derived from sale or use of resources in the period. In other words costs are *matched* to the accounting period in which they are assumed to help produce revenue. Costs written off in this way are said to have been *expensed.* It is this idea of period-by-period matching of costs and revenues, termed the *matching concept* or *accruals concept,* which lies at the root of accounting profit measurement.

Matching requires that resources remaining unused at the end of the current accounting period are carried forward as costs for future periods – which helps to explain why assets are put into the balance sheet at cost rather than at, say, the amount for which they could be sold. That applies to the general approach: variations will become evident later.

The preparation of the final accounts from the accounting records at the end of a period is largely concerned with separating the amounts which should be matched to the current period as costs and revenue from those which should appear as assets and claims in the balance sheet. The first step is the compilation of a trial balance from the balances remaining at the end of the period immediately prior to profit calculation. (In the context of Fig. 2.2 that would have been before entries 7, 8a, 8b and 9 had been made.)

The principles of final adjustments will be considered in relation to Fig. 2.3. In the first two columns are shown the trial balance that might have derived from the accounts of Weaver at the end of a further year's trading ending 31 December 19–1. During the year Weaver increased his firm's rate of output and sales. Halfway through the year he introduced new capital of £8,000 (added to the £520 balance at 31 December 19–0), purchased and mortgaged a £15,300 30-year lease on a shop for the sale of his products, and bought shop fixtures and fittings for £2,000.

The items in Fig. 2.3 have been conveniently arranged so that the upper section relates to the profit calculation: amounts in the upper part of the first two trial-balance columns are *prima facie* those representing costs and revenues. However, certain final adjustments need to be made, and these are shown in the third and

Fig. 2.3 Worksheet for final accounts, 31 December 19–1.

	Trial balance		Final adjustments		Items for profit calculation and balance sheet	
	Dr £	Cr £	Dr £	Cr £	Dr £	Cr £
Profit calculation items						
Cost of goods sold	12,000				12,000	
General expenses	2,180				2,180	
Depreciation – leasehold property			**1a** 255		255	
– fixtures and fittings			**1b** 90		90	
Bad debts			**2a** 25		25	
Doubtful debts			**2b** 45		45	
Discounts allowed	120		**3** 10		130	
Mortgage interest	600		**4** 120		720	
Insurances	250			**5** 50	200	
Drawings	2,000				2,000	
Sales		20,000				20,000
Interest on bank deposit		110		**6** 40		150
Discounts received		90				90
Taxation			**7** 1,060		1,060	
Balance sheet items						
Leasehold property	15,300				15,300	
Accumulated depreciation on leasehold property				**1a** 255		255
Fixtures and fittings	2,000				2,000	
Accumulated depreciation on fixtures and fittings				**1b** 90		90
Materials	900				900	
Work-in-progress	1,300				1,300	
Finished goods	1,500				1,500	
				2a 25		
Sundry debtors	1,830		**5** 50	**2b** 45	1,800	
				3 10		
Bank deposit account	920		**6** 40		960	
Bank and petty cash	400				400	
Capital		8,520				8,520
12% mortgage on property		12,000				12,000
Sundry creditors		580		**4** 120		700
Taxation due				**7** 1,060		1,060
	£41,300	£41,300	£1,695	£1,695	£42,865	£42,865

Note: Figures and letters in bold print (e.g. **1a**) refer to final adjustment items discussed in the text.

fourth columns of Fig. 2.3. Each adjustment is numbered and explained in order below. (Weaver's double-entry accounts incorporating the final adjustments are provided at the end of this chapter, in Fig. 2.4.)

1. Depreciation

Weaver's acquisition of leasehold property and fixtures and fittings during 19–1 introduces a new element of profit measurement. Both are long-lived assets which will yield their benefits through use over many years rather than by swift consumption or disposal in the manner of the current assets considered earlier. Such items are called *fixed assets,* because the long periods for which they are usually held makes them a relatively fixed or permanent feature of the firm's asset structure.

Fixed assets may have long lives, but, with the notable exception of freehold land, they can rarely be assumed to last for ever. So, in accordance with the matching concept, the costs of fixed assets are matched over their expected lives to the accounting periods which are assumed to benefit from their services. The amount charged in this way to the profit calculation of an accounting period is called 'depreciation', and the remaining amount of the asset carried forward to succeeding periods is shown in the balance sheet at cost less accumulated depreciation.

That may seem a roundabout way of explaining depreciation, which a dictionary would define more simply as a loss in value through wear and tear. But that everyday definition does not entirely fit orthodox accounting: the procedure of writing off the original cost of an asset over its expected life does not necessarily produce an estimate of value in the sense of a price at which the asset might be bought or sold.

In accounting, the term 'depreciation' is not confined merely to physical assets which are subject to wear and tear, but the word *amortization* is sometimes used, particularly by Americans, to describe the process of writing off the cost of 'non-physical' assets over their lives – such as the limited right to use of property which Weaver's lease provides.

The most common depreciation approach adopted in accounting is the *straight-line method* which makes an equal depreciation charge to each accounting period over the asset's expected life. The annual depreciation charge is calculated by dividing the asset's cost, minus any anticipated salvage value at the end of the asset's life, by the years of expected useful life. Whether the straight-line method is necessarily appropriate for all fixed assets need not detain us here; depreciation methods will be reconsidered more fully in Chapter 8.

Weaver's lease on his shop, which was acquired for £15,300, has a 30-year life. Since the lease will be valueless at the end of 30 years the annual depreciation charge can be calculated simply as

$$\frac{£15{,}300}{30} = £510$$

However, the lease was acquired halfway through 19–1, so that only 6 months' depreciation need be charged against revenue of that year. Consequently, £255 is shown as a debit in the first section of the adjustment columns of Fig. 2.3, that amount forming part of the depreciation charge in the profit calculation.

The corresponding £255 credit appears as item (**1a**) in the lower section of Fig. 2.3. This amount, to which would be added a further £510 depreciation in each successive year, is termed a *provision.* A provision is an amount provided for an estimated decline in an asset's 'value to the business'; the word can also be used to describe an amount provided for an estimated liability such as a 'provision for taxation'.

A provision for accumulated depreciation is deducted from the cost of the relevant assets in the balance sheet; consequently Weaver's leasehold property would be reduced by accumulated depreciation in his balance sheet.

The depreciation of the £2,000 fixtures and fittings acquired halfway through

19–1 follows the same pattern, except that the expected useful life of these assets is 10 years and the assets are assumed to have a salvage value of £200 at the end of that time. Thus a full year's charge for depreciation would be

$$\frac{£2{,}000 - £200}{10} = £180$$

The half-year's depreciation of £90 is shown as final adjustment (**1b**), appearing as a debit in the profit and loss section and as a credit for the balance-sheet adjustments.

2. Bad and doubtful debts

When sales are made on credit a firm faces the normal business hazard that some customers will fail to pay, whether deliberately through the evasion of their debts or through eventual insolvency. Consequently, in preparing a firm's final accounts it is always necessary to consider the amount by which debtors should be reduced for bad debts and doubtful debts.

A debt which is not expected to be collected is considered 'bad' and is written off completely in the accounts. An example of the double entry for writing off a bad debt incurred by John Bloggs is shown below.

John Bloggs		Bad debts		Profit and loss	
Balance b/d £25					
	Bad debt £25 ⟶	Bloggs £25	P & L £25 ⟶	Bad debt £25	

The first entry to the bad debts account might take place at any time of year, although transfer of an accumulated total to profit and loss would occur when final accounts are prepared. In Fig. 2.3 the entries have been made, for convenience, at the end of the year; item (**2a**) shows £25 debit to profit and loss, with a corresponding credit of £25 reducing sundry debtors for the balance sheet. The information in the bad debts account should act as a memorandum to ensure that Bloggs is not forgotten if a future opportunity to recoup the debt presents itself.

A firm with a sound financial control system should have a well-established procedure for determining when a debt is to be considered bad, after exhausting a specific routine of reminders, solicitors' letters, court actions, etc. The greater the debt the more it is worth spending on an attempt at collection; pursuit of small debts soon becomes financially unsound. Of course, in order to minimize such debt problems, firms adopt credit-control procedures to ensure that slow payers do not get more credit and credit limits are adhered to.

A firm should also provide for debts which are not yet considered bad but which have been outstanding for a length of time which makes collection doubtful. For example, it may be possible to examine past results and estimate that 50 per cent of debts outstanding over 4 months eventually prove bad. For that approach it is necessary to prepare a statement of the *ageing of debtors*, this has nothing to do with the customers' senility but lists amounts outstanding for 1 month, 2 months, etc. Such a statement can be prepared very much more easily by a firm using a computer-based, data-processing system than by one which relies on more traditional accounting processes. The latter might use a rougher estimating approach – say, 1 per cent of the total amount of outstanding debtors at the end of the year might be assumed uncollectable.

Whatever the basis of the estimate, the firm would proceed to make a *provision for doubtful debtors* of the resulting amount. The first year such a provision was made it would be recorded in the books by entries for the full amount of the provision as follows:

Provision for doubtful debts

	P & L £45 →

Profit and loss

Provision £45	

The adjustment is shown as item **(2b)** in Fig. 2.3. For the balance sheet the provision would be deducted from total debtors to give a net figure, but the provision would remain in the accounting records just like accumulated depreciation – until the end of the next accounting period. It would then be *increased or decreased* by a transfer to the profit and loss account, the purpose being to adjust the provision for the amount of doubtful debts outstanding at the end of that year. Thus, if it were decided to reduce the provision to £35 that would be accomplished by a debit of £10 to the provision account and a £10 credit to the profit and loss account.

3. Cash discounts allowable

A different sort of provision concerns those debtors who are expected to pay promptly. Weaver allows a cash discount for prompt payment, a fairly common practice among UK firms. Assuming that he allows a discount of 2 per cent for payment within 14 days, there will be some debtors outstanding at 31 December 19–1 who have made purchases within the previous fortnight and who are therefore entitled to a cash discount if they pay promptly. The proportion of debtors who will take advantage of the discount could be estimated from past experience; a more 'prudent' approach would assume that all debtors entitled to the discount will take advantage of the facility – either way the figure must be an estimate.

Figure 2.3 assumes that the estimated discount allowable to Weaver's debtors at 31 December 19–1 was £10. Final adjustment 3 shows a debit of £10 which will be added to the discounts allowed for the profit calculation, to give £130 in total. The corresponding £10 credit could either be taken to a provision account along the lines of the doubtful debt provision, or, more simply, it could be carried forward in the discounts allowed account as a balance ready to offset the amounts actually allowed in the succeeding year:

Discounts allowed

19–1		19–1	
Charged during year	£120	P & L	£130 →
Balance c/d	10		
	£130		£130
		19–2	
		Balance b/d	10

Profit and loss 19–1

Discounts allowed	£130	

The reader may notice that no similar adjustment has been made to discounts received of £90, which Weaver received for prompt payment on his purchases. There would be no anticipation of discounts receivable, even though Weaver may be entitled to discounts from creditors for purchases made near to the end of the accounting year *and* he may intend to take them. The reason lies in the 'prudence' viewpoint of the accounting conventions: likely costs are allowed for, but likely revenue is usually ignored.

4. Mortgage interest

Weaver's 12 per cent mortgage of £12,000 on his leasehold property was incurred halfway through the accounting year. Assuming that no variations in the balance of the mortgage occurred during that period, Weaver should have paid £720 for 6 months' interest on the mortgage. However, the trial balance shows that only £600 has been paid. Consequently a final adjustment of £120 is shown in Fig. 2.3; the interest debit for the profit calculation is increased to £720 and the corresponding £120 credit increases sundry creditors for the balance sheet. In the mortgage interest account the entries would follow the pattern illustrated above for discounts allowed – with £120 appearing as a credit balance ready to offset the cash payment which should be made early in the succeeding year:

Mortgage interest

19–1		19–1	
Bank	£600	P & L	£720 →
Balance c/d	120		
	720		720
		19–2	
		Balance b/d	120

Profit and loss 19–1

Mortgage interest	£720	

This type of item requiring final adjustment is called an *accrual*; it involves a liability that 'accrues' in the sense that it arises through the lapse of time. Rent,

Fig. 2.4 Weaver's double-entry accounts for 19–1.

Bank, petty cash, deposit account

Balance 1 Jan. 19–1	140	Wages	8,200
Cash sales	2,600	Creditors	6,880
Debtors	15,630	General expenses	2,180
Interest on deposit	110	Mortgage interest	600
	40	Insurances	250
Capital	8,000	Drawings	2,000
Mortgage	12,000	Leasehold property	15,300
		Fixtures	1,750
		Balances c/d	960
			400
	£38,520		£38,520
Balances b/d 1 Jan. 19–2	960		
	400		

Capital

		Balance 1 Jan. 19–1	520
		Bank	8,000
Balance c/d	10,055	P & L	1,535
	£10,055		£10,055
		Balance b/d 1 Jan. 19–2	10,055

Creditors

Discounts	90	Balance 1 Jan. 19–1	40
Bank	6,880	Materials	7,260
Balance c/d	580	Fixtures	250
	£7,550		£7,550
		Balance b/d 1 Jan. 19–2	580†

Debtors

Balance 1 Jan. 19–1	180	P & L– bad debt	25
Sales	17,400	Discounts	120
		Bank	15,630
		Balance c/d	1,805
	£17,580		£17,580
Balance b/d 1 Jan. 19–2	1,805*		

Discounts allowed

Debtors	120	P & L	130
Balance c/d	10		
	£130		£130
		Balance b/d 1 Jan. 19–2	10*

Discounts received

P & L	90	Creditors	90

Finished goods

Balance 1 Jan. 19–1	100	P & L	12,000
Work-in-progress	13,400	Balance c/d	1,500
	£13,500		£13,500
Balance b/d 1 Jan. 19–2	1,500		

Fixtures and fittings

Bank	1,750		
Creditors	250		

Fixtures and fittings – depreciation

		P & L	90

General expenses

Bank	2,180	P & L	2,180

Insurances

Bank	250	P & L	200
		Balance c/d	50
	£250		£250
Balance b/d 1 Jan. 19–2	50*		

Interest on deposit account

P & L	150	Bank	150

Fig. 2.4 (cont.)

Leasehold property

Bank	15,300		

Leasehold property – depreciation

		P & L	255

Materials

Balance 1/Jan./19–1	40	Work-in-progress	6,400
Creditors	7,260	Balance c/d	900
	£7,300		£7,300
Balance c/d 1/Jan./19–2	900		

Mortgage interest

Bank	600	P & L	720
Balance c/d	120		
	£720		£720
		Balance b/d 1/Jan. 19–2	120†

Mortgage loan

		Bank	12,000

Profit and loss

Finished goods	12,000	Sales	20,000
General expenses	2,180	Discounts received	90
Depreciation:		Interest on deposit a/c	150
fixtures	255		
property	90		
Debtors – bad	25		
Provision for doubtful debts	45		
Discounts allowed	130		
Mortgage interest	720		
Insurances	200		
Drawings	2,000		
Taxation	1,060		
Capital a/c	1,535		
	£20,240		£20,240

Provision for doubful debts

		P & L	45*

Sales

P & L	20,000	Bank	2,600
		Debtors	17,400
	£20,000		£20,000

Taxation

		P & L	1,060

Wages

Bank	8,200	Work-in-progress	8,200

Work-in-progress

Balance 1/Jan. 19–2	100	Finished goods	13,400
Materials	6,400	Balance c/d	1,300
Wages	8,200		
	£14,700		£14,700
Balance b/d 1/Jan. 19–2	1,300		

* Balance of sundry debtors and prepayments for balance sheet is made up as follows:

		£
Debtors		1,805
Less		
Provision for doubtful debts	45	
Discounts allowable	10	
		55
		1,750
Insurance prepayment		50
		£1,800

† Balance of sundry creditors for balance sheet is made up as follows:

	£
Creditors	580
Mortgage interest outstanding	120
	£700

salaries and subscriptions are other examples of items that can involve accruals; the actual date on which payment has to be made is irrelevant, it is the build-up of liability that must be recorded.

5. Insurances

Just as an accrual arises from receiving benefits over time which have not yet been paid for, it is commonplace to pay in advance for benefits which will be derived over time. Such an amount is termed a prepayment, and requires a final adjustment which is precisely opposite to that for an accrual.

Weaver paid £250 for insurances during the year 19–1. Of that amount it will be assumed that £100 was a year's fire insurance on the leasehold property bought halfway through the year – which means that Weaver still has £50-worth of fire insurance cover due to him. The necessary final adjustment credits insurance expenses with £50, which reduces insurance expenses to £200 for the profit calculation. For the balance sheet the corresponding debit provides a £50 addition to sundry debtors, which should strictly become 'sundry debtors and prepayments'. The details of the double entry in the accounts are as follows:

Insurances

Bank	£250	P & L	£200 →
		Balance c/d	50
	£250		£250
19–2			
Balance b/d	50		

Profit and loss

→ Insurances	£200		

6. Interest on bank deposit

It was said earlier that the mere likelihood of revenue was not recognized in accounts. But when revenue is accrued due to the firm, so that the firm has a *legal* right of recovery, that is more than a likelihood and the amount is recognized by a final adjustment. That recognition is, of course, subject to the debtor being considered capable of paying the amount accrued.

Weaver had a bank deposit account on which interest of £40 was accrued due at 31 December 19–1 but was not yet entered in Weaver's accounts. The necessary final adjustment credits £40 to revenue for the profit calculation and increases the bank deposit account with a corresponding debit.

7. Taxation

Weaver would be liable for tax on the profits of his business. Although the calculation of that liability would normally start with accounting profit, various amendments would be made in line with the tax rules for determining taxable profit. Moreover, the level of tax to be borne by Weaver as a sole trader would depend on his personal circumstances. Such aspects are not appropriate for consideration here;

it is sufficient to assume that Weaver's tax liability, which he would have to meet in a year's time, has been estimated at £1,060.

The final adjustment in Fig. 2.3 debits £1,060 against profit and loss and raises a taxation creditor of that amount for the balance sheet.

All the final adjustments for 19–1 in the Weaver example have now been considered. Although it has taken some time to explain each item, the worksheet approach in Fig. 2.3 is exceedingly swift – once the principles are understood. This method is commonly used by accountants because the totals provide an overall check on double-entry adjustments. Student readers are recommended to test the time-saving properties of the method for themselves, by simply inserting final adjustment alongside trial-balance figures provided in an examination paper; the resulting amounts provide all that is needed to 'plug into' a set of final accounts – which are to be considered in Chapter 3.

However, the reader may find it helpful to see Weaver's transactions for the year and final adjustments recorded in double-entry accounts, and a condensed version of these records appears in Fig. 2.4. Inevitably, the examples have covered only major principles, not every conceivable type of transaction.

Notes and references

1. The reader who seeks a more extensive treatment of double entry might refer to H. C. Edey, *Introduction to Accounting*, Hutchinson (1966) or F. Wood, *Business Accounting 1*, Longman (1972).

Chapter 3

Accounting summaries

A firm's financial reports at the end of an accounting period consist of statements summarizing the figures in the basic accounting records. Each summary is intended to convey a specific aspect of a firm's financial affairs.

The balance sheet is a statement of a firm's resources, and the claims on those resources, *at a point in time.* An understanding of the progress of a firm's activities requires further statements which show *movement over time.* Certain movements are revealed in the profit statements, which explain how the ownership claim changed in the accounting period since the last balance sheet (apart from new capital introduced). Movements affecting other balance-sheet items are the concern of the third major accounting summary: the funds flow statement.

In this chapter each type of accounting summary will be considered in turn, commencing with profit statements and the balance sheet which together make up the traditional final accounts. All the figures relate to Weaver's accounts considered in Chapter 2, and in particular the final accounts will be derived from the work-sheet in Fig. 2.3.

3.1 The profit statements

Profit calculations are normally prepared in interconnected sections, with each section providing a summary statement of one stage of the firm's transactions.

The first stage for a manufacturing firm which produces its own goods (as opposed to wholesale or retail firms which purchase ready-made goods) is to bring together the costs of manufacture in a *manufacturing account.* That involves important problems which are deferred until Chapter 4, so no manufacturing account is shown for Weaver's production. Instead it is assumed for simplicity that Weaver's cost of goods manufactured for 19–1 was made up of material and wage costs, in the manner previously discussed for his operations in 19–0. The calculation involved was shown in the work-in-progress account in Fig. 2.4, and the resulting £13,400 for cost of finished goods manufactured has been transferred into the trading account in Fig. 3.1.

1. Trading account

The purpose of the trading account is to calculate *gross profit,* which is the difference between sales revenue and cost of goods sold.

The cost of goods sold is obviously made up of the cost of opening stocks (of finished goods) plus the cost of goods manufactured during the year, less the closing stock of finished goods left at the end of the year. The resulting cost of goods sold of £12,000 in fact appeared as the first item in Weaver's trial balance – so that Fig. 3.1 merely demonstrates how that figure could have been derived.

Fig. 3.1 Weaver's profit statements.

	£	£
Trading account for year ended 31 Dec. 19–1		
Sales		20,000
Less Cost of goods sold:		
Opening stock of finished goods	100	
Cost of goods manufactured	13,400	
	13,500	
Less closing stock of finished goods	1,500	12,000
Gross profit		£ 8,000
Profit and loss account for year ended 31 Dec. 19–1		
Gross profit		8,000
Interest on deposit account		150
Discount received		90
		8,240
Less General expenses	2,180	
Depreciation	345	
Bad and doubtful debts	70	
Discounts allowed	130	
Mortgage interest	720	
Insurances	200	3,645
Net profit before taxation		4,595
Taxation on profit of the year		1,060
Net profit after taxation		£ 3,535
Appropriation account for year ended 31 Dec. 19–1		
Net profit after taxation		3,535
Proprietor's drawings		2,000
Retained profit (to proprietor's capital account)		£ 1,535

Why bother to calculate gross profit? The figures may be used in several ways – all of which have pitfalls for the unwary. The uses commonly involve expressing gross profit as a ratio or percentage of either cost (of goods sold) or sales, which in Weaver's case give:

$$\frac{\text{gross profit}}{\text{margin on cost}} = \frac{\text{gross profit}}{\text{cost of goods sold}} = \frac{£8{,}000}{£12{,}000} = 0{\cdot}66 \text{ or } 66\tfrac{2}{3} \text{ per cent}$$

$$\frac{\text{gross profit}}{\text{margin on sales}} = \frac{\text{gross profit}}{\text{sales}} = \frac{£8{,}000}{£20{,}000} = 0{\cdot}4 \text{ or } 40 \text{ per cent}$$

The two measures are merely different ways of saying the same thing[1].

Business enterprises often express their prices as a percentage markup on cost; these expected margins may be compared with actual gross profit margins achieved. Alternatively, comparisons may be made between profit margins on sales of different periods – for example, a 52 per cent margin in one period might be compared with a 49 per cent margin in the succeeding period. However, such a comparison is hardly very informative, unless the three different potential sources of change can be disentangled:

1. When, as is usual, the firm sells a mixture of products at different profit margins, the product mix may have changed;
2. Profit margins for individual products (i.e. prices relative to costs per unit) may fluctuate;
3. Differences may arise through stock losses from pilfering, etc.

The analysis of such differences would need a more sophisticated accounting system than Weaver's. But the internal accounting methods of many firms can effectively distinguish the separate elements; for example, retail chain stores calculate category 3 of the above list and call it 'shrinkage' – which provides a check on individual stores.

For the banker, however, the gross profit margin can contribute to an exceedingly rough check on the plausibility of a customer's financial expectations *when nothing better is available.* A customer's cash projections which assume changes from past experience on profit margins require justification, an issue which is examined in Chapter 4.

2. Profit and loss account

Weaver's profit and loss account (or 'P & L') in Fig. 3.1 commences with gross profit previously calculated. To this amount are added those credit items from the trial balance which are not of a trading nature, which in this case are interest on deposit account and discounts received.

From the resulting total revenue of £8,240 are deducted those expense debits which were not taken into the cost of manufacture. The result is net profit before taxation, from which estimated tax of £1,060 is deducted. The final figure of £3,535 for net profit after taxation is, of course, the central indicator of the firm's financial performance, and represents Weaver's increased command over resources arising from the firm's operating activities during the year.

3. Appropriation account

The appropriation account shows what happens to the firm's available profit. It records Weaver's withdrawals of £2,000 during the year, and the remaining retained profit is taken to his capital account in the balance sheet. For a company the retained profit would not be added directly to capital, but would be taken to a separate account and given a title such as 'revenue reserve', 'retained profit' or merely 'profit and loss account balance'.

A separately labelled appropriation account is not an essential feature of the profit statements – often the appropriation items are shown in a subsection at the end of the profit and loss account. But the distinction between charges against profit (which belong in the profit and loss account proper) and appropriations of profit is fundamentally important. The latter comprise all distributions to owners (e.g. dividend distributions) plus any transfers to 'reserves' which are a part of ownership interest; all other debits in the profit statements are charged against profit. The point of the distinction is that profit is an indicator of the ongoing viability of the firm, whereas appropriations show what happens to the rewards.

3.2 The balance sheet

Weaver's balance sheet in Fig. 3.2 has been presented, like the profit statements, in 'narrative' format rather than the more traditional double-sided layout. Normally,

Fig. 3.2 Weaver's balance sheet.

Balance sheet at 31 Dec. 19–1

19–0 £		£	£
	Fixed assets		
	Leasehold property, at cost	15,300	
–	*Less* accumulated depreciation	255	15,045
	Fixtures and fittings, at cost	2,000	
–	*Less* accumulated depreciation	90	1,910
	Current assets		
	Stocks, at cost:		
40	Materials	900	
100	Work-in-progress	1,300	
100	Finished goods	1,500	
180	Sundry debtors and prepayments	1,800	
	Bank deposit account	960	
140	Bank and petty cash	400	6,860
£560			£23,815
	Capital		
	At 31 Dec. 19–0	8,520	
520	Retained profit 19–1	1,535	10,055
	Long-term debt		
–	12% mortgage, secured on leasehold property		12,000
	Current liabilities		
–	Current taxation	1,060	
40	Creditors	700	1,760
£560			£23,815

narrative presentations show current liabilities as a deduction from current assets, to give net current assets – but for Weaver's balance sheet the worksheet order of Fig. 2.3 has been retained. Weaver's previous year's balance sheet for 31 December 19–0 is also shown for comparison purposes, the figures being derived from Fig. 2.2.

There are certain broad guidelines to the presentation of balance sheets: assets and liabilities are *grouped* under headings for similar items (fixed assets, current assets, etc.) and then put in order of *liquidity* for assets and in order of *urgency* for claims. In most British balance sheets the least liquid assets and the least urgent claims appear first.

1. Assets

Fixed assets are traditionally shown at historical cost, less accumulated depreciation. It should be noted that what constitutes cost means not merely the purchase price but also necessary costs incurred in acquiring and installing relatively permanent assets. Thus, Weaver bought his leasehold property at £15,000 but incurred £300 legal fees on the acquisition; the latter has been legitimately 'capitalized' instead of being charged against profit in the year of acquisition (although some firms may 'prudently' choose to write off the £300 immediately). Similarly, the purchase price of fixtures and fittings might have been £1,600 and their cost of installation £400, making up the £2,000 shown in the balance sheet.

Current assets were discussed earlier as those which would normally be 'turned over' during the operating cycle of the firm. Alternatively, they can be regarded as assets that would normally be realized in the next accounting period – within a year. But a firm with an exceptionally long operating cycle (e.g. shipbuilding) might well include among its current assets some work-in-progress that would be held for more than a year.

Accounting conventions on asset valuation make a sharp distinction between fixed and current assets. Although historical cost is traditionally the starting-point for determining the amounts at which both types of asset appear in the accounts, current assets are reduced to 'market value' if that falls below cost. In practice the rule is largely concerned with stocks, which in the UK are shown at the lower of cost or net realizable value, and with debtors, which are shown after deductions for bad and doubtful debts.

For fixed assets the traditional view is that price changes should be ignored. The historical cost of a wasting asset, apart from anticipated residual value, should be written off against profit over its expected life. However, more recent developments which recognize price changes will be met later.

There are assets which do not fit happily into either the fixed or current categories, but which are usually given separate headings of their own. Such assets are more often met in the accounts of companies than sole traders, and they are not represented in Weaver's accounts. Investments, either in the shares of other companies or in interest-bearing securities like government stocks, provide one example; however, if investments are held for short-term liquidity purposes they may be placed among current assets. The other major items are intangible assets.

Up to now discussion has been confined to *tangible assets* which are physical assets (like buildings, machinery, stocks, etc.) and financial assets involving well-defined legal rights against specific outsiders (e.g. debtors, bank deposits, investments). On the other hand, *intangible assets* are non-physical assets which either involve rights, often ill defined, against outsiders in general or represent anticipated future benefits which may not attach to a specific physical asset.

The intangible assets most often met in accounts are patents, trademarks and goodwill. All of them can have substantial value in the sense of future expected benefits to a firm, but the amounts at which they are shown in a firm's books are usually even more a matter of historical accident than most accounting figures. Thus, a patent bought from its inventor by a firm might be shown at its purchase price of £1 m., whereas another equally important patent registered by the firm itself could be shown at a few hundred pounds – and the costs of the research team which developed that patent would have been charged against profits. Similarly, goodwill is only shown in accounts when it represents the excess cost of a *purchased* interest in a business over the amount at which the net assets have taken into the purchaser's books at some past date; the amount says nothing about current values. Firms almost inevitably have a current market value greater or less than the book values of their assets minus liabilities, but because that difference has not been 'purchased' it does not appear in the accounts.

The accounting treatment of intangibles varies; patents are depreciated over their expected life and trademarks are commonly shown at nominal values, while goodwill is commonly treated in the accounts of UK firms as a fixed asset. Further consideration will be given to intangibles in company accounts in Chapter 8.

2. Claims

On the claims side of the balance sheet all items relating to the ownership claim appear together as a group. That is not difficult to achieve in the case of a sole trader like Weaver, for whom retained profit of the year has merely been added to capital. But for companies which may have more than one class of share capital and different types of reserves, it is important that the proprietors' stake in the business be distinguished clearly. Certainly the ownership claim has no connection with 'loans' or long-term debts, which should occupy a separate segment of their own.

Current liabilities are the counterpart to current assets, in that they represent short-term commitments which are normally payable within a year; items which can be outstanding for rather longer periods may be included. Bank overdrafts, which are technically repayable on demand, should appear among current liabilities.

3.3 Funds flow statements

Although funds flow statements have been prepared in a variety of forms for many years, it is only recently that their presentation in annual accounts has become general practice. Consequently, accounting conventions are by no means as well established as for the other two major summaries. There are differences of opinion over what such statements should contain, how they should be presented – and even over what they should be called.

In accounting, as in everyday language, the word 'funds' can have several meanings. The three most important senses of the word are working capital, cash and 'all financial resources'. Any one of those concepts of funds could be adopted in a funds flow statement; the first is the most common, although firms do employ other approaches (including hybrid concepts).

Fig. 3.3 Funds Flows.

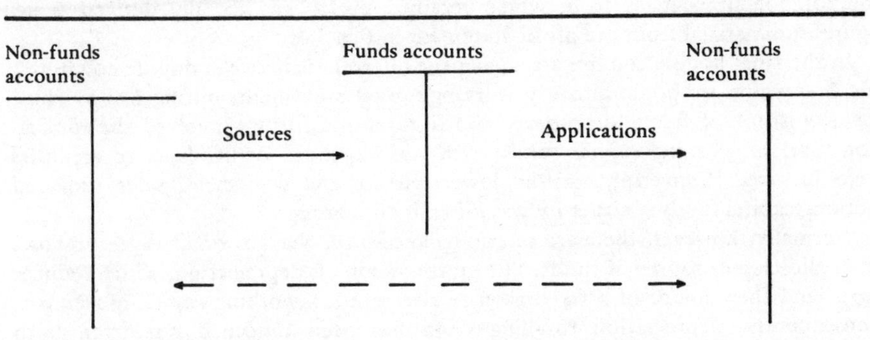

The concept of funds determines which flows (movements) should be disclosed in the statement. Funds can be viewed as a double-entry account, as shown in Fig. 3.3. Flows into the account are debits which provide sources of funds, and flows out of the account are credits representing applications (uses) of funds. Transactions between other, non-funds, accounts do not affect funds and so are irrelevant. In principle, therefore, a funds flow statement should summarize the entries which would appear in a funds account – no more and no less. In practice, the approach is usually modified by showing only the net effect of certain funds movements.

As for what the statements should be called, the preferred title of the UK accountancy profession is *statement of source and application of funds*[2]. The implication of a single source and single application is a minor, if unimportant, mystery; most statements involve a variety of different sources and applications. A commonplace abbreviation in discussion is *funds statement*, which is only slightly briefer and less correct than 'funds flow statement' adopted in this book. Perhaps the most accurate title for orthodox statements is used by the American profession: *statement of changes in financial position.* That term has the merit of indicating that most statements explain changes between balance sheets without disclosing all details of funds movements – as will be seen in the 'add-back' method of calculating funds generated from operations, which is to be described below.

1. Working-capital flows

The working-capital approach to funds concentrates on movements which increase or decrease current assets minus current liabilities. In effect, such a statement explains the reasons for the change in working capital during a period.

This viewpoint fits conveniently with the principles on which the balance sheet and profit statement are prepared. It will be remembered that profits and costs do not depend merely on cash transactions, but include transactions involving debtors and creditors. Consequently, most (although not all) of the transactions summarized in a firm's final accounts involve working-capital movements.

A worksheet showing the calculation of Weaver's working capital funds flows in 19–1 is shown in Fig. 3.4. The information is based entirely on figures previously shown in Figs. 3.1 and 3.2.

In the first and second double columns of the worksheet are listed the amounts from Weaver's balance sheets at 31 December 19–0 and 19–1. However, the retained profit amount in the 19–1 balance sheet has been replaced by details of the component changes from which retained profit was actually derived – i.e. figures summarized from the profit statement in Fig. 3.1.

In the final double column are shown the differences between double columns 1 and 2 – which are predominantly working-capital movements during 19–1. Thus, the acquisition of freehold property and fixtures and fittings involved the application (use) of working capital funds; cash was expended or liabilities to creditors were incurred. Conversely, in the lower part of the worksheet, sales provided working capital funds – either by way of cash or debtors.

Normally, however, there are certain balance-sheet changes which do not involve an application or source of funds. The most common is depreciation, which reduces profit and the amount of a fixed asset – clearly not a working capital movement. Consequently, depreciation totalling £345 has been cancelled out from both 'applications' and 'sources' in Fig. 3.4. Other transfers between *non-funds* accounts

Fig. 3.4 Worksheet for funds flow 19–1.

	Balance sheet 31 Dec. 19–0 [1]		Final accounts 19–1 [2]		Changes (differences between [1] and [2])	
	Dr £	Cr £	Dr £	Cr £	'Applications' £	'Sources' £
Leasehold property			15,300		15,300	
depreciation				255		₵ 255
Fixtures and fittings			2,000		2,000	
depreciation				90		₵ 90
Stocks	240		3,700		3,460	
Sundry debtors and prepayments	180		1,800		1,620	
Bank accounts and cash	140		1,360		1,220	
Capital at 31 Dec.		520		8,520		8,000
Retained profit [£1,535 in 19–1; see below]						
Mortgage				12,000		12,000
Current taxation				1,060		1,060
Sundry creditors		40		700		660
	£560	£560				
Components of £1,535 retained profit:						
Sales				20,000		20,000
Other income items				240		240
Cost of goods sold			12,000		12,000	
General expenses			2,180		2,180	
Depreciation			345		₵ 345	
Other expenses			1,120		1,120	
Taxation			1,060		1,060	
Proprietor's drawings			2,000		2,000	
			£42,865	£42,865	£42,305	£42,305

Note: ₵ = cancelled out against an opposite change of the same amount, adjusting for items not involving movement of funds.

showing up as both applications and sources would be similarly eliminated. For example, if Weaver had increased his capital by introducing into the business £20,000 freehold property which he owned, both sides of that transaction could be eliminated as non-working-capital funds movements.

The treatment of taxation is more complicated. The view adopted here is that amounts owing for tax are current liabilities and therefore any movements affect working capital funds. Consequently the amount of £1,060 charged in the profit and loss account has not been cancelled against the £1,060 *increase* in tax liability from the balance sheets. (That increase is, of course, only coincidentally equal to the current year's tax charge because there happened to be no tax liability in the preceding year's balance sheet.)

The funds flow statement derived from the detailed movements in the worksheet is shown in presentation A of Fig. 3.5. Under the heading of 'operations' are shown the gross amounts of funds flows relating to the ordinary operating activities of the firm: sales, less cost of goods and so on. The resulting figure of £4,940 'funds

Fig. 3.5 Working-capital flows.

Weaver's funds flow statement for year ended 31 Dec. 19–1

	£	£
Presentation A – detailed movements		
Sources		
Operations		
Sales		20,000
Other income		240
		20,240
Less Cost of goods sold	12,000	
General expenses	2,180	
Other expenses	1,120	
		15,300
Funds generated from operations		4,940
Less Taxation		1,060
Net funds generated from operations		3,880
Other sources		
Capital introduced	8,000	
Mortgage loan	12,000	
		20,000
		23,880
Applications		
Distributions – proprietor's drawings	2,000	
Purchase of fixed assets	17,300	
		19,300
		4,580
Increase in working capital		
Increase in stocks	3,460	
Increase in debtors	1,620	
(Deduct) increase in creditors	(660)	
(Deduct) increase in tax liability	(1,060)	
	3,360	
Movement in net liquid funds – increase in cash balances	1,220	
		4,580
Presentation B – 'add-back' method		
Sources		
Operations		
Profit before tax		4,595
Adjustment for items not involving movement of [working capital] funds:		
Depreciation		345
Funds generated from operations		4,940

Remaining items appear as in presentation A above.

generated from operations' is the amount by which working capital would have increased in the absence of tax and non-operating movements.

From funds generated has been deducted the current taxation figure of £1,060, to give 'net funds from operations' of £3,880. The increase in tax liability also appears towards the end of the statement, as part of the explanation of the change in working capital. This treatment of tax is controversial, and an alternative view would be that tax should only appear as an *application* of funds when it is actually paid[3]; in Weaver's case no tax would appear in the statement for 19–1. However, that would not be consistent with the working-capital approach to funds being adopted here.

The other movements shown under presentation A are self-explanatory.

The detailed disclosure of operating items adopted in presentation A is in fact rare. Instead, the usual procedure *adds back non-funds items to profit* as a method of deriving 'funds generated from operations'. That 'add-back' method is shown in presentation B of Fig. 3.5; the remaining items would appear in exactly the same way as in presentation A.

Why is the 'add-back' procedure almost always adopted? One possible reason is that it originally avoided disclosure of expense items that were not legally required to be shown in company accounts. Whatever the reason, the adding back of depreciation can delude people into believing that depreciation is a source of funds. That such a belief is false can be proved very simply by considering what would have happened if Weaver's depreciation had been increased by £1,000 to £1,345. Presentation A would be unaffected; in presentation B the profit before tax would be reduced by £1,000 and depreciation would be increased by £1,000 – *leaving funds generated from operations unchanged* at £4,940.

There is another unfortunate confusion over working-capital funds generated from operations. That amount is popularly described, particularly in the financial press, as 'cash flow'. A quick look at the operating items in presentation A will confirm that they are *not* purely cash transactions. Anyone who took the popular use of the term 'cash flow' literally, and assumed that Weaver's operations in 19–1 had generated £4,940 in *cash* would be sadly disappointed; it will be shown in the next subsection that Weaver's operations in reality generated cash of only £270.

The misuse of the term is so deeply entrenched that it is advisable to be on guard whenever it is used; in this book inverted commas around 'cash flow' will warn that working capital is really referred to. Certainly the banker who is interested in a firm's capacity to generate funds for the repayment of borrowing should be careful to distinguish between working-capital flows and genuine cash flows.

An example may help to illustrate the sort of difficulties that can arise on the points made above. In the following quotation (*Financial Times*, 12 December 1973) both an apparent confusion over depreciation and an ambiguous use of 'cash flow' are combined: 'another aspect of [the company's] financial policy worth highlighting for the benefit of other small companies is that it has adopted a tough 20 per cent annual depreciation on plant and machinery. This . . . helps the cash flow.'

It seems that the writer was using 'the cash flow' in the common journalistic sense of working-capital funds generated by operations. The almost universal add-back method of presenting funds flow statements appears to have led him to believe that higher depreciation would increase the funds generated – a view that has already been shown to be false. Nor would it matter if the writer had been genuinely referring to *cash* flows; it should be evident that an increase in depreciation cannot generate an extra penny in cash.

It is possible that the writer of the quotation had in mind that increased depreciation could act as a brake on company distributions to shareholders. Depreciation reduces profit, and the company which has neither current profit nor retained profits from earlier years cannot legally pay a dividend. But in that case higher depreciation would be an unnecessarily misleading and roundabout way of doing what the company could do directly – by deciding not to declare a dividend.

What could have been said was simply that the company's depreciation policy was particularly cautious, and the company's profit was therefore all the more credible. The introduction of the term 'cash flow' merely introduced confusion – confusion which is, regrettably, not uncommon [4].

2. Cash flows

A genuine cash-flow approach to funds would define funds as cash, comprising physical cash (notes and coins) and amounts in bank accounts. At its simplest a funds flow statement could be provided by combining a firm's bank account and petty cash account. Such near-cash items as readily marketable securities could be brought within the scope of a funds concept concerned with liquid resources, but the narrower definition of cash will be adopted here.

In Weaver's case the bank deposit and current accounts, plus petty cash, would comprise his cash funds. The movements in those accounts can be summarized to provide Weaver's funds flow statement on a cash basis.

In Fig. 3.6 presentation A shows the detailed cash movements for Weaver's funds flow statement. The first section relates to operations, and shows actual *receipts and payments of cash* arising from operating activities. Cash received at the time of sale is shown separately from amounts received from debtors – information which would be helpful in the interpretation of accounts if it were included in funds flow statements. It will be observed that operating payments are not identified with the costs listed in the previous working-capital statement (Fig. 3.5) but coincide with the amounts which appeared in Weaver's *bank account* in Fig. 2.4. The differences between the working-capital and cash viewpoints arise from amounts owing to creditors and from prepayments.

At the risk of labouring the point, the contrast between the £270 cash generated by operations in Fig. 3.6 and the £4,940 working-capital funds generated by operations in Fig. 3.5 deserves emphasis. Both amounts are not strictly flows in themselves but the residual effect of different flows; however, only the £270 is in any sense Weaver's *cash flow* from operations. Expanding firms usually have to tie up a significant proportion of their resources generated from operations in the non-cash components of working capital, and Weaver's business is no exception.

The remaining items of presentation A show sources and applications of cash relating to non-operating transactions: all the transactions would have gone through the bank account. The movements are, in fact, almost the same as those which appeared at this stage in Fig. 3.5 because most of the transactions were made directly for cash without the intervention of debtors or creditors. But there is one exception. Weaver bought £17,300 fixed assets in 19–1 and only paid for £17,050; a fixed asset purchased for £250 remains to be paid for. The £250 appeared among Weaver's creditors in his balance sheet, and therefore did not involve a cash movement in 19–1 (see creditors in Fig. 2.4).

The full disclosure of cash movements in a firm's funds flow statement would be exceedingly unusual, although traditional 'receipts and payments accounts' prepared by some non-profit-making bodies effectively provide the same informa-

Fig. 3.6 Cash flows.

Weaver's funds flow statement for year ended 31 Dec. 19–1

	£	£
Presentation A – detailed movements		
Sources		
Operations		
Cash sales		2,600
Receipts from debtors		15,630
Interest on deposit account		150
		18,380
Less payments Wages	8,200	
Purchases	6,880	
General expenses	2,180	
Mortgage interest	600	
Insurances	250	
		18,110
Cash generated from operations		270
Other sources		
Capital introduced	8,000	
Mortgage loan	12,000	
		20,000
		20,270
Applications		
Proprietor's drawings	2,000	
Tax paid	–	
Purchase of fixed assets	17,050	
		19,050
Increase in cash and bank balances		£ 1,220
Presentation B – 'add-back' method		
Sources		
Operations		
Profit before tax		4,595
Adjustments for items not involving movement of [cash] funds:		
Depreciation	345	
Increase in creditors [£660 minus £250 creditor for fixed asset]	410	
Less increase in stocks	(3,460)	
increase in debtors	(1,620)	
		(4,325)
Cash generated from operations		270
Remaining items appear as in presentation A above.		

tion. However, a few firms do adopt the 'add-back' method shown in presentation B of Fig. 3.6. This is similar in principle to the add-back method considered earlier for working capital: amounts which do not involve movements of funds are added to (or deducted from) profit. In order to calculate the residual effect of operations on cash it is necessary to adjust profit for the non-cash changes in working capital.

The £270 'cash generated from operations' in presentation B is derived by adjustments which exclude non-operating elements. Thus the £250 creditor for fixed assets, mentioned earlier, has been excluded from the change in creditors. That amount would be offset against the £17,300 fixed-asset purchase, to give the same £17,050 payment as was shown previously in presentation A. Consequently, all non-operating items would be identical in both presentations.

In practice, adjustments like Weaver's £250 creditor for fixed assets would be likely to be ignored in the add-back method. They would certainly have to be ignored by anyone who attempted to derive 'cash from operations' on the basis of Weaver's final accounts, without access to Weaver's basic accounting records. In that case the £660 increase in creditors between the 19–0 and 19–1 balance sheets would appear in the adjustments to profit, giving 'cash from operations' of £520. Purchase of fixed assets would appear as £17,300. Consequently, the add-back method for cash flows is likely to involve approximations; nevertheless, those approximations can on occasion be useful.

3. *All financial resources*

The widest possible view of funds flow is that of 'all financial resources'. A statement based entirely on this view would summarize all movements in the firm's claims and assets, so that no movements would be excluded on the grounds that they did not involve 'funds'.

For the most part the presentation of funds flow statements on this basis would be very similar to presentation for the working-capital concept, because the overwhelming majority of transactions involve working capital. The major additional movements disclosed would involve rather unusual non-operating items; some examples are given below, but the list is not exhaustive.

(a) Transfers between capital or long-term debt and fixed assets would qualify for disclosure. Thus, if Weaver had introduced freehold property worth £25,000 into the business, giving a corresponding £25,000 increase in his capital, the former would appear as an application of funds and the latter as a source. Those movements would not, of course, have appeared in statements adopting the working capital or cash concepts.

(b) When a firm, particularly a company, acquires another business it often makes an issue of capital in exchange for both fixed assets and (net) current assets. Clearly, the capital issue would appear as a source and the assets acquired would qualify as an application in the 'all financial resources' approach.

(c) Firms are increasingly moving away from traditional historical cost accounting by revaluing fixed assets and long-term investments in their accounts. Such revaluations normally involve an increase in assets in the balance sheet and a corresponding transfer to revaluation reserve (increasing ownership claim). Other types of revaluation also find their way into accounts: for example, when changing exchange rates affect the value placed on overseas fixed assets. Depreciation is also merely a form of revaluation, in a uniformly downward direction. All such movements would strictly be eligible to appear in an 'all financial resources' funds flow statement.

In practice, the 'all financial resources' approach is not adopted in full. But it is commonly used to modify the usual working-capital approach, particularly by the disclosure of acquisition movements of the type described in (b) above and less frequently by the presentation of some limited aspects of revaluation such as those relating to exchange-rate changes.

It has been seen that views of funds are diverse, presentation of statements can cause misunderstanding, and the use of terminology is not always precise. Such problems mean that the banker must be alert in using funds flow statements in the assessment of financial changes. The general tendency for statements to show working-capital movements by the add-back method [5], on the lines of presentation B in Fig. 3.5, does at least mean that the banker knows what to expect.

Notes and references

1. Each ratio can be derived from the other, irrespective of the money amounts involved. Thus, where P is gross profit, with P/C gross profit on cost and P/S gross profit on sales:

   $$\text{gross profit on sales} = 1 - \frac{1}{1 + (P/C)}$$

   which in Weaver's case is

   $$1 - \frac{1}{1{\cdot}66} = 0{\cdot}4$$

   similarly, gross profit on cost is

   $$\frac{1}{1 - (P/S)} - 1, \quad \text{giving } \frac{1}{1 - 0{\cdot}4} - 1 = 0{\cdot}66$$

2. *Statement of Standard Accounting Practice 10 [SSAP 10]: Statements of Source and Application of Funds*, Institute of Chartered Accountants in England and Wales (1975). For an earlier survey of practices in Canada, the United Kingdom and the United States see *The Funds Statement*, Accountants International Study Group (1973): published jointly by the American Institute of Certified Public Accountants, and the Institutes of Chartered Accountants in Canada, England and Wales, Ireland and Scotland.
3. For an example of a statement adopting that approach, see Appendix B.
4. See, for example, Chapter 6 of R. K. Jaedicke and R. T. Sprouse, *Accounting Flows: Income, Funds, and Cash*, Prentice-Hall (1965).
5. *SSAP 10* (see note 2 above), which is unsatisfactorily vague in many respects, does not specifically discuss the add-back method, but it effectively supports that approach by using it in its examples.

Chapter 4

Costs, revenues and cash flows

4.1 Preliminaries

Chapter 3 explained the rudiments of the three major accounting summaries that are normally relied upon by external users of accounts. This chapter attempts to provide additional perspective by looking at underlying assumptions about costs and at the problems of forward estimates. Very broadly it might be said that whereas the predominant viewpoint of Chapter 3 was from the outside looking back, this chapter is rather more concerned with the inside looking forward.

In dealing with the affairs of his business customer the banker commonly has access to financial information which is primarily prepared for internal management use – either because the information is volunteered by the customer or because the banker seeks it. What information is available does, of course, vary considerably in both quantity and quality between firms; in general the larger the firm the more financial information there will be for management purposes.

Accounting figures, whether intended for external or internal use, can relate either to the past or to the future, and it will be convenient to distinguish between:

reports which contain figures relating to the past; and
budgets or *forecasts* which contain figures relating to expectations of the future.

The sort of internal accounting reports a banker would be interested in do not differ in principle from the summaries considered so far, and further figure examples are therefore not necessary here. The important differences are that when internal reports are available they are more frequently produced (e.g. monthly profit statements), are more detailed on such matters as costs, and are not subject to the audit which external reports undergo. Their timeliness is their great advantage; external reports are normally only available annually and then it is usually several months after the end of the financial year before preparation and audit are completed – by which time the information may be decidedly stale. Clearly, swiftly prepared internal figures do not have the same status as audited external reports, but they can be used for an updated view of a firm's financial affairs when a borrowing request is under consideration and also to monitor a firm's progress during the period of an advance.

When a banker considers a borrowing request he employs, either explicitly or implicitly, forecasts of some sort about the customer's finances. The customer's own forecasts therefore have some significance; the preparation of budgets for the planning and control of activities is an important function within the well-run firm[1]. The budgets most frequently prepared, and of particular interest to the banker, are short-term budgets of 1 year or less.

The succeeding sections of this chapter attempt some guidance towards a discriminating view of what lies beneath the surface of accounting figures. Costs are given precedence because their accounting treatment is often both complex and financially significant. Sections 4.2 and 4.3 look at ways in which costs may be assumed to change with levels of activity and at some implications of accounting treatments. These lead into budgeting in section 4.4. Finally, in the uncertain light of what has gone before, section 4.5 takes a simplified view of some budget examples.

4.2 Cost behaviour

When a firm proposes to increase its output by 10 per cent is it reasonable to expect total costs to increase by less than 10 per cent, exactly 10 per cent or more than 10 per cent? Such questions are concerned with cost behaviour – the way costs change with the level of activity. As with most important questions, the answers are not clear-cut – they depend among other things on the context in which the output change takes place.

There are several different and controversial ways of viewing cost behaviour [2]. The approaches outlined here provide simple 'models' of general tendencies; being simple they are incomplete, but they can provide insight for different purposes. Although they contribute to management decisions it will be seen in section 4.3 that yet another approach is commonly used in accounting records.

The emphasis in this chapter is on short-term costs (and revenues) over a period of months or a year; investment decisions involving a longer viewpoint are excluded. In this section and the next all price changes in what is bought or sold (e.g. through inflation) are excluded. Finally, output will be assumed to equal sales until stock implications are considered in section 4.3.

1. Individual cost movements

An obvious way of looking at cost behaviour is to examine the movement of individual cost items with changes in the firm's level of activity. Figure 4.1 provides six examples; levels of costs on the vertical axis are plotted against the volume of output on the horizontal axis, and each example might represent the behaviour of a different cost item.

(a) The rent of a firm's factory might be fixed at £5,000 per year; the cost would be the same irrespective of the number of units of output produced in the factory. If the firm sought to produce more and more units it would at some stage have to spend more money on increased factory space; the rent remains unchanged only over a limited range of activity. Such a cost which remains constant over a certain range of activity is termed a *fixed cost*. The implied range of activity is the current capacity of the firm – the output which could be produced without additional premises, plant and equipment.

(b) What is a fixed cost is merely a matter of degree. Those resources which have to be acquired in 'slices' capable of servicing a range of output can be viewed as '*step-costs*' which take a step upwards when an additional slice of the resource is acquired. Thus a firm which needs an additional supervisor for every 1,000 units of output would have a pattern of supervision costs as illustrated in Fig. 4.1(b).

Fig. 4.1 Individual cost movements.

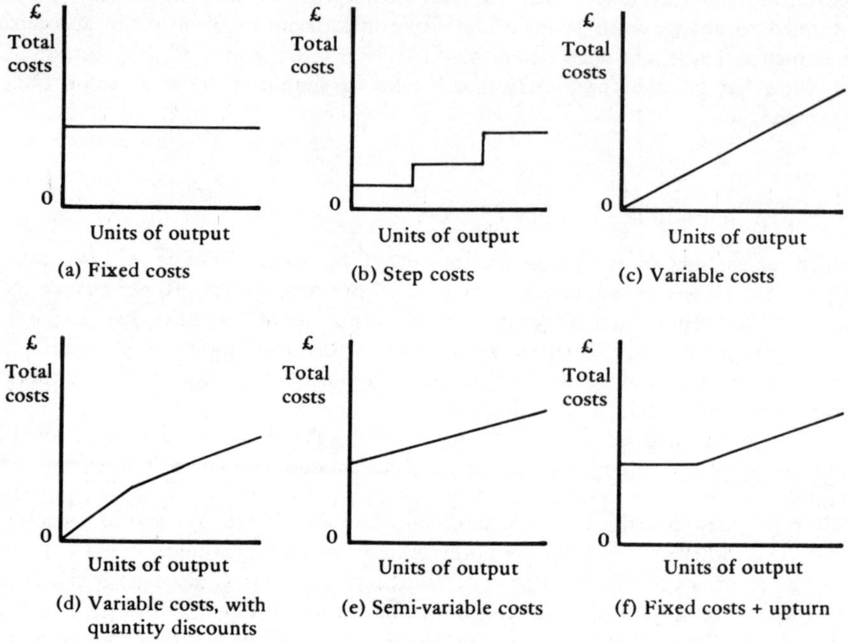

(c) If a unit of production requires 3 kilograms of material costing £2 per kilogram, the firm's total costs increase by £6 for every unit produced. In practice, costs rarely behave so consistently (wastage and quality may vary), but in accounting the simplifying assumption is normally made that such costs change in direct proportion to output – in a straight line, as illustrated in Fig. 4.1(c). These costs are termed *variable costs.*

(d) Suppliers may give 'quantity discounts' for large purchases, so that a firm's material cost *per unit* could decline with output – for example, £2 per kilogram might be paid for 1,000 kilograms of material, but £1.95 per kilogram for 5,000 kilograms, and so on. The pattern of costs might then take the shape illustrated in Fig. 4.1(d).

In other circumstances material costs could increase at a faster rate than output: for example, if local suppliers are limited in capacity the firm would incur extra costs by buying further afield. Therefore the usual assumption that materials involve linear variable costs is not a cast-iron rule.

(e) The use of some resources involves an initial basic charge plus additional costs proportionate to the use of the resources. Electricity may be priced on this basis, with a standing quarterly charge plus a price per kilowatt of electricity consumed; if output is geared to electrically powered machines the costs would take the form shown in Fig. 4.1(e).

The pattern is merely a combination of fixed and (linear) variable costs; costs with such characteristics are usually called *semi-variable* costs.

Depreciation is sometimes assumed to have such a cost pattern, made up of a fixed-cost element for loss of value through age plus variable costs for greater usage – but the usual straight-line method treats depreciation simply as a fixed cost.

(f) Under some circumstances production wages could have a pattern like Fig. 4.1(f). A work force, with guaranteed weekly wages, operating a mechanized production line could give relatively fixed costs over a large range of output. Output close to full capacity could involve additional shifts or overtime payments, causing an upturn in costs.

In fact, production wages are usually assumed to be variable costs. That is plausible where production techniques permit reasonably swift adjustment of manning levels with output changes. But towards the limits of capacity a disproportionate upswing in costs through overtime, etc. remains likely.

Some costs are not related to the firm's output but to other activities, particularly sales (which in the real world do not necessarily equal output). A simple example is commission on sales. Firms usually relate such costs to projected sales for budgeting, but for the banker the point is not likely to be material.

Other costs are often difficult to relate to the level of activity. Administration costs should normally be semi-variable, but any sizeable organization is at risk from Parkinson's Law: '. . . the number of officials and the quantity of work are not related to each other at all. The rise in the number of those employed is governed by Parkinson's Law and would be much the same whether the volume of work were to increase, diminish or even disappear' [3].

Expenditure on such items as advertising and research and development (R & D) can often be adjusted by management in the short term without much regard for activity levels. But long-term effects are important: for example, in some circumstances advertising can affect sales over many years[4]. Consequently, such expenditures are more like investments than the short-term costs considered here.

Although accountants estimate individual cost movements for certain internal purposes, more simple overall cost classifications also have their uses.

2. The fixed/variable cost classification

The fixed/variable cost classification divides costs simply between those that remain fixed over some assumed range of activity and those that vary with activity. Variable costs are usually assumed to vary *linearly* with activity and semi-variable costs are divided into their fixed and variable elements as described earlier.

Management control of costs within firms is often partially based on this assumption of cost behaviour. More relevant here, however, is the simple overall view provided by the 'break-even chart'.

The break-even chart is merely a graph showing fixed and variable costs for a given range of output (implicitly the current capacity of the firm or department), with the addition of a sales revenue line at a constant price per unit. The cost and revenue relationships take the form shown in Fig. 4.2(a), and assume the declining average cost per unit and constant sales price shown in Fig. 4.2(b).

Fig. 4.2 The break-even chart approach.

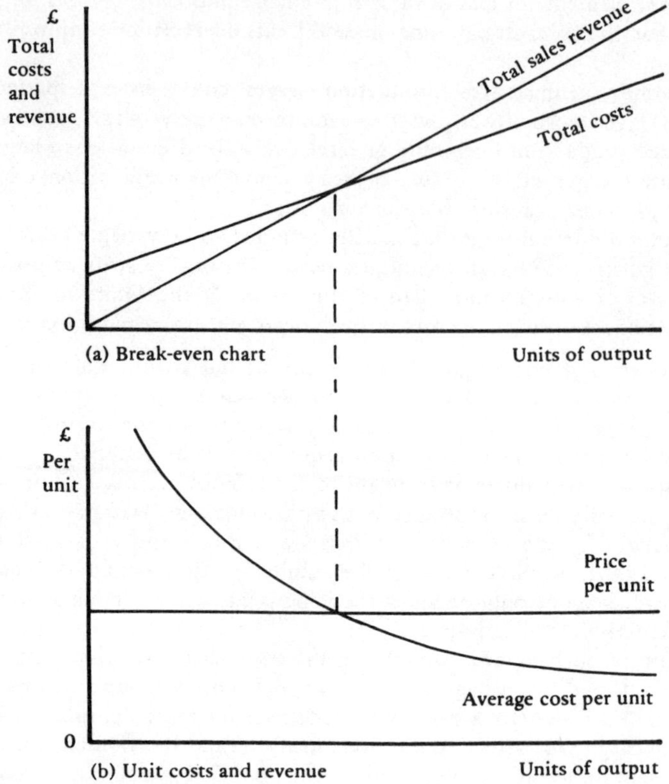

Ignoring for the present the limitations of the break-even chart, what can it offer? It can provide a framework for appreciating the financial viability of operations at different levels of activity and the relative 'riskiness' of different cost structures.

These aspects will be examined with Fig. 4.3, which shows in its upper section estimated cost and revenue graphs for Assemblers Ltd (*A*) and Manufacturers Ltd (*M*), on a monthly basis. The figures in the lower section of the illustration can be ignored for the moment.

Both firms produce goods which are sold at £10 per unit, and each can produce a maximum of 1,000 units per month.

Firm *A* incurs fixed costs of £1,600 per month and by purchasing components for assembly it incurs substantial variable costs of £6 per unit. Firm *M*, on the other hand, manufactures from raw materials. It therefore has substantial fixed costs for premises and equipment totalling £4,400 per month. Its variable costs are, however, relatively low at £2 per unit.

Fig. 4.3 Cost behaviour and risk.

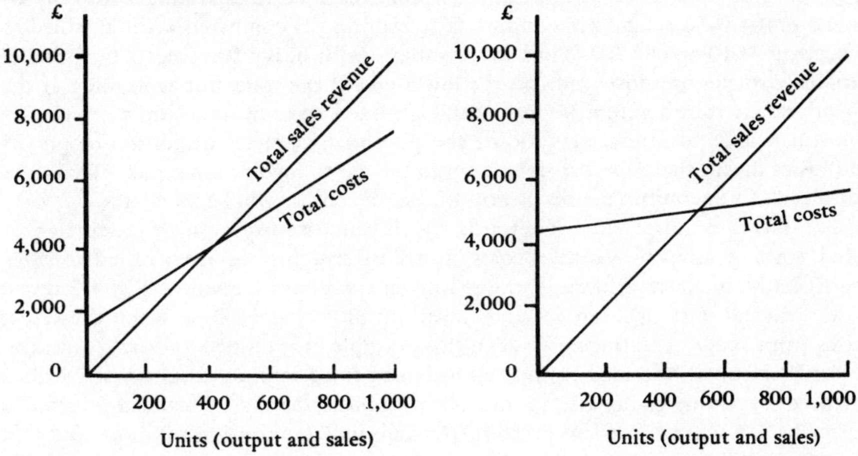

	Assemblers Ltd			Manufacturers Ltd	
Unit sales and output	200	600	1,000	600	700
	£	£	£	£	£
Sales revenue	2,000	6,000	10,000	6,000	7,000
Less:					
Fixed costs	(1,600)	(1,600)	(1,600)	(4,400)	(4,400)
Variable costs	(1,200)	(3,600)	(6,000)	(1,200)	(1,400)
Profit (loss)	(£800)	£800	£2,400	£400	£1,200
Probabilities	0·3	0·4	0·3	0·5	0·5
Profit weighted by probabilities	(£240)	£320	£720	£200	£600
'Expected' profit		£800		£800	

The firms are markedly different in their break-even points – the level of sales (= output) above which a profit is made. Break-even points can be found by calculating the sales quantity at which costs equal revenues, as follows:

$$Pq = F + Vq$$

where P is the selling price per unit, q the quantity of goods produced and sold, F the fixed cost per period and V the variable cost per unit.

Putting in the known values for P, F and V for each company gives for *A* Ltd:

$10q = 1{,}600 + 6q$; $\quad 4q = 1{,}600$
so that $q = 400$

and for *M* Ltd:

$10q = 4{,}400 + 2q$; $\quad 8q = 4{,}400$
so that $q = 550$

Firm *A* needs to sell 400 units to break even. Firm *M*, however, must sell 550, as its relatively heavier fixed costs have to be 'spread' over more sales before profit is achieved. But once above the break-even point, each additional units adds only £4 to *A*'s profit (£10 selling price minus £6 variable cost) compared with £8 added to *M*'s profit (£10 minus £2). Thus the company with heavy fixed costs but smaller variable cost per unit loses more at the lower end of the scale, but gains more at the upper end. It can therefore be said that high fixed costs make a firm more vulnerable financially to sales fluctuations; the potentially greater dispersion of profits and losses means that *M*'s *cost structure* can be said to involve more risk. (That does not mean *M*'s operations are necessarily riskier overall, as will be seen later.)

The increased dispersion of rewards which can arise from a high proportion of fixed costs relative to variable costs in a cost structure is often called *leverage* (particularly in North America); the graphs in the upper section of Fig. 4.3 reveal how the total cost line can act as a 'lever' on profits and losses. When the effect arises from fixed operating costs, as in this example, it is termed *operating leverage.* A similar result is obtained from the burden of fixed interest costs when a firm is financed by loans, giving rise to the term *financial leverage.* Financial leverage is normally known as *gearing* in the UK and will be considered more fully in Chapter 5. Whatever the sources, leverage/gearing is an important element in the assessment of a firm's financial viability.

However, the dispersion of rewards arising from leverage is only potential; much also depends on the level of sales. Firm *A* could have a *wider* spread of profits and losses than *M.* To demonstrate this point it is necessary to harp back to estimates of probabilities which were introduced in section 1.2.

Management, or anyone else, considering a firm's activities will be aware that some levels of sales are 'more probable' than others (on past experience and expected economic climate). In fact, although notions of probabilities are inherent in most decisions, they are rarely made explicit; nevertheless, it would be possible to estimate probabilities for different sales levels, to give a 'probability distribution' for sales. For simplicity it will be assumed that *A* has three probable sales levels, while *M* has only two:

A		M	
Unit sales	Probabilities	Unit sales	Probabilities
200	0·3		
600	0·4	600	0·5
1,000	0·3	700	0·5
	1·0		1·0

The lower section of Fig. 4.3 shows the profit or loss the companies would make at each probable sales level. The contemplated results for *A* range from a loss of £800 to a profit of £2,400, whereas *M* shows only moderate profits of £400 or £1,200. The probabilities suggest that, if they applied over many months, 30 per cent of months would yield a loss of £800 for *A*, and so on. Consequently, the probabilities can be used to calculate an 'average' anticipated profit, termed the *expected profit,* which is derived from multiplying each profit or loss by its probability and totalling the results. The outcome is an expected profit of £800 for each company. Whether the identical expected profit means that the companies are equally attractive in their probable profits is a matter of attitude to risk: *A*, with its wider dispersion of rewards and losses, is the more 'risky' of the two. Yet it was observed that *M*'s cost structure involved more risk. The point is that leverage is *one* element affecting risk; it must be considered in relation to the firm's overall operating and financial context – not only the demand for the firm's products as illustrated here but also vulnerability to price changes, labour relations and so on.

The fixed/variable cost classification has provided a simplified framework for looking at the implications of cost structures, but its limitations must be borne in mind. When a firm's output is made up of many different products, each with different variable costs and different profit margins, the simple break-even chart used here is inadequate for many purposes. Moreover, the straight lines of the break-even chart are likely to be merely convenient approximations.

3. An economic view of costs

The traditional view of short-run costs in economics does not adopt the straight-line relationships discussed abôve, but instead assumes that added costs of producing additional units increase disproportionately at some stage of output. Total costs turn upwards towards the limits of capacity, as shown in Fig. 4.4(a), giving average costs which first decline with output and then rise again – in the shallow U-shape shown in Fig. 4.4(b).

Fig. 4.4 Traditional economic view of costs.

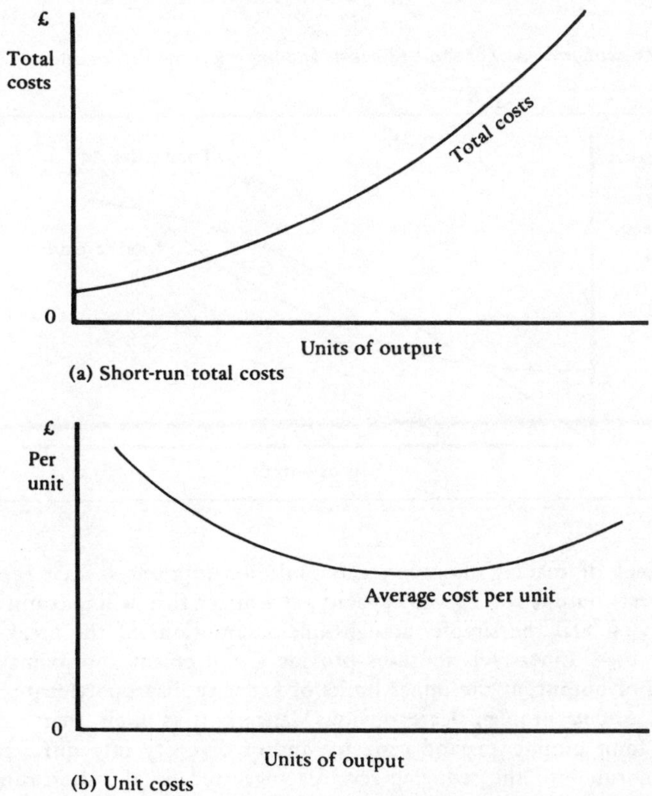

The assumption that *short-run* total costs increase disproportionately towards the limits of capacity uses the idea of 'diminishing returns'. With a fixed resource (e.g. land for a farm) and given technology, the production yielded from each additional slice of other resources (labour, etc.) must eventually diminish – which is merely another way of saying that costs per unit of output increase. The argument applies equally to fixed resources like factory premises and equipment; eventually problems of overtime, congestion, etc. must cause increases in unit costs.

However, in the *long run*, when for the individual firm *all* resources can be considered capable of expansion and there may be technological improvements, the diminishing returns argument is not applicable. Indeed, there may be economies of scale from the use of larger, more sophisticated equipment, job specialization, etc. Markets provide a limit to sales at any given price, but for the multiproduct firm there are many 'markets'. In the final analysis managerial ability sets the limits to profitable expansion.

Returning to the short run, for a single product the behaviour of revenue with increasing sales depends on the market in which a firm is operating. In a 'perfect' market, in which the firm's own sales satisfy only a miniscule part of total demand, all output of the individual firm may be saleable at a constant price per unit. In that case the previously assumed straight line for revenue is reasonable. But if a firm supplies a large part of the market for its product(s) it may have to reduce the average price per unit in order to increase sales, producing smaller total revenue increases. The latter situation is assumed in Fig. 4.5.

Fig. 4.5 An economic view of short-run costs and imperfect market for sales.

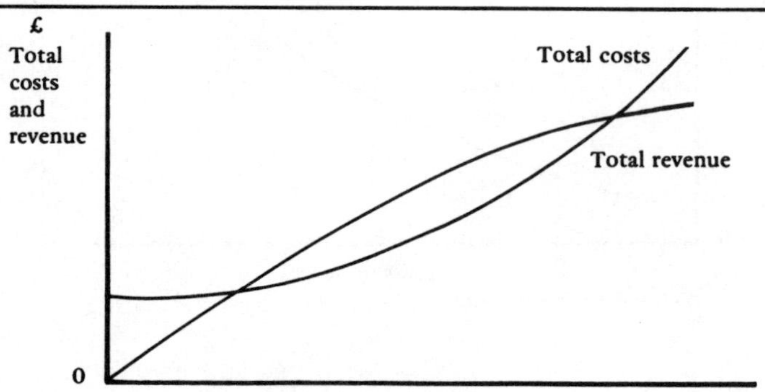

The effect of making short-run economic assumptions is that there is some optimal (best) output for a given capacity, at which a firm will maximize its profit. Both this view and the simpler straight-line assumptions of the break-even chart have their uses. Linear relationships provide a convenient approximation over a wide range of output; at the upper limits of capacity disproportionate increases in costs (and pricing problems) are obvious dangers. It is likely that a firm would choose to limit output, expand capacity and/or diversify into different products rather than run into the reducing rewards suggested by the short-run economic analysis, but that analysis serves as a reminder that avoidance is not automatic.

4.3 Production cost information for accounts

The traditional method for routine recording of costs owes little to the ideas of cost behaviour considered so far, but depends on a division between direct and indirect costs. A *direct cost* is one which can be readily identified with units of output[5]; a cost which is not so identified is termed either an *indirect cost* or an *overhead cost.*

The costs more commonly treated as direct costs are direct materials and direct wages. This means that materials used for production, and wages paid to workers directly engaged in making a product, are specifically recorded as costs of that product as they are incurred. Most firms would, of course, have many product accounts.

Indirect costs of production include both those costs which cannot be identified with individual products (e.g. factory rent, depreciation) and other costs which are merely too trivial to identify separately (e.g. glue in a furniture factory). Consequently they include both fixed and variable elements; often those elements are subdivided for certain internal budgeting control purposes, but that is *not* usually extended to the calculation of product costs for external reporting purposes. Sometimes the facts that indirect costs tend to be predominantly fixed costs and that direct costs are broadly variable leads people to interpret the indirect/direct cost split as though it were the same as the fixed/variable classification – but that must be understood as an exceedingly rough approximation.

Indirect costs are *allocated* in some way to units of production, and a variety of methods are available. Some allocation methods use indicators of activity like machine hours or direct labour hours worked. They are based on the argument that products which occupy the most hours in production also make most use of the facilities represented by indirect costs; consequently the indirect costs are allocated to products in proportion to production hours. Thus, if a factory's indirect costs are £100,000 in a period in which 50,000 machine hours are worked, the units of product A which take 10,000 machine hours to produce would be charged with £20,000 indirect costs (£2 per machine hour).

Other allocation methods, which are simpler to operate, adopt direct costs (individually or in total) as a basis for allocation. Thus, if the factory's indirect costs are again £100,000, with direct costs £200,000, the units of product A may incur £30,000 direct costs – leading to an allocation of £15,000 indirect costs (50p per £1 of direct cost).

Different, equally acceptable, allocation methods can therefore give different figures. Although some accountants would argue in favour of particular allocation methods, the choice is frankly an arbitrary one. Whatever method is chosen would be adopted consistently, but the scope for different methods provides a reminder of the estimated nature of calculations for stocks and work-in-progress in the balance sheet and for the profit statement.

The approach of allocating indirect costs to products is termed *absorption costing*; the philosophy is that indirect costs must be 'absorbed' over units of production. The method is central to conventional calculations of costs of manufactured goods and stocks for final accounts, and the essence of the convention is expressed in the following statement of standard practice: '... "costs" of stocks and work-in-progress should comprise that expenditure which has been incurred in the normal course of business in bringing the product or service to its present location and condition. Such costs will include all related production overheads, even though these may occur on a time basis'[6].

Thus, all production (manufacturing) costs are included in the above definition[7]. Excluded are overhead costs (indirect costs) relating to marketing and distribution, administration and general management. The line between production and non-production costs may sometimes be difficult to draw, but 'accounting judgement' on this aspect is minor compared with the allocation bases mentioned earlier.

Production cost information can be summarized at the end of an accounting period in a manufacturing account, as the first stage of profit calculation. An example of such an account, together with a trading account, is given in Fig. 4.6. Opening work-in-progress and production costs of the period are debited to the manufacturing account, and closing work-in-progress and the cost of manufactured goods transferred to the trading account are credited. Hidden behind such figures are assumptions which have important implications for profit measurement.

Fig. 4.6 Manufacturing and trading accounts.

Manufacturing account

	£		£
Opening work-in-progress	300	Closing work-in-progress	400
Direct materials consumed	700	Cost of goods manufactured	5,900
Wages for direct labour	500		
Wages for indirect labour	300		
Factory rent	2,500		
Power expenses	400		
Depreciation of machinery	1,600		
	£6,300		£6,300

Trading account

	£		£
Opening stock of goods	3,540	Sales	10,000
Cost of goods manufactured	5,900	Closing stock of goods	2,600
Gross profit	3,160		
	£12,600		£12,600

Note: A common alternative presentation would show closing work-in-progress as a deduction from the total on the left-hand side of the manufacturing account. Similarly, closing stock of goods could be deducted from the sum of opening stock and cost of goods manufactured – to give cost of goods sold, on the lines already illustrated in Fig. 3.1.

Costs of stocks (including work-in-progress) produced in one period are carried into the next accounting period, which can have a considerable impact on profits when there are variations in unit costs of production arising from different levels of sales and output between periods. Moreover, there is more than one method for calculating the 'cost flows' of stocks – determining the costs of units sold and of those which remain in stock at the end of the period. This will be demonstrated with the aid of Fig. 4.7, which shows the effect of four different stock valuation methods. The first is *not* conventionally acceptable because it does not include all production costs. The remaining three acceptably include all production costs, but use different *cost-flow* assumptions. All three cost-flow assumptions would be acceptable in some countries, but the last one is not favoured in the UK.

Each method in Fig. 4.7 relates to *M* Ltd, the firm in section 4.2 which had fixed costs of £4,400 per period and variable costs of £2 per unit produced [8]. For the present purposes *M* is assumed to have the following units of output, sales and stocks for its first three accounting periods:

Period	Opening stock Units		Output Units		Sales Units		Closing stock Units
1	0	+	700	−	700	=	0
2	0	+	1,000	−	400	=	600
3	600	+	800	−	1,000	=	400

The calculations in Fig. 4.7 summarize information which would go into manufacturing and trading accounts; costs like administration and advertising which would appear in the profit and loss account are ignored. Nevertheless it will be convenient to refer to the figures broadly as profit calculations: principles are unaffected by the omission of those P and L account costs.

Fig. 4.7 Cost treatments for stock valuation. (cont. on p. 50)

	Period 1		Period 2		Period 3	
Stocks valued at:	Units	£	Units	£	Units	£
1. Variable costs						
Variable production costs	700	1,400	1,000	2,000	800	1,600
Opening stock	–	–	–	–	600	1,200
					1,400	2,800
Less closing stock	–	–	600 @ £2*	1,200	400 @ £2*	800
		1,400		800		2,000
Fixed production costs		4,400		4,400		4,400
Cost of goods sold	700	5,800	400	5,200	1,000	6,400
Gross profit (loss)		1,200		(1,200)		3,600
Sales	700	£7,000	400	£4,000	1,000	£10,000
2. All production costs – FIFO (first-in-first-out)						
Production costs	700	5,800	1,000	6,400	800	6,000
Opening stock	–	–	–	–	600	3,840
					1,400	9,840
Less closing stock	–	–	600 @ £6·40*	3,840	400 @ £7·50*	3,000
Cost of goods sold	700	5,800	400	2,560	1,000	6,840
Gross profit		1,200		1,440		3,160
Sales	700	£7,000	400	£4,000	1,000	£10,000

Fig. 4.7 (cont.)

	Period 1		Period 2		Period 3	
Stocks valued at:	Units	£	Units	£	Units	£
3. All production costs — weighted average of period						
Production costs	700	5,800	1,000	6,400	800	6,000
Opening stock	–	–	–	–	600	3,840
					1,400	9,840
Less closing stock	–	–	600 @ £6.40*	3,840	400 @ £7.03*	2,812
Cost of goods sold	700	5,800	400	2,560	1,000	7,028
Gross profit		1,200		1,440		2,972
Sales	700	£7,000	400	£4,000	1,000	£10,000
4. All production costs — LIFO (last-in-first-out)						
Production costs	700	5,800	1,000	6,400	800	6,000
Opening stock	–	–			600	3,840
					1,400	9,840
Less closing stock	–	–	600 @ £6.40*	3,840	400 @ £6.40*	2,560
Cost of goods sold	700	5,800	400	2,560	1,000	7,280
Gross profit		1,200		1,440		2,720
Sales	700	£7,000	400	£4,000	1,000	£10,000

* Calculations of unit costs for stock valuations.

Variable costs:	$\frac{\text{variable costs}}{\text{units produced}}$	$\frac{£2,000}{1,000} = £2$	$\frac{£1,600}{800} = £2$
First-in-first-out (closing stock at cost of *latest* units produced):	$\frac{\text{variable + fixed costs}}{\text{units produced}}$	$\frac{£6,400}{1,000} = £6.40$	$\frac{£6,000}{800} = £7.50$
Weighted average of period:	$\frac{\text{variable + fixed costs + opening stock valuation}}{\text{units produced + units of opening stock}}$	$\frac{£6,400}{1,000} = £6.40$	$\frac{£9,840}{1,400} = £7.03$
Last-in-first-out (closing stock at cost of *earliest* units produced):	$\frac{\text{variable + fixed costs}}{\text{units produced}}$	$\frac{£6,400}{1,000} = £6.40$	$\frac{£6,400}{1,000} = £6.40$

1. Variable-cost valuation for stocks

If variable costs were used for stock valuations the fixed costs would be charged in full against profit of the current period, and no part would be eligible to be carried forward to succeeding periods in the stock valuation.

The use of the variable-cost valuation for stocks would yield profits or losses which are *the same* as those shown previously for *M* in Fig. 4.3. At sales of 700 units profit is £1,200, while at the lower sales of 400 units there is a £1,200 loss; at 1,000 units profit is £3,600. The reason is simply that the stock valuation method is consistent with the assumptions about cost behaviour adopted in Fig. 4.3: if the company is to produce at all it must meet its fixed costs of £4,400 each period, and all units produced incur additional costs of £2 per unit.

2. 'All production costs' valuation – with FIFO

The inclusion of all production costs in costs calculations causes variations in cost per unit when output changes. When output is high the fixed-cost element is spread over a larger number of units, so that average cost of production declines – which is a desirable state of affairs *provided* the goods can be sold.

Differences in unit costs require a decision on which units are assumed to be sold, and which units are left in stock (a decision which would also have to be made for the variable-cost approach when variable costs per unit are not constant). Most commonly, the oldest stock is assumed to be sold first – an assumption termed 'first-in-first-out' or FIFO. Firm *M*'s profit calculations on this basis are shown in the second section of Fig. 4.7, although the FIFO aspect does not affect the figures until period 3.

In the first period gross profit is again £1,200 – because output equals sales, and in any case there are no opening or closing stocks. But the second period shows £1,440 profit – in sharp contrast to the £1,200 loss under 'variable costing'. Here, 600 units of closing stock have been valued at a production cost of £6·40 per unit, which carries forward costs of £3,840 into the next period. But only £1,200 of those are variable costs; the remaining £2,640 are fixed costs. It is the allocation of £2,640 fixed costs to closing stocks which gives £1,440 gross profit instead of the £1,200 loss under variable costing. Thus, by this method, although *M* was able to sell *less* units in period 2 it made a *greater* profit – through increased production.

In period 3, with sales at 1,000 units, the FIFO approach assumes the opening stock of 600 units (cost £3,840) is sold – plus half the 800 units produced in the period. The other 400 units are carried forward at production cost of £7·50 per unit, of which only £2 per unit represents variable costs and the remainder (£5·50 × 400 = £2,200) consists of fixed costs. The result is a gross profit of £3,160, which is £440 lower than that obtained under the variable-cost approach because:

fixed costs in opening stocks were	£2,640
fixed costs in closing stocks were	£2,200
additional fixed costs borne in period 3	£ 440

The period 3 figures are consistent with those in the manufacturing account example shown earlier in Fig. 4.6, apart from the minor difference that stocks were there assumed to be held partially as work-in-progress.

3. 'All production costs' valuation – weighted average of period

Another common, and conventionally acceptable, cost-flow assumption is that stocks are valued at some form of average cost over the period. The *weighted average* method is shown in Fig. 4.7, where costs of the period are added to cost of opening stock and the resulting total is divided by the sum of units produced plus units in the opening stock.

There are no opening stocks to affect the average calculation in *M*'s first two periods, so the only difference from FIFO occurs in period 3. Closing stocks are valued at £7·03 per unit, derived from averaging £9,840 over 1,400 units. The result is a lower closing stock valuation than with FIFO, and consequently a lower gross profit of £2,972. The difference between that figure and the £3,600 under the variable-cost valuation can be explained in the same manner as before:

fixed costs in opening stocks were 600 @ £4·40	£2,640
fixed costs in closing stocks were 400 @ £5·03	£2,012
additional fixed costs borne in period 3	£ 628

Thus, cost-flow assumptions affect the amounts of costs transferred between periods, but not the basic principle that shifting occurs. The cost-flow assumptions of FIFO and weighted average of the period, plus a different method of averaging, are most commonly adopted in the UK.

4. 'All production costs' valuation – with LIFO

The important feature of this method is that it charges goods to the profit calculation at *roughly current cost of the period* – because the latest goods are charged out first. M's sales in period 3 included 200 old units, so they were charged against profit at the old cost and all the new production was charged at the new cost. This tendency of LIFO to charge profit with up-to-date costs leads some people to argue that it is a useful method, particularly in times of inflation.

However, LIFO has the disadvantage of giving an out-of-date balance sheet valuation, sometimes years out of date.

LIFO is entirely acceptable under UK company law, but both the tax authorities and the accountancy profession have been opposed to its use. Consequently it is hardly ever adopted in a firm's main accounts, although a similar method (base stock) has some support. LIFO is often used in the USA.

Figure 4.7 has shown that variable-cost valuation would tend to give a *sales-linked profit figure,* whereas stock valuation based on production costs which include the fixed-cost elements in overheads gives a profit which is *partially linked to the level of production.* In practice, the variable cost method is *not* adopted for stock valuation in external reports, although an approximation using direct costs was a rarely used but acceptable method in Britain until a statement of standard accounting practice decreed in 1975 that overheads should be included in stock valuation. Consequently, virtually all valuations of manufactured stocks and work-in-progress include overheads (on bases which should be stated in the final accounts), which can have implications in interpreting accounts.

When a firm adopting a conventional stock valuation method has heavy fixed costs *and* a build-up of manufactured stocks and work-in-progress it is advisable to treat the profit figure with considerable caution. This is not merely because disposal of stocks may prove difficult, but because in order to reduce stocks it may be necessary to reduce future production levels – leading to increased unit costs of production and lower profits.

Finally, three further points need to be made:

(a) The example concerned a simple, single-product firm. In reality the picture would be made much more complicated by a variety of products and by changing prices (for inputs and sales). However, as a broad generalization the comments in the preceding paragraph about stock build-up would apply when manufactured stocks and work-in-progress increase as a proportion of sales.

(b) Summary accounts (like the manufacturing account in Fig. 4.6) do not distinguish specifically between fixed and variable costs, so a broad judgement on the weight of fixed costs would have to depend on classification of the individual cost items listed in the accounts.

(c) Stock valuations are subject to two 'safety checks' required by standard accounting practice. Absorption of overheads over units of production should be based on 'normal level of activity, taking 1 year with another'. That means that if production falls below 'normal', the costs of unused capacity are charged against profit as a period cost (rather like the fixed costs in part one of Fig. 4.7) – but the emphasis remains on *production* rather than sales. If the resulting costs of stocks or work-in-progress are above net realizable value (price less selling and/or completion costs) the accounting valuation is reduced to the lower figure.

4.4 The budgeting process

There are no guidelines of 'standard practice' for budgeting and internal information as there are for external financial reports. What will be provided here are a few indications of what could be described as a middlebrow approach, which would not normally be fully implemented in a small business but which does not explore the quantitative techniques available to the large organization.

Budgets are most commonly prepared a year in advance, and tend to be finalized in a bout of decision-making a few weeks before the year's commencement. There may be month-by-month subdivision of the figures to reflect seasonal fluctuations during the year, although in volatile industries a 3- or 6-month budget period may be adopted instead. Less usual is the 'rolling budget' which is prepared, say, a year in advance but is updated continuously on a monthly or quarterly basis. Whatever the form of the short-run budgets, they are likely to be formulated in the light of broad plans for the firm's development in the succeeding few years.

The budgeting process is by no means a passive matter of contemplating what will happen to the firm, but should involve deliberate and active search of available opportunities. Interrelationships between demand, prices, costs, resources and financing mean that a number of attempts must usually be made before the component elements fit together for the 'best' solution – or at least a satisfactory one. Computer facilities can be invaluable in calculating alternative solutions, but whatever the mechanics of preparation the resulting budgets can be divided into four major categories:

1. *Sales budgets* are prepared for product classes, and commonly provide a starting-point for preparing the other budgets – subject to amendments as preparation proceeds.

   In sales budgeting the anticipated economic environment, competition and marketing activities are all relevant. Many firms are 'price-takers', adopting prices set by competitors or recommended by their suppliers: their sales budget problem becomes one of estimating external price changes and consequent sales volume. Other firms are 'price-makers' who fix prices (government legislation permitting) in an attempt to achieve the most profitable combination of price and volume. The latter group is by no means confined to large firms, but includes every firm whose products are not identical with those of its competitors and every firm which sells 'individualized' items from garage repair services to antiques.

2. *Cost budgets* are divided into production and non-production sections. Within the firm these budgets control activities and expenditure, and they are therefore subdivided according to the responsibilities related to segments of the firm. On the production side, budgets are often built up from *standard costs* which set cost 'benchmarks' for particular operations; these are later compared with actual results for controlling costs.
3. *Resource budgets* cover the different resources needed to implement the firm's projected activities. Approach and time scale depend on the nature of operations: a shipbuilder would adopt much longer-range preplanning for materials than, say, a catering establishment. Apart from materials, examples of resource budgets are the capital budget (for fixed assets and perhaps long-term financing) and the cash budget – although the latter is effectively a summary budget.
4. *Summary budgets* piece together the effects of the other budgets, and would normally be presented as a projected profit statement and balance sheet looking like the usual reports considered in Chapter 3.

    The cash budget (which on an annual basis could look rather like Fig. 3.6) would fill the role of a funds flow statement.

Within the firm, budgets are involved in two roles: planning and control. Planning is concerned with what ought to happen, whereas control involves regulating progress as activities proceed. Firms operating a full budgetary-control system prepare frequent comparisons between budgets and actual results; on the production side daily standard cost comparisons may be made. On an overall basis, comparisons between budgets and results are commonly made monthly to monitor progress; the banker may see such reports for a similar purpose.

It must be appreciated that the major purpose of internal budgets in a control system is to encourage the best use of resources rather than to make cautious forecasts. The viewpoint of what should be achieved may be legitimate for the management of activities within the firm, but for financing purposes some leeway needs to be allowed for mishaps. Budgets could be prepared showing different results for a range of probable outcomes (on the lines of the lower section of Fig. 4.3), but in practice business budgets finally opt for a single outcome. Consequently, in any consideration of figures based on internal budgets, the banker should bear in mind not only that the figures represent one of a range of probable outcomes, but also that the point chosen on the range can be influenced by management attitudes in the budgeting process.

The banker's concern centres on the summary budgets, particularly the cash budget. A month-by-month cash projection is most relevant for the banker, who can make use of estimates of cash fluctuations and maximum borrowing in an overdraft situation.

Budgets need not depend on well-developed accounting systems: prudent people were budgeting long before accounts as we know them were invented ('For which of you, intending to build a tower, sitteth not down first, and counteth the cost, whether he have sufficient to finish it?' Luke xiv. 28). Simple budgets can be prepared for the one-man firm by examining the pattern of transactions in previous years and making adjustments for assumed changes. Clearly, such projections have less significance than careful analyses backed by an ongoing budgetary-*control* system, but they can provide useful guidance for short-term financing. A similar approach can be adopted by the banker as a rough check on the plausibility of estimates provided by the customer, an aspect which will be considered in section 4.5.

4.5 Budget credibility

A banker can ask to see summarized budgets for a firm when considering lending, but the importance he attaches to obtaining such budgets, and the attention he gives to the detailed figures, must depend on the lending context. At one extreme a firm's operating budgets would be of little assistance in assessing a bridging loan for purchase of new premises if the loan is to be well covered by security on the old premises awaiting sale; the banker's risk relates predominantly to the saleability of the old premises. At the other extreme, in dealing with working-capital lending to a firm which has repeatedly broken lending conditions, a banker's requirement for budgets can provide a framework for financial discipline and the exploration of improvements to the firm's finances.

Fig. 4.8 Weaver's budget summaries. (cont. on p. 56)

Actual 19–1 £		Profit statement year ending 31 Dec.	£	Budgeted 19–2 £
20,000		Sales		30,000
		Less Cost of goods sold:		
	100	Opening stock of goods	1,500	
	13,400	Cost of goods manufactured	18,400	
	13,500		19,900	
	1,500	Closing stock of goods	1,900	
12,000				18,000
8,000		Gross profit		12,000
150		Interest on deposit account		–
90		Discounts received		130
8,240				12,130
	2,180	*Less* General expenses	4,000	
		Depreciation [property £510,		
	345	fixtures £180, vehicle £400]	1,090	
	70	Bad and doubtful debts	130	
	130	Discounts allowed	200	
	720	Mortgage interest	1,380	
	–	Bank interest	120	
	200	Insurances	230	
3,645				7,150
4,595		Net profit before taxation		4,980
1,060		Taxation on profit of the year		1,200
3,535		Net profit after taxation		3,780
2,000		Drawings		2,400
£1,535				£1,380

Fig. 4.8 (cont.)

Actual 19–1 £		Balance sheet at 31 Dec.			Budgeted 19–2 £
		Fixed assets	**Cost** £	**Accumulated depreciation** £	
15,045		Leasehold property	15,300	765	14,535
1,910		Fixtures and fittings	2,000	270	1,730
–		Motor vehicle	2,000	400	1,600
			19,300	1,435	17,865
		Current assets			
		Stocks, at cost:			
	900	Materials		1,125	
	1,300	Work-in-progress		1,625	
	1,500	Finished goods		1,900	
	1,800	Sundry debtors and prepayments*		2,260	
	960	Bank deposit account		–	
	400	Bank and petty cash		730	
6,860					7.640
£23,815					£25,505
		Capital			
	8,520	Opening balance		10,055	
	1,535	Retained profit		1,380	
10,055					11,435
		Long-term debt			
12,000		12% mortgage, secured on leasehold property			11,000
		Current liabilities			
	1,060	Taxation: due 19–3		1,060	
	–	due 19–4		1,200	
	700	Sundry creditors†		810	
1,760					3,070
£23,815					£25,505

* Sundry debtors and prepayments:

		£
Debtors		2,300
Less Provision for doubtful debts	70	
Discounts allowable	20	
		90
		2,210
Insurance prepayment		50
		£2,260

† Sundry creditors:

	£
Creditors	700
Mortgage interest outstanding	110
	£810

Fig. 4.9 **Weaver's cash budget for year ending 31 December 19–2.**

	Jan.	Feb.	Mar.	Apr.	May	June
	£	£	£	£	£	£
Receipts:						
Cash sales	150	180	250	250	250	250
Debtors	1,750	1,250	2,000	2,500	2,500	2,000
	1,900	1,430	2,250	2,750	2,750	2,250
Payments:						
Wages	700	800	900	900	850	750
Purchase creditors	580	580	680	680	580	400
General expenses	300	300	320	320	320	320
Mortgage interest	120	120	120	120	120	120
Bank interest						50
Insurances		80				100
Drawings	200	200	200	200	200	200
Vehicle purchase	2,000					
	3,900	2,080	2,220	2,220	2,070	1,940
Net receipts (payments)	(2,000)	(650)	30	530	680	310
Bank balance (overdraft) 1 Jan. £1,360 balance	(640)	(1,290)	(1,260)	(730)	(50)	260

	July	Aug.	Sept.	Oct.	Nov.	Dec.	Year
	£	£	£	£	£	£	£
Receipts:							
Cash sales	250	180	250	360	360	480	3,210
Debtors	1,500	1,000	2,500	3,750	3,250	2,000	26,000
	1,750	1,180	2,750	4,110	3,610	2,480	29,210
Payments:							
Wages	800	1,000	1,100	1,100	950	850	10,700
Purchase creditors	400	800	1,100	950	750	500	8,000
General expenses	320	320	360	360	380	380	4,000
Mortgage interest	120	110	110	110	110	110	1,390
Bank interest						70	120
Insurances					50		230
Drawings	200	200	200	200	200	200	2,400
Vehicle purchase							2,000
Mortgage repayment	1,000						1,000
	2,840	2,430	2,870	2,720	2,440	2,110	29,840
Net receipts (payments)	(1,090)	(1,250)	(120)	1,390	1,170	370	(630)
Bank balance (overdraft)	(830)	(2,080)	(2,200)	(810)	360	730	

To recognize the banker's interests in a customer's budgets is not to suggest that the figures can be passively accepted as a revelation of the future. On the contrary, budgets can be used to expose and challenge assumptions which might otherwise remain hidden. The banker can employ three elements in a judicious use of a customer's short-term budgets:

1. By testing the plausibility of the figures, in the light of past known performance and the banker's assessment of the economic environment facing the firm.
2. By discovering whether the budgets are linked to the control process within the firm, or whether they have been prepared for the banker's benefit. This aspect is not so much concerned with the figures themselves, but with gleaning some insight into the coherence of the internal control system and, by implication, managerial competence.
3. By ensuring that the success of lending is not too closely dependent on the achievement of the budgets. That, of course, concerns not only the possibility of allowing 'safety margins' in using the budget figures but depends on overall assessment of financial structure, security, etc.

Only the first of these elements requires consideration here. Some points will be illustrated by assuming that Weaver has prepared summary budgets for 19–2 to support his application for an overdraft; it is the plausibility of the budgets, not the lending itself, which is being examined. The projected profit statement and balance sheet, with comparative figures for 19–1, appear in Fig. 4.8; the monthly cash budget is shown in Fig. 4.9. The figures are detailed for explanatory purposes, but a sense of proportion in looking at any such estimates is important – what are important are the big figures and the assumptions on which they are based.

The budgets will be examined under six headings. The first is general, and the others relate mainly to particular budgets – but interrelationships between budgets are relevant throughout.

1. Consistency

It may seem obvious that budgets should be consistent with the last set of final accounts; for example, Weaver's opening £1,360 balance in his cash budget is made up of £960 from closure of his deposit account and £400 bank and petty cash balance. Early receipts from debtors and payments to creditors should also reflect balances outstanding in the previous balance sheet; for Weaver most of the debtors and all the purchase creditors at the end of 19–1 appear in the first month of the 19–2 cash budget (many firms have longer credit periods).

That does not mean the banker can expect budgets to link straightforwardly with the last set of audited accounts. Only if Weaver and his accountant had worked feverishly on the New Year bank holiday 19–2 would Weaver's astonished banker get both audited accounts and budget on the first banking day in January. Audited accounts for companies are usually available about 5 or 6 months after the end of the accounting year, although longer delays are commonplace – particularly for small firms. Thus the link between the last audited accounts and budgets must be *un*audited accounts and/or estimates. Weaver might reasonably present his unaudited accounts for 19–1 and his 19–2 budgets towards the end of January. Alternatively, by May he might have his audited accounts and provide the banker with budgets for which the first few months' transactions would represent the actual results. The banker can check that transactions in any link period are consistent with the behaviour of the bank account.

The other aspect of consistency may also appear obvious: the budget summaries should be internally consistent (e.g. sales, receipts from debtors and debtors in the balance sheet). But the bank is often provided with only a profit forecast and/or a cash budget. It is then important to consider the implications for the missing element (e.g. balance-sheet structure).

2. Sales

The sales figure is crucial in its impact on profit, cash flows and working capital (e.g. stocks, debtors). For most firms, sales are also difficult to forecast accurately. Consequently, if any figure in the budget deserves a close look it is this one.

As an outsider concerned with the plausibility of projected sales the banker can consider three major aspects: past sales trends, the likely competitive situation for the firm in its industry, and price inflation or deflation. Doubts on any of these points deserve a convincing explanation from the customer.

Weaver shows projected sales of £30,000 in Fig. 4.8, as a 50 per cent increase on 19–1. Assuming a moderately expansionary market for the firm's products and a rate of inflation of, say, 10 per cent, the increase looks distinctly optimistic. But Weaver expanded facilities substantially in the second half of 19–1. He explains that whereas sales to June 19–1 were £8,000, the sales in the second half were £12,000 – an annual rate of £24,000. Thus the projected increase in the annual rate for 19–2 is 25 per cent, of which 10 per cent represents 'inflationary' price increases and only the remainder is a genuine sales volume change. The budgeted sales become more credible, although the 19–2 cash budget reveals a seasonal pattern, with more sales in the second half – which suggests that Weaver could be optimistic to project a full year's sales on the best half of 19–1.

3. Costs

In looking at costs, the simple assumption that some elements will remain fixed and the remainder will tend to vary linearly with output is not a bad *starting-point.* However, all the qualifications about cost behaviour mentioned in section 4.2, and the possibilities of changing prices for inputs, must be borne in mind.

Weaver has assumed in his profit budget that cost of goods sold will again be 60 per cent of sales, which is not implausible for his peculiar production cost calculation, in which cost of goods is made up of materials and wages only – presumably variable. In the more usual situations where overheads (predominantly fixed) are included in the production cost calculation similar problems to those discussed in section 4.3 may be relevant, but firms do not usually *budget* for large *increases* in manufactured stocks, so overheads are unlikely to 'swell' the budgeted profit significantly.

A cautious rule of thumb might be to assume, in the absence of evidence to the contrary, that average production costs will increase in proportion to output, but that a decline in output will yield a corresponding reduction in only direct materials and direct wages (the latter dependent on the problems of reducing labour hours or the labour force).

Weaver's general expenses include certain overheads, such as workshop rent, which would normally be fixed costs. The budgeted increase to £4,000 might, however, reflect a 'step cost' expansion of facilities – and Weaver had previously got away with low general expenses.

The only other cost items worth mentioning are depreciation (which included £400 on a newly-purchased motor vehicle) and mortgage interest on £12,000 in the first half-year and on £11,000 in the second half. The overall result in the profit budget is a lower retained profit for 19–2, despite the substantial sales increase.

4. Working capital (excluding cash)

There can be certain economies of scale in working-capital items; for example, to double sales may not require the doubling of goods held in stock. However, for short-term budgets involving relatively small changes in scale such benefits are unlikely to be either substantial or reliable, and an assumption that working-capital items will generally change in line with output or sales is a plausible and fairly cautious starting point. Briefly, materials, work-in-progress and creditors would *tend* to change with the level of production, and debtors with sales, while finished goods provide the buffer between sales and output.

Weaver's materials and work-in-progress are budgeted to increase 25 per cent over 19–1. That is lower than the increase in production (37 per cent increase, from £13,400 to £18,400, in cost of goods manufactured in the projected profit statement). However, his activities expanded considerably in the latter part of 19–1 and his earlier arguments about sales would be relevant; the percentage increase in stocks of materials and work-in-progress is the same as the assumed sales increase.

Weaver's budgeted debtors and creditors are roughly in line with changes in output and sales. The liabilities for 2 years' tax in the budgeted balance sheet may be puzzling; the reason is that the tax rules allow a specific time lag before payment, which allows for taxable profits to be agreed. Weaver would in fact have to pay half of the £1,060 tax (on 19–1 profit) on 1 January 19–3, which would make a swift hole in his budgeted bank balance.

5. Fixed assets and long-term debt

The purchase of fixed assets is relatively simple to budget for, given the firm's intentions. The only problem, apart from finding the money, is likely to involve price changes. However, where fixed assets are being constructed for or by the firm, the hazards of time delays and cost escalation are significant. There are techniques for tackling such problems, but they are outside the scope of this book [9].

Weaver's projected purchase of a motor vehicle for £2,000 and his £1,000 mortgage repayment (see cash budget and balance sheet) are self-explanatory. A lending banker may well question whether they are both necessary.

6. Timing of cash flows

The timing of receipts and expenditures can be crucial for a firm's liquidity. The timing of some payments is relatively inflexible if the firm is to survive; wages and insurances are good examples. Other payments offer some flexibility: stocks can provide some freedom on materials, payments to creditors can be delayed – although not too long or too frequently. For receipts there are two major elements: seasonal fluctuations in sales and the period of credit allowed to customers. In all these aspects the firm should be able to derive reasonable estimates from past experience, although it is worth remembering that there is some tendency for credit periods to 'stretch' in times of economic stringency.

In examining a cash budget the banker can gain a rough idea of the plausibility of the timing pattern from past experience on the bank account. Covering short-term fluctuations is, of course, traditionally acceptable overdraft lending for the banker – who looks for a 'good swing' between debit and credit balances in the lending period.

Weaver has allowed a credit period of about a month for both debtors and creditors, which was mentioned earlier as being shorter than for most firms, but is justified by the balances outstanding at the end of 19–1. The other items do not raise issues of principle, except that Weaver's seasonal sales pattern may be difficult to establish on the basis of 1 year's experience of rapidly expanding sales.

Notes and references

1. The reader who wishes to pursue this topic will find introductory treatments in H. C. Edey, *Business Budgets and Accounts*, Hutchinson University Library (1960) and in the earlier part of F. Wood and J. Hellings, *Accounting and Finance*, Polytech Publishers and Longman (1975).
2. For more extensive, but readable, treatments of costs see Chapter 6 of C. I. Savage and J. R. Small, *Introduction to Managerial Economics*, Hutchinson University Library (1967) or Chapter 5 of D. C. Hague, *Managerial Economics*, Longman (1969).
3. C. Northcote Parkinson, *Parkinson's Law, or the Pursuit of Progress*, Murray (1959).
4. Evidence of a sophisticated nature on long-term advertising effects appears in K. S. Palda, *The measurement of cumulative advertising effects*, Prentice-Hall (1964).
5. Some definitions of direct cost would include a cost which can be identified with a particular segment of a business for internal control purposes, but that aspect is not relevant here.
6. *Statement of Standard Accounting Practice 9 [SSAP 9]: Stocks and Work-in-progress*, Institute of Chartered Accountants in England and Wales (1975), paragraph 3.
7. When a firm is engaged in a lengthy production process for goods *under contract* the valuation of work-in-progress can also include an estimated profit element. That aspect is outside the present consideration of costs.
8. Firm *M* is chosen because the heavy fixed costs in its cost structure make profit more dependent on the choice of stock valuation basis. The effect on profit for *A*, the other company considered in section 4.2, would have been less dramatic.
9. Techniques involving the use of critical path analysis for the control of time and costs of large projects are widely used, particularly in the construction industry – where the banker might come across the techniques in connection with lending. An easy introduction, although with emphasis on time rather than cost, is provided by K. G. Lockyer, *An Introduction to Critical Path Analysis*, Pitman (1967). Cost aspects are emphasized in C. Staffurth (ed.), *Project Cost Control Using Networks*, Operational Research Society and Institute of Cost and Works Accountants (1969).

Chapter 5

Tax flows

5.1 The tax context

Taxation is a technical and complex subject in which the banker is unlikely to become deeply involved unless he owes allegiance to a specialist tax advisory department. But for a variety of reasons a lending banker needs some awareness of the tax context in which businesses operate. Tax payments occurring at lengthy intervals can cause peak borrowing requirements and impose temporary strains on a firm's liquidity, tax considerations can materially affect assessment of projects undertaken by a firm, and interpretation of accounting information can be assisted by some knowledge of the tax structure. For such reasons it is impossible to ignore taxation in assessing a firm's financial affairs.

There are three major bases for levying taxes: on income, on wealth or assets and on expenditure. In these groups the main UK taxes are:

1. Income tax on individuals and unincorporated businesses; corporation tax on companies and associations. These taxes also cover 'capital gains', arising on the sale of 'capital assets'.
2. Capital transfer tax, arising on the transfer of wealth between individuals. For local government purposes there is also a tax (called 'the rates') on all property assets – with the notable exception of agricultural property.
3. Value added tax, and a variety of taxes on specific items of expenditure. In the latter category some of the largest revenue raisers are taxes on tobacco, hydrocarbon oils, alcohol and betting.

Business enterprises are heavily involved in the first group of taxes, not merely because business income is taxed but because employers are required to deduct income tax from their employees' earnings. PAYE (pay-as-you-earn) income tax deducted by the employer normally has to be paid to the Inland Revenue within 14 days of the end of the month in which the tax was deducted.

In a sense business firms also act as collectors for the different taxes in group 3; the taxes are levied on firms but are almost invariably recouped by them through selling prices. The group 3 taxes are all payable to the Customs and Excise authorities; the duties on specific goods are normally levied on import or on manufacture.

This chapter will skim the surface of certain topics which are intended to assist understanding of the background to tax information in accounts, timing of the payments and the impact of tax on capital structure. Consequently, only certain broad principles concerning two elements of groups 1 and 3 will be considered: the taxation of business income and value added tax[1]. But it must be said that what is a broad principle one year could be history the next; although there are some curiously ancient elements in the UK tax system it is also prone to confusingly frequent changes. Rates of tax are, of course, even more subject to change – and any rates of tax or allowances used in examples will be merely illustrative.

Section 5.6 summarizes the treatment of tax in accounts.

5.2 Taxation of unincorporated businesses

A businessman or an accountant will commonly refer to a tax bill on business profits as 'a Schedule D assessment'. That is because sole traders and partnerships are assessed for tax on their profits under Case I or II of 'Schedule D'. Arising from bygone days when such a distinction presumably meant something, Case I applies to profits of trade and Case II applies to professions and vocations; for most practical purposes the rules are identical. Other 'cases' and 'schedules' are used for different types of taxable gains and income[2].

The calculation of taxable business profit uses accounting profit as a *starting-point,* but a number of important legal rules give rise to adjustments – so that in reality taxable profits are very closely defined by law. Some of the more important aspects of these rules are as follows:

1. Expenditure must be incurred 'wholly and exclusively' for the purposes of the business if it is to be allowed for tax. For example, a shopkeeper's expenses in running a car may be charged against his accounting profit, but the tax authorities will need to be convinced that the expenditure is for business purposes before allowing the deduction for tax. Moreover, there is one class of expenditure which is *not* allowable for tax even though it is incurred 'wholly and exclusively' for the business – that is business entertaining, although entertainment of *overseas* customers can be deducted for tax.
2. Capital outlays are not deductible for tax purposes. Thus a shopkeeper who spends money on repairing and improving his premises might 'prudently' write off the whole amount against accounting profit, but for tax calculations only the repairs would be deductible.
3. Accounting depreciation is not allowed for tax purposes, but instead the law provides for specific *capital allowance* on fixed assets to be deducted in calculating taxable profits. Capital allowances will be considered more fully in section 5.4.
4. A capital gain, arising from the sale of a business asset in excess of cost, is taxable at a lower rate than business profit on ordinary trading transactions. A continuing firm would rarely have to pay tax on such gains anyway, because 'roll-over' relief allows any capital gains to be set against the cost of acquiring new business assets (which need not be identical replacements). However, a firm which repeatedly buys and sells assets of a particular type will be treated as trading in those assets – and any surplus will be taxed as ordinary business profits.
5. Relief is given for that part of the change in value of a firm's stocks which is considered to arise from 'inflationary' price changes[3].

From the above list, which applies equally to the taxation of company profits, it should be evident that only very rarely are taxable profits equal to accounting profits – usually taxable profits are lower.

Apparently, small business customers will sometimes imply to a bank manager that their audited accounts are prepared for tax purposes and consequently understate profit and present an unduly gloomy picture of their financial position [4]. Three major possibilities are involved:

1. The customer may not understand the tax procedures. Although audited accounts provide the starting-point for tax calculations, the tax authorities do not naïvely accept any accounting profit presented to them, but apply legal rules for adjustments of the sort listed earlier.
2. A permissibly cautious view may have been taken in the accounts in determining the value of stocks and work-in-progress, which the customer may consider are worth more. A banker is unlikely to favour the customer's optimism above the prudent view of value.
3. The accounts may have been prepared on falsified information; for example, some cash transactions may have been deliberately omitted from the books. The polite euphemism for that is tax evasion, but it is as much theft from other taxpayers as if the customer had stolen from the banker's till. The banker's response to suspicions in this direction must be a matter for his conscience. In any event, phantom cash cannot assist a lending decision – what does not go through the books cannot go through the bank account.

Consequently, any argument that a set of audited accounts deserves tc be viewed sympathetically because it has been prepared for tax purposes deserves short shrift.

The timing of tax payments is related to the tax year, which runs from 6 April to the succeeding 5 April. Those curious dates have an ancient history. The year used to run to 25 March, but the UK's change to the Gregorian calendar altered the date by 11 days to 5 April – in the year 1752!

Business profits under Schedule D are assessed on what is termed a *preceding year basis* (although special rules apply to the opening and closing years of a business). The preceding year basis means that tax is assessed annually on the taxable profits of the accounting period which ended in the preceding tax year.

Figure 5.1 shows the assessment basis for three different individuals, A, B and C. Their accounting years end on different dates between 6 April 19–1 and 5 April 19–2; in each case taxable profits for those years would be assessed in the following tax year – 19–2/3. The *rates* of personal income tax applying to the profits would, of course, be those applicable to the tax year 19–2/3.

Payment of tax under Case I or II of Schedule D is due in two equal instalments on 1 January and 1 July of the tax year. Thus if A had a tax liability of £1,000 on profits for his accounting year ended 6 April 19–1, he would be due to pay £500 on 1 January 19–3 and £500 on 1 July 19–3. He gets a respite of almost 21 months between the end of his accounting year and his first tax instalments; consequently the £1,000 tax liability would appear in two balance sheets (at 6 April 19–1 and 6 April 19–2).

On the other hand, B and C, with different accounting years, would nevertheless have to pay their taxation on the same dates as A. In contrast with A's 21-month 'tax holiday', C's time lag is less than 9 months; the full tax liability would appear in the balance sheet at 5 April 19–2, and the second instalment would still be outstanding in the succeeding balance sheet.

Time lags between the end of the accounting year and the dates of tax payments provide a breathing space for profit calculation and the agreement of tax liability

Fig. 5.1 Preceding year basis for taxing business profits.

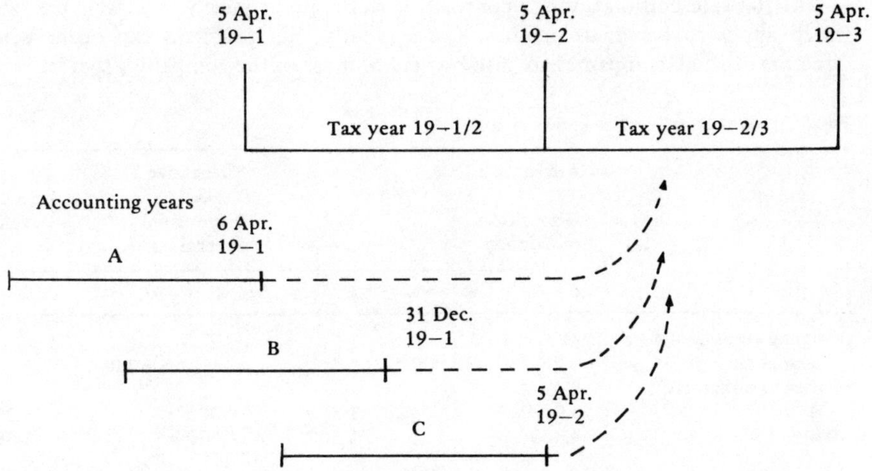

with the Inland Revenue. They also mean that tax rates are not known for certain until after the profits are earned: tax rates are announced in the spring budget so that the tax rates for 19–2/3 would be announced about March 19–2 and enacted in a Finance Act a few months later.

A sole trader's tax liability on business profits will depend on his personal tax reliefs and overall income. As is well known, income tax is levied on a 'progressive basis' which bears most heavily on large incomes. Thus, allowances are given for personal circumstances, and then a fairly wide band of income is charged at *basic rate* (around 30–35 per cent in recent years); thereafter increasing rates of tax are charged on successive slices of income.

In the case of a partnership, the firm would be assessed according to the personal circumstances of each partner and his share of the profits. However, each partner remains jointly and individually liable for the whole of the firm's tax liability – in the usual manner of a partner's legal responsibilities for partnership transactions.

5.3 Corporation tax

Companies, including unincorporated associations such as building and co-operative societies, are assessed on their business profits for corporation tax. The basis of assessment is Case I of Schedule D, so that the rules for determining taxable profits correspond with the examples given for individuals in section 5.2. The major differences of corporation tax arise from the rates of tax levied on profits, from the treatment of profit distributions and from the timing of tax payments.

Corporation tax is levied on taxable profits at a flat rate which has been about 50 per cent in recent years. Companies pay a 'small companies rate' which is 10 percentage points lower (i.e. around 40 per cent) when profits are below a certain level[5], and there are similar concessions to building societies and co-operative societies. Capital gains get an abatement which effectively means that they are liable to the same 30 per cent tax rate as the capital gains of unincorporated businesses; the 'roll-over' relief also applies.

The flat-rate corporation tax contrasts with the progressively increasing tax rates which apply to personal incomes. Consequently, tax problems can occur when directors of small companies are also owners of most of the company's shares.

Fig. 5.2 Directors' salaries and taxation.

	Alternative 1			Alternative 2		
	Disposition of earnings		Tax	Disposition of earnings		Tax
	£	£	£	£	£	£
Company earnings before salaries and tax		30,000			30,000	
Salaries to directors:*						
A	8,000		1,500	14,000		3,300
B	8,000		1,500	14,000		3,300
		16,000			28,000	
Taxable profit (at corporation tax 40%)		£14,000	5,600		2,000	800
Total tax			£8,600			£7,400

* Assumed that the directors have no other sources of income and the personal tax liability of each director is determined as follows:

	£	Tax rate (%)
Personal reliefs	3,000	0
Liable at basic rate	11,000	30
Next	2,000	40
	etc.	etc.

Assume for simplicity that two directors own all the shares in a company, so that its earnings are entirely at the directors' disposal. As long as the directors' top rates of personal income tax are below the rate of corporation tax there are tax advantages in drawing salaries rather than allowing taxable profits to increase. Figure 5.2 provides a simplified example in which personal income tax and corporation tax combined would be greater if directors' salaries were £8,000 each (alternative 1) than if they were £14,000 (alternative 2).

What if the directors want to draw lower salaries and retain the surplus in the company for expansion? There is no reason why the directors' thrift should deprive them of their personal tax reliefs – so the higher salaries would usually be paid, but the surplus would be immediately lent back to the company as directors' loans, usually interest free. This is often a reason for the appearance of directors' loans in the accounts of small companies.

The situation is less simple when such aspects as dividends and the timing of tax payments have to be considered, but the importance of tax considerations remains.

At the other extreme, when personal tax rates of the individual controlling a company are higher than the flat rate corporation tax, there can be potential tax advantages in *retaining* profits: the individuals may in due course be able to realize gains through the sale of shares attracting the favourable capital gains tax rate. For this reason there are special tax rules applying to *close companies* – companies controlled by five or less participants. These rules broadly require a close company to pay out dividends to its shareholders under certain conditions. Nowadays any investment income and at least half the property income (both after tax) must be distributed to shareholders. Trading profits also used to come within these rules, but they were exempted in 1980 as a measure intended to benefit smaller companies.

Dividends are important for corporation tax in other respects. When a company pays a dividend to its shareholders it must also pay over to the Inland Revenue an amount which is equivalent to basic rate income tax. Thus, if a company pays £700 in cash to its shareholders as a dividend when the basic rate of income tax is 30 per cent, it must also pay £300 to the Inland Revenue. From the company's point of view the £300 represents *advance corporation tax (ACT)* levied at $\frac{30}{70}$ of the dividend payment, the ACT being set off against the company's eventual corporation tax liability on that year's profits. From the UK shareholders' viewpoint, however, the dividend represents gross income of £1,000 for tax purposes, and the individual shareholders get *imputed* credits totalling £300 for having borne tax on the dividend.

The practical effect of the system is that the tax authorities collect basic rate income tax at source. An individual UK shareholder whose total income makes him liable for tax at a higher rate will be assessed for extra tax on the dividend, but conversely an individual with a small income below the tax threshold (or a charity) can obtain a refund for the imputed tax credit. The reason for 'imputing' tax credits, rather than plainly calling them allowances for tax deducted, arises from certain international agreements affecting tax on overseas dividend payments. The method, applicable in the UK since 1973, gives rise to the term *imputation system of corporation tax.*

When a company *receives* a dividend from another UK company in which it owns shares, the income is not subjected to corporation tax a second time. Such receipts are called *franked investment income* and are immune from corporation tax in the hands of the recipient company. When that company in turn comes to pay out a dividend it can do so without paying ACT on that part of the distribution which equals the franked investment income; this franked investment income flows through to the final shareholders without further tax burden.

Unlike earlier UK systems of company taxation which favoured retained profits, the imputation system ensures that business profits bear the same flat rate corporation tax irrespective of the source or disposal of the profit. However, it maintains the long-standing difference in treatment between debt interest and the rewards from shares – which can have important implications for company financing.

Interest is an allowable deduction in calculating taxable profits, but dividends are paid (or profits retained) only after corporation tax is met. Figure 5.3 shows a situation in which a company is considering raising £10,000 for expansion. Prospective lenders and shareholders are assumed to require a gross return (before personal tax) of £1,000 per year, representing 10 per cent on their investment. If shareholders wanted more than debt holders in order to compensate for risk, that would merely accentuate the tax differences being demonstrated here.

The company needs to earn only an additional £1,000 (before interest and tax) in order to pay lenders an amount equivalent to £1,000 gross – because interest is a *charge on income* allowable for tax purposes. Normally the company would have to

Fig. 5.3 Tax effects on debt and share financing.

	Debt		Shares
	£		£
Company viewpoint			
Required earnings before interest and tax (additional to existing earnings)	1,000		1,400
Charges on income, allowable for tax	1,000		–
Earnings liable to corporation tax	–		1,400
Corporation tax at, say, 50%	–		700*
Net profit available for dividends	–		£ 700
Security holder viewpoint			
Gross income	1,000		1,000
Less basic rate income tax at, say, 30%	300	('imputed')	300
Net receipt	£ 700		£ 700

* The company would pay £300 ACT on the dividend, with the balance of £400 'mainstream' corporation tax later. The example assumes for simplicity that the dividend is paid in the year in which the profit is earned. A proposed dividend which is paid in the succeeding year would complicate the timing of the tax payments, but would not affect the principle being demonstrated.

deduct income tax at the basic rate from the interest payments, and pay the tax to the Inland Revenue. Thus the lenders get £700 net, after tax at the basic rate. Had the lending been short-term the company would not deduct tax – but the recipient would remain liable for income tax, so the net effect would be the same.

If funds were raised by shares, and the corporation tax rate were 50 per cent, the company would need to earn an additional £1,400 in order to pay £700 in dividend from those earnings. On payment of the dividend the company would make a £300 ACT payment which, from the shareholder's viewpoint, would be 'imputed' as income tax and would put them into the same position as the lenders. The remaining £400 corporation tax would be payable later. Similar arguments would apply if, as is quite likely, the new shareholders would be equally content to see the company retain its earnings for expansion rather than distribute them – £1,400 would have to be earned in order to retain £700.

Consequently there is a distinct, if unintentional, bias in the tax system towards debt finance – which is most pronounced when company tax rates are high. Clearly this bias will only have effect where there is some degree of choice between debt and equity financing, and for companies with taxable profits against which they can offset the interest charge. There is a similar tax effect for unincorporated businesses, but their limited access to long-term debt finance makes it less important.

Turning to the timing of corporation tax liabilities, three aspects will be considered in turn.

1. Tax rates and the accounting period

The rate of corporation tax is determined annually in the Finance Act and applies to profits earned *in the previous year to 31 March*. For example, the 19–3 Finance

Act would set the corporation tax rate for the previous year from 1 April 19–2 to 31 March 19–3. Consequently, company accounts are commonly prepared before the relevant corporation tax rate has been fixed; companies normally provide for tax on the basis of the current rate and make an adjustment in the succeeding year's accounts if the rate changes.

When there is a change in tax rate and a company's accounting period overlaps 2 tax years, the taxable profits are apportioned on a time basis. Figure 5.4 shows the effects of such a tax rate change: a company with an accounting year ending on 31 December would have one-quarter of its profits taxed at the old corporation tax rate, and the remaining three-quarters would be taxed at the new rate.

Fig. 5.4 Corporation tax and the accounting period.

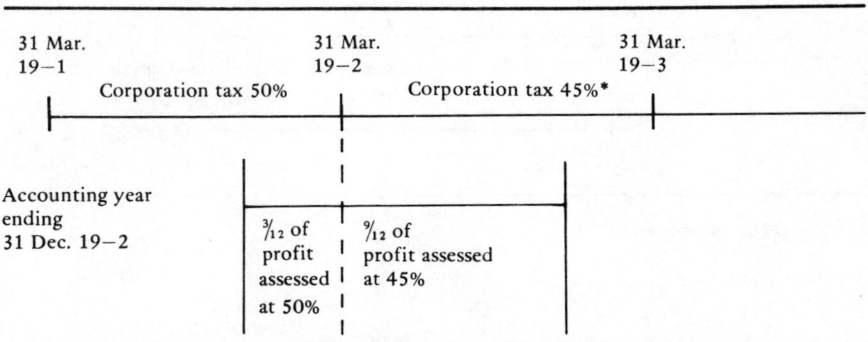

* Rate determined in Finance Act 19–3

2. *Timing of mainstream corporation tax payments*

The amount of a company's corporation tax assessment, *after* allowing relief for advance corporation tax paid dividends, is commonly termed *mainstream* corporation tax – although the term does not have legal significance.

There are two different rules for determining when a company's mainstream corporation tax is payable. The first rule applies to companies which had a taxable accounting period in the year to *5 April 1965*: they get precisely the same interval from the end of their accounting period to the date of payment as they got in 1965, subject to a minimum period of 9 months. In fact, until 1965 companies paid income tax, and were subject to the 'preceding year basis', in the same way as unincorporated businesses – so the determination of their tax payments was identical to that considered in section 5.2 (and Fig. 5.1), except that companies paid tax in only one instalment on 1 January.

Figure 5.5(a) shows the timing of corporation tax payments for three companies which have been operating since before 1965. *A* Ltd and *B* Ltd are required to pay their mainstream corporation tax (after allowance for ACT payments) on 1 January 19–3. The '9-months minimum' rule would give *C* Ltd a few extra days, with payment due 5 January 19–3. If any pre-1965 company changed its accounting date the *interval* would remain the same: thus if *B* Ltd changed its accounting year to end on 31 March its tax payments would be due 12 months later, on 1 April.

Fig. 5.5 Timing of mainstream corporation tax: (a) pre-1965 companies; (b) post-1965 companies.

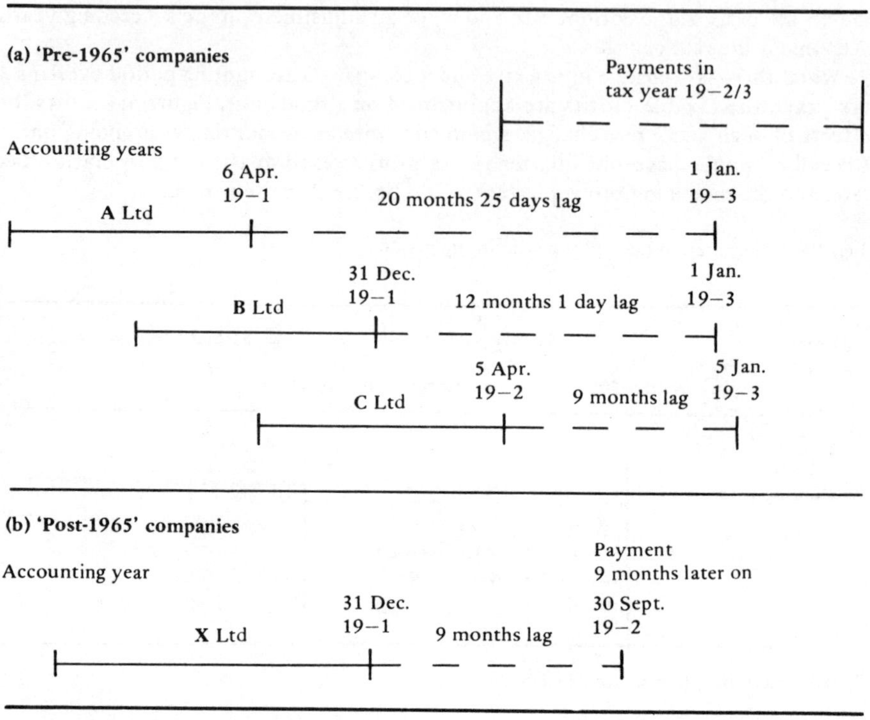

The alternative rule applies to post-1965 companies which were never subject to the old income tax system. Such a company is simply required to pay corporation tax 9 months after the end of its accounting year, whenever that may be. Figure 5.5(b) shows that *X* Ltd, with its accounting year ending on 31 December 19–1, would be liable to pay its tax on 30 September 19–2.

3. ACT payments and set-off

It was said earlier that whenever a dividend is paid there must also be an ACT payment to the Inland Revenue – except to the extent that the dividend represents franked investment income. The mechanics of payment require companies to make returns of dividends paid in quarterly periods ending 31 March, 30 June, 30 September, 31 December *and* at the end of each accounting period. Payment of the ACT must be made to the Inland Revenue within 14 days of the end of the return period.

An ACT payment is set off against corporation tax liability on the profits of the accounting period in which the dividend payment was actually made. Thus, if each of the companies in Fig. 5.5 had paid a dividend on 1 April 19–1, the due dates for any ACT payment and the dates on which ACT is relieved against corporation tax liability would be as shown below.

Dividend payment made 1 April 19–1 by:	ACT payment due by:	ACT payment offset against the company's corporation tax due on:
A Ltd	20 April 19–1	1 Jan. 19–3
B Ltd	14 July 19–1	1 Jan. 19–3
C Ltd	19 April 19–1	5 Jan. 19–3
X Ltd	14 July 19–1	30 Sept. 19–2

5.4 Capital allowances and deferred taxation

Accounting profits are rarely the same as taxable profits: that was established in section 5.2. One major source of difference, between accounting depreciation and capital allowances for tax, has implications which will be considered in this section.

The amount of depreciation which should be provided in accounts for long-lived assets is a matter of judgement, and for the sake of uniform tax treatment capital allowances are determined by law and substituted for depreciation in calculating taxable profits. In recent decades, however, the allowances have become much more than a substitute for accounting depreciation; they have become a weapon in the armoury of national economic management. Rates of allowances have been set at a high level in recent years, with the intention of encouraging capital investment.

Capital allowances are given for specific classes of assets, and apply equally to incorporated and unincorporated businesses – although for simplicity discussion will be confined to companies.

Plant and machinery constitutes a major class of assets which, since 1972, have been given a *first year allowance* of 100 per cent of cost. This allowance can be deducted in full against taxable profits in the year of acquisition.

Less generous allowances apply to other assets; for example, motor cars are much less favourably treated. They get a *writing down allowance* of 25 per cent each year (subject to a limit for expensive cars), calculated on the reducing balance of unrelieved expenditure brought forward each year. There are also different allowance rules for such assets as agricultural buildings, mines and oil wells – but the other major category concerns industrial buildings.

Industrial buildings are eligible, in the year of acquisition, for an allowance which works like the first-year allowance for plant and machinery. This time, however, it is called an *initial allowance*; in 1981 it was set at 75 per cent of cost. In addition the asset gets a writing-down allowance of 4 per cent per year. But this allowance, unlike that for cars, is given on a straight-line basis commencing in the first year. Thus, a company which purchased an industrial building for £100,000 would, with a 75 per cent initial allowance and 4 per cent writing-down allowance, get £79,000 deducted from taxable profits in the first year and £4,000 thereafter until the balance was exhausted.

In contrast to industrial buildings, most commercial premises get no capital allowances whatever. The exception is certain expenditure for the construction or extension of hotels, which since 1978 have been eligible for an initial allowance of 20 per cent and a writing-down allowance of 4 per cent per year. Consequently, it is worth bearing in mind that whereas outlays on industrial buildings bring swift tax savings there are few corresponding financial implications for the company purchasing other buildings.

Capital allowance rules are more complex than has been suggested here – for example, different procedures may apply to second-hand assets. It must also be remembered that *a company has to be earning profits in order to get the benefit of allowances*, although allowances can be carried back against earlier profits to some extent – and can be carrried forward against future profits indefinitely. In recent years companies that have not had enough profits to make full use of their capital allowances have often turned to leasing, where the provider of lease finance gets the benefit of the tax allowances. Accounting implications of leases will be considered in Chapter 8. Complications aside, the central issue to be understood is that the impact of capital allowances on cash flows is very substantial indeed. The principles on which such cash effects can be related to a firm's investment decisions will be considered in Chapter 7.

Capital allowances are by no means the only 'investment incentives' provided by governments. Many financial inducements are available for investment in areas of the UK which have above-average unemployment (usually everywhere except the South and Midlands). These subsidies, which include cash grants and assistance with factory premises, can be important in the assessment of the financial affairs and plans of customers. Information on the prevailing range of incentives can be obtained from any office of the Department of Industry [6].

However, the immediate concern is with the effects of generous capital allowances on the presentation of company accounts. Figure 5.6 shows figures for a company which bought a machine with an estimated 5-year life for £5,000 in 19–1. With a first-year capital allowance of 100 per cent and corporation tax rate at 50 per cent the acquisition reduces the company's 19–1 tax charge by £2,500. But in the financial accounts the asset is depreciated at £1,000 per year for 5 years. In the absence of any accounting adjustments the £12,000 net profit after tax in 19–1 looks distinctly healthier than the £9,500 in 19–2.

Fig. 5.6 Capital allowance effects without deferred tax adjustments.

	19–1 £	19–2 £
Tax figures		
Accounting profit before depreciation	21,000	21,000
Capital allowance	5,000	–
	16,000	21,000
Corporation tax at 50%	£ 8,000	£10,500
Accounting figures		
Accounting profit before depreciation	21,000	21,000
Depreciation	(1,000)	(1,000)
	20,000	20,000
Corporation tax	(8,000)	(10,500)
Net profit after tax	£12,000	£ 9,500

To the many users of accounts who attach importance to the figure for net profit after tax, the effect of a low tax charge in a year of exceptionally heavy investment might arouse unjustified expectations for the future – unjustified because the profits of later years would bear accounting depreciation without the corresponding tax relief. Problems of this type can be tackled with the use of a deferred tax account, which trickles the capital allowance effects into the profit calculation in line with accounting depreciation.

The operation of a deferred tax account will be demonstrated in two different situations.

1. The single-asset case

Figure 5.7 shows how the deferral of tax benefits would work for the £5,000 asset (with 5-year life) considered earlier in Fig. 5.6. The £5,000 first-year capital allowance exceeds depreciation by £4,000. That difference, at a corporation tax rate of

Fig. 5.7 The single-asset case.

In each year:

taxable income before capital allowances = accounting profit before depreciation = £21,000

Corporation tax 50% throughout.

		Deferred taxation account		Corporation tax for profit and loss account [debit]	Corporation tax payable [creditor]
		Dr	Cr		
	£	£	£	£	£
Year 19–1					
Machine purchased	£5,000				
Capital allowance	5,000				
Depreciation in accounts	(1,000)				
Timing difference	£4,000				
Deferred tax transfer at 50%			2,000	2,000	
Corporation tax payable				8,000	8,000
Year 19–2					
Depreciation in accounts	£1,000				
Deferred tax transfer at 50%		500		(500)	
Corporation tax payable				10,500	10,500
Year 19–3					
Depreciation in accounts	£1,000				
Net effects of transfers, as 19–2		500		10,000	10,500
Year 19–4					
Depreciation in accounts	£1,000				
Net effects of transfers, as 19–2		500		10,000	10,500
Year 19–5					
Depreciation in accounts	£1,000				
Net effects of transfers, as 19–2		500		10,000	10,500

50 per cent, provides an early tax benefit of £2,000. Recognition of the benefit for accounting purposes is deferred by crediting £2,000 to the deferred tax account and correspondingly debiting corporation tax for the profit and loss account. The procedure produces a corporation tax charge of £10,000 for the 19–1 profit and loss account – and for succeeding years if the company's gross earnings remain unchanged.

The deferred tax account would be reduced from 19–2 onwards by £500 per year. In 19–5 the balance would become zero, and the process would start again in 19–6 if a replacement asset were purchased. Unfortunately the solution is less neat for a multi-asset firm.

2. *The annual purchase case*

Figure 5.8 shows a similar situation to the previous one, except that a new machine is now purchased each year. The income information and the last two columns of corporation tax figures have been omitted because they would be treated in a similar way to Fig. 5.7 and the use of increasing income figures would be unnecessarily distracting; the issue this time really affects the deferred taxation balance.

The assets grow to five machines by 19–5, after which annual purchase would represent annual replacement for a stable group of assets. The deferred taxation

Fig. 5.8 The annual purchase case.

Corporation tax 50% throughout.
Machine purchased each year for £5,000, first-year capital allowance 100%.

			Deferred taxation account		Balance
			Dr	Cr	Cr
	£		£	£	£
Year 19–1					
Capital allowance machine 1	5,000				
Depreciation in accounts	1,000				
Timing difference	£4,000	50%→		2,000	2,000
Year 19–2					
Capital allowance machine 2	5,000				
Depreciation in accounts (two machines)	2,000				
Timing difference	£3,000	50%→		1,500	3,500
Year 19–3					
Capital allowance machine 3	5,000				
Depreciation in accounts (three machines)	3,000				
Timing difference	£2,000	50%→		1,000	4,500
Year 19–4					
Capital allowance machine 4	5,000				
Depreciation in accounts (four machines)	4,000				
Timing difference	£1,000	50%→		500	5,000
Year 19–5					
Capital allowance machine 5	5,000				
Depreciation in accounts (five machines)	5,000				
Timing difference	0				5,000

account grows to £5,000 and will remain at that figure for as long as the company continues to replace one machine per year at £5,000 – which, if one believes in the immortality of companies, might be for ever. However, the constant price is implausible – what happens if the replacement cost rises?

With increasing replacement costs the deferred tax balance would not in fact reach stability at 19–5, but would continue to grow. If each succeeding machine cost more than its predecessor, the capital allowances would keep ahead of the depreciation charges and the timing differences would keep piling up.

The treatment of timing differences has caused great problems for accountants. Not only is there the effect on normally reported profits, the deferred tax can also be viewed as a provision for the tax liability that could arise if the assets were sold. At one time an accounting standard required that all timing differences should be covered in a deferred tax account. But many companies were unhappy to make large transfers out of profit when it seemed most likely that asset replacements would bring continuing tax reductions. As a consequence, the present standard on deferred tax[7] makes the important concession that provision need not be made for recurring timing differences – where there is stable or growing investment.

However, that concession is far from saying that deferred tax need not be provided. It must be provided where timing differences are not recurring (as in the single-asset case in Fig. 5.7), which would occur with very irregular or declining capital expenditure.

The conditions which must be satisfied if amounts are not to be provided for timing differences are:

(a) the company is a going concern;
(b) the directors are able to foresee on reasonable evidence that no liability is likely to arise from the reversal of timing differences for at least three years ahead; and
(c) there is no indication that changes after that period are likely to lead to liabilities.

Capital allowances are not the only source of timing differences. When fixed assets are revalued in accounts there is no tax bill – but tax could be payable eventually if the assets were sold at that price. Similarly, a gain on sale of a fixed asset will get roll-over relief (mentioned earlier) if a replacement asset is bought – but tax could become due eventually if that asset is sold in turn without roll-over relief. Deferred tax would have to be provided in such cases unless the conditions above are satisfied.

Some minor timing differences arising from short-term differences between the accounting and tax bases must also be provided for. In addition, the deferred tax account is a temporary home for advanced corporation tax adjustment, to be considered in section 5.7.

The overall result of the standard is that the deferred tax account represents a possible liability for tax. In this view the deferred amounts ought to be carried at the current tax rate and adjusted (through the profit and loss account) for any change in tax rate. This would seem to be the majority view among UK companies[8]. But the standard also allows an alternative method, which would keep to the original tax rate.

The standard requires a note disclosing the potential amount of deferred tax for *all* timing differences. Thus information on both the full and limited deferral is given. (See note 18 to Good Practice Ltd in Appendix B.)

What does all this mean to the banker? Apart from the financing implications of capital allowances, it means that the banker will come across amounts of deferred tax on the fringes of the long-term liabilities section of customers' balance sheets. (For an example, see the balance sheet of Good Practice Ltd in Appendix B.) Unlike the position under the previous standard, these amounts can be regarded as genuinely possible liabilities. Thus for balance sheet ratios they represent funds provided by outsiders rather than owners. But the liability is only *possible*, and conversion into a liability for payment should release corresponding funds to the company (e.g. tax cannot be payable on a revaluation gain until the asset is sold). If the banker wants to consider the implications of payment, an initial rule of thumb might be to offset the deferred tax amount against fixed assets – since disposal of fixed assets could give rise to a tax liability.

5.5 Stock relief

It was explained earlier that taxation on business profits uses accounting profit as a starting point. On this basis a business that buys goods at £10 and sells them at £15 would be taxed on a profit of £5. But during inflation, when prices in general are rising, the business might find that it could only replace the goods at £13. If the business replaced the goods it would be able to withdraw only £2 from the business if trade was to continue at the same level. Yet the firm would be taxed on £5 unless some form of relief was given.

Stock relief deals with this problem. The method in use since 1980 gives relief based on an *all stocks index*, which is published monthly by the Department of Industry. The relief is given on stocks over £2,000, in proportion to the increase in the all stocks index over the period. It seems that a decrease in the all stocks index, and a corresponding charge, is unthinkable.

The method of calculating stock relief is illustrated in Fig. 5.9. This approach would apply equally to companies or unincorporated businesses.

For the purpose of the relief, stocks comprise raw materials, work-in-progress and finished goods.

Fig. 5.9 Stock relief calculations.

For the year ended 31 December 19–1 a business has:

Taxable profits (before stock relief)	£60,000
Opening stocks 1 January 19–1	£30,000
Closing stocks 31 December 19–1	£37,000

The all stocks index published monthy by the Department of Industry shows:

December 19–0	170
December 19–1	187

Stock relief is calculated as:

$$(\text{opening stock} - £2{,}000) \times \frac{\text{increase in all stocks index}}{\text{opening all stocks index}}$$

which in this case come to:

$$(£30{,}000 - £2{,}000) \times \frac{187 - 170}{170} \qquad = £2{,}800$$

Thus the taxable profit will be:

taxable profits before stock relief – stock relief

£60,000 – £2,800 = £57,200

A business would only be liable to repay the stock relief if it ceases to trade or its activities become negligible. But in any case the maximum repayment would be for 6 years' relief. These features have convinced accountants that the present system of stock relief does not involve timing differences which might be reversed for a going concern. Consequently, stock relief would not normally affect deferred tax, even in the note which shows the potential amount of all timing differences.

5.6 Value added tax

Value added tax (VAT) is levied on the sale of a wide range of goods and services in the UK. Although a firm is liable for tax on its sales (output) it can offset against that liability any VAT suffered on goods or services purchased (inputs). Thus the firm pays tax only on the difference between its taxable output and taxed inputs – the *value added* by the activities of labour and capital of the firm.

Fig. 5.10 Taxation of value added.

	Before VAT		VAT at 10%		
Sales	10,000	+	1,000	←	Collected from customers
Purchased inputs subject to VAT	(7,000)	+	(700)	←	Paid to suppliers
'Value added'	3,000		300	←	VAT payable
Wages and salaries	(2,000)				
Net profit	£1,000				

Figure 5.10 shows how the tax would operate for a firm subject to a single VAT rate of 10 per cent. The purchased inputs subjected to VAT would include not only purchased material but also equipment and a wide range of services from window cleaning to legal fees. As Fig. 5.10 shows, wages, salaries and profit comprise the major elements of value added.

Different rates of VAT can apply to different goods and services, and the rates of tax can be changed by the government much more swiftly than tax rates on income and profits.

For those goods and services which are not subject to VAT there are two categories:

1. *Zero rated.* Items in the zero-rated group, mainly food, are entirely free from VAT. That means that not only do the *sales* of a firm in the zero-rated category escape VAT, but that when the firm has *purchased* items (e.g. equipment) which have borne VAT a refund of the tax on inputs can be obtained.
2. *Exempt.* This category is largely concerned with activities which would be awkward to bring within the VAT system, such as insurance and banking. Very small businesses can also be treated as exempt. Here any sales of exempt goods or services are not subject to VAT, but no refunds are available for any VAT borne on inputs.

VAT has two implications of particular interest to the banker. The first is that firms have to produce regular returns for VAT purposes which can provide up-to-date financial information; the second is that the collection and payment of VAT can improve or weaken a firm's cash flows.

Firms must account regularly to the Customs and Excise authorities for VAT collected on sales, less amounts of VAT paid on inputs. The information has normally to be provided every 3 months on the Customs and Excise 'VAT form 100'; the return and payment of tax must normally be made within 1 month of the end of each quarter. Thus a firm with a VAT quarter ending February would have to pay by the end of March; the month in which a firm's VAT quarter ends is fixed by the tax authorities. However, a firm can apply for a monthly return period – and a zero-rated firm seeking swift refunds of VAT borne on inputs would usually apply.

Whatever the VAT return period, a banker who wants to keep a close eye on a borrower's business activities can ask his customer to produce the regular quarterly copies of 'VAT 100'. The banker can use the information on sales and inputs in conjunction with bank transactions to get some idea of developments in debtors and creditors (e.g. the difference between sales on VAT 100 and receipts through the bank account in the corresponding period should be roughly equal to the change

Fig. 5.11 VAT cash flows, 'credit taking' firm.

Three-month tax period, VAT rate 10%.
Inputs subject to VAT £7,000 per month + VAT £700. Credit period 1 month.
Sales subject to VAT £10,000 per month + VAT £1,000. Sales for cash.

	Month 1	2	3	4	5
	£	£	£	£	£
VAT paid		(700)	(700)	(700)	(700)
VAT collected	1,000	1,000	1,000	1,000	1,000
Net	1,000	300	300	300	300
VAT to Customs and Excise				(900)	
Cumulative VAT effect on cash flows	1,000	1,300	1,600	1,000	1,300 etc.

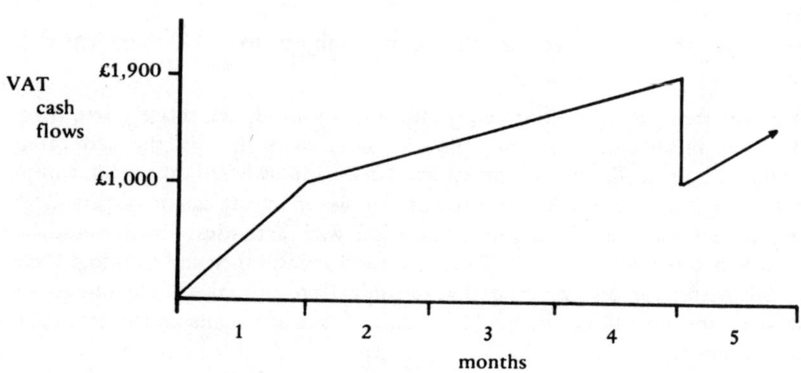

in debtors during the period). The VAT forms are not, of course, anywhere near as informative as full accounting reports, but they do have the merit of being readily available – the small business cannot offer the usual excuse that the information would be too troublesome to prepare. Curiously, bankers in fact very rarely make use of quarterly VAT returns [9].

Fig. 5.12 VAT cash flows, 'credit giving' firm.

Three-month tax period, VAT rate 10%.
Inputs subject to VAT: £7,000 per month + VAT £700. Credit period 1 month.
Sales subject to VAT: £10,000 per month + VAT £1,000. Credit period 2 months.

Month	1	2	3	4	5
	£	£	£	£	£
VAT paid		(700)	(700)	(700)	(700)
VAT collected			1,000	1,000	1,000
Net	–	(700)	300	300	300
VAT to Customs and Excise				(900)	
Cumulative VAT effect on cash flows	–	(700)	(400)	(1,000)	(700) etc.

Assume that a firm sells goods at the same rate at which it purchases them (i.e. stock build-ups or run-downs are ignored). If such a firm gets longer credit periods than it gives, it will be collecting VAT before it makes the corresponding VAT payments – so that VAT has a favourable effect on cash flows. This is demonstrated in Fig. 5.11, where a firm subject to a VAT rate of 10 per cent buys goods on 1 month's credit and sells for cash. After month 1 the firm would have VAT collected, but awaiting settlement, of between £1,000 and £1,900. The amounts would not, of course, be specifically earmarked in cash but would have its impact on the firm's cash balance.

The VAT effect on cash flows is reversed when a firm gives more credit than it receives (although a firm always gets a period of credit from Customs and Excise on its own value added). An example is shown in Fig. 5.12, where 1 month's credit is obtained on inputs as before, but this time 2 months' credit is given on sales. The firm pays over VAT to suppliers before the corresponding receipts from customers, and the unfavourable effect on cash flows is as high as £1,000.

A firm which has a monthly VAT return period and is zero-rated (e.g. a food producer) would normally obtain refunds for VAT borne on inputs about 1 month after submitting its returns. If its inputs are bought at an even rate throughout each month the firm would get VAT refunds *on average* about 1½ months after goods are acquired. VAT would consequently be recouped before payment if the firm gets a credit period above 1½ months from its suppliers – and conversely under 1½ months.

The cash-flow implications of VAT are of most concern to firms and their bankers when the rate of tax is changed; a rate change will affect financial expectations. An increase in VAT rate on a firm's sales would tend to reduce demand for the firm's products – but for the 'credit-taking' firm there will be some offset in improved VAT cash flows. For example, an increase in VAT to 15 per cent might reduce the inputs and sales of the firm in Fig. 5.11 by one-tenth to £6,300 and £9,000 respectively (both before VAT). So net cash flows from trading would be lower, although by how much would depend on the proportionate reduction of wages, etc. But the change would lead to an *increase* in the 'cumulative VAT effect on cash flows' – which would be £350 higher at £1,350 in month 1 (15 per cent of £9,000), £1,755 in month 2 (£1,350 plus £405) and so on.

For the credit-giving firm an increase in VAT would, of course, be uniformly detrimental (and a decrease uniformly beneficial). The moral is, however, that VAT affects financing in different ways which need to be considered in relation to the attributes of the individual firm.

5.7 Taxation in accounts

Some aspects of the treatment of tax in accounts have already been touched upon. This section will bring together certain basic points which affect accounting presentation [10] ; the effects are summarized in Figs. 5.13 and 5.14.

The points involved are considered under three heads.

1. Interest and dividends

The requirement that basic rate income tax shall be deducted at source from long-term interest affects both payments and receipts of companies. A company must make returns for income tax deducted from payments, and can offset any income tax borne on its receipts in the same return period. The return periods end on 31 March, 30 June, 30 September, 31 December and the end of the accounting year (i.e. the same return periods as for ACT).

A balance of income tax owing to the Inland Revenue must be paid within 14 days of the return period. Thus, in Fig. 5.13 the balance of £1,800, representing the difference between amounts deducted and borne in the quarter ending 31 December 19–1, will be payable by 14 January 19–2. With an accounting year ending 31 December the £1,800 will appear among creditors in the balance sheet – although not as a separate tax liability because it represents an amount owed by the company as a collecting agent. Had the balance been in the other direction (e.g. £700 debit only on the income tax account) it would be set off against the company's mainstream corporation tax liability on profit of the period. The £1,000 paid in bank interest is unaffected by all this; it is, of course, paid gross without income tax deduction.

Note that although the company received only *net* long-term interest of £1,400 the effect of the income tax entry is to raise interest to its gross (pre-tax) amount, so that £2,000 interest appears in the profit and loss account (see Fig. 5.14). There is a *partial* similarity in the treatment of £3,500 received by Cap Ltd from another UK company; as franked investment income that is 'grossed up' by the addition of £1,500 tax credit (for ACT). However, that amount is not offset against anything but is charged as part of taxation of the period (shown separately in Fig. 5.14). The result of this treatment of dividends received is a rather artificial representation of the £1,500 tax borne by the other company on behalf of Cap Ltd.

In contrast with the 'grossing up' of dividends received, the dividends paid and proposed are shown at their net amount excluding tax credit. The reason is that although ACT is payable, it will be offset against corporation tax. For the £8,400

Fig. 5.13 Tax on interest and dividends – Cap Ltd. (cont. on p. 82)

Return period (and accounting period) ending 31 Dec. 19–1
Basic rate of income tax 30%
Rate of ACT $^{30}/_{70}$

Interest

Interest received

P & L	2,000	15 Nov. Bank	1,400
		Income tax	600 →
	£2,000		£2,000

Income tax

15 Nov. Deduction from interest received	→ 600	1 Oct. Deduction from interest paid	2,400 ←
Balance c/d	1,800		
	£2,400		£2,400
		1 Jan. Balance [payable to Inland Revenue by 14 Jan.]	1,800

Debenture interest

1 Oct. Bank	5.600	P & L	8,000
Income tax	2,400		
	£8.000		£8,000

Bank interest

20 Dec. Bank	1,000	P & L	1,000

Dividends

Dividends received

P & L	5,000	12 Oct. Bank	3,500
		Tax credit	1,500 →
	£5,000		£5,000

Tax attributable to dividend income (for P & L account)

12 Oct. Imputed tax credit	→ 1,500	P & L	1,500

Dividends paid and proposed

15 Dec. Bank	8,400	P & L	8,400
		P & L	2,800

Advance corporation tax

		15 Dec. ACT (net, £3,600 – £1,500) on paid dividend	2,100 →
		[payable to Inland Revenue by 14 Jan.]	
		31 Dec. ACT on proposed dividend	1,200 →

Corporation tax

		Balance	25,000
→	2,100	P & L	30,000

ACT recoverable

→	1,200		

Fig. 5.13 (cont.)

Other items to complete double-entry balances for Fig. 5.14

Bank

Opening balance	4,950	1 Oct. Debenture interest	5,600
12 Oct. Dividend received	3,500	15 Dec. Dividend paid	8,400
15 Nov. Interest received	1,400	20 Dec. Bank interest	1,000
Balance c/d	5,150		
	£15,000		£15,000
		Balance b/d	5,150

Deferred taxation

		Opening balance	35,600
		P & L	4,000

Sundry creditors

		Trade creditors	92,650
		PAYE	2,700
		VAT	5,000

Revenue minus costs

P & L	80,000	19–1	80,000

Capital and reserves

		Opening balances	184,000
		19–1 Retained profits	47,300

Sundry assets

Balances	536,000		

Debenture stock

		Balance	100,000

dividend paid in the last quarter of the year there is a notional ACT liability of $\frac{30}{70}$ – i.e. £3,600. But that is reduced by the £1,500 tax credit on franked investment income, so that £2,100 is payable by 14 January. That amount is therefore raised as a creditor (credit ACT, debit corporation tax) and forms part of the £3,300 ACT among creditors in the balance sheet (see Fig. 5.14).

Similarly, for the proposed dividend of £2,800 (appearing as a creditor in the balance sheet) there will be ACT of $\frac{30}{70}$ to pay, amounting to £1,200. When that amount is paid it will be available to offset against corporation tax on *19–2* profits – which have not yet been earned. Therefore for the 19–1 accounts the £1,200 ACT recoverable is not offset against corporation tax but is offset against deferred taxation in the balance sheet, from whence it will re-emerge to offset corporation tax on next year's profits.

2. Corporation tax and deferred taxation

The accounts in Fig. 5.14 show the treatment of corporation tax and deferred taxation, the bases for which have already been discussed.

The UK corporation tax charge of £30,000 in the profit and loss account might have been calculated as 40 per cent (small companies rate) on taxable profit of £75,000, after capital allowances.

The current year's capital allowance is assumed partially deferred, although there would be some release of past deferrals to match depreciation. The assumed net deferral of £10,000 capital allowances at the 40 per cent tax rate produces a transfer to deferred taxation of £4,000, which is recorded in the double-entry accounts in Fig. 5.13.

Fig. 5.14 Tax in final accounts – Cap Ltd.

Profit and loss account for year ended 31 Dec. 19–1

	£	£
Trading profit before interest		96,000
Interest received on quoted investments		2,000
Dividends received on quoted investments		5,000
		103,000
Less interest charges: Debenture interest	8,000	
Bank interest	1,000	
		9,000
Profit before taxation		94,000
Taxation*		35,500
Profit after taxation		58,500
Dividends – interim paid	8,400	
final proposed	2,800	
		11,200
Transferred to reserves		£47,300

* The taxation charge based on profit of the year was made up as follows:

UK corporation tax at 40%	30,000
Tax attributable to dividend income	1,500
Transfer to deferred taxation [e.g. capital allowances £10,000 at 40%]	4,000
Overseas taxation	–
	£35,500

Balance sheet at 31 Dec. 19–1

Share capital and reserves		231,300
Deferred taxation [£39,600 – ACT recoverable £1,200]		38,400
Debenture stock		100,000
Current liabilities:		
Creditors [including income tax £1,800, ACT £3,300, PAYE £2,700 and VAT £5,000]	105,450	
Bank overdraft	5,150	
Taxation – corporation tax payable 1 Jan. 19–1	25,000	
corporation tax payable 1 Jan. 19–2	27,900	
Proposed dividend	2,800	
		166,300
		£536,000
Sundry assets		£536,000

Note: Information in square brackets would not normally be disclosed in accounting reports.

3. VAT and PAYE

VAT levied on a taxable firm is treated in the accounts as though the firm were merely a collecting agent. Thus, any VAT on inputs acquired by the firm are debited to a VAT account, and VAT collected on sales is credited. The balance represents the amount the firm owes to (or occasionally is owed by) the Customs and Excise authorities, and would be paid over periodically as described earlier.

At the end of the accounting year any credit balance outstanding on the VAT account would be shown as part of creditors in the balance sheet – as demonstrated in Fig. 5.14.

However, VAT on some inputs is not deductible (e.g. on motor cars), nor would a so-called exempt firm (which does not pay VAT on sales) be able to offset VAT on inputs. Consequently, such amounts would be treated as costs, and would be charged against profit calculation or to the cost of fixed assets as appropriate.

It was said earlier that income tax deducted from the pay of employees under PAYE must be accounted for monthly to the Inland Revenue. Amounts outstanding at the end of the year appear among creditors, as shown in Fig. 5.14.

These examples have demonstrated that a variety of different tax liabilities are included in the balance sheet, not all of them immediately apparent.

Notes and references

1. For the reader who wants more information on taxation there are many sources available. A cheap and readable introduction is provided by *The British System of Taxation*, HMSO, which is updated periodically. For a most capable but readable critique see J. A. Kay and M. A. King, *The British Tax System*, Oxford University Press (1980). For comprehensive, up-to-date and superbly indexed guides used by professional accountants, there are the annual *Tolley Guides* published by Tolley Publishing Co.
2. Other cases under Schedule D are: III – interest receivable; IV and V – overseas income; VI – miscellaneous income. The remaining schedules are: A – property income; B – woodlands; C – interest, etc. paid by paying agents; E – emoluments; F – dividends.
3. General principles of accounting treatment of price changes will be considered in Chapter 9.
4. See, for example, L. S. Dyer, *A Practical Approach to Bank Lending*, Institute of Bankers (1974), p. 21.
5. £90,000, with 'taper relief' for profits between £90,000 and £225,000, 1981/82.
6. Some banks produce their own information booklets on investment incentives.
7. *Statement of Standard Accounting Practice 15; Accounting for deferred taxation*, Institute of Chartered Accountants in England and Wales (1978).
8. In a survey of 300 large companies, of whom 226 had a deferred tax balance, '171 appeared to use the liability method'. *Survey of Published Accounts 1981–82*, Institute of Chartered Accountants in England and Wales. This survey also showed that almost half the companies (142 out of 300) made at least some provision for capital allowances in deferred tax.
9. Bankers examined VAT returns in less than 1 per cent of the cases of company borrowing surveyed in Appendix E.
10. Presentation of tax in accounts (in addition to the deferred tax standard SSAP 15) are set out in *SSAP 5 – Accounting for value added tax* (1974) and *SSAP 8 – The treatment of taxation under the imputation system in the accounts of companies* (1974). Both are available from the Institute of Chartered Accountants in England and Wales.

Chapter 6

Discounting cash flows

6.1 Investment projects

One of the traditional considerations of a banker in examining a borrowing request is the *purpose* for which the funds are to be used. The implication of this concern with purpose is that the banker seeks some reassurance, in the case of business lending, that the funds will be employed in ways likely to enhance rather than diminish the firm's financial viability.

Where the purpose of a firm's borrowing is not purely short-term, but relates to some outlay intended to yield benefits beyond the current year, it is convenient to call the venture an investment project. It is with the rudiments of financial assessment of investment projects that this chapter is concerned.

Bankers vary in the attention they give to customers' justifications of individual investment projects. The sort of arguments that may be advanced against any attention to the assessment of particular projects are as follows:

1. Banks do not lend to projects but to firms, so that the overall financial viability of the borrowing firm is the banker's proper concern.
2. Technicalities of assessing projects are best left to the customer, while the banker concentrates on assessing the firm's managerial capacity.
3. Banks, at least UK clearing banks, do not indulge in long-term lending and should therefore confine themselves to ensuring that the borrowing firm can repay in the short run.

Taking each of those arguments in turn:

1. Individual projects are the ingredients which determine a firm's overall viability; a project which is relatively large for the firm has obvious implications which deserve serious attention.
2. A banker who has no understanding of the most elementary principles for assessing investment projects is likely to be in some difficulty in communicating with competent professional managers, and he will be unqualified either to judge or to guide the efforts of less well-endowed firms which seek financial assistance.
3. A rigid preference for short-term lending would be denied by many clearing bankers[1]; moreover, investment projects can have substantial financial impact even when the repayment period for borrowing is intended to be fairly short.

There are, therefore, respectable reasons for paying some attention to the bases on which investment projects can be assessed, and for acquiring an understanding of the analytical framework within which cash receipts and outlays, profitability, time and cost of capital can be related[2].

Any assessment of an investment project, indeed any decision, requires a choice to be made – either between several options or between doing something and doing nothing. How should such a choice be made? *Ignoring non-financial considerations and (temporarily) risk and inflation aspects,* two very simple rules offer themselves:

more rather than less: preference should be given to the project offering the highest rate of return.

sooner rather than later: the project offering the swiftest return should be preferred, to lighten interest costs and/or release funds for other profitable employment.

Unfortunately, a decision based on one rule *alone* is insufficient. For example, assume that Quilp has £1,000 to lend. Rock would 'repay' £100 in each of years 1 and 2 but £1,400 in year 3, Solid would 'repay' £900 in year 1 and £400 in year 2, whereas Trust would 'repay' £500 per year for 3 years. As Quilp has only £1,000 available for lending, he can choose only one option: the options are *mutually exclusive.* The cash payments would cover both interest and principal, would be made at the end of the relevant years and would be certain. Which alternative should Quilp adopt?

Fig. 6.1 Quilp's investment options

		Rock	Solid	Trust
Time		£	£	£
0		(1,000)	(1,000)	(1,000)
1		100	900	500
2		100	400	500
3		1,400	–	500
Simple annual rate of return on investment	$\left[\frac{\text{(Receipts} - \text{outlay) } 100}{\text{outlay} \times \text{project life}}\right]$	**20%**	15%	$16\frac{2}{3}$%
Payback period		$2\frac{4}{7}$ years	**$1\frac{1}{4}$ years**	2 years

The 'best' result under each decision rule is shown in bold type.

Figure 6.1 shows the application of the simple decision rules to Quilp's investment options. The 'more rather than less' rule is represented as *simple annual rate of return on investment.* That expresses the difference between Quilp's cash receipts and outlay as a percentage of outlay, averaged over the life of the investment. Rock comes out as the best option on this basis.

Another widely used method adopts a *payback period,* which reflects the rule 'sooner rather than later'. Payback measures the expected length of time for repayment of the original outlay, and this time it is Solid which comes out best – with the shortest payback period of 1¼ years.

Clearly, there must be something wrong with rules which concentrate on only one facet of a decision. What is needed is a device which will incorporate both the 'more' and 'sooner' rules together – which is the concern of section 6.2.

6.2 Compounding and discounting at interest

The 'sooner rather than later' rule reflects the fact that an amount of money *now* is worth more than the same amount in the future[3] because there are costs of waiting – in foregone opportunities for investment or consumption, or through payment of interest to the providers of funds. A rate of interest expresses the costs of waiting, and therefore cash flows over time can be translated into 'worth' on a common time basis by applying an appropriate interest rate.

In what follows it will be convenient to use the word *amount* for a payment or receipt in a stream of cash flows, and *value* for the result of translating amounts on to a common time basis by application of an interest rate.

Translation of the amounts in cash flows on to a common time basis can be achieved in any one of three different ways, by

1. *Compounding* the amounts forward to a future time;
2. *Discounting* the amounts back to the present;
3. Translating the amounts into a uniform series of values at regular intervals, termed *annual values* when an annual interval is adopted.

Any one of these three ways, if used correctly, is equally valid in assessing investment projects. But because the present is the common time element for all alternatives when decisions have to be made, cash flows are almost invariably discounted back to a *present* value – thus the term *discounted cash flow* is popularly attached to the technique under consideration.

Principles will be explained in relation to Fig. 6.2, which provides four diagrams (with figure examples) of interest calculations. The diagrams reflect the three different approaches mentioned above. Diagram 1 shows compounding and diagram 2 discounting. Diagram 3 is, however, another discounting approach which provides a bridge to annual values in diagram 4. The bases for each diagram will be examined in turn.

1. Future value of a present amount

The idea of compounding at interest will be familiar to readers, even if the mathematics are not.

An amount of £1 deposited now in a bank deposit account at interest of 10 per cent per year will obviously increase to £1·10 at the end of year 1. At the end of year 2 interest of 10 per cent on £1·10 (i.e. £0·11) will be added to make the deposit £1·21, and so on in succeeding years. The process can be reduced to a formula by using two symbols:

r interest on £1 for one time period (i.e. at 10 per cent per period, $r = 0{\cdot}10$);
n number of time periods for which interest is to be compounded.

Applying these symbols to the bank deposit example, an amount of 1 deposited at r per year will earn r at the end of 1 year, so that the deposit becomes $1 + r$. At the end of a second year the deposit gets not merely interest on the principal of 1, but also interest on the previous year's interest. The value to which the deposit will have accumulated at the end of the second year can consequently be expressed as

$$(1 + r)(1 + r) = (1 + r)^2$$

At 10 per cent per year interest, £1 will amount at the end of 2 years to

$$(£1{\cdot}10)(£1{\cdot}10) = £1{\cdot}21$$

For the addition of each period's interest therefore, the expression for the value of the deposit can be multiplied again by $(1 + r)$. At the end of three periods the

Fig. 6.2 Diagrams for interest factors.

① Future value of £1

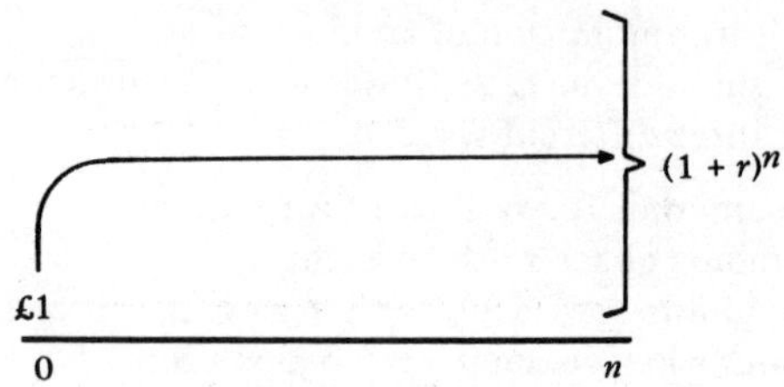

Examples at 10%
(r = 0.10)

$(1 + r)^n$

Year 1	1·100
Year 2	1·210
Year 3	1·331

② Present value of £1

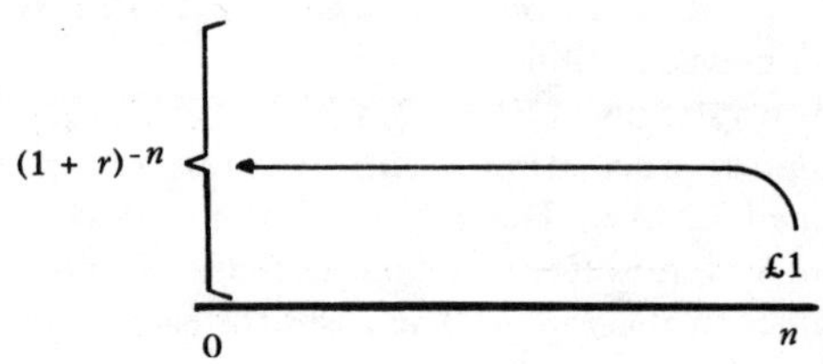

Reciprocal of ①

Year 1	$\frac{1}{1{\cdot}100}$	= 0·909
Year 2	$\frac{1}{1{\cdot}210}$	= 0·826
Year 3	$\frac{1}{1{\cdot}331}$	= 0·751

③ Present value of £1 received per year

$$a_{\overline{n}|r} = \frac{1 - (1 + r)^{-n}}{r}$$

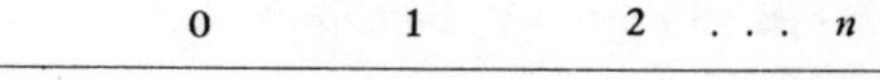

Summed from ②

Year 1	0·909	
Year 2	+0·826	= 1·735*
Year 3	+0·751	= 2·486*

* Should in fact be 1·736 and 2·487; differences arise from rounding.

④ Annual value (or periodic value) of £1 received now

$$a_{\overline{n}|r}^{-1} = \frac{r}{1 - (1 + r)^{-n}}$$

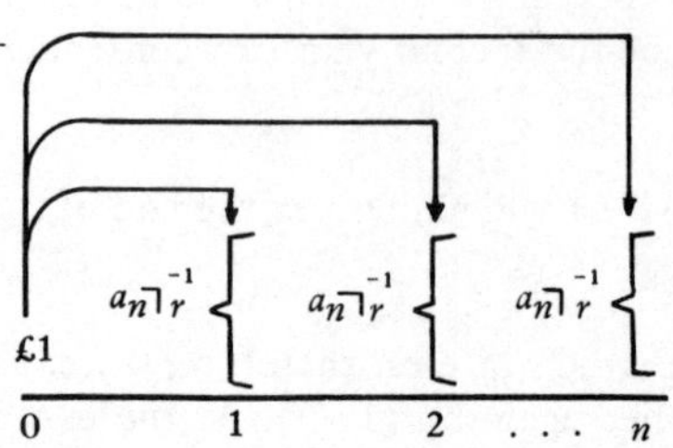

Reciprocal of ③

Year 1	$\frac{1}{0{\cdot}909}$	= 1·100
Year 2	$\frac{1}{1{\cdot}735}$	= 0·576
Year 3	$\frac{1}{2{\cdot}456}$	= 0·402

expression equals $(1 + r)^3$, at the end of four periods $(1 + r)^4$ and so on. It can be seen that at the end of n periods the value of the deposit will be given by $(1 + r)^n$, so that

future value of an amount of 1 now = $(1 + r)^n$

Figure examples of the values obtained at 10 per cent are shown on the right-hand side of the first diagram in Fig. 6.2. For an amount other than 1 it is necessary to multiply by the amount involved, thus:

present amount × $(1 + r)^n$ = future value (1)

Thus, £900 after 2 years at 10 per cent will become

£900 × 1·21 = £1,089

It would be inconvenient to calculate $(1 + r)^n$ – and the other expressions to be considered shortly – every time interest calculations were to be made. Therefore tables of pre-calculated factors are widely used, and such factors are increasingly incorporated as facilities in pocket calculators. For the benefit of readers, tables for $(1 + r)^n$, and the next two formulations from Fig. 6.2, are provided in Appendix A at the end of this book. Readers unfamiliar with such tables are advised to follow through into the tables the figures from Fig. 6.2 as each group is explained.

Although Fig. 6.2 is concerned only with annual compounding or discounting, the tables can be used for any period. For example, interest could be compounded at 5 per cent every half-year; that might be referred to as compounding at '10 per cent per year with half-yearly rests'.

2. Present value of a future amount

The formula for *discounting* a future amount back to a present value is simply the previous formula upside down – its reciprocal, which can be written either as $1/(1 + r)^n$ or more commonly as $(1 + r)^{-n}$.

The derivation simply involves switching $(1 + r)^n$ to the other side of equation (1), which, with suitably adjusted wording, becomes:

$$\text{present value} = \frac{\text{future amount}}{(1 + r)^n} = \text{future amount} \times (1 + r)^{-n} \qquad (2)$$

The factor $(1 + r)^{-n}$ is commonly represented more shortly by v^n; the factor for, say, discounting an amount 3 years hence back to a present value at 10 per cent per year could be represented as $v^3_{0\cdot 10}$.

Figure 6.2 shows that the present value (PV) of 1 due 1 year hence is 0·909, the PV of 1 due 2 years hence is 0·826 and so on. That means someone to whom money is worth 10 per cent per year would regard the offer of £1 in a year's time as equivalent to £0·909 now, an offer of £1 in 2 years' time as having a value of £0·826 now, and so on. A little arithmetic will confirm that £0·909 would indeed accumulate at 10 per cent to £1 in a year, whereas £0·826 would take 2 years (assuming that parts of a penny are recognized for the purposes of calculation).

The $(1 + r)^{-n}$ formulation is the central element in 'discounted cash flow'. Bankers who are in the habit of thinking in terms of accumulating interest are liable to find the discounting approach much less easy to understand than compounding – and may be tempted to dismiss discounting as an unnecessary optional extra. But quite apart from the fact that firms which consider interest in investment appraisal do so in discounting terms, the notion of discounting is essential equipment for anyone who wants to understand the ingredients of valuation, from commercial property to stock market securities. Some aspects of valuation will be touched upon in Chapter 7.

3. Present value of an annuity

A series of cash flows occurring at regular intervals is called an annuity. As the name suggests, the interval implied is a year, but constant amounts at other time intervals can be accommodated in the formulation which will be developed.

These regular cash flows (or at least expectations that they will be regular) are quite common in business decisions. It would be tedious to multiply each identical amount by the PV factors for each year; instead a new table of factors can be derived by successive addition of the factors for $(1 + r)^{-n}$.

In Fig. 6.2 this process is demonstrated, so that at 10 per cent per year the annual amounts of £1 at the ends of years 1, 2 and 3 would have a PV of £2·486. In familiar banking terms that means that someone who paid £2·486 into a deposit account could, with interest at 10 per cent, withdraw £1 at the end of each of the 3 succeeding years. The addition of factors for $(1 + r)^{-n}$ which had previously been rounded to the nearest unit provides a minor complication in Fig. 6.2; the factors 1·736 and 2·487 will be adopted in the following examples, for consistency with the tables. In practice, tables are calculated directly from the formula which is derived as follows:

$$a_{\overline{n}|r} = (1 + r)^{-1} + (1 + r)^{-2} \cdots + (1 + r)^{-(n-1)} + (1 + r)^{-n} \qquad (3a)$$

where $a_{\overline{n}|r}$ is the symbol which represents 'the present value of periodic amounts of 1 at the end of each of n periods, with interest rate r per period'.

The equation, which merely represents what was done arithmetically in Fig. 6.2, can be multiplied both sides by $(1 + r)$ to give:

$$(1 + r)\, a_{\overline{n}|r} = 1 + (1 + r)^{-1} \cdots + (1 + r)^{-(n-2)} + (1 + r)^{-(n-2)} + (1 + r)^{-(n-1)} \qquad (3b)$$

Subtracting equation (3a) from (3b) gives:

$$r \cdot a_{\overline{n}|r} = 1 - (1 + r)^{-n},$$

so that

$$\text{present value of annuity of 1 per period} = a_{\overline{n}|r} = \frac{1 - (1 + r)^{-n}}{r} \qquad (3c)$$

The reader should note particularly that this formula, for which factors are given in the third table of Appendix A, relates to periodic amounts which commence at the *end* of the first period. If, however, the amounts commence at the *beginning* of the first period (i.e. at time 0) the first amount obviously does not need discounting – so it carries a weight of 1, and the remaining amounts can be given the weight from the table of factors. For example, at 10 per cent per year:

PV of £500 per year for 3 years, commencing at the end of year 1 is
£500 × 2·487 = £1,244

but

PV of £500 per year for 3 years, commencing *immediately* (time 0) is
£500 × (1 + 1·736) = £1,368

The figures for the factors used above are those shown in the third section of Fig. 6.2.

4. Annual value of a present amount

The formula for compounding a single amount, $(1 + r)^n$, was reversed into discounting by putting it upside down. The same technique can be used to reverse the time direction of the annuity formula. Thus, whereas

$$\text{future stream of periodic amounts} \times \frac{1-(1+r)^{-n}}{r} = \text{present value of annuity}$$

switching $\frac{1-(1+r)^{-n}}{r}$ to the other side and adjusting wording gives

$$\text{future stream of periodic values (annual value)} = \text{present amount} \times \frac{r}{1-(1+r)^{-n}}$$

Since the last expression in this equation is merely the reciprocal of the expression in (3c), the earlier shorthand $a_{\overline{n}|r}$ can now become a reciprocal $a_{\overline{n}|r}^{-1}$ and the new formula can be summarized as

$$\text{future stream of periodic values (or annual values) from an amount of 1} = a_{\overline{n}|r}^{-1}$$

$$= \frac{r}{1-(1+r)^{-n}} \qquad (4)$$

In Fig. 6.2 the fourth section on the right-hand side shows how the factors for equation (4) can be derived as reciprocals of the factors previously calculated alongside diagram 3 (which represented equation (3c)).

No table corresponding to equation (4) has been provided in Appendix A because annual (or periodic) values can be calculated directly from the third table for $a_{\overline{n}|}$. Thus, to find the annual value over 4 years which can be derived from £5,000 at 8 per cent per year, it is merely necessary to *divide* £5,000 by the annuity factor:

$$\frac{£5{,}000}{a_{\overline{5}|0\cdot08}} = \frac{£5{,}000}{3\cdot31} = £1{,}511 \text{ per year}$$

The meaning of the results can again be easily understood by returning to the bank deposit example. What annual value for 1 year could be derived from the deposit of £1 at 10 per cent in a bank account? Clearly £1·10 could be withdrawn at the end of the year, which is the factor given in Fig. 6.2. But what annual value for 2 years could be derived from the deposit of £1? The deposit account would look like this:

Time		In £		Out £	Balance £
0	Deposit	1·000			1·000
1	Interest	0·100	Withdrawn	0·576	0·524
2	Interest	0·052	Withdrawn	0·576	0·000

The withdrawals are shown to be the same as the annual value calculated alongside the fourth diagram in Fig. 6.2.

The annual value calculation has a wide variety of practical applications. It provides the usual repayment basis for mortgages, it can help to answer questions about the minimum cash flows which would be needed to justify a particular investment, and so on.

5. Future value of an annuity

Constant amounts have so far been considered in relation to the present (i.e. the discounting viewpoint) but it is equally possible to look at such amounts in terms of accumulation to future values (i.e. the compounding viewpoint).

Appropriate factors can be obtained by summing the compound interest factors $(1 + r)^n$ from the first table of Appendix A. Thus the first column below shows what annual amounts of £1 at the *beginning* of each year for 5 years would accumulate to at 8 per cent per year; the second column shows the same thing where the annual amounts were paid at the *end* of each year.

Invested at 8 per cent, time:	Amounts of £1 at *beginning* of each year would by end of year 5 accumulate to:	Amount of £1 at *end* of each year would by end of year 5 accumulate to:
	£	£
0	1·469	–
1	1·360	1·360
2	1·260	1·260
3	1·166	1·166
4	1·080	1·080
5	–	1·000
	£6·335	£5·866

The second column, for annual amounts paid at the *end* of year, represents a factor for which tables are commonly prepared. It can be used in connection with a *sinking fund,* where constant periodic amounts are invested at interest to produce a particular future value – for example, for the redemption of a loan. Thus if Mudside County Council has obtained a loan of £100,000 which is repayable in 5 years' time, and it is decided amounts are to be provided at the end of each year and invested at 8 per cent per year to meet redemption, the amount required is

$$\frac{£100{,}000}{5{\cdot}866} = £17{,}047 \text{ per year}$$

These provisions for redemption would, of course, be in addition to whatever interest was payable on the loan while it remained outstanding.

6.3 Net present value

The treatment of the mechanics of interest calculations has cleared the way for the incorporation of interest in the analysis of investment projects. Quilp's investment options can now be reconsidered.

Assume that Quilp has to pay interest at 10 per cent per year on his £1,000, and that the three options considered previously are the only ones open to him – except that he could reinvest at 10 per cent per year any surplus after meeting interest payments. The interest rate represents Quilp's *cost of capital,* a term which will be reconsidered later. Clearly, Quilp would prefer the option which provides the greatest surplus after allowing for his cost of capital.

The factors developed in Fig. 6.2 have been applied to Quilp's investment options in Fig. 6.3, to discount the cash flows back to the present. Thus for the Rock option the PV of £100 1 year hence is £90·9 (rounded to £91), and so on. The amounts of £500 per year promised by Trust have been discounted by using the annuity factor 2·487. Anyone who enjoys arithmetic could, of course, produce the same present value for Trust by separately discounting each annual amount (£500 × 0·909; £500 × 0·826, etc.). The discounted cash flows produce a PV for each option, from which is deducted the initial outlay of £1,000 to produce the *net present value* (NPV).

Fig. 6.3 Quilp's investment options – NPV.

Time	Rock	£	Solid	£	Trust	£
	Interest 10%		Interest 10%		Interest 10%	
1	£100 × 0·909	91	£900 × 0·909	818	Annuity	
2	£100 × 0.826	83	£400 × 0·826	330	£500 × 2·487	1,244
3	£1,400 × 0·751	1,051				
	PV	1,225		1,148		1,244
0	Outlay	(1,000)		(1,000)		(1,000)
	NPV	£225		£148		£244

Note: Calculations rounded to nearest £1.

NPV represents the *worth* of an option at the given interest rate. If Quilp had £225 in cash now he could, with the aid of his borrowed £1,000 and interest at 10 per cent, precisely reproduce the cash flows offered by Rock – i.e. the Rock option is equal to £225 cash now, if the cash flows are certain and cost of capital is 10 per cent per year.

It now transpires that Trust offers the best option of the three, with an NPV of £244. In contrast, the rule of 'more rather than less' in Fig. 6.1 pronounced in favour of Rock, while the 'sooner' viewpoint chose Solid. The combination of 'more' *and* 'sooner' in the discounting approach has provided a new, rather more rational, decision. It is this combination of the two elements which leads many firms to adopt discounting in assessing investment projects.

It would have been perfectly legitimate to have assessed Quilp's investment options by compounding the cash flows instead of discounting them. The result would have produced a net future value or *net terminal value* (NTV) at the end of the third year for each option, which would be equal to the NPV compounded at 10 per cent per year for 3 years (£224·9 × 1·331 = £300, etc.). The decision would therefore be unchanged; the Trust option would still be the best. However, if that approach is adopted it must be remembered that options must always be compared at a *common date,* which for NTV means the *terminal* or latest end date among the options. Also amounts must be compounded for the *difference* between the time of the cash flow and the chosen end date. Thus the calculation of NTV for Solid, for comparison with other options at *year 3,* would proceed as follows:

	£
£900 compounded for 2 years £900 × 1·210	1,089
£400 compounded for 1 year £400 × 1·100	440
Terminal value at year 3	1,529
Less outlay compounded 3 years £1,000 × 1·331	1,331
NTV at year 3	£ 198

The NTV method will not be considered further, because it is rarely used by firms and the comparison of future values will not help in the understanding of the principles under consideration.

6.4 DCF yield

One straightforward decision rule is favoured by many businessmen: the higher the percentage rate of return on investment, the better. However, it has been seen that the simple rate-of-return method of calculation adopted in Fig. 6.1 ignores the timing of cash flows.

With the aid of discounting it is possible to improve the calculation. The question posed is: 'What rate of interest would be needed to produce the expected cash flows from the outlay on a particular project?' The solution rate is usually called *DCF yield* by businessmen or internal rate of return by economists.

The calculation problem is that of finding the rate of interest which will discount the receipts from the project back to a present value which equals the project outlay [4]. The rate has to be discovered by trial and error when irregular cash flows are involved, although there is a swifter process when cash flows take the form of an annuity.

For example, returning to Quilp's investment options, what is the DCF yield of the Trust option which offered an annuity of £500 for 3 years? Find the factor for $a_{\overline{3}|}$ which will make the PV of the 3-year £500 annuity equal to the £1,000 outlay:

$$a_{\overline{3}|?} \times £500 = £1{,}000$$
$$\therefore\ a_{\overline{3}|?} = 2$$

A search of the appropriate interest table in Appendix A reveals:

$$a_{\overline{3}|0\cdot22} = 2\cdot042$$
$$a_{\overline{3}|0\cdot24} = 1\cdot981$$

Consequently the DCF yield of the Trust option is about 23 per cent. On the other two options, it is clear they must yield more than 10 per cent, because they both gave positive NPVs at that rate. Calculations which discount the cash flows to approximately equal the £1,000 outlay are shown in Fig. 6.4.

Comparison of Figs. 6.3 and 6.4 provides a disconcerting difference in the ranking of the Rock and Solid options:

Ranking	**Fig. 6.3**	**Fig. 6.4**
1	Trust	Trust
2	Rock	Solid
3	Solid	Rock

Fig. 6.4 Quilp's investment options – DCF yield.

	Rock		**Solid**		**Trust**	
Time		£		£	£	£
	Discounting at →	18%		22%	22%	24%
1	£100 × 0·847	85	£900 × 0·820	738	£500 × 2·042 = 1,021 (years 1–3)	£500 × 1·981 = 991 (years 1–3)
2	£100 × 0·718	72	£400 × 0·672	269		
3	£1,400 × 0·609	853		–		
	PV	1,010		1,007	1,021	991
0	Outlay	(1,000)		(1,000)	(1,000)	(1,000)
	NPV	£10		£7	£21	£(9)
	Approximate DCF yield	18%		22%	23%	

Note: Calculations to nearest £.

Thus, if the choice were simply between Rock and Solid, NPV at 10 per cent would favour the former and DCF yield the latter. The reason is that different interest rates for discounting attach different relative weights to early and late cash flows: high rates treat the late cash flows more severely. Comparing Figs. 6.3 and 6.4, the switch in discounting Rock's third-year £1,400 from 10 per cent to 18 per cent cuts that amount's importance to the project, whereas in Solid the bulk of the cash received in the first year gets *relatively* better treatment through the switch to a higher interest rate.

A firm making a decision on financial grounds would, of course, only adopt an investment project which offered a DCF yield higher than the firm's cost of capital. Consequently the use of DCF yield, with its concern for high rates, is relatively more favourable to projects with large early cash flows than is NPV; bankers may well have a similar bias.

Another important conflict between the methods can occur when mutually exclusive projects involve different outlays. The implications can be seen by considering the options set out in Fig. 6.5.

Middleton, a businessman with a cost of capital of 10 per cent per year, has an opportunity to acquire a 3-year lease on a workshop for £1,000. He can let the workshop at £500 per year or spend a further £800 on equipment – so that the workshop could be rented out at £850 per year. The equipment and lease would be valueless at the end of 3 years. Since Middleton can only choose *one* alternative use for the workshop it is evident that, as in the previous Quilp example, the options are mutually exclusive.

Figure 6.5 shows that the NPV method favours the second option with its NPV of £314, while DCF yield suggests the first option. What has happened is demonstrated in the final column of Fig. 6.5, headed 'difference'. The second option requires additional investment of £800 and offers an additional £350 per year – giving an NPV of £70 and a DCF yield of 15 per cent. It is the £70 which has boosted the second option's NPV, while the 15 per cent has dragged down the average DCF yield for that option.

Clearly, if the cash flows are *certain* and Middleton's cost of capital is indeed 10 per cent per year (i.e. he can either get more funds or reinvest at that rate), then he should take the second option – because it increases his wealth by £70. NPV makes more sense than DCF yield because, to put it dramatically, the yield method would prefer a return of 30 per cent on £100 to 29 per cent on £1 m.

However, the dramatics can be overdone. Decisions are rarely made on the basis of a single indicator[5]; before reaching a decision firms commonly look at both NPV and yield, and also consider qualitative elements (e.g. impact on workforce, customer goodwill). When the reality of risk is introduced some firms prefer the yield method because its results are proportional to the funds at risk – but there are better and more specific ways of looking at risk.

Fig. 6.5 Mutually exclusive options with different outlays – NPV versus DCF yield.

		Option 1		**Option 2**		**Difference**	
Time		Interest 10%	£	Interest 10%	£	Interest 10%	£
1 2 3		£500 × 2·487 =	1,244	£850 × 2·487 =	2,114	£350 × 2·487 =	870
0	Outlay		(1,000)		(1,800)		(800)
	NPV		£244		£314		£70
	Approx. DCF yield	(calculated previously – Fig. 6.4)	23%	$\left(a_{\overline{3}\rceil}? = \frac{1,800}{850} = 2{\cdot}118\right)$	20%	$\left(a_{\overline{3}\rceil}? = \frac{800}{350} = 2{\cdot}286\right)$	15%

6.5 The cash flows

The analysis of an investment project can only be as good as the estimation of cash flows on which it is based. Forecasting of any sort is a complex and difficult process, and it becomes more hazardous as the forecast periods grow more distant. Indeed, sceptics are sometimes inclined to take the view that the accident rate on forecasts makes them a total waste of time – which is rather like saying that the incidence of road accidents is so high that one should drive with one's eyes shut.

Some ways of tackling problems of risks and price changes will be mentioned in section 6.5 but initial assumptions about cash flows have to be made. As with other quantitative techniques, sophistication in forecasting tends to increase with the size of firm; most really large companies nowadays employ a range of computer models relating to the economic environment in which they operate. In the smaller firm, forecasting is generally more sporadic; that may help to explain why smaller firms are prone to invest at the top of the business cycle instead of in advance of an upswing – i.e. there is a danger in reacting to the firm's *current* economic environment instead of planning for the future. More perceptive small firms do, of course, exploit specialized knowledge and anticipate developments in their own narrow market areas.

The reader who wishes to pursue the techniques of forecasting will find a number of books available[6]. In general, however, the banker's main concerns with specific forecasts would be to consider their plausibility in the context of his own assessment of the firm's economic environment, and to interrelate them with judgements about the firm's overall capabilities.

Incorporation of forecast figures into a cash-flow analysis in itself involves principles which can help the banker to understand the financial ramifications of an investment decision. Some basic points will be made in relation to an example, the cash flows for which are set out and discounted in Figs. 6.6 and 6.7.

MAX LTD EXAMPLE

Among its many activities Max Ltd has a workshop making fusterns, a product with a declining market. In the next 3 years operating cash receipts after meeting operating outlays (i.e. ignoring depreciation) are expected to be £15,000, £10,000 and £5,000. The workshop assets are as follows:

	Original cost	Book value (cost less accumulated depreciation)	Realizable value now
	£	£	£
Workshop	70,000	50,000	40,000
Equipment	24,000	6,000	—
Stocks + debtors − creditors	10,000	10,000	10,000

If the workshop continues in operation until the end of the third year it could then be sold for £30,000. The equipment would be valueless, but the working capital would be liquidated at book value.

The directors of Max Ltd are considering re-equipping the workshop to produce gimbles. Equipment would cost £98,000 and it would be necessary to maintain working capital of £25,000 – but against that £13,000 would be received from selling the old equipment and liquidating working capital, so that net outlay would be £110,000. Receipts after meeting outlays (i.e. ignoring depreciation) are expected to be £30,000 per year for 10 years. At the end of that time the building plus equipment would sell for £30,000 and working capital would be liquidated.

The directors assume a cost of capital of 16 per cent per year before tax. The corporation tax rate is 50 per cent and the £98,000 equipment outlay will be eligible for first-year tax allowance.

The following points relate to Fig. 6.6, where options are discounted at 16 per cent; tax aspects will be added in Fig. 6.8.

1. Opportunities

All known opportunities should be considered – and wherever existing assets are involved an ever-present possibility is disposal. There may be non-financial reasons why a firm would not contemplate disposal until the financial aspects become very pressing, but the availability of the option must be borne in mind.

By including all three options in Fig. 6.6 it has been possible to confine the analysis purely to *cash* flows. Clearly option 1 is not 'costless' even though it does not involve any cash outlay at year 0; the cost involved is that of foregoing the best available alternative (which turns out to be disposal in Fig. 6.6).

Sometimes it is convenient to impute asset values instead of staying strictly with cash flows. Thus the cost of option 1 could have been shown as £50,000, to produce a negative NPV of £800. However, strict adherence to cash flows is less likely to cause confusion.

Fig. 6.6 Investment options, Max Ltd – before tax.

	Year 0	1	2	3 . . . 10	PV calculations at 16% per year	
	£000s					
Option 1 – Fusterns						
Receipts		15	10	5	*	23·6
Sale [30 + WC 10]				40	40 X 0·641 =	25·6
					NPV	49·2
Option 2 – Gimbles						
Receipts		30 ——————→		30	30 X 4·833 =	145·0
Sale [30 + WC 25]				55	55 X 0·227 =	12·5
						157·5
Outlay	(110)					(110·0)
					NPV	47·5
Option 3 – Disposal						
Sale [40 + WC 10]	50				NPV	50·0

* (15 X 0·862) + (10 X 0·743) + (5 X 0·641) = 23·6.
Note: Calculations to nearest £100. WC = working capital.

2. *Bygones*

'Bygones are bygones' is a good slogan for decision-making; what matters is not what was paid for an asset but what can be done with it now. That applies whether or not the asset has been depreciated; only by luck will the written-down book value based on historical cost have any relationship to current opportunities. Thus the £50,000 and £6,000 book values of Max's workshop and equipment do not enter into Fig. 6.6 because they have nothing to do with alternative cash flows.

Past costs which are irrelevant to decisions are often referred to as *sunk costs.*

3. *Depreciation*

No depreciation is included in the calculations. The reason is simply that costs of assets are recorded as outlays when acquired; to deduct depreciation from receipts would be to charge the assets twice, which is obviously invalid.

4. *Working capital*

It must be admitted that the 'receipts' for the options in Fig. 6.6 would in fact be the differences between sales and costs involving working-capital movements. Thus the receipts are the same as 'funds generated by operations', for which the term 'cash flow' was shown to be a misnomer in Chapter 3. In the present context, however, there are good reasons for the approach.

It would be possible to incorporate cash flows month by month or quarter by quarter (with adjustment of the discounting rate), but for most projects that would be over-zealous. Instead it is usual to assume that 'funds generated by operations' are in fact cash flows received at the end of the year; in addition it is necessary to estimate the working capital likely to be tied up over the life of the project. This is demonstrated in Fig. 6.7, which elaborates the first year's figures of option 2 in Fig. 6.6.

Fig. 6.7 Max Ltd – option 2, year 1.

	Actual cash flow year 1				**Outstanding end-year (for balance sheet)**		**Total**
	Jan.–Mar.	Apr.–June	July–Sept.	Oct.–Dec.			
	£000s throughout						
Sales	–	30	50	40	Debtors	30	150
Cost outlays	(12)	(32)	(36)	(28)	Creditors	(12)	(120)
Net	(12)	(2)	14	12		18	30
					Stocks	7	
					Working capital	25	

Sales total £150,000 and cost outlays total £120,000 over a full year, which explains the £30,000 net receipts per year shown in Fig. 6.6. But the debtors take about 3 months to pay up, and some credit is obtained on costs. Consequently there is a net amount of £18,000 tied up in debtors minus creditors which, together with £7,000 assumed to have been invested in stocks, provides the working-capital requirement of £25,000.

It can now be seen that Fig. 6.6 (which adopted typical assumptions) erred somewhat towards caution in assuming that working capital would be laid out immediately and that net receipts do not come in until the end of the year. A banker is unlikely to object to this; what he should check if he becomes involved in considerations relating to an investment project is that *some* appropriate allowance has been made for working-capital requirements – omissions are by no means rare.

Working capital will be phased out with the ending of a project, and for the ongoing firm it is usually fair to assume realization in the normal course of business rather than at any 'forced sale' losses. Normal stock wastage and bad debts are implicit in the projected receipts.

5. Tax

In Chapter 5 it was seen that the early tax reliefs provided by capital allowances are designed to have an incentive effect on investment. A rational assessment of an investment project must therefore incorporate some consideration of the impact of tax on cash flows[7]. Amendments have been made to the Max Ltd calculations to incorporate tax in Fig. 6.8; the principles involved will be considered in turn.

(a) *The tax rate* of 50 per cent stated in the example will not necessarily remain unchanged indefinitely, but in the absence of grounds for assuming a change in rate the current level provides a reasonable assumption. A partnership in which personal tax rates differed between partners could present difficulties – merely reflecting that the interests of the partners would not be identical; some average rate could be adopted.

(b) *Cost of capital* is 16 per cent per year before tax. With a 50 per cent tax rate half of the rewards will go in tax, so the company will seek a *post-tax* return of the remainder – i.e. 8 per cent.

(c) *Timing of tax payments* is determined by rules considered in Chapter 5. Precise calculations can be made when timing is crucial to the decision (e.g. by discounting at quarterly intervals) but a year's time lag in cash payments and refunds has been adopted here.

(d) *Capital allowances* like that for option 2 reduce taxable profits (with the usual time lag) and can therefore be treated as a tax receipt equal to the eligible investment at the ruling tax rate. The recognition of the capital allowance tax relief transforms option 2 relative to the other options – which is the reason for going to all this trouble. One qualification must be borne in mind: a company must have sufficient profits overall to absorb the capital allowances if it is to get swift benefits from the tax relief.

(e) *Sale of fixed assets* can lead to labrynthine tax complexities, which can only be sketched here. Any gains from sale over original cost will be taxable at the special (lower) gains rate, although for the continuing firm the payment can be postponed indefinitely by purchasing other assets which get the 'roll-over' relief mentioned in Chapter 5. Where an asset has received capital allowances on original cost, tax will be clawed back to the extent that the allowances were over-generous – so that tax is effectively levied at the full current rate on the difference between any unrelieved asset balance and the lower of sale price or original cost.

In the Max Ltd example it has been assumed that the costs of the workshop and old equipment had been fully allowed for capital allowances, so that the sale prices are taxable in all cases. This assumption is implausible so far as industrial buildings allowances on the workshop are concerned, but it eases the calculations and makes no difference to the choice of best option.

Comparison of the NPVs in Figs. 6.6 and 6.8 shows that tax considerations transform option 2 from last among three close choices into the leader by a very wide margin. The size of the margin owes something to the tax assumptions on sale of assets, but most of the impact arises from the capital allowance relief of £49,000. When tax can make such large differences to investment projects it might be thought that consideration of tax would be standard practice, but apparently only about half of British companies take tax into account when making investment decisions[8].

6. *Replacements and the time horizon*

Often investment decisions in a continuing enterprise involve a choice between replacing an asset now or later, which can give 'open-ended' streams of alternatives. Thus, if there is a choice between retaining machine A which is owned by the firm and has a 3-year life, and replacing with a new machine B which has a 10-year life, there can also be the prospect of an improved machine C (or otherwise replacement B) as a successor to A in 3 years' time – and so on. These possibilities are shown diagrammatically in Fig. 6.9.

There are ways of dealing with a series of alternatives which are more complex than can be considered here. But a convenient, if arbitrary, way out is to cut off the end of the series by assuming a time horizon and some quite arbitrary amount for the asset at that point. Any such amount implicitly values the series of cash flows

Fig. 6.8 Investment options, Max Ltd – after tax.

	Year 0	1	2	3	4 . . . 10	11	PV calculations at 8% per year	
	£000s							
Option 1 – Fusterns								
Receipts		15	10	5			*	26·4
Sale (30 + WC 10)				40			40 × 0·794 =	31·8
								58·2
Tax			(7·5)	(5)	(2·5)		†	(23.3)
					(15)			
							NPV	34·9
Option 2 – Gimbles								
Receipts		30 →			→ 30		30 × 6·710 =	201·3
Tax relief			49				49 × 0·857 =	42·0
Sale (30 + WC 25)					55		55 × 0·463 =	25·5
								268·8
Outlay	(110)							(110·0)
Tax			(15) →			→ (15)	‡	(86·3)
						(15)	(15) × 0·429 =	(6·4)
							NPV	66·1
Option 3 – Disposal								
Sale (40 + WC 10)	50							50·0
Tax		(20)					(20) × 0·926 =	(18·5)
							NPV	31·5

* (15 × 0·926) + (10 × 0·857) + (5 × 0·794)
† (7·5 × 0·857) + (5 × 0·794) + (17·5 × 0·735)
‡ (15 × 6·710) × 0·857

Note: Calculations to nearest £100.

Fig. 6.9 Replacement sequence.

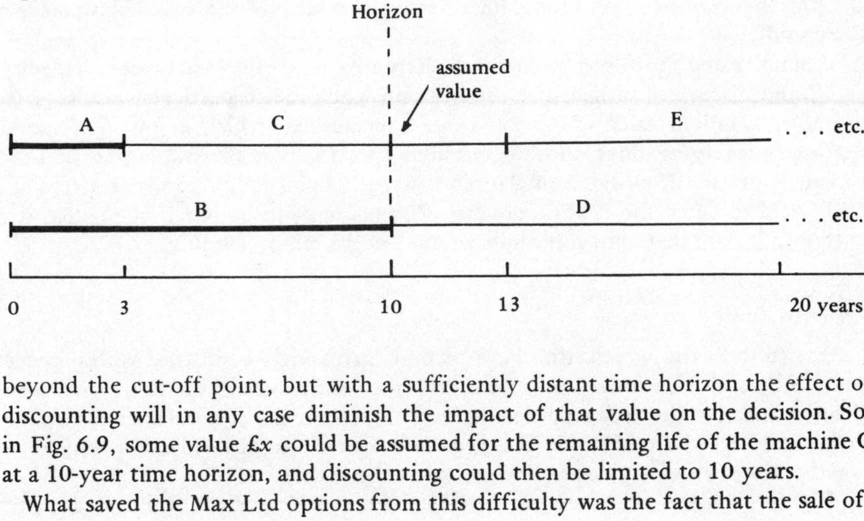

beyond the cut-off point, but with a sufficiently distant time horizon the effect of discounting will in any case diminish the impact of that value on the decision. So, in Fig. 6.9, some value £x could be assumed for the remaining life of the machine C at a 10-year time horizon, and discounting could then be limited to 10 years.

What saved the Max Ltd options from this difficulty was the fact that the sale of *all* assets associated with the alternatives were incorporated at some stage in each set of cash flows. Had the fustern equipment occupied a part of a multiproduct factory, the closure of which was not contemplated, it would be important to consider what would fill the vacuum after year 3. The horizon approach might then be necessary.

6.6 Cost of capital, risk and inflation

A firm's 'true' cost of capital is like the Holy Grail – often sought, but rarely found. Fortunately, perfection is not essential for financially satisfactory solutions.

If a firm has virtually unlimited access to funds, its cost of capital is the rate of return which it must provide to be suppliers of those funds. Since most firms are financed from a mixture of sources, the calculation of some average cost of capital is commonplace – which should, of course, relate to current and future financing costs, not the past.

For the firm with limited access to funds the cost of undertaking one project is the return foregone on the next-best project – so cost of capital is an opportunity cost, representing the estimated rate which could be earned elsewhere. No funds are costless; the cost of employing a firm's own accumulated liquid resources on an investment project is the next-best alternative use foregone.

Clearly, a firm should adopt a cost of capital which is at least as high as the average rate at which it raises its funds – normally above the banker's lending rate. Beyond that is a matter for the firm's judgement of opportunities – but subject to the following remarks on risk and inflation.

The most common method of dealing with risk in investment decisions is simply to increase the discounting rate (or required yield) for riskier projects; the choice of rate is essentially a matter of hunch.

A much rarer, but more rational, approach assigns probabilities to different levels of cash flows (sales, production costs, etc.). From this information is calculated a probability distribution of DCF yields or NPVs. More than pencil and paper is needed for the calculations, but the results provide a genuine overall picture of the risks involved [9] – on similar lines to the distributions of probable outcomes in Chapter 4.

A simpler and quite commonly used alternative is to ask, 'What would happen if . . .?', and discover how sensitive the decision would be to particular events – for example, a fall in sales of 10 per cent. The method, which enjoys the title of *sensitivity analysis,* does allow decision-makers to explore risk implications. A variant is to ask, 'How far would receipts have to fall for NPV to become zero and DCF yield to equal the cost of capital?' For example, in option 2 of Fig. 6.6 it is easy to calculate that annual receipts would have to fall by £9,800:

$$\frac{\text{NPV}}{a_{\overline{10}|0\cdot16}} = \frac{47{,}500}{4{,}833} = £9{,}800$$

One form of risk which firms have become increasingly concerned with in recent years is that of inflationary price changes. In an inflationary situation providers of finance find that they get repaid in 'lighter' money which has a lower ability to buy real goods. They therefore tend to require a higher rate of return to compensate; whether the return fully compensates is not at issue here.

For the analysis of investment projects a firm can estimate in inflated money terms, forecasting changes in money costs, revenues and cost of capital year by year. If it does that, it is appropriate to discount at the money rate of return which is actually required by lenders and investors. That is the method implied in this chapter, because the rates used have been at the sort of level that would normally include some inflationary compensation.

However, it is entirely valid and often more convenient to estimate in 'real terms'. This can be done by making estimates in current money and ignoring purely proportionate inflationary changes. However, it is important to use some assumed 'real' inflation-free cost of capital. For example, if money cost of capital is expected to be 14 per cent and inflation is expected at 10 per cent per year, the real rate of interest is *approximately* 4 per cent – the difference between the two[10].

In fact, firms often use neither approach, but instead estimate in current money (consistent with real terms), using the prevailing cost of capital. The latter tends to be enlarged by investor expectations of inflation, so that 'non-inflated' cash flows are discounted at a rate which is at least partially 'inflated'. When this occurs the result errs towards caution.

Notes and references

1. For example: 'The trend towards medium-term finance, which requires such close attention, arises because sophisticated industrial plant needs funding in periodic large amounts . . . medium-term lending has grown and the total represents about a quarter of the bank's lending to manufacturing industry.' Derek Weyer, Senior General Manager, Barclays Bank (*Investors Chronicle*, 20 Feb. 1976).
2. The reader who wishes to pursue the topic of investment appraisal in depth is referred to two well-established texts which represent different shades of opinion in this area. They are: H. Bierman and S. Smidt, *The Capital Budgeting Decision*, Macmillan, New York (1980) and A. J. Merrett and A. Sykes, *The Finance and Analysis of Capital Projects*, Longman (1973). A less demanding book is J. R. Franks and H. Scholefield, *Corporate Financial Management*, Gower Press (1974).
3. Changes in the purchasing power of money through inflation or deflation are still being ignored.
4. Possible complications of negative cash flows in the later years of the project's life will be ignored here; they can lead to more than one solution rate for DCF yield.
5. A survey reported in *The Director* (Nov. 1970) showed that use of more than one method was commonplace among the eighty-three companies (of varying size) which were surveyed – and discounting methods were slightly more often used than payback and 'simple annual return'.

   Methods used for evaluating capital expenditure products (percentage of eighty-three companies)

	All methods used %	Main methods %
Payback period	49	23
'Accounting' or 'simple' rate of return	41	25
Discounted cash flows (including internal rate of return – DCF yield)	52	25
Present value	12	4
Necessity criteria (i.e. other factors more important than specific financial justifications)	38	20
Other methods	23	8

   Note: The second column does not total 100% because a few respondents placed equal weight on the methods.

The phrase 'discounted cash flow (including internal rate of return – DCF yield)' does not distinguish between the use of NPV with DCF yield and the use of DCF yield alone – but the latter is almost certainly more common than use of present value (i.e. NPV) alone.

6. For example: J. Morrell (ed.), *Management Decisions and the Role of Forecasting*, Penguin (1972); W. K. Benton, *Forecasting for Management*, Addison Wesley (1972).
7. Consideration of the effect of tax on decisions has become something of a patriotic duty – at least so far as industrial investment is concerned. A central criticism that 'the influence of taxation and capital allowances on profitability are often inadequately considered' appeared in a government-sponsored pamphlet which also summarized discounting techniques relatively simply: *National Economic Development Council, Investment Appraisal*, HMSO (1971).
8. The survey in *The Director* mentioned in note 5 showed that 53 per cent of the companies took taxation into account in making investment decisions.
9. For further explanation see D. B. Hertz, 'Risk analysis in capital investment', *Harvard Business Review* (Jan.–Feb. 1964).
10. In fact the real rate is 3.6 per cent, given from 1.14/1.10 = 1.036. For a book which contains a great deal of interest on investment in inflationary conditions see B. Carsberg and A. Hope, *Business Investment Decisions under Inflation*, Institute of Chartered Accountants in England and Wales (1976).

Chapter 7

Financial structure

7.1 Choices in finance

This chapter is largely concerned with exploring the background to the claims side of the balance sheet – how firms, particularly companies, may be financed and why. However, the financing considerations will focus not on institutions (where to raise the money) but on instruments (the rights and implications of different sorts of claims). Running through the choices of financial structure there will be the themes of risk and cost, and the problems of balancing the two.

The ultimate risk a firm faces is that of insolvency: the inability to pay debts as they fall due. For the individual or partnership insolvency can lead to bankruptcy, the seizure of assets for the benefit of creditors and certain legal disabilities. For companies, under consideration here, insolvency can lead to liquidation in a creditors' winding up – with consequences which, in financial terms, correspond to bankruptcy.

Note that the definition of insolvency relates to the short-term ability to pay debts as they fall due. It is not enough that a company could meet its commitments if it were given time; its creditors may not choose to wait. Consequently, in considering financial structure, some attention must usually be paid to the time scales of assets and liabilities: finance cannot be entirely divorced from the purposes for which it is employed. For many companies this comes down to ensuring that current assets exceed current liabilities by some respectable margin, but for other companies, particularly financial institutions, it can involve careful balancing of the timing (maturity dates) of assets and liabilities.

On the cost side, Chapter 6 made the point that in one sense funds are never costless – there is always some alternative use for resources, which is an opportunity cost. Company managements are usually very conscious that cost in this sense has to be balanced against the benefits of a safety net of current assets, including bank balances. In another sense, that of 'out-of-pocket' costs of various *sources* of finance, there are substantial variations: for example, from interest-bearing loans to apparently interest-free creditor balances. Here a company has to balance the benefits of low-cost finance against the risks of not meeting payments on demand, and sometimes there are hidden costs to be considered (e.g. higher prices for generous credit from suppliers).

The financial structures achieved by companies are not rigid 'once-for-all' affairs, but are affected by changes in the economic environment. An example is provided by Fig. 7.1, which shows comparative percentages of assets and liabilities for UK companies in 1967 and 1977.

Figure 7.1 shows that owners' funds, in share capital and reserves, slipped from 52 per cent to 42 per cent of total finance. This was largely because the profits retained by companies did not keep pace with inflation. Long-term borrowing also fell, as many companies avoided new long loans at what were thought to be high interest rates. So the importance of current liabilities increased. As a result, current assets covered liabilities less than 1½ times in 1977, compared with 1¾ times in 1967.

Fig. 7.1 Financial structure of UK listed companies 1967 and 1977.

	1967		1977	
	%		%	
ASSETS				
Fixed assets				
Tangible fixed assets, net of depreciation	41		35	
Goodwill	3		3	
		44		38
Investments		5		5
Current assets				
Stocks and work-in-progress	24		28	
Debtors	23		23	
Cash	4		6	
		51		57
		100		100
FINANCE				
Share capital and reserves				
Ordinary shares	21		10	
Preference shares	3		1	
Capital and revenue reserves	28		31	
		52		42
Deferred taxation		4		6
Long-term loans		13		10
Minority interests in subsidiaries		2		2
Current liabilities				
Bank overdrafts and loans	6		10	
Creditors	18		27	
Current tax	3		2	
Dividends and interest due	2		1	
		29		40
		100		100

Notes:
1. Source: *Annual Abstract of Statistics*, HMSO.
2. 1967 figures based on 1,993 companies; 1977 cover 975 companies.
3. Companies included are those engaged mainly in manufacturing, distribution or construction; excluded are companies with main interests in agriculture, shipping, insurance, banking, finance, property or overseas activities.

Of course, individual company balance sheets may differ greatly from these average summaries, which cover only large companies. But the figures are a good starting point for looking at financial structure.

Two items of finance in Fig. 7.1 can be dismissed immediately. Deferred tax was considered earlier in Chapter 5; it can be considered as finance from the tax man. Minority interests in subsidiaries concern groups of companies, and are explained in Appendix D; the amounts are a form of ownership finance.

7.2 Ownership finance

Certain legal rules, which do not affect unincorporated businesses, apply to company finance.

The normal company has limited liability, and is limited by shares. This means that owners are not personally liable for the company's debts; they can only lose the shares (and the reserves belonging to them).

A share represents a portion of the capital of a company, and ownership of a share gives membership of the company. Beyond that, however, different rights may attach to shares of different classes.

Shares of UK companies must have a *nominal value* or *par value*, which is the monetary amount of the share (e.g. 1p or £1). These amounts make up the share capital, which can involve four main stages:

(a) *Authorized share capital* is the total the company *may* issue; it is recorded with the Registrar of Companies and can only be changed by a general meeting of members.
(b) *Allotted share capital* is the total allotted to members; it must not exceed the authorized share capital.
(c) *Called up share capital* is the amount members have been called upon to pay into the company; it is often called *issued share capital*.
(d) *Paid up share capital* is the amount actually paid in.

In practice the first two are often different, because a company can then allot new shares at short notice. But nowadays most shares are fully paid when they are allotted, so that differences between (b), (c) and (d) are rare. By law a company must give information on these points in its annual accounts; for an example see the accounts of Good Practice Ltd in Appendix B, particularly note 19.

Whether a company must have a minimum share capital depends on whether it is a public or private company.

(a) *A public company* must end its name with 'public limited company' or its Welsh equivalent 'cwmni cyfyngedig cyhoeddus', or the abbreviations PLC or CCC. Any public company must have allotted share capital above a certain minimum, which is currently £50,000.
(b) *A private company* is simply any company that is not a public company. Its name must be followed by 'limited' or its Welsh equivalent 'cyfyngedig' or the abbreviations Ltd or Cyf. There is no minimum share capital for a private company, but any company must have at least two members, so a practical minimum might be two shares of 1 pence each! A private company must not offer to the public any of its shares or debentures (explained later).

1. Ordinary shares

Ordinary shares comprise the most common class of share by far, as can be seen from Fig. 7.1, and the word 'shares' without qualification generally means ordinary shares. They have *residual* rights to what is left after meeting the requirements of other claimants, whether for income (i.e. the annual profit calculation) or for capital (i.e. on liquidation of the company), and ordinary shares are often referred to as *equity*. However, there may be residual claims by preference shares, to be discussed later.

Normally each ordinary share entitles its holder to one vote in company meetings, for the appointment of directors and so on. But capital structures sometimes flout the one-share-one-vote principle.

The nominal value of a share is unlikely to bear any resemblance to its current market value, and may not even represent the amount which the existing shareholder paid for the share or the price at which the share was originally issued. For example, Fig. 7.2 shows accounting entries for Sameric Ltd, which was established with an issue at par of 4,000 shares of 50p each (since the company has only one class of shares, they must be ordinary shares). The company prospered and acquired another business at a price of £10,000, in exchange for an issue of shares. But by this time shares in Sameric Ltd were worth £5 apiece, so that it was only necessary to issue £1,000 nominal capital, made up of 2,000 shares of 50p each. The balance of £9,000 had to be placed in a *share premium account*; this is a form of 'capital' reserve which the Companies Acts do not allow to be distributed as dividends.

Fig. 7.2 Share issues for Sameric Ltd.

Sundry assets		Issued share capital (shares of 50p each)		Share premium	
(1) £2,000			(1) £2,000		
(2) £10,000			(2) £1,000		(2) £9,000

The registration of share transfers between individual shareholders does not take place in the accounting records proper, but in a separate share register. So Sameric's original shares might have been transferred many times before the second share issue occurred, but the entries in Fig. 7.2 remain unchanged.

For most small companies share issues provide a very limited potential source of finance. Existing shareholders may not have personal resources to subscribe for further shares, and yet they commonly will not want to lose control to new outside subscribers. In fact, most private companies restrict the rights of existing shareholders to transfer their shares (e.g. by requiring shares to be offered first to existing shareholders). Moreover, private individuals would often hesitate to become 'minority outsiders' in a small company, where personality considerations can be almost as important as in a partnership. But there are some financial institutions which are prepared to take equity stakes in thriving smaller companies[1].

Raising finance by selling shares to the general public is legal only for public companies. Such investors would want a good market for their shares. A company must be quite large and meet very strict rules for a Stock Exchange listing, although a market in the shares of smaller unlisted (public) companies is being developed.

When share capital is raised from existing shareholders of any company the method used is termed a *rights issue*. Shareholders are given the right to subscribe to new shares in the company in proportion to their existing shareholdings. Thus, after the share issue in Fig. 7.2, Sameric Ltd might have given its shareholders the right to subscribe, at a price of £1, to one new 50p nominal value share for every share currently held.

Compared with the market price of £5 per share mentioned earlier, the rights issue may appear to be a bargain. The £5 per share would give a market valuation of £30,000 to the company's 6,000 shares prior to the rights issue, so the introduction of a further £6,000 (if all rights are taken up) might be assumed to raise the valuation of the company to £36,000. But the new valuation would be divided over 12,000 shares, giving £3 per share. A shareholder who previously had one share worth £5 plus £1 in cash would, after taking up the rights, have two shares worth about £3 each. Thus, rights issues give nothing away to the shareholders; the valuations will really depend on whether the firm can use the new funds profitably. However, when the price of a rights issue is significantly below the market value of the existing shares the individual shareholder, in order to avoid loss, needs either to take up the rights *or* to sell them (buying and selling rights for listed companies is normal Stock Exchange practice). Otherwise, in this example, he would lose about £2 on each of his old shares without corresponding compensation.

2. Preference shares

Preference shares provide preference for dividend distributions before ordinary shares – if a dividend is to be paid at all.

Most preference shares are *non-participating* and are entitled only to a fixed percentage dividend on their nominal values, although there is no legal duty to pay as in the case of loan interest. On the other hand, *participating* preference shares give certain rights to additional dividends linked to those declared on ordinary shares.

Preference shares are normally *cumulative* (an assumption which can be made in the absence of a contrary statement in accounts). This means a dividend undeclared in any year is carried forward, and any backlog must be paid before an ordinary dividend. Preference shares are generally entitled only to repayment of nominal values on liquidation of a company – before ordinary shares and, of course, after all debts have been met. But the terms of the shares sometimes permit participation in a surplus on liquidation.

The small part of preference shares in UK balance sheets is evident in Fig. 7.1. Preference shares are similar to debt in giving a limited return to the providers of finance, and yet preference dividends are not deductible for tax purposes. Consequently, preference dividends suffer the tax disadvantages considered for dividends in general in Chapter 5, and with few offsetting advantages these shares are now rarely issued.

The tax system has affected preference shares in another way: shares issues prior to 6 April 1973, when the imputation system came into effect, have their original rates of dividend reduced by three-tenths. This is, in fact, not an alteration of the returns obtained by shareholders (except to the extent that tax rates change subsequently) but is an adjustment for the imputed tax credit which shareholders now get, and which replaced the old system of deduction of income tax at source.

3. Reserves

Reserves are the largest part of shareholders' interests in most companies. Reserves which arise from retained profits are usually called revenue reserves or simply 'profit and loss account'. These will normally contain past conventional accounting profit; they are essentially the same as the accumulated realized profits (less any losses) from which the 1980 and 1981 Companies Acts allow dividend payments.

Other reserves may have titles like 'capital reserve' which show that they are not intended for distribution as dividends. One such reserve that must be kept separate by law is the *revaluation reserve*, arising from gains on revaluation of assets still held by the company.

Another reserve balance which is not distributable is the share premium account. Apart from minor technical purposes, the only way a company can wipe out a share premium account is by using it to issue *bonus shares*. Bonus shares, often called a *scrip issue*, can also be a method of capitalizing any other reserves.

Figure 7.3 demonstrates the effect of capitalizing the share premium account and part of the reserves of Sameric Ltd which were previously shown in Fig. 7.2. On the left-hand side is shown the balance sheet before the issue; on the right-hand side there appears the balance sheet after the company made a bonus issue of five shares for every 50p share held. The £9,000 balance in the share premium account and £6,000 of the revenue reserves have been transferred to share capital.

Fig. 7.3 Bonus issue for Sameric Ltd.

Balance sheet before bonus issue				Balance sheet after bonus issue			
	£		£		£		£
Issued share capital: 6,000 shares of 50p	3,000	Sundry assets	54,000	Issued share capital: 36,000 shares of 50p	18,000	Sundry assets	54,000
Share premium account	9,000						
Revenue reserves	17,000			Revenue reserves	11,000		
	29,000				29,000		
Sundry liabilities	25,000			Sundry liabilities	25,000		
	£54,000		£54,000		£54,000		£54,000

What are the practical results of the capitalization? One is that the directors' borrowing powers may have been increased: the rules commonly adopted by companies for the management of their affairs [2] limit directors' borrowing powers to the level of issued share capital. But those borrowing powers specifically exclude temporary loans from a company's bankers, and in any case the outsider is not under an obligation to enquire into such management arrangements.

A second result is that Sameric's freedom to pay dividends from reserves has been diminished by £6,000; a lending banker who had been concerned about potential dividends could have achieved a similar effect by imposing lending conditions (e.g. in a security document).

A third likely consequence is that Sameric Ltd had first to increase its *authorized* share capital – and to pay *pro-rata* charges to the Registrar of Companies for the privilege. The large reserve balances remaining on UK company balance sheets in Fig. 7.1 suggest that such costs are not always outweighed by the benefits of capitalization.

Bonus shares do not in fact give shareholders anything they do not already own; the slice of the company owned by each shareholder is unchanged. Thus if Sam held 2,000 shares of 50p before the bonus issue he would have 12,000 shares of 50p after the issue. Both slices are one-third of the company's ownership claim and the assets and liabilities are unchanged.

However, where *Stock Exchange listed* companies are involved, it is commonly said that a large number of medium-priced share units assists marketability (and therefore total market values) more than a smaller number of high-priced shares. Some listed companies make fairly regular bonus issues (e.g. one share for ten held); bonus issues in any case tend not to dominate existing capital as much as in the Sameric example.

4. Redemption and reduction of share capital

A company may issue shares (ordinary or preference) which are redeemable, at the option of the company or the shareholder. A company may also purchase any of its own shares from shareholders who want to sell, subject to certain safeguards[3].

Redeemable shares may be redeemed from the proceeds of a new issue of shares. In this case the new shares simply replace the old ones in the balance sheet.

A company may also redeem shares, or buy back its own shares, out of its existing cash. Two alternative methods may be used:

(a) *A capital redemption reserve* may be set up, by transferring from distributable reserves an amount equal to the share capital which is being cancelled. This reserve is rather like a share premium account; it can only be used for bonus issues, so overall capital is maintained.
(b) A *private* company may reduce its share capital by any shortfall between the price paid for the shares and the available reserves (both distributable and non-distributable). Certain safeguards must be met, including a declaration of solvency from the directors. A public company cannot use this option.

7.3 Long-term debt

Any division between long and short-term debt is arbitrary – but convenient. Debt repayable in less than 1 year is clearly short-term, and comes into the later section on working capital. Five years is another common dividing line, which is used for the legal disclosure rules on company accounts (see note 16 of Appendix B). Thus it could be said that medium term is between 1 and 5 years, and long term is over 5 years. The latter would be rather more usual for the types of debt to be considered here.

1. Debentures and loan stock

Companies raise long-term finance (and, often, medium-term finance) from three major sources: financial institutions such as insurance companies and merchant banks; trading associates such as suppliers; and, in the case of larger companies, from the 'investing public' – which is nowadays composed more of institutions than of individuals. Usually the term *loan* describes block borrowing from a single source, whereas *debenture* or *loan stock* describes units of debt sold to a variety of purchasers.

Debentures and loan stocks are normally divided into units rather like shares (£5 debenture in *X* Ltd). They specify an interest rate and a redemption period (e.g. between 1989 and 1993). They are also frequently subject to a trust deed, under which a trustee (such as a bank) would be empowered to intervene on behalf of holders if conditions of borrowing are not fulfilled; failure to pay interest is an obvious breach.

'Unsecured loan stock' is a term met in the accounts of the most creditworthy giant companies, but companies usually have to provide some form of security to obtain long-term loans. The term 'debenture' is usually employed when security is involved, and, of course, bankers use that word to indicate a document taking security over a company's assets to support even fluctuating short-term lending. But in general usage the word 'debenture' applies to the amount of debt, not the security itself.

A debenture may be secured on specific assets of the company (e.g. property) or by a floating charge over the company's pool of assets. This book is not concerned with the legal complexities of security, but briefly a specific charge prevents the borrower from disposing of the asset without first redeeming the loan, whereas a floating charge leaves the company free to deal in the assets until the charge 'crystallizes' through a breach in the lending terms. The lender on a specific charge can recoup first against the specific asset, whereas the lender on a floating charge has rights against assets ahead of unsecured creditors. Debentures which have equal rights on a floating charge with an earlier issue are said to rank *pari passu* with that earlier issue; subordinated issues rank after other lenders in the same way.

It is not unusual for debentures to be issued at a discount on their face or nominal value and/or to be made redeemable at a premium. So, for example, a £100 debenture might be issued at 98 (sold for £98) and redeemable at 101. In each case the borrowing cost is increased above the 'coupon' or contractual rate of interest.

Discounts may be written off to the profit and loss account over the life of the debenture, and a provision can be built up in a similar manner to meet a premium. The amounts would be determined on a straight-line basis. However, the problem may be avoided because the Companies Act 1948 quite irrationally permits discounts on issue of debentures, or premiums on their redemption, to be written off against a share premium account.

Finally, when redemption of debentures occurs the necessary cash will frequently come from a fresh issue, although the company may have accumulated sufficient cash. In the latter case there is no reason why such accumulation should be formalized, but a company could have made the sort of sinking fund calculation shown at the end of section 6.2.

Sinking funds can be formalized in accounting records, although they appear more frequently in accounting textbooks than in company accounts. A transfer would be made annually from the profit and loss account to the credit of a *sinking fund account,* which is really a form of reserve account. What is more significant is that a corresponding amount would be invested in *sinking fund investments* (debit sinking fund investments account and credit cash account). Reinvested income on investments would result in corresponding increases in the sinking fund account and the investment account. At the end of it all the investments would be used to produce cash with which to eliminate the debentures – leaving the sinking fund account to revert to a reserve which, at least legally, would be available for dividends.

2. Convertible loan stocks

A convertible loan stock is a hybrid: it combines the usual characteristics of a debenture with option to convert into ordinary shares in the future. So £100 of stock redeemable in 1996–1999 might be convertible at the holder's option into thirteen ordinary shares between 1989 and 1991 or into eleven ordinary shares between 1992 and 1996.

Convertible issues provide the stockholder with the attractive choice of converting into shares if the company does well or retaining the relatively secure income and value of the loan stock if it does not. For this reason convertibles are often part of the package offered when one company seeks to buy out the shareholders of another company in a takeover bid.

7.4 Yields and values

A company's capacity to raise finance is determined by its ability to provide returns to investors and lenders. The required yields are not, of course, static; they may change through a shift in the financial status of a company, and they change almost continuously with developments in the economic environment. In both cases expectations of the future are the determining elements: the reliability of the company's earnings, anticipated effects of inflation and so on.

For financial instruments which have already been issued, a change in required yield implies a corresponding change in market value. For example, assume a company issued £10,000 of 8 per cent debentures at par some years ago. The debentures are redeemable in 5 years' time at a premium of £1 per £100. The prevailing rate of interest for borrowing with comparable risk is now 10 per cent per year. Since prospective holders can obtain 10 per cent elsewhere they can be assumed to discount the anticipated cash flows at that rate.

Figure 7.4 shows that the cash flows associated with the debentures, when discounted at 10 per cent, produce a PV of £9,305 – which, ignoring market imperfections and transfer costs, should represent the current market price of the debentures. At that market value the company could repurchase the debentures (if cash were available) and make a 'gain' of £695.

Such gains or losses to the borrower, with corresponding losses or gains to the lender, inevitably occur with interest-rate changes. Consequently, companies are commonly influenced by their views on future interest-rate developments when deciding the timing of long-term debt finance.

Fig. 7.4 Valuation of £10,000 8 per cent debentures.

Time (years)	1	2	3	4	5		PV at 10%
	£	£	£	£	£		£
Interest receipts	800	800	800	800	800	800 × 3·791	3,033
Redemption at premium					10,100	10,100 × 0·621	6,272
							£9,305

Similar reasoning on valuation can be applied to ordinary shares. There is some yield required by shareholders (which may be influenced by the degree of risk attaching to the shares) at which expected cash flows from dividends and the eventual sale of shares can be discounted to provide a value. Shareholders might, of course, have different views and arrive at different values – but if they act rationally on their beliefs they will sell shares with a PV below current market price, and buy in the reverse situation. As a result market prices will be determined by an interaction of views on PV; the fact that investors may not formalize their decisions in quite the way described here is not important.

It is the required yield at which the market as a whole would discount the expected cash flows of a share which can be regarded as the company's cost of equity capital – with its implications for decisions on investment and raising of new funds. Unfortunately, neither the required yield nor the expected cash flows of investors as a whole are easily discovered; only the market price of a share is known for sure, and not even that if the company is unlisted. Consequently, required yields can only be approximations.

There are, however, two commonplace measures used in connection with share prices which link with yields and discounting. These are price/earnings ratio and dividend yield, both of which are published daily alongside share price information in papers like the *Financial Times*.

Price/earnings ratio (or *PE ratio*) is the ratio of current share price to earnings per share. Earnings per share is itself a widely used term meaning the most recent

Fig. 7.5 Price/earnings ratio and dividend yield.

Company data

Profit, after taxation and preference dividends 19–1	£750,000
Ordinary dividends, paid and proposed for year 19–1	£360,000
Ordinary shares issued: 4,000,000 of 50p nominal value each	£2,000,000
Market price of ordinary share at 15 March 19–2	£1·50
Earnings per share (£750,000 ÷ 4,000,000)	18·75p
Dividends per share (£360,000 ÷ 4,000,000)	9p

P/E ratio at 15 March 19–2

Either

$$\frac{\text{market price of share}}{\text{earnings per share}} = \frac{£1{\cdot}50}{18{\cdot}75\text{p}} = 8$$

or

$$\frac{\text{market price of share} \times \text{issued shares}}{\text{profit, after tax and preference dividends}} = \frac{£1{\cdot}50 \times 4{,}000{,}000}{£750{,}000} = 8$$

Earnings yield:

$$\frac{18{\cdot}75\text{p}}{£1{\cdot}50} \quad \text{or} \quad \frac{£750{,}000}{£1{\cdot}50 \times 4{,}000{,}000} = 12\tfrac{1}{2}\%$$

Dividend yield at 15 March 19–2

Either

$$\frac{\text{dividends per share}}{\text{market price of share}} = \frac{9\text{p}}{£1{\cdot}50} = 6\%$$

or

$$\frac{\text{ordinary dividends}}{\text{market price of share} \times \text{issued shares}} = \frac{£360{,}000}{£1{\cdot}50 \times 4{,}000{,}000} = 6\%$$

year's (net) profit after tax and preference dividends, divided by the number of shares in issue. Two alternative methods of calculating the PE ratio are shown in Fig. 7.5. The ratio is sometimes turned upside down and called *earnings yield*, which expresses the company's earnings per share as a percentage of share price.

By convention the expression of dividends in relation to share price is invariably in the form of a yield. *Dividend yield* is found by expressing the company's dividends per share in the preceding year as a percentage of the current share price. Alternatively, it can be derived from total dividends, as shown in Fig. 7.5.

PE ratios are widely used as benchmarks in the valuation of shares. In the comparison of shares of listed companies a frequent starting-point is to consider whether 'similar' companies in terms of apparent risks have similar PE ratios. Their use in this connection does imply that past earnings indicate future earning capacity.

Another common use is the adoption of a particular PE ratio to determine the purchase price of share capital of an unlisted company which has no readily available market price guidelines. The share capital of *X* Ltd might be purchased at a PE ratio of, say, 5 in relation to the latest agreed annual profits; thus profits of £20,000 would give a valuation of £100,000. Accountants are prone to express this approach as '5 years purchase of the maintainable profits' – where maintainable means some average of *past* profits excluding extraordinary items. Neither side to such a transaction seriously assumes that profits will not fluctuate, but what the calculation implies is that an annuity of £20,000 *for ever* is being discounted back at 20 per cent per year.

To explain the last assertion it is necessary to recall that the formula for the present value of an annuity developed in section 6.2 (subsection 3) was

$$a_{\overline{n}|r} = \frac{1 - (1 + r)^{-n}}{r}$$

As the future periods represented by n become very distant, and n becomes very large, so $(1 + r)^{-n}$ becomes very small indeed. That is hardly surprising – few of us would assign much value to the prospect of £1 in 100 years' time. Consequently the $a_{\overline{n}|r}$ formula approaches the limit:

$$\frac{1 - 0}{r} = \frac{1}{r}$$

$1/r$ represents the formula for the present value of a *perpetuity*: an annuity which runs for ever. That is precisely the implication of the PE ratio calculation; when r is 20 per cent per year (the earnings yield is 20 per cent) the perpetuity factor is 5 (the PE ratio is 5). The third table of Appendix A shows that an interest rate of 20 per cent produces a PV factor of about 5 when n equals 50; at this level of interest distant amounts add hardly anything to a valuation.

A similar approach to valuation could be adopted by using dividend yield – although it would be clearly inappropriate to, say, a controlling interest in an unlisted company where power over earnings would be associated with control. Consider a share with a dividend of 14p in the preceding year, which the calculation implies is the annual dividend for future years; valuation at a required yield of 7 per cent produces:

$$\text{annual dividend} \times \frac{1}{r} = 14\text{p} \times \frac{1}{0{\cdot}07} = £2{\cdot}00$$

Users of PE ratios and dividend yields are well aware that earnings on dividends will not continue at a static level indefinitely; adjustment for expectations is made in the acceptable level of the ratio or yield. Thus the valuation of a 'growth' company on the stock market would produce a high PE ratio and low dividend yield.

The relative importance of earnings and dividends in share valuation, with consequent effect on financing costs and strategy, is a difficult and controversial issue[4]. At the risk of oversimplifying, it can be said that in the long run earnings – and particularly the ability of a company to inspire investors with confidence in its *future* earnings – are the really crucial elements for share valuation and for a company's capacity to raise new capital.

As for dividends, it would seem that for the share valuation of a listed company a change in the level of payment is more important than the size of the dividend relative to earnings. Companies generally attempt to maintain their dividend levels, and an increase in dividend is likely to be taken as a signal by investors that future earnings are anticipated to be maintainable at a rather higher average level than in the past. Conversely a dividend cut is commonly taken to imply that the company has little confidence in its future earnings. Such 'informational content' of dividends may therefore have an important *short-term* impact on share price and, in extreme cases, a corresponding impact on investor confidence. For such reasons the dividends of listed companies are not optional extras which can be varied with minor or temporary fluctuations in financing requirements; they involve serious policy implications.

7.5 Debt and equity relationships

Debentures rank before shares in their rights to income and to repayment on liquidation. This precedence supports the usual assumption that, for any given amount of funds to be raised by a company, the interest which lenders require on debentures will be less than the yield required by investors in relatively more risky ordinary shares[5].

The lower debenture interest rate leads to the traditional view that the introduction of some 'moderate' amount of long-term debt can reduce the average cost of capital – which means improving the value of the firm. This point can be demonstrated with an example.

Jake has a business which has expected earnings of £800 per year. He intends to convert the business into a company, raising funds from outside investors. The required yield on equity for this kind of firm is 16 per cent per year, so the company could be established with the issue of 5,000 ordinary shares of £1 each at par (i.e. £800 × 1/0·16 = £5,000). The average cost of capital is obviously 16 per cent per year.

Alternatively, the company could raise £2,000 of 10 per cent debentures and issue 3,000 ordinary shares of £1 each. An extreme, but conveniently simple, version of the traditional view might be that the debt element introduced is so 'moderate' that the prospective shareholders would not require any increase in their required yield. If that were the case it would be possible for Jake to raise £3,750 by issuing the shares at a premium – reducing his average cost of capital to 14 per cent, thus:

	Income		'Extreme traditional' valuation	Average cost of capital
	£		£	
10% debentures	200		2,000	
Ordinary shares	600	600 × 1/0·16	3,750	
	£800		£5,750	$\frac{£800}{£5,750} \approx 14\%$

However, a closer look at the effect of the debentures on the capital structure makes it very doubtful whether ordinary shareholders would be prepared to accept a prospective yield of 16 per cent. Unless the company's £800 earnings before interest are entirely certain (which is unrealistic) the commitment to pay £200 per year in interest must increase the risk for the residual income.

It was seen earlier in section 4.2 that the effect on a cost structure of an increase in fixed costs relative to variable costs was to extend the spread of potential profits and losses. The process was called leverage or gearing, and it was pointed out that the similar effect of long-term interest in a capital structure was termed *gearing* in the UK. The example used on that occasion (Fig. 4.3) can be developed to provide some insight into Jake's financing problem.

Jake's £800 anticipated earnings equal the expected profit of £800 in Fig. 4.3 (although this time the period involved is a year). Assuming that Jake's business had an underlying cost structure and associated sales probabilities identical with those of Assemblers Ltd in Fig. 4.3, the probability distribution of earnings would be as follows:

Probability	Earnings
0·3	£800 loss
0·4	£800 profit
0·3	£2,400 profit

The effect of gearing on this distribution of earnings is shown in Fig. 7.6. With an all-equity capital structure of £5,000 nominal value shares, the shareholders

Fig. 7.6 Effect of gearing.

Without gearing: percentage return on shares of £5,000 nominal value			
Profit (loss)	(£800)	£800	£2,400
Percentage return on £5,000 nominal value	(16%)	16%	48%
Probability	0·3	0·4	0·3
Weighted percentage return on £5,000 nominal value	(4·8%)	6·4%	14·4%
Expected percentage return on nominal value		16%	
With gearing: percentage return on shares of £3,000 nominal value, after £2,000 debentures			
Earnings (loss) before interest	(£800)	£800	£2,400
Debenture interest	(£200)	(£200)	(£200)
Profit (loss) after interest	(£1,000)	£600	£2,200
Percentage return on £3,000 nominal value	(33⅓%)	20%	73⅓%
Probability	0·3	0·4	0·3
Weighted percentage return on £3,000 nominal value	(10%)	8%	22%
Expected percentage return on nominal value		20%	

could *lose* as much as 16 per cent of the nominal value in a year – or they could make as much as 48 per cent. When these percentages are weighted for probabilities they come back to the overall 16 per cent originally assumed as the required yield. With the introduction of gearing the range of percentage returns becomes very much greater. Shareholders could lose a third of the nominal value of their shares in any year or they could make a return as high as 73½ per cent. Risks have increased.

The riskier geared capital structure produces an expected annual yield of 20 per cent on nominal value. There is a school of thought that believes the increased yield would merely compensate for the increased risk on ordinary shares, so that a company's overall value (and therefore cost of capital) would not be affected by capital structure. Thus, instead of selling for £3,750, the shares in Jake's company would sell for only £3,000, to give the same average cost of capital for both the geared and ungeared company:

	Income		'Risk-adjusted' valuation	Average cost of capital
	£		£	
10% debentures	200		2,000	
Ordinary shares	600	$600 \times \frac{1}{0{\cdot}20}$	3,000	
	£800		£5,000	$\frac{£800}{£5{,}000} = 16\%$

It is plausible that shareholders should seek some increase in their rewards in exchange for an increase in risk; whether the required yield would always increase so as to leave the value of the company unchanged is debatable[6] but it is cautious assumption. However, the tax benefits of debt considered in Chapter 5 are undisputed, and those advantages do act to make some degree of debt financially attractive.

The effect of gearing in increasing risk for shareholders brings with it an inevitable increase in risk for all claimants against the company, including bank lenders. The size of the buffer provided by shareholder resources is proportionately reduced with gearing and made more vulnerable to trading fluctuations. Consequently, there will be some level of gearing beyond which suppliers and banks would be reluctant to give credit – even if long-term lenders could initially be found to provide such gearing. No rigid rules can be laid down regarding acceptable gearing levels, in particular because it is necessary to look at the underlying operating structure (with associated risk) of the company and at the overall financial commitments.

A contractual commitment to pay a fixed sum each year on rental of equipment can have a very similar gearing/leverage effect as interest on debt to purchase the same equipment – yet only the latter approach would be reflected in the balance sheet.

Two qualifications need to be made about the relevance of the preceding discussion to the sort of consideration of gearing which arises in the interpretation of accounts. The first is that the arguments on yields related to market values, while the interpretation of accounts involves book values which reflect the market situation with varying degrees of imperfection. The second qualification is that concentration on long-term debt, although simplifying the analysis, should not be taken as implying that short-term debt has any lesser impact for risk-assessment purposes. Debt involves a whole spectrum of timing, and it is the overall effect which is important in assessing risk. Consequently, for interpretation purposes there is a lot to be said for examining the relationship between *total* debt (including current liabilities) and equity (represented in accounts by share capital plus reserves).

However, it will be remembered that the long-term borrowing powers of companies are commonly limited in relation to issued share capital. In fact the one-to-one ratio of long-term debt to issued share capital is still regarded by some people as a rule-of-thumb limit for industrial companies, although many financially reputable companies have long operated with gearing above that level.

7.6 Working capital

A firm's task in maintaining a viable working-capital structure is in many ways more complex than the choices involved in long-term financing. Share capital and long-term debt, once determined, will remain unchanged for substantial periods, and even decisions on dividends/retentions are relatively infrequent. In contrast, working-capital relationships depend not only on any policy decisions made by the firm but also on the firm's administrative capacity to apply such policy to very large numbers of transactions, on fluctuations in trading levels and on the behaviour of customers and suppliers in changing economic circumstances.

Problems of controlling working capital have received increasingly serious attention, and in particular sophisticated techniques have been developed for stock control[7]. All that can be provided here are a few pointers to the influences on working capital. Some general implications of trade credit will be considered before examining creditors, debtors and stocks in turn.

1. Trade credit

Among the considerations affecting the granting of trade credit and its terms are administrative convenience, questions of competitive power and trade customs.

Administrative convenience may be served on both sides of a transaction by separating the delivery of goods or services from cash collection; at an everyday level a newspaper agent may deliver daily but require payment weekly. Generous trade credit can be an alternative to price competition, and can be used as a way of discriminating between customers. Often, however, it seems that credit periods may be a matter of custom in different trades, and indeed in different countries. For example, in Europe the experience of European subsidiaries of American corporations points to substantial national differences; one study[8] of average collection periods showed:

	Days
Belgium/Luxembourg	82·0
Denmark	75·0
France	85·0
Germany	55·2
Italy	109·0
Netherlands	60·3
UK	71·6

Perhaps not entirely unconnected with the above is some evidence[9] concerning UK companies which suggests that credit-taking/giving increases substantially in times of economic stringency; it is, of course, plausible that when funds are tight firms should attempt to 'leapfrog' in their credit-taking. The evidence indicates that in the periods studied these changes were most marked in the accounts of small firms – but that they lost out significantly more to debtors than they gained from creditors; in other words small firms tended to get 'squeezed' when money was tight.

The extent to which small companies offer longer credit terms was shown by a survey of UK companies in 1973[10]. Average terms of payment required were under 45 days for 93 per cent of large companies and 94 per cent of medium-sized companies – but for only 86 per cent of small companies. Credit periods offered are not necessarily kept, and some indication of the administrative capacity to control amounts outstanding is given by the delay in despatch of invoices: despatch within a week was achieved by 67 per cent of large companies and 76 per cent of medium-sized companies, but by only 34 per cent of small companies.

Trade credit is costly to the provider, in terms of loss of use of funds, the administrative costs of reminders and possibly eventual bad debts – although in some cases these costs may be offset by higher profit margins. Firms often attempt to deal with these costs by offering discounts for prompt payment (typically up to 5 per cent) or by charging interest; in the UK the former is the more popular method. In the survey mentioned above, 35 per cent of the companies offered discounts for prompt payment, and 11 per cent charged interest on overdue accounts. Smaller companies were more generous in offering discounts, while the charging of interest was predominantly the preserve of the large and medium-sized companies – which is not surprising, because small firms might be expected to favour swift cash flow and minimal paperwork, whereas larger companies commonly have wider access to funds and electronic data-processing systems for their credit control.

2. Creditors

In its approach to decisions on trade creditors a company should rationally balance discounts or interest charges against its own cost of capital. For example, one of the company's suppliers might offer a discount of 5 per cent for payment within 7 days. If the alternative is a further 2 months' credit, the cost of that credit is 5 per cent for every 2 months – which is more than 30 per cent per year (actually 34 per cent compound). Since that is likely to be well above the company's cost of capital, it would be worthwhile to take the discount. On the other hand, a low rate of discount could be below the company's cost of capital, giving no incentive for early payment. The reasoning can be reversed for interest on overdue accounts, but in that case the company must be careful not to put its creditworthiness in jeopardy.

Thus, it is entirely rational for a firm to treat different creditors in different ways, *provided* the terms of trade credit encourage such behaviour. This is a point to be borne in mind when interpreting accounts or looking at the detailed composition of a borrower's creditors.

3. Debtors

In determining its policy on trade debtors a firm has four major options open to it.

The most severe is not to give credit at all, but to require all sales to be for cash. This approach obviously applies to many retail establishments, and credit-card services have often taken over the credit-giving function of retailers. It has also been successful for many 'cash-and-carry' wholesalers, but the formula cannot be applied universally.

The second option is an administrative solution, which involves efficient credit control: the checking of the creditworthiness of customers, the establishment and observance of individual credit limits, the punctual issue of invoices, statements and reminders, and the pursuit of legal action on non-payers. The third option, the discount/interest approach considered earlier, is merely a device for reducing some of the administrative problems and costs, not an alternative solution. A firm should, of course, only offer a discount which is less than the prospective benefits from early receipts (in terms of cost of capital plus administrative savings and, conceivably, lower bad debts). As for charging interest on overdue accounts, the firm would have the difficult task of pitching this above its cost of capital plus other costs of delay – without offending too many customers.

The fourth possibility is for the firm to deal with its debtor problems by entering into a *factoring agreement*. Factoring[11] involves the sale of trade debts, usually on a continuing basis, to a factor – a firm specializing in the provision of financial and administrative services for trade debt. Invoices are despatched in the usual way, but debtors make their payments to the factor, who maintains debtor accounts and takes collection responsibility. The factor then makes guaranteed payments to the client firm at specific intervals after the despatch of invoices. In addition, the factor would be prepared to make advance payments (up to 80 per cent of debtors). Alternatively, there is a variation known as 'invoice discounting' or 'confidential invoice factoring' which merely provides for an advance of up to 80 per cent on sale of debtors – but the firm obtaining finance continues to collect payments as a trustee for the provider of finance. Obviously charges are made for these services, and a firm must compare these costs with available alternatives.

The effect of factoring transactions in the accounts is that debtors are replaced by whatever cash is received plus whatever balance is owed by the factor for the balance of debts outstanding. Consequently, when advance payments are involved, the debtor balance which appears in the firm's balance sheet can substantially understate the amount of credit being allowed to the firm's customers. There is, however, nothing in the Companies Acts or standard accounting practice which specifically requires the use of factoring to be disclosed in accounting reports.

4. Stocks and work-in-progress

Stocks can be held for three purposes: to meet the normal transactions of a business, to serve as a safety stock for fluctuations in demand and delivery times, or for speculation on an expected increase in price. Stock can also, unfortunately, be held for no purpose at all.

Where stocks of any volume and complexity are held, a basic requirement for stock control is a continuous inventory system. This is simply a record of the physical quantities of goods, updated for movements as they occur. Without some such system it is necessary to rely entirely on physical checks for the assessment of stock levels – and the potential for understocking or overstocking, and also for undetected pilferage, are substantial.

As for the level of stocks, there is often a tendency for individuals within an organization to be more conscious of the disadvantages of being out of stock than of the costs of stockholding. The costs of carrying stocks include not only the firm's cost of capital on funds tied up but also losses through deterioration and obsolescence of stocks. Moreover, there are also costs involved for each delivery made (administration, handling, etc.).

There are highly developed techniques available for determining the minimum cost level of safety stocks and for calculating the economic order quantity for transaction purposes (which in turn determines the average stock level). Widely used computer models incorporating these techniques can update estimates as demand changes, but even relatively simple calculations can lead to significant savings on stockholding. However, it should be noted that the purpose of the techniques is to minimize costs, not stocks; stockholding could conceivably increase with the introduction of the techniques if stocks were previously too low, although in practice that is exceedingly unlikely.

An important characteristic of stock-control techniques is that the basic economic order quantity formula for transaction purchases is related to the *square root* of demand (and is often called the 'square root formula'). Consequently a doubling of sales does not require a doubling of stocks – although this only applies to increases in the scale of *existing* products; for the addition of a new product there can obviously be no economies of scale based on stocks of old items.

Work-in-progress is a working-capital item which often causes concern to both firms and their bankers. But no generalization can be made here apart from the obvious one that the swift conversion of work-in-progress into completed production hinges on the firm's operating efficiency. Certain accounting aspects, particularly on long-term contracts, will be examined in Chapter 8.

Notes and references

1. Ten specialists in this area are listed in R. Strong, *Raising Finance for the Smaller Company – Accountants Digest*, Institute of Chartered Accountants in England and Wales (1974).
2. Table A of the Companies Act 1948, which sets out model articles of association; companies can adopt different articles.
3. The legal rules on these matters appear in Companies Act 1981, sections 45–62.
4. A succinct treatment of this and related conceptual issues in financing appear in A. A. Robichek and S. C. Myers, *Optimal Financing Decisions*, Prentice-Hall (1965); some mathematics are involved.
5. Yet published yields on long-term debt are often higher than earnings yields on ordinary shares. Among the reasons are the effect of inflation expectations in increasing money interest rates and the fact that earnings yields on ordinary shares reflect past, not expected, money earnings. Arguments and assumptions about debt/equity relationships therefore relate to 'real terms' after adjusting for expected growth and money changes.
6. The basic proof on this issue depends on investors' exploitation of price differences between geared and ungeared companies; see Robichek and Myers, op. cit.
7. For a straightforwardly readable account on working capital see M. Grass (ed.), *Control of Working Capital*, Gower Press (1972). A good analytical survey, but not for the innumerate, is contained in D. R. Mehta, *Working Capital Management*, Prentice-Hall (1974).
8. The figures relate to the credit experience at 31 March 1973 of US manufacturing corporations with subsidiaries in EEC countries and appear in P. R. A. Kirkman, 'The management of trade debtors', *Accountancy* (April 1974), pp. 42–52. The original source of the figures was the Credit Research Foundation, New York.

9. See E. W. Davis and K. A. Yeomans, *Company Finance and the Capital Market; University of Cambridge, Department of Applied Economics, Occasional Paper 39*, Cambridge University Press (1974), particularly Chapter 7. The *average* total assets in years 1966 to 1970 for companies in the sample were: small, under £100,000; medium, under £1m.; large, around £17–22m.
10. *Credit Management Databook*, Gower Reference Publications (1973). Size definitions were: small, sales under £1m.; medium, sales £1–10m.; large, sales over £10m.
11. For further consideration see M. Forman and J. Gilbert, *Factoring and Finance*, Heinemann (1976).

Chapter 8

Content of company accounts

8.1 Introductory

There are three major influences on the content of company accounts: legal rules, the conventions adopted by professional accountancy bodies and, in the case of listed companies, Stock Exchange requirements and recommendations.

To dispose of the last item first, a company which is 'listed', with its shares quoted on the Stock Exchange, must abide by the rules set out in the *Stock Exchange's Admission of Securities to Listing*. Many of these rules are concerned with the proper conduct of financial announcements. Of those which affect accounts, the more important concern the announcement of half-yearly and preliminary results and, in the annual report, the presentation of a geographical analysis of results and the inclusion of a statement of directors' reasons where any standard accounting practice has not been adopted. These points are self-explanatory and need not be considered further.

Legal rules for companies are contained in the Companies Acts 1948 to 1981; the Acts in between are 1967, 1976 and 1980. Major parts of the 1980 and 1981 Acts began a common approach to company law within the countries of the European Community. The detailed rules for accounting disclosure appear in the 1981 Act, and section 8.2 will look at how they work.

Company law states the minimum that company accounts should show. How the figures are obtained, and how much extra disclosure may be needed to give a clear picture, are generally matters for accounting conventions. In the UK and Ireland the main conventions are provided in the *Statements of Standard Accounting Practice* (SSAPs) of the Accounting Standards Committee (ASC)[1]. The national standards operate within a broader set of international standards developed by the International Accounting Standards Committee, which represents accountants in many countries.

Before an accounting standard is adopted it is published as an *exposure draft* for discussion and criticism, and accounts are sometimes influenced by exposure drafts. Many standards also affect unincorporated businesses, but all of the standards apply to companies – although not every company is affected by every standard.

Among the reasons for the importance of standards is the need for a company's accounts to have an audit certificate. Under the Companies Act 1948 a company's accounts must be audited by a qualified accountant; nowadays this is normally done by a firm of accountants acting as auditors. A great deal depends on the judgement of the auditors, who will *qualify* their certificate if they are not satisfied. How serious this is depends on what is said; obviously any critical statement can have financial implications.

However, a controversial feature of standards is the way they narrow permitted practices and make accounts more uniform in their calculations. Standards have sometimes done this by excluding long established practices which were more 'prudent' than those adopted in the standards. Moreover the rigid application of a standard might sometimes give a misleading result for a company. So a company may decide not to comply with a standard for good reasons. In such cases, if the auditors agree with the company's approach they can say so in their report – but they must draw attention to the departure from the standard. From time to time some very reputable companies have chosen to ignore certain aspects of the standards: Barclays Bank, Imperial Chemical Industries, Tate and Lyle, and the Wedgwood Group are examples.

It is therefore important that the banker should fully understand the nature of any comments in the auditors' certificate. Company directors are normally quite prepared to include the company's auditors in discussions with the bank when significant borrowing is at issue (although as much for financial as audit opinion); opposition by the directors to such a proposal would in itself raise doubts.

Major aspects of standards and conventions will be outlined in later sections. Matters concerning taxation and funds flow statements were covered in earlier chapters and will not be considered again.

The only way of gaining a real understanding of company accounts is by studying them. A sample report and accounts for Good Practice Ltd, a private company, appears towards the end of this book in Appendix B. As the name suggests, this is an example of good accounting practice which satisfies standards and the Companies Acts; it was prepared by Arthur Young McClelland Moores & Co, chartered accountants. This example, which gives comments on disclosure on each left-hand page, is both a reference point and the vital final stage for matters discussed in sections 8.2 to 8.5. But it does not attempt to show all disclosure requirements, and in particular illustrates a company without subsidiaries or associated companies (these will be explained later).

8.2 Statutory requirements

Certain fundamental rules concerning company accounts appear in the Companies Act 1948. These include requirements to keep proper books of account, to present a balance sheet and profit and loss account to a general meeting of the company at least once a year, to have the annual accounts audited, to prepare a directors' report on the affairs of the company and to send the report and annual accounts to all members and debenture holders. A company which controls the affairs of other companies must also provide group accounts, which are to be considered in section 8.7.

Since the 1967 Act all companies must send their accounts, and certain other information, in an annual return to the Registrar of Companies; these returns can be read by the general public on payment of a fee. However, the Companies Act 1981 allows small and medium-sized companies to file *modified accounts*. A company qualifies if it meets two of the following three criteria:

	Small	Medium
Turnover (=sales) less than	£1.4m.	£5.75m.
Total assets less than	£0.7m.	£2.8m.
Employees less than	50	250

A small company can file a balance sheet with very brief notes and it need not file either a profit and loss acount or a directors' report. A medium-sized company may omit only a few details, of which turnover is the most important. *Yet all companies must prepare full accounts and a directors' report for their shareholders.* Thus modified accounts are a matter of secrecy, not less paperwork. A banker who is shown modified accounts by a company customer should insist on seeing the full accounts which must have been prepared for shareholders. Modified accounts will be ignored here.

Since the 1976 Act there have been time limits on the filing of accounts and their circulation to shareholders. Private companies are required to submit their accounts within 10 months of the end of their normal accounting period; the maximum delay for public companies is 7 months. However, there seems to be little policing of these rules.

There is an overriding requirement that a company's accounts should give a *true and fair view* of the state of affairs of the company and of the profit or loss for the year. The phrase 'true and fair view' is audaciously vague, but it suggests that the overall information in the accounts is more important than playing the legal rules. In practice it puts much weight on the opinion of the auditors, who include the phrase 'true and fair view' in their audit certificate if they are satisfied with the accounts.

The 1981 Act requires that certain 'accounting principles' shall be observed. In fact these are merely longstanding accounting conventions[2]. The four principles are that a company's business shall be assumed to be a *going concern*, accounting policies should be applied with *consistency*, amounts should be decided on a *prudent basis* and all *accrued income and charges* should be brought into accounts.

A company can choose between the conventional methods of historical cost accounting rules and 'alternative accounting rules'. The latter are largely current cost (to be considered in Chapter 9) but selling price valuations would be permitted for some assets. However, if a company opts for the alternative rules for its main accounts it still has to give considerable historical cost details.

The two main areas of disclosure, the accounts and the directors' report, will be considered in turn:

1. Balance sheet and profit and loss account

The detailed rules in accounts appear in Schedule 1 of the Companies Act 1981. They apply to all companies except banks, insurance companies and certain shipping companies[3].

Appendix C of this book reproduces Schedule 1, except for special provisions on groups and investment companies. Readers are advised to refer to it for the rules applying to ordinary companies, which can then be seen in operation by turning to Good Practice Ltd in Appendix B. Note that comparative figures for the previous year are required for the figures in the accounts.

Much of Schedule 1 is self-explanatory, if legalistic. Only the more difficult and important issues will be considered here; the letter S will indicate section numbers in Schedule 1.

A major feature of the rules is that accounts must be presented in a standard format. There are two alternative formats for the balance sheet; although the words vertical and horizontal do not appear in the Schedule, they are implied in the methods:

1. Vertical, showing net current assets and ending with capital and reserves (the usual modern narrative method).
2. Horizontal, showing assets alone on one side of the balance sheet and liabilities (including capital and reserves) on the other.

Similar vertical or horizontal alternatives are available for the profit and loss account. But there is a further sub-division between formats showing both cost of sales and gross profit (particularly suitable for retailing or wholesaling companies) and formats listing raw material costs, etc. Thus:

1. Vertical, deducting cost of sales, distribution costs and administrative expenses from turnover (= sales).
2. Vertical, commencing with turnover and changes in stocks and work-in-progress, and deducting costs of materials, staff costs, depreciation, and so on.
3. Horizontal, with charges and income (debit and credit) separately listed. The charges deduct cost of sales, etc, as in 1 above.
4. Horizontal again, but this time with costs along the lines of format 2.

In using the formats a company can leave out the wording for any items for which there is no amount in that year, or can show amounts in greater detail. Some limited grouping of items is also permitted.

In the balance sheet the treatment of current assets and liabilities deserves mention. The debtors included under current assets must show separately any amount falling due after more than one year (note 5 to balance sheet formats). Similarly creditors for amounts due within one year (including debenture loans where relevant) are grouped together, while there must be a separate section for amounts due after one year (note 13 to balance sheet formats).

Apart from the standard formats, a great deal must be shown in notes to the accounts. These include the disclosure of accounting policies (on such matters as depreciation) and extensive notes to both the balance sheet and the profit and loss account. So, for example, a company must disclose the amount of depreciation charged in the year (S.19 of Schedule 1) even though it has adopted Format 1 or 3 for its profit and loss account – where depreciation will have been merged into cost of sales, distribution costs and/or administrative costs. Similarly items like interest, rents from land, hire of plant and machinery (but *not* rents paid for buildings) and auditors' remuneration must be disclosed.

Schedule 1 does not mention directors' remuneration, but this must be disclosed under the 1948 Act. Further details must be given when total remuneration is above a certain level, currently £40,000. (See Good Practice Ltd note 5 and comments.)

The disclosure rules often refer to *provisions*. These are defined in S.87 and S.88 as:

(a) amounts providing for depreciation or diminution in value of assets; and
(b) amounts retained as reasonably necessary for the purpose of providing for any liability or loss which is either likely to be incurred, or certain to be incurred but uncertain as to amount or as to the date on which it will arise.

For category (a) full details of provisions concerning fixed assets must be disclosed (S.42), but there is no corresponding requirements for current assets. Consequently a provision for bad debts need not be shown (unless it is so significant as to come within the overall need to show a 'true and fair view'). Thus a banker who wants to find out how big a provision has been deducted from trade debtors in the balance sheet will usually have to ask the customer.

The most common type, (b) item, is a provision for tax (appearing in the balance sheet and profit and loss account formats) which will be estimated but not agreed at the accounting date.

There is a special type of *potential* liability which is not likely, but might occur. This is a *contingent liability*; no provision would normally be made for this, but its existence would be stated in a note to the balance sheet. The term is not defined by law but accountants would regard it as a loss contingent on one or more uncertain events[4]. A good example is a guarantee of a supplier's bank overdraft, which would only become a real liability if the supplier defaulted (see note 24 to Good Practice Ltd accounts). A company is required by S.50 to disclose:

1. Details of any charge on the assets of the company to secure the liabilities of any other person, including, where practicable, the amount secured.
2. For any other contingent liability not provided for:
   (a) the amount or estimated amount of that liability;
   (b) its legal nature; and
   (c) whether any valuable security has been provided by the company in connection with that liability, and if so what.

Distinct from provisions are *reserves*, which in the widest sense may be any part of the shareholders' equity apart from shares. If companies are allowed to transfer provisions and reserves without disclosure, there is a real danger that they will use 'hidden reserves' to manipulate declared profits. Consequently S.46 requires a note to the balance sheet when any amount is transferred:

(a) to or from any reserves; or
(b) to any provisions for liabilities and charges; or
(c) from any provision for liabilities and charges otherwise than for the purpose for which the provision was established.

The profit and loss account must also show any transfer affecting reserves, and dividends paid or proposed (S.3(7)).

The 1980 Companies Act allows dividends to be paid only from accumulated realized profits, less losses. In fact what is a realized profit can be a matter of judgement; consequently Schedule 1 of the 1981 Act (S.90) says in effect that realized profits are profits calculated according to generally accepted accounting principles (i.e. standards).

Disclosure of particular interest to bankers concerns any security over its assets that a company may have given to creditors. (Security given for any other purpose was considered with contingent liabilities above.) S.48(4) requires a note to the balance sheet showing for each item of creditors:

(a) the aggregate amount of any debts included under that item for which any security has been given; and
(b) an indication of the nature of the securities so given.

However, the legal disclosure rules do not cover the twilight area of *reservation of title*. This concerns situations in which a firm's suppliers have a clause in their conditions of sale which reserves ownership in goods until amounts due are paid (commonly called a Romalpa clause[5]). Much depends on the particular wording and circumstances, but the supplier may in effect have security over a variable pool of goods. Auditors have decided that for material amounts a note should be shown, relating to trade creditors (see Good Practice Ltd, Note 15).

2. The directors' report

The directors' report to be presented to shareholders with the annual accounts contains information which, although not always of a purely accounting nature, can be of considerable interest to the banker. The company's auditors are required to consider whether the directors' report is consistent with the accounts, and to state in their report if they are *not* satisfied.

The required contents of the directors' report stem from several Companies Acts and comprise:

(a) A fair review of the development of the business during the year and its position at the end of it.
(b) Principal activities, and any changes during the year.
(c) Recommended dividends.
(d) Amount carried to reserves.
(e) Significant changes in fixed assets, and if the market value of land is considered by the directors to be substantially different from book value, an indication of the difference. In practice such a comment on land would be rare: directors tend to get land professionally revalued if they consider there is a substantial difference between market and book value.
(f) Names of persons who were directors at any time during the financial year.
(g) Directors' personal contracts with the company, apart from service contracts.
(h) Directors' interests in the shares and debentures of the company (or group), and any arrangements between the company and its directors involving the acquisition of shares or debentures in this or any other company.
(i) Particulars of important events affecting the company (or subsidiaries) which have occurred since the end of the year.
(j) An indication of likely future business developments.
(k) An indication of research and development activities.
(l) Details of any acquisitions by the company of its own shares.
(m) If political or charitable donations exceed £200, the purposes and amount of the money donated. For political purposes individuals or parties receiving more than £200 must be named.
(n) Where the company employs 250 or more persons, details of its employment policy toward disabled persons.

Requirement (i), concerning important events since the end of the year, is an attempt to cover changes affecting the company between the accounting date and the issue of the report. A similar effort on the accounts is SSAP 17[6] for post balance sheet events, which requires the balance sheet to reflect additional evidence on valuation which comes in after the end of the accounting year. This standard also covers the auditor's disclosure of window-dressing transactions intended to make the balance sheet look healthier than it really is at the end of the year (window-dressing is discussed in Chapter 10).

8.3 Intangible fixed assets

Intangible assets were defined earlier in Chapter 3 as non-physical assets which either involve rights against outsiders in general or represent anticipated future benefits which may not attach to a specific physical asset.

The Companies Acts do not define intangibles, but the list in the balance sheet formats makes it clear that three major types are envisaged: development costs, goodwill, and a group of concessions, patents, licences, trade marks and so on. Although the valuation of the last group may be problematical, their conventional accounting treatment is not unduly difficult; their historical cost is written off over their expected lives, which are usually limited in law.

Development costs arise from research and development (R & D) expenditure, which is incurred to obtain future benefits from new techniques and products. Although R & D is often a matter for big companies it can also be important to some quite small firms (e.g. in scientific instruments). An accounting standard on R & D[7] states that both research and development costs should normally be written off. However, in certain circumstances development costs may be carried forward to future periods; in particular the project must be reasonably certain to be technically and commercially viable. Such development costs would then be written off over the periods which benefit.

The legal rules seem to have the accounting standard in mind, and state that development costs may only be included in the balance sheet 'in special circumstances' (Schedule 1, S.20). A note must show the period for writing off the costs and the reasons for capitalizing them.

Goodwill arises from the excess cost of a purchased interest in a business over the amount of net assets taken into the purchaser's books. Since companies often buy control of other companies, goodwill commonly arises in group accounts (to be considered in section 8.7). UK accountants have had great difficulty in agreeing on a treatment for goodwill. Some would argue that the goodwill should be left in the balance sheet so long as the underlying business is viable; others would view goodwill as a wasting asset, while others see the uncertain value of goodwill as a reason for writing it off against reserves in the year of acquisition. The last view is the most popular.

The 1981 Act requires that goodwill should be written off over a period which does not exceed its useful economic life (S.21). Although this gives wide scope to the company, it is clear that goodwill should be written off. Amortization over a period would be charged through the profit and loss account.

Certain items are specifically mentioned as not being eligible for treatment as assets (S.3(2)). These are preliminary expenses in setting up a company, expenses and commission on the issue of shares or debentures, and the costs of research. However, when debt securities are issued by a company at a discount, that discount can be treated as an asset, and written off annually. Although not a genuine intangible, such an asset does not fit any other category either.

8.4 Tangible fixed assets

Accounting conventions on tangible fixed assets are in a state of transition. The basic and long-established convention is that fixed assets, being held for use by the company, are recorded at historical cost. The cost is then written down to some assumed salvage value over the expected life of a wasting asset. The purpose is that of 'spreading' the cost of the asset over the accounting periods benefiting from its services. The resulting amount of cost, less depreciation, at which the asset is recorded in the balance sheet during its life is a value only in the limited sense of being a *book* value; accountants have in the past studiously avoided giving the impression that the accounting conventions are intended to show fixed assets in balance sheets at amounts approximating to market values.

In recent years property assets have often been the subject of occasional revaluations – in accounts which are otherwise largely based on conventional historical cost. Provided the revaluations are conducted and certified by professional valuers, they are acceptable to auditors; disclosure rules for revaluation under the 1981 Companies Act are set out in Schedule 1, S.34 and S.43.

Consequently, quite apart from the coherent attempts to reflect price changes in accounts which are to be considered in Chapter 9, 'value' has become an acceptable term in relation to fixed assets in traditional accounts – even if its meaning is not always clear. The depreciation standard SSAP 12[8] defines depreciation as: 'a measure of the wearing out, consumption or other loss of *value* of a fixed asset which can arise from use, effluxion of time and obsolescence through technological and market changes'.

In the application of this definition, 'value' is taken to mean either original cost or some subsequent valuation; the charge for depreciation would be based on whatever amount appears in the books. In the year of revaluation a note would be disclosed in the accounts showing the subdivision of the depreciation charge between original cost and that part relating to the change in valuation.

The standard requires buildings to be depreciated, although not, of course, any freehold land on which the buildings are erected. The argument is that all buildings have a limited life, and any increases in market value which may arise in land and buildings do not detract from the need to charge the profit calculation with costs of the asset's dwindling life. However, a separate standard, SSAP 19[9], applies to investment properties. These are properties not occupied by the company or group, the disposal of which would not materially affect any manufacturing or trading operations. Such properties appear in the balance sheet at their open market valuation, and only leasehold property need be depreciated (particularly when the unexpired term is 20 years or less).

The 1981 Act requires all fixed assets to be depreciated over their 'useful economic lives', which supports the SSAP 12 approach to buildings. There are also requirements to distinguish between freehold and leasehold buildings, with a further subdivision between long leases with more than 50 years left to run and short leases below that period.

SSAP 12 avoids the problem of which methods should be adopted to determine the allocation of depreciation to accounting periods. *Any* depreciation pattern is conventionally acceptable. Although the straight-line method, with its constant annual charge, is by far the most popular there are several other established approaches; the following two examples are not exhaustive.

The *reducing balance method* has some support in the UK, particularly for motor vehicles. With this method an asset costing £1,000 might be depreciated at, say, 25 per cent per year on written-down value (i.e. the reducing balance). First-year depreciation would be £250, second-year £187.50 (25 per cent of £750) and so on.

The *unit of service method* may be used for mineral rights, or less commonly for equipment, where the service-unit potential of the asset is divided into the asset's cost to give a depreciation cost per service unit. Thus, if an asset expected to yield 1,000 units of benefits costs £1,000 the depreciation each year would be based on £1 per unit consumed.

What should determine the depreciation pattern is the way in which net services are yielded by the asset. In this it can be borne in mind that the net services given by assets are often highest in their early years of life, before increasing costs of repairs and decreasing competitiveness of production take effect. The straight-line method of depreciation in itself cannot be described as 'prudent' in such cases – although much depends on the assumption made for the useful life of the asset.

When experience or changed circumstances show that an asset's value is less than the amount shown in the accounts, it is sensible to revise the accounts. The 1981 Act (Schedule 1, S.19(2)) requires a provision to be made for any reduction in value which is expected to be permanent. There are broadly similar, but less clear, requirements on underdepreciation in SSAP 12. A simple example of an adjustment to a fixed asset is shown in Fig. 8.1.

For the banker interested in the firm's future operating viability, it should be remembered that the extra charge (£134 in the example) represents 'bygones'. It should be non-recurring (in a more realistic longer-term fixed asset) if the firm has now got the position right.

Fig. 8.1 Permanent reduction in value of a fixed asset.

Asset purchased for £1,000
Originally determined depreciation: £200 per year for 5 years
In year 2 expected economic life reduced to 3 years; consequent permanent reduction in value.

Year	Fixed asset		Accumulated provision for depreciation	
0	Cash 1,000			
1				P & L 200
2				P & L 333 + 134 adjustment
3				P & L 333

8.5 Stocks and work-in-progress

The treatment of stocks and work-in-progress is the subject of *SSAP 9*[10]. This adopts the long-established basic convention for the valuation of stocks and work-in-progress in UK accounts: *lower of cost or net realizable value*. Simple as that may appear, there are three aspects which need clarification: what is cost, what is net realizable value, and how are the two compared?

1. *Cost* is unambiguous where purchased items (not manufactured within the firm) are concerned: in orthodox historical cost accounts it is the cost at which the items were acquired. When the goods are manufactured within the firm, however, standard practice requires the inclusion of production overheads in the cost calculation; the definition involved and the substantial impact fixed overheads can have on profit measurement have already been examined in section 4.3.

   The first-in-first-out and average cost assumptions of cost flows which were also explained in section 4.3 are acceptable and normally adopted in the UK. But the standard does not approve of certain methods that would charge out cost of goods against revenue at approximately current prices (as opposed to historical cost) while leaving stocks at old (usually very old) prices. These are the base stock method, which treats a basic level of stock like a fixed asset, and last-in-first-out, which charges the cost of the *last* goods acquired against revenue. The former is adopted by a few UK companies but the latter is not (although it sometimes appears in UK group accounts via US subsidiaries). Any of these methods is legally acceptable; see Appendix C, S.27(2).

2. *Net realizable value* is defined as the actual or estimated selling price less all further costs to completion and all costs to be incurred in marketing, selling and distributing.
3. *Comparison of cost against net realizable value* should be made either in respect of each item of stock and work-in-progress separately, or by comparing similar groups. Comparison of *total* net realizable value against total cost, which is less 'prudent' in its valuation but used to be acceptable, is no longer orthodox.

The position is very different on the valuation of work-in-progress relating to long-term contracts for which the work involved exceeds a year: the 'lower of cost or net realizable value' rule does not apply. Traditionally, firms undertaking long-term contracts have been permitted by accounting conventions to anticipate unrealized profit on the contracts by adding to the valuation of work-in-progress an estimated amount of profit on the work performed so far. A firm undertaking long-term contracts would otherwise have 'lumpy' profit recognition on the completion of contracts which could cause substantial fluctuations in reported earnings.

SSAP 9 adopts the position that appropriate recognition of unrealized profit on contracts is not merely permitted, but *should* be undertaken: 'The amount at which long-term contract work in progress is stated in periodic financial statements should be cost plus any attributable profit, less any foreseeable losses and progress payments received and receivable'.

There are no reservations stated on this issue in the actual statement of standard accounting practice, although in an explanatory note it is recognized that 'many businesses ... carry out contracts where the outcome cannot reasonably be assessed'. But attributable profit should be recognized when 'it is considered that their outcomes can be assessed with reasonable certainty', although 'the judgement involved should be exercised with prudence'. Judgement in this context would be a matter for the auditors as well as the directors.

An example of the way in which the valuation might be derived is given in Fig. 8.2. Three contracts are shown, which are assumed to represent the only activities of the company. Only the usual production costs are eligible for inclusion in the valuation; administration and selling costs would be charged directly against profit.

Note that the proportion of time elapsed on each contract does not necessarily relate very closely to the proportion completed (i.e. the work achieved). Moreover, in estimating final costs some cautious consideration needs to be given to possible price rises and production delays – although as a possible offset for some contracts the bulk of expenditure on materials may have been incurred early on. Consequently the amount spent so far as a proportion of estimated final costs need not necessarily coincide with the proportion completed. But the proportions of both time spent and expenditure so far can provide rough checks on the plausibility of work achieved.

In Fig. 8.2 the valuation of Contract A includes two-thirds of the anticipated profit of £45,000. For Contract B, however, the entire anticipated loss of £16,000 is deducted from the valuation, on the usual prudence principle that *all* foreseeable

Fig. 8.2 Valuation of long-term contract work-in-progress.

Caret Ltd contract information for year ended 31 Dec. 19–1

	Contracts A £000s	B	C	Company totals £000s
Expenditure				
Materials	50	20	10	80
Labour	32	18	5	55
Depreciation	10	6	1	17
Other production costs	18	10	4	32
Contract expenditure to 31 Dec. 19–1	110	54	20	184
Administration				20
Selling expenses				15
Total expenditure to 31 Dec. 19–1				219
Date of commencement	1 Feb. 19–1	1 Mar. 19–1	1 Nov. 19–1	
Estimated completion date	31 Mar. 19–2	31 Aug. 19–2	30 Sept. 19–2	
Proportion of time elapsed	$\frac{11}{14}$	$\frac{10}{18}$	$\frac{2}{11}$	
Estimated proportion completed	$\frac{2}{3}$	$\frac{1}{2}$	$\frac{1}{6}$	
Contract price	195	120	99	
Less estimated final costs	150	136	66	
Estimated profit (loss)	45	(16)	33	
Attributable profit (loss)	$\frac{2}{3} \times 45 = 30$	All (16)	Contract under 1 year	
Valuation of work-in-progress				
Contract expenditure above	110	54	20	
Attributable profit (loss)	30	(16)	–	
Valuation for balance sheet	140	38	20	198

losses are provided for. Contract C is not eligible for treatment as a long-term contract because it is expected that it will be completed within the year. As a result the total valuation for work-in-progress on the contracts would appear in the balance sheet at £198,000.

One further requirement of standard *SSAP 9* worthy of note is that stocks and work-in-progress should be subclassified in financial statements. That involves the disclosure of separate totals for raw materials, finished goods and work-in-progress where appropriate. These details, which are also required by the legal balance sheet formats, can be helpful for the interpretation of trends in assets and stock turnover.

8.6 Leases and hire purchase contracts

In recent years companies have financed an increasing proportion of their fixed assets through lease, partly for tax reasons. Leasing accounted for one-eighth of all new UK investment in plant and machinery in 1980. This growth has posed accounting problems, and the ASC has made controversial proposals for a standard on the topic[11]. The standard would apply to the UK only and, for legal reasons, not to Ireland.

A lease can be any contract between a lessor (who owns an asset) and a lessee who hires the asset for a specified period. Two types of lease are distinguished in the proposed standard:

1. *A finance lease* ensures that the lessee pays virtually all of the purchase price of an asset, plus financing and other costs. Normally these amounts are paid in rentals over an initial period of years during which the lease cannot be cancelled; thereafter the lessee would have the right to lease indefinitely at a peppercorn rent. Thus in effect the lessee gets the risks and rewards of ownership, although without formal legal title to the asset.
2. *An operating lease* is any lease which does not qualify as a finance lease. In particular an operating lease would not give the lessee a rental holiday after the initial period of payments. Operating leases cause no real accounting problems; under the standard rentals would feature as costs or income in the accounts in the normal way.

A major attraction of the finance lease is connected with tax allowances. 100 per cent capital allowances on plant and machinery (considered in Chapter 5) are of little use to a company which has no taxable profits. But financial institutions with large taxable profits can take advantage of the capital allowances by buying eligible assets and leasing them out. The tax advantages are partly passed on to the lessee and both parties benefit; even the government's aim of stimulating investment through capital allowances is fulfilled.

The finance lease has almost the same financial effects as taking a loan and buying an asset. Payments have to be met and the lessee has full control of the asset. Yet traditionally there would be no sign of this in the balance sheet; just a note to the profit and loss account of the amount for hire of plant and machinery, as required by the Companies Acts. This 'off balance sheet' finance would not come into balance sheet analysis on matters like gearing.

Consequently the proposed standard would require lessees to record any finance lease in the balance sheet as an asset and as an obligation to pay future rentals. Any asset subject to a finance lease, including leasehold property, would come within the standard. The procedure would apply also to hire purchase contracts (where ownership does in fact pass to the hire purchaser in completion of the conditions of the contract).

Corresponding rules would apply to the lessor's side of the transaction; the balance sheet would show a debtor at the amount of the net investment of the lease. Most lessors already make calculations of the general sort envisaged; their reservations stem largely from tax changes that might stem from implied ownership rights in the lessee's balance sheet.

1. Accounting by lessees

The proposed standard does not specify detailed calculation methods for lease obligations, but its wording and guidance notes[12] point in certain directions.

Figure 8.3 illustrates the calculation of lease obligations for a company and gives an example of the asset and liability disclosure in the balance sheet at the end of the third year. Note that the asset has a longer expected life than the lease.

Fig. 8.3 Example of obligation under finance lease.

A company entered into a finance lease commencing 1 January 19–1. The first rental of £200 was paid in advance and £200 rental was paid for four further years. The asset could have been bought for £760, has an expected economic life of 8 years and will be depreciated on the straight-line basis at £95 per year.

	Actuarial method		Sum of the digits		Straight line finance charge
	£		£		£
19–1 1 Jan. Price of asset	760		760		760
Rental in advance	(200)		(200)		(200)
	560		560		560
31 Dec. Interest 16% of £560	90	£240 × $\frac{4}{10}$	96	$\frac{£240}{5}$	48
Obligation 31 Dec. 19–1	650		656		608
19–2 1 Jan. Rental	(200)		(200)		(200)
	450		456		408
31 Dec. 16% of £450	72	£240 × $\frac{3}{10}$	72	$\frac{£240}{5}$	48
Obligation 31 Dec. 19–2	522		528		456
19–3 1 Jan. Rental	(200)		(200)		(200)
	322		328		256
16% of £322	51	£240 × $\frac{2}{10}$	48	$\frac{£240}{5}$	48
Obligation 31 Dec. 19–3	373		376		304
19–4 1 Jan. Rental	(200)		(200)		(200)
	173		176		104
16% of £173	27	£240 × $\frac{1}{10}$	24	$\frac{£240}{5}$	48
Obligation 31 Dec. 19–4	200		200		152
19–5 1 Jan. Rental	(200)		(200)		(200)
				$\frac{£240}{5}$	48
	–		–		–

Example of balance sheet at 31 Dec. 19–3

	Actuarial method	Sum of the digits	Straight line finance charge
Assets			
Leased asset under finance lease	760	760	760
Less accumulated depreciation (3/8ths)	285	285	285
	£475	£475	£475
Liabilities			
Obligation under finance lease	£373	£376	£304

Of the methods used, the *actuarial method* is based on the sort of interest calculations considered in Chapter 6. The interest rate could be calculated in the manner of a DCF yield (internal rate of return).

The *sum of the digits method* gives a good approximation to the interest charge in the actuarial method, and is easier to calculate. The digits are the years of the lease 1 + 2 + 3 + 4 = 10, with the last put first for the proportion 4/10ths, etc. £240 is the finance charge, the difference between the lease payments (5 × £200 = £1,000) and the asset price £760. The proportions have been calculated over 4 years rather than 5 years because this fits more closely to the correct actuarial figures when rental is paid in advance. The sum of the digits method is more commonly called 'the rule of 78' in the finance industry because it first came into use for 12 month credit contracts where the base of the monthly proportion would be 1 + 2 + . . . 12 = 78.

The straight-line charge merely divides the finance charge of £240 over the 5 payments of the lease (4 years would not have given a much better result in this case). It does not reflect the greater amount of borrowing in the early years, but it is simple. It has been suggested by the ASC as a possible method for the smaller company.

2. Accounting by lessors

In principle the same sort of calculations would be made for lessors. However, the effect of 100 per cent capital allowances, and in some cases regional development grants, makes it usual to consider the net cash flows after tax. Moreover, because most lessors have a very large number of transactions, the calculations are rather more complicated. But staying with the simple figures in Fig. 8.3, the lessor's balance sheet on 31 December 19—3 could show as a debtor:

Net investment in finance lease	£373

8.7 Group accounts

The need to produce group accounts was mentioned earlier. Three basic questions deserve consideration here: *What* is a group, *why* have group accounts, and *how* are the accounts to be prepared?

A group is a collection of companies controlled by a single *holding company*. The Companies Act 1948 defines a company as a subsidiary of another if that other *either* holds more than half the nominal value of its share capital *or* controls the composition of its board of directors. A group consisting of the holding company *A* and its subsidiaries *B*, *C* and *D* could take the form shown in Fig. 8.4, where each arrow indicates a holding of more than half the nominal value of the subsidiary company.

The shareholders of *A* Ltd would receive group accounts as well as the balance

Fig. 8.4 *A* Ltd and subsidiaries.

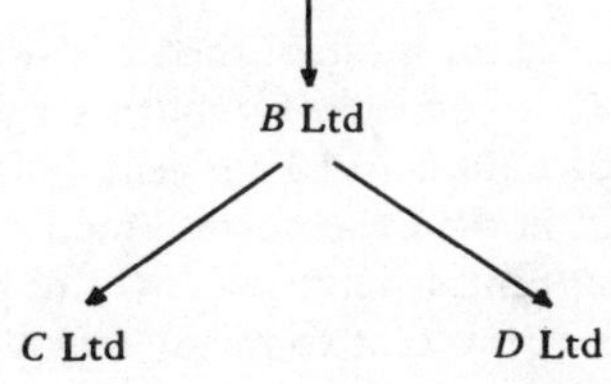

sheet of the holding company. However, the shareholders of *B* Ltd, who might include some 'minority' outsiders, would not receive group accounts for that company and *its* subsidiaries because *B* Ltd is itself a subsidiary.

Under UK law it is not possible for a company to hold shares in its holding company (unless purely as a trustee, or if the shares were held before the 1948 Act). Consequently the scope for contorted financial structures is reduced.

The reasons for the existence of groups are diverse. It is usually much simpler for one company to acquire shares in another company than to undertake the legal complexities of transferring the assets and liabilities of an acquired business; once started, the subsidiary relationship may be allowed to persist. There may be advantages in setting up a joint venture in which outside minority shareholders can participate; for example, in a subsidiary established in an overseas country. Perhaps most important from a banking viewpoint is the fact that the limited liability of each company in the group compartmentalizes financial liability: the creditors (including bank lenders) of a subsidiary can claim only against the assets of that company, and they have no automatic legal rights against any assets held by the holding company.

A reason sometimes advanced for a group structure is that financing opportunities can be more successfully exploited. If that means higher gearing can be achieved at low cost, the notion is unlikely to be successful nowadays because the disclosure of a group financial structure is one answer to the earlier question: why have group accounts? This can be shown by examining an exaggerated 'pyramid' gearing structure with the help of Fig. 8.5.

Fig. 8.5 'Pyramid' financing and group accounts.

	Profit and loss account		Balance sheet		
	[*i* = interest]	[*d* = dividend]	Share capital +	10% Debentures	= Assets
	£		£	£	£
A Ltd	*i* 10	*d* = 50	100	100	Shares in *B* ~~200~~
	~~60~~ ↑				
B Ltd	*i* 20	*d* = ~~60~~	~~200~~	200	Shares in *C* ~~400~~
	~~80~~ ↑				
C Ltd	*i* 40	*d* = ~~80~~	~~400~~	400	Productive assets 800
A Group (Consolidated accounts)	Interest 70	Dividend 50	£100 +	£700 =	£800

Assume that a company, *A* Ltd, is established with £100 share capital and £100 in 10 per cent debentures. That company establishes a wholly owned subsidiary, *B* Ltd, having a share capital of £200 and 10 per cent debentures of £200. The funds of *B* Ltd are in turn invested in the £400 share capital of *C* Ltd, and that company raises a further £400 in 10 per cent debentures. If *C* Ltd purchases productive assets which yield a return of 15 per cent, that company will have earnings before interest of £120 per year – which will permit an annual dividend of £80 after paying interest, as shown in Fig. 8.5. *B* Ltd will in turn be able to pay a dividend of £60, while the holding company will be able to provide its shareholders with a return of 50 per cent on their investment of £100.

In the absence of information on the relationship between the companies each company individually would not appear abnormally high in its gearing. But the returns to the shareholders *and debenture holders* at the apex of the pyramid are clearly vulnerable to fluctuations in the earnings of the underlying assets as the result of the gearing of prior debt lower down the pyramid. For example, if the earnings of the underlying assets were halved (to £60) there would be no income passing up to *A* Ltd to meet the interest on its debentures.

Group accounts cut through the barriers between companies *by eliminating those amounts in the separate company summaries which arise from inter-company transactions* – and totalling the result. This is the basic principle of consolidation on which group accounts are prepared. The final line of Fig. 8.5 shows that when the transfers of dividends between the three companies are eliminated it becomes evident that the group as a whole has paid out £70 in interest and £50 in dividends from its £120 earnings. Similarly, when investments in shares are cancelled out against the shares themselves the highly geared balance sheet of *A* Ltd and its subsidiaries emerges – with £100 share capital and £700 debentures.

The elimination is not usually as simple as Fig. 8.5 might suggest. When investments in a subsidiary are acquired at a cost which exceeds the related share capital and reserves, the difference normally appears as 'goodwill arising on consolidation' in the group accounts. When subsidiaries are not wholly owned, a claim representing the interests of minority shareholders must also appear in the balance sheet.

The other major reason for the presentation of group accounts is that without them (and without certain other aspects of disclosure of the current Companies Act) a holding company could use the earnings of subsidiary companies as 'secret reserves' from which appropriate dividends could be trotted out to boost the apparent profitability of the holding company in a bad year.

The Companies Acts do not give detailed instructions on how group accounts are to be prepared. Even the accounting standard on group accounts, SSAP 14[13], is concerned with broad issues. Consequently on some minor issues the accounting conventions permit more than one method of approach. The overriding principle of consolidation and its implications for understanding the financial state of a group are not affected by these peripheral problems.

The techniques of consolidation can be dealt with most conveniently as a separate topic, and an outline on the preparation of group accounts is provided[14] in Appendix D.

8.8 Associates' profits, gains and extraordinary items

The content of a company's profit and loss account is influenced by accounting conventions on certain important issues which are largely outside the Companies Acts; these issues are to be considered in this section.

The Companies Acts draw the line for subsidiaries at 50 per cent of nominal value of share capital; at that level of ownership or below there is no need for group accounts. Yet a company which owns 49 per cent of the share capital of another company may clearly have a significant influence on the policies of that other company. Should the financial implications of that ownership be entirely ignored in accounts?

The accounting profession's answer[15] is to include certain profit figures in the accounts of an investing company which owns shares in an *associated company*. A company (which is not a subsidiary of the investing company or group) is an associated company if the investing company owns at least 20 per cent of the voting share capital – and the investing company's interest is 'long-term' and provides 'significant influence'.

The crux of the procedure is that instead of merely showing dividends received in its profit and loss account, as with a normal minority investment, the investing company shows its share of profits (less losses) in the associate. The approach is shown in Fig. 8.6, where Gog Ltd is assumed to own 30 per cent of the voting share capital of its associated company, Magog Ltd.

Magog is assumed to have earned £300,000 profit before tax, so that £90,000 is shown in Gog's profit and loss account – with a corresponding tax charge of £45,000. Of the remaining £45,000, the associate paid over a dividend of only £10,000; consequently £35,000 of the amount recognized in the profit and loss account is in fact still retained by Magog Ltd. The other side of the double entry in Gog's books would be a debit increasing investment in the associated company by £35,000.

The moral of this example is that, of Gog's apparent retention of £55,000, only £20,000 is wholly under its control. Although this example is extreme, the point is worth remembering when a company includes significant profits from associates in its accounts.

The treatment of associated companies is, in a sense, a revaluation of investments. But the accounting conventions adopt a different view where the revaluation of fixed assets is concerned. In a nutshell, the rules[16] are that when fixed assets are revalued any unrealized surplus or deficit is taken straight to reserves without passing through the profit and loss account. However, if the reserves are insufficient to meet a deficit, any excess deficit should be charged in the profit and loss account. (Appropriate adjustments would be made for assumed tax effects.)

The general problem of how to treat unusual gains and losses in accounts is the subject of an accounting standard on 'extraordinary items'[17]. The basic principle at stake is that if a company can pick and choose which unusual items to put through the profit calculation and which to put straight to reserve there is a danger of 'creative accounting': gains into the profit and loss account but losses 'hidden' away against reserves. The following attempts to summarize the effects of a contentious and complex standard.

(a) *Extraordinary items* are those derived from events outside the ordinary course of business (e.g. discontinuance of a significant part of the business). These go to the profit and loss account, but in a separate section as shown in Fig. 8.6.
(b) *Prior year adjustments* are 'rare and limited to items arising from changes in accounting policies or from the correction of fundamental errors' (e.g. a change in valuation basis of stocks). Only these items go direct to reserves.
(c) Unusual items like abnormal charges for bad debts or stock write-offs, exchange differences from conversion of foreign currencies and most adjustments for prior year tax estimates, would be charged against profit in the usual way (although particularly large amounts may be disclosed separately to give a 'true and fair view').

Fig. 8.6 Gog Ltd group profit and loss account, incorporating results of associated companies.

		£000s
Turnover (of Gog Ltd and subsidiaries)		1,000
Operating profit (of Gog Ltd and subsidiaries)		170
Share of profits less losses of associated company		90
Profit before taxation		260
Taxation: Gog Ltd and subsidiaries	85	
Associated company	45	
		130
		130
Minority interests		15
Profit after taxation before extraordinary items		115
Extraordinary items		–
Profit attributable to members of Gog Ltd		115
Dividends		60
Net profit retained		55*

*Retained by Gog Ltd and subsidiaries	20
Retained in associated company	35
	55

Such items deserve attention by the banker because they can be very substantial in relation to ordinary operating results. If the unusual item is one of which it can be said 'bygones are bygones' then it can be excluded from the assessment of operating viability irrespective of its accounting treatment. An item may, however, raise doubts or questions about management's control of activities which need to be pursued (e.g. exceptional bad debts).

Notes and references

In the following:

SSAP = Statement of Standard Accounting Practice

ICAEW = Institute of Chartered Accountants in England and Wales

All SSAPs can also be obtained from the accountancy institutes listed on page 6, note 3.

1. A book containing all current material on SSAPs is published annually, and can be slightly less expensive than buying several standards separately: *Accounting Standards: the full texts*, ICAEW annually.
2. *SSAP 2: Disclosure of Accounting Policies*, ICAEW (1971).
3. Banks, insurance companies and certain shipping companies are still subject to special disclosure rules in the Companies Act 1948. The main effect is to allow hidden reserves – but the *clearing banks* now disclose fully. European Community disclosure rules for such companies are in the pipeline.
4. See *SSAP 18: Accounting for contingencies*, ICAEW (1980). The standard also refers to contingent gains, which 'should be disclosed only if it is probable that the gain will be realized'. When realization becomes reasonably certain accrual, not contingency treatment, becomes appropriate.
5. After the first law case in the UK in which such a clause was used successfully: *Aluminium Industrie Vaassen BV v. Romalpa Aluminium Ltd, (1976), 2 All E.R. 552*. See *Journal of Business Law* (1976), pp. 209–213, and for subsequent cases *Journal of Business Law* (1979), pp. 215–218, and (1980), pp. 5–7.

6. *SSAP 17: Accounting for post balance sheet events*, ICAEW (1980).
7. *SSAP 13: Accounting for research and development*, ICAEW (1977).
8. *SSAP 12: Accounting for depreciation*, ICAEW (1977).
9. *SSAP 19: Accounting for investment properties*, ICAEW (1981).
10. *SSAP 9: Stocks and work in progress*, ICAEW (1975).
11. *Exposure Draft 29: Accounting for leases and hire purchase contracts*, ICAEW (1981).
12. *Guidance notes on ED29*, Accounting Standards Committee 1981.
13. *SSAP 14: Group Accounts*, ICAEW (1978).
14. Two introductory books are B. S. Topple, *Byrne's Consolidated Accounts*, Student Publications (1970) and R. E. Ellmer, *The Mechanism of Consolidated Accounts*, Heinemann (1974). For comprehensive treatments of this subject see J. C. Shaw (ed.), *Bogie on Group Accounts*, Jordan (1973) and R. M. Wilkins, *Group Accounts*, ICAEW (1975).
15. *SSAP 1: Accounting for the results of associated companies*, ICAEW (1971, revised 1982).
16. These points made on revaluations are not strictly rules, but are made in Exposure Draft 16: Supplement to 'Extraordinary items and prior year adjustments' ICAEW (1975). As this material has not been converted into a standard it is a matter of guidance rather than a requirement, but it is generally followed in practice.
17. *SSAP 16: Extraordinary items and prior year adjustments*, ICAEW (1974–1978).

Chapter 9

Accounting for price changes

9.1 Specific and general price changes

In 1626 Peter Minuit bought an island for about $25. The island was Manhattan, which developed into the immensely valuable business section of New York City. Had that well-known purchase from the American Indians been conducted in the manner of later financial practices, the Peter Minuit Corporation might still be in existence – with a property asset shown at a cost of $25 in the balance sheet.

The basic problem of pure historical cost accounting is that many of the figures it provides are merely history, even if their age is measured in months or years rather than centuries. Moreover, the history is likely to involve an undisclosed mixture of dates, so that the Peter Minuit Corporation would be perfectly orthodox in adding the cost of property bought for $1 m. in 1976 to its earlier property bought in 1626 and showing the result, 'property at cost $1,000,025'. Of course, some elements in 'conventional' accounts do reflect value changes (e.g. stock at lower of cost or net realizable value) but there is no coherent view.

If accounts are to provide figures which are *informative*, in the sense of communicating something about the current (or at least recent) position of the firm and its production/consumption of resources, the measures adopted must relate to economic conditions at the time of the accounts rather than over a series of earlier accounting periods. Until recently such views were considered heretical, but frequent and substantial price changes in recent years have led the financial community in the UK and elsewhere to accept the inevitability of a reform of accounting procedures. In particular, there has been increasing scepticism of the 'prudence' of profit figures which are calculated by charging costs (e.g. depreciation) for consumption of resources calculated on historical cost bases far below current price levels.

The phrase 'current price levels' introduces a central and controversial question: If accounts are to be modified to reflect price changes, *which* price changes are appropriate?

There is a crucial distinction between *specific* price changes for individual goods and changes in the *general* level of prices. Specific price changes in any period can and do vary enormously between different goods – for example, in the UK in the first half of the 1970s most forms of electronic calculating equipment declined substantially in price, whereas prices of many oil products approximately trebled. The overall impact of individual price changes constitutes the change in the general price level, which really means the price change for some 'average' collection of goods. It hardly needs to be said that it is an increase in the *general* price level, involving a decline in purchasing power of money, which is called inflation. However, the popular phrase *inflation accounting* is often applied to accounts which include either type of price change.

Measurement of price changes from either viewpoint involves problems. In considering the specific price of an individual asset, should the price adopted be that at which the firm can currently buy a similar partly-used asset (termed *current cost* or *replacement cost*) or should it be the prevailing selling price, with due allowance for costs of disposal (*net realizable value*)?

Some aspects of this issue will be considered in section 9.3, but here two points can be made to indicate why current cost finds more support than net realizable value. The first is the opinion that the economic viability of a continuing business depends on selling goods in excess of the cost of obtaining replacement resources (not necessarily physically identical, but at a corresponding cost level). The second is that the adoption of selling prices for long-lived assets would often lead to most of the assets' acquisition cost appearing as the first year's depreciation – because specialist assets, when second-hand, are usually difficult to sell separately at a good price. For example, a restaurant's ovens or a petrol station's pumps could be sold as separate assets at only a fraction of their buying price after a few weeks' use.

Thus the current cost view emphasizes *profit* measurement for the firm as a *continuing* entity, and in the latter respect is consistent with the basic notion of continuity considered in Chapter 1. The alternative selling price approach would provide balance-sheet figures reflecting the 'break-up' values of separable assets. Although net realizable values would undoubtedly be of interest to the banker as an indicator of the safety net provided by the firm's assets, such values have at present little prospect of being included as a standard basis for accounting reports. Consequently, in interpreting accounts which have been adjusted for price changes the banker must not be tempted to regard them (if unconsciously) as though the balance-sheet values represented net realizable values.

With the adoption of specific prices there remains the administrative task of discovering current prices. In principle this should not be too difficult for the goods in which the company deals, although practice is another story. But for fixed assets, good second-hand markets are rarely available, so some reference has to be made to the new price of a similar asset – less appropriate depreciation. Even so, the problems of finding individual asset prices will often lead to the adoption of a *price index* for recording of price changes in particular assets or groups of assets in accounts. For example, instead of trying to find prices for individual desks, chairs, tables, etc. it is more usual to use an index (prepared on a sample of prices) for the price of office furniture. If that index rose from 120 to 132 in the period the accounting figures for office furniture would be amended correspondingly by 10 per cent.

Returning at last to the general price level, the problems are: which measure to use and why? The issues involved in the second question will emerge in sections 9.2 and 9.3; all that is needed now is a measure of the change in the general price level. Clearly, this has to be an index representing a collection of goods. There are indices available reflecting price changes over all goods bought in a country, but they are not available sufficiently frequently or swiftly for accounting purposes. The *retail price index* (RPI), representing retail prices of some 'typical' collection of goods purchased by individuals, has the advantages of being published monthly and of being widely accepted as a measure of price changes. Consequently the RPI, which accountants commonly refer to as providing a measure of *current purchasing power,* offers the most convenient indicator of changes in the general price level.

9.2 Five profit concepts

The best way to understand the issues involved in accounting for price changes is to see the effects on some fairly simple figures. This section will compare five different profit concepts, all relevant to recent developments in accounting practice.

The first method, which merely ignores price changes, is the basis for conventional accounting. The second method updates original cost for changes in the purchasing power of money. But the remaining three approaches all revalue assets at estimated current cost. Thus they give identical balance sheet totals; they disagree only on the division between profit and capital reserves. The five concepts to be considered are:

1. *Historical cost profit* – sales minus original cost.
2. *Current purchasing power (CPP)* – sales minus the current purchasing power of the original cost.
3. *Current cost with operating and holding gains* – gains from selling and holding assets, after adjustment for specific price changes.
4. *Current cost: real terms* – gains from selling and holding assets, after adjustment for specific price changes *and* deductions for maintained purchasing power of the firm's equity.
5. *Current cost: SSAP 16* – gains from selling, after specific price adjustments for maintaining the operating capability and financial structure of the firm.

Each of these methods has a place in the British accountancy profession's stumbling efforts on price changes. Despite criticism over many years, *historical cost* is still the main method in all but a few firms; accounts showing price changes are normally supplementary statements.

In 1974 a poorly prepared provisional standard[1] was issued, which required *CPP accounts* for companies listed on the Stock Exchange. But the next year a government committee produced the Sandilands Report[2], which favoured the method of *current cost with operating and holding gains*. So the Accounting Standards Committee (ASC) dropped its CPP views and in 1976 proposed a new standard[3] for current cost with operating and holding gains – although some extra figures broadly showed *current cost: real terms*.

The 1976 proposals were generally soundly based on ideas that had been developed over many years. Unfortunately the proposals were also very wordy and were to apply rapidly to *all* businesses. This was too much for most chartered accountants, who had not yet got used to the idea that anything was wrong with historical cost accounts. In a grassroots revolt against the leaders of their profession the chartered accountants voted against the 1976 proposals. The ASC went back to the drawing board.

By 1980 the ASC agreed on Statement of Standard Accounting Practice 16[4], which applies to large companies. Strangely the ideas behind SSAP 16 are more complicated, and in this writer's opinion less sensible, than the 1976 proposals. Although SSAP 16 is the profession's latest attempt it may not be the last, and it is worth noting that developments in other countries have generally had more in common with methods 2 and 3.

The five concepts are illustrated in Fig. 9.1. This shows the trading results for a new business which commenced the accounting period with the following balance sheet[5]:

	£		£
Capital	3,050	Stocks	4,000
Loan (interest free)	950		
	£4,000		£4,000

During the period the replacement cost of the firm's stock of goods rose by 50 per cent, and the retail price index increased by 10 per cent. At the end of the period the firm sold three-quarters of its stock for £4,500 to a customer; this amount appears as a debtor in the balance sheet at the end of the period. The unrealistic assumptions that this was the only transaction, that it took place right at the end of the period, and that no interest was payable on the loan, are all made to simplify the arithmetic without affecting the arguments.

A further problem is evaded by assuming that the business is a new one; for an existing business the balance sheet at the beginning of the period would need to reflect price changes up to that time.

1. Historical cost

In this familiar method, £3,000, representing three-quarters of the £4,000 historical cost of goods, is deducted from sales revenue to give a profit of £1,500. The remaining stocks are shown in the balance sheet at £1,000.

2. Current purchasing power (CPP)

The CPP method adjusts for changes in the value of the *monetary unit* rather than for changes in specific prices of the firm's resources. It does not seriously challenge the idea of historical cost, but merely translates 'old' money asset outlays into 'new' money without considering what may have happened to the specific prices of the assets.

In Fig. 9.1 the goods sold (line 2) involved an outlay of £3,000 in old £s. Since the general price level has risen 10 per cent that outlay is equal to £3,300 in inflated £s, derived by multiplying the historical cost by the retail price index at the end of the period (110) and dividing by the index at acquisition (100). In this example stocks were conveniently acquired at the beginning of the period and (partly) sold at the end; in more realistic situations index adjustments from the average date of acquisition and the average date of sales would have to be made. In line 3 the gain of £1,200 from sale of goods is comparable with the £1,500 profit calculated under historical cost; some allowance has been made for the fact that the purchases were made in 'heavier' money than the sales.

The *monetary gain* makes more sense than the previous calculation. It represents something which has become familiar to many people: the gain from incurring debts in old £s and repaying later in inflated, less valuable, £s. At the beginning of the period the firm incurred a debt of £950, fixed in money terms, which the firm still owed in inflated £s at the end of the period. To command the same general purchasing power the payment would have had to be increased by 10 per cent to £1,045; the difference is the monetary gain from owing money during the period. A corresponding monetary loss could have been incurred if the firm had held money or claims expressed in money, but the firm was not owed any money until the last moment of the period.

Fig. 9.1 Five approaches to profit calculation.

	[1] Historical cost	[2] CPP		Current cost: [3] Operating/holding gains		[4] Real terms		[5] SSAP 16	
	£		£		£		£		£
Profit and reserves									
1. Sales	4,500		4,500		4,500		4,500		4,500
2. *Less* cost of goods sold	3,000	$\times \frac{110}{100}$	3,300	$\left(£3,000 \times \frac{150}{100}\right)$	4,500		4,500		4,500
3.			1,200	Operating gains	0	Operating gains	0	Operating profit	0
4. Monetary gain $\left(£950 \times \frac{10}{100}\right)$			95			As in [2]	95	Gearing adjustment 19% of £1,500	285
5. Profit	£1,500		£1,295					Current cost profit	£285
6. Holding gains: Realized				$\left(£3,000 \times \frac{50}{100}\right)$	1,500	$\left(£3,000 \times \frac{50-10}{100}\right)$	1,200	As in [3] *Less* gearing adjst.	1,500 (285)
7. Unrealized				$\left(£1,000 \times \frac{50}{100}\right)$	500	$\left(£1,000 \times \frac{50-10}{100}\right)$	400	As in [3]	500
8.				Total gains	£2,000	Total real gains	£1,695		
9. Capital reserve		As in [4]	£305			(£3,050 × 10%)	£305	Current cost reserve	£1,715
Ending balance sheets									
10. Opening equity	3,050	$\times \frac{110}{100}$	3,355		3,050	$\left(£3,050 \times \frac{110}{100}\right)$	3,355		3,050
11.				Holding gains	2,000	Real holding gains	1,600	Current cost reserve	1,715
12.						Monetary gain	95		
13. Profit	1,500		1,295	Operating gains	0	Operating gains	0	Current cost profit	285
14. Closing equity	4,550		4,650		5,050		5,050		5,050
15. Loan	950		950		950		950		950
16.	£5,500		£5,600		£6,000		£6,000		£6,000
17. Stocks	1,000	$\times \frac{110}{100}$	1,100	$\left(£1,000 \times \frac{150}{100}\right)$	1,500		1,500		1,500
18. Debtor	4,500		4,500		4,500		4,500		4,500
19.	£5,500		£5,600		£6,000		£6,000		£6,000

Readers should not assume that a monetary gain represents the *net* benefit from owing money. It has been mentioned elsewhere that interest rates have a tendency to rise in inflationary periods to compensate for a prospective decline in purchasing power, and there may also be hidden costs in the prices charged by suppliers who give long credit terms. Consequently a monetary gain will normally be a counterpart to costs elsewhere in the profit calculation; whether the firm derives a net benefit from owing money depends on the relative size of those costs.

The firm commenced the period with a capital of £3,050 in old £s. Just to keep in line with inflation the owners' wealth needs to be 10 per cent higher in new £s before a genuine profit is made. Thus an amount of £305 is calculated as a capital revenue in line 9, and is added to opening equity as a price level adjustment in the balance sheet (line 10).

As for profit, that is £1,295 (lines 5 and 13). In effect that is historical cost profit (£1,500) plus asset revaluation (stocks £100) minus the equity adjustment (£305).

On the assets side of the balance sheet those assets whose value is *not* fixed in money terms (stocks alone in this case) are converted into new £s in the same way as cost of goods earlier.

3. Current cost – operating and holding gains

This approach adjusts for specific price changes only, and ignores general prive-level changes. Thus, cost of goods sold (line 2) is converted from cost at the date of acquisition (index 100) to replacement cost at disposal (specific index 150). Disposals occurring throughout a period would require more complex adjustments.

The important point emerges that, *in terms of prevailing prices, the firm is not operating at a profit* (line 3); *it is selling goods only at the price at which it could replenish its stocks*. However, because the firm held stocks which cost £4,000 over a period in which replacement cost rose 50 per cent, it made what is termed a *holding gain* of £2,000. £1,500 has been *realized* (line 6) by selling three-quarters of the stocks; the remaining £500 (line 7) is an *unrealized* gain on stocks still held. It is no coincidence that the £1,500 realized gain equals the profit previously derived by the historical cost method: *that approach merges realized holding gains into profit without revealing their existence*.

In the balance sheet holding gains (line 11) augment equity. General price changes are ignored, so only stocks require adjustment by conversion from historical cost to replacement cost. The £500 increase in stock valuation is the counterpart to the unrealized holding gain mentioned above.

4. Current cost – real terms

This approach incorporates both specific price changes and CPP adjustments. It represents the plausible view that a firm gains no real advantage from a 10 per cent increase in the specific money prices of the assets it holds if prices in general have also risen by 10 per cent. Thus for 'real profit' the specific price changes are first calculated along CCA lines, and then the 'illusory' elements reflecting the erosion of general purchasing power of the monetary unit are deducted.

In Fig. 9.1 the charge for cost of goods sold in line 2 remains at £4,500, as in the previous method, because that expresses the real current costs in inflated £s at the end of the period.

As in the previous method, the important point emerges that the firm's operations are merely breaking even in terms of prevailing prices; line 3 shows that sales only just cover the firm's current costs.

The monetary gain has been incorporated on precisely the same basis as under the CPP method: again it represents the gain from the loan incurred in old £s which is repayable in inflated, less valuable £s.

Real holding gains are more complex. In order to produce a real gain on specific assets the prices of the firm's assets must have moved up the price escalator faster than prices in general. If the prices had increased by only 10 per cent it should be evident that no real holding gain would have emerged. So the excess of the specific price rise over the change in purchasing power (50 per cent minus 10 per cent) gives the real holding gains of £1,200 and £400. Clearly, real holding losses would have occurred if the specific price increase had been below 10 per cent.

It is no coincidence that the £1,200 real realized holding gain (line 7) equals the £1,200 profit before the monetary gain under the CPP method (line 3). Just as historical cost failed to reveal that profit was entirely composed of £1,500 holding gain, so the CPP method failed to reveal that CPP profit was largely composed of a £1,200 real holding gain.

The £305 capital reserve on line 9 is exactly the same as in the CPP method. This raises the owner's opening wealth of £3,050 by 10 per cent in line with inflation, before real gains are considered to have been made.

The balance sheet items all follow from earlier calculations. The opening equity has been increased by the capital reserve, and gains totalling £1,695 have been transferred to the balance sheet. Stocks are revalued at current cost; the loan and debtor both remain fixed in money terms.

Note particularly that the closing equity, representing owners' wealth, is the same as in the previous current cost method; all the other balance sheet totals are also the same. This is because assets and liabilities are valued in the same way under both methods. The important difference between the methods is in the division of gains. The previous method simply showed all gains, but the real terms method divides between gains needed to maintain the purchasing power of equity (£305) and the remaining real gains.

5. Current cost – SSAP 16

This approach keeps to specific price changes, along the lines of method 3. But it sets aside amounts considered to be needed to maintain the operations of the business at current costs; these amounts are holding gains after adjustment for the way the firm is financed.

Thus in the present example it would be argued that the firm should not distribute its holding gains to owners if the present level of operations is to be maintained; it will need to replace the stock at current cost as it is sold. So the holding gains of £2,000 are transferred to a *current cost reserve*, like a capital reserve, which maintains the capital needed to operate the firm.

However, the firm is partly financed by borrowing. Assuming the same proportion of operations can be financed in that way in the future, that proportion of *realized* holding gains can be taken as profit – which could be withdrawn by the owners. That is the reason for the gearing adjustment. The gearing proportion is calculated from average borrowing in relation to total financing:

$$\frac{\text{opening + closing loan}}{\text{opening + closing equity and loan}} \qquad \frac{950 + 950}{4{,}000 + 6{,}000} = 19\%$$

This 19 per cent of *realized* holding gains of £1,500 is taken as profit to the owners (at the expense of the lenders); thus £285 is added to operating profit to give current cost profit in line 5. The idea behind the gearing adjustment is similar to that of the monetary gain, except that the gearing adjustment implies future financing whereas the monetary gain merely explains the past. The gearing method shows benefits of borrowing when prices have increased, but without recognizing general price changes.

The important feature of SSAP 16 is that it mixes profit and financing issues. It does not simply measure the increase in the firm's resources, it also estimates that part of the increase (transferred to current cost reserve) that would need to be set aside to finance the present level of operations with the present financing pattern.

This section has introduced some basic issues; the next section looks more closely at SSAP 16 and its application.

9.3 Current cost accounting under SSAP 16

In the UK current cost accounting (CCA) follows the methods set out in SSAP 16. Like any other standard it has no legal force, but the influence of professional accountants as auditors has brought most of the companies concerned into line.

It is important to understand that SSAP 16 does not replace historical cost accounts. It brings CCA as additional information, and only for large firms, in the hope the use of CCA will gradually increase. Thus:

1. Current cost accounts must be supplied in addition to historical cost accounts. This is normally done by preparing supplementary CCA statements, but the main accounts can be in current costs with supplementary historical cost figures.
2. The standard applies to companies with shares or loan capital listed on the Stock Exchange and to large companies outside the disclosure exemptions of the 1981 Companies Act (see Chapter 8). However, the standard does not apply to some businesses, such as insurers, property companies and long-term investment firms.

Although SSAP 16 is called a method of current cost accounting, it does not always use current cost values. Its central idea of value is *value to the business* – taken from the Sandilands Report, which in turn borrowed from writers on valuation. Essentially value to business is the amount of loss a firm would suffer if it were deprived of an asset (ignoring insurance). This value is given by one of the following:

1. Net current replacement cost – the current replacement cost of an identical asset, net of depreciation where appropriate.
2. Net realizable value.
3. The amount recoverable from further use of the asset – which might be estimated as the present value of expected future cash flows from the asset (Chapter 6).

In most cases the current cost (value 1) will be below at least one of the other two amounts, because firms are in business to sell or use their assets at a profit above current costs. In such cases a firm deprived of the asset would normally go out and replace at current cost. *Thus value to the business is normally current cost.*

However, consider a company which owns a modern petrol filling station. The filling station was on a main road until a bypass was built; now tràde is terrible. Assume therefore that both net realizable value and the amount recoverable from further use are well below current cost (of the site plus replacement equipment). The company could sell out or continue to run at the reduced cash flows for the life of the equipment; it should choose whichever gives the greater value. The *value to the business* is the greater of those two values; it is not current cost because the company would not replace if it had a choice.

To cover such situations the standard says:

Value to the business is:
(a) net current replacement cost, or, if a permanent diminution in value below net current replacement cost has been recognized,
(b) recoverable amount, which is the greater of net realizable value of an asset and the amount recoverable from its further use.

In the current cost balance sheet the methods of valuing assets and liabilities (ignoring minor exceptions) are:

1. *Land and buildings, plant and machinery, stocks and intangible assets except goodwill* – at their value to the business. These are the items that really matter in CCA.
2. *Investment in associated companies* – the investing company proportion (see Chapter 8, section 8.8) of the associated company's net assets on a CCA basis.
3. *Other investments* (except any treated as current assets) – at directors' valuation, with reasons if different from mid-market values.
4. *Goodwill* – the conventional basis, which for present purposes is historical cost.
5. *Current assets except stocks above* – historical cost.
6. *All liabilities* – historical cost.

The Sandilands Report recognized that changes in the market values of long-term liabilities were in principle similar to price changes in assets. But neither that report nor SSAP 16 applied price changes to liabilities.

Companies may calculate current costs from their own purchasing experience, but it is normal to use published indices for different classes of assets. The UK Government Statistical Service publishes a regular series[6].

The main features of SSAP 16 accounts will be explained with the aid of historical cost accounts of Bigshot PLC[7] in Fig. 9.2, which are converted to current cost accounts in Fig. 9.3. The layouts follow balance sheet format 1 of the Companies Act 1981.

Note that the current cost profit calculation in Fig. 9.3 starts with historical cost trading profit and then makes current cost adjustments. This is the most common method; the accounts could start with full current cost figures, but that is rare.

The example uses price increases throughout for simplicity, but the same principles would apply (with reversed adjustments) for a fall in prices.

Fig. 9.2 Historical cost accounts and price indices for Bigshot PLC.

		£m.	£m.
Profit and loss account information for 19–2			
Sales			1,400
Less	Opening stock	156	
	Purchases	1,024	
	Closing stock	(196)	
	Cost of goods sold		984
Gross profit			416
Less	Depreciation	50	
	Other running costs	255	
	Interest	20	325
Profit before taxation			91
Corporation tax			25
Profit after taxation			66
Dividends			30
Retained profit			36

Balance sheet at 31 December 19–2

Comparative figures 19–1 £m.			
500	Fixed assets purchased 1 January 19–1		500
50	*Less* depreciation (10% straight line)		100
450			400
156	Stock	196	
151	Trade debtors	160	
(12)	Bank (overdraft 19–1)	10	
		366	
(117)	Trade creditors	136	
(19)	Current tax	25	
(20)	Proposed dividend	30	
		191	
	Net current assets		175
(200)	Debenture loan		(150)
(45)	Deferred taxation		(45)
344			380
	Capital and reserves:		
200	Share capital		200
109	Reserves at 1 January	144	
35	Profit for the year	36	
			180
344			380

Price indices for fixed assets and stock

	Fixed assets	Stock
1 January 19–1	80	*
Average for November/December 19–1	*	120
31 December 19–1	90	123
Average for 19–2	96	130
Average for November/December 19–2	*	140
31 December 19–2	104	142

*indices not relevant

Stock, debtors and creditors all turn over, on average, once every two months.

Fig. 9.3 Current cost accounts for Bigshot PLC.

		£m.	£m.
Current cost profit and loss account for the year ended 31 December 19–2			
Turnover			1,400
Historical cost trading profit before interest			111
Less Current cost operating adjustments:			
Depreciation adjustment		10	
Cost of sales adjustment [COSA]		27	
Monetary working capital adjustment [MWCA]		5	42
Current cost operating profit			69
Gearing adjustment [33% of 42]		(14)	
Interest on borrowing		20	6
Current cost profit before tax			63
Corporation tax			25
Current cost profit attributable to shareholders			38
Dividends			30
Retained profit to revenue reserves			8
Current cost balance sheet at 31 December 19–2			
Fixed assets: gross current replacement cost	$\left[500 \times \frac{104}{80}\right]$		650
Less depreciation	$\left[\frac{2}{10} \times 650\right]$		130
Net current replacement cost			520
Current assets			
Stock	$\left[196 \times \frac{142}{140}\right]$	199	
Trade debtors		160	
Bank		10	
		369	
Creditors falling due within one year			
Trade creditors		136	
Current tax		25	
Proposed dividend		30	
		191	
Net current assets			178
Debenture loan			(150)
Deferred taxation			(45)
			503
Capital and reserves			
Share capital			200
Revenue reserves [Historical cost reserve 144 + retained current cost profit 8]			152
Current cost reserve – see Note below			151
			503
Note – Current cost reserve			
Realized:			
Current cost adjustments			42
Gearing adjustment			(14)
Unrealized:			
Fixed asset revaluation [Net CRC 520 – Net HC 400]			120
Stock [Current cost 199 – historical cost 196]			3
			151

1. Fixed assets and depreciation

Asset price changes normally bring two types of adjustment. One is for the price change in assets which have been held for part of the year, but are sold or used up (partly or fully) by the end of the year. These are the *realized* holding gains considered earlier. The other type of adjustment concerns price changes on assets which are still held at the end of the year; these are the *unrealized* holding gains.

The first type brings an increased charge (debit) to the profit and loss account. Depreciation on assets used during the year involves just such a charge. Bigshot charged £50m. depreciation in its historical cost accounts. But the price index for its fixed assets had risen from 80 on 1 January 19–1, when the assets were bought, to an average of 96 during 19–2. The average price index is normally chosen for the year's depreciation because the assets depreciate throughout the year; thus an average does rough justice to different prices during the year. The calculation for the depreciation adjustment in Fig. 9.3 is therefore:

$$\text{Historical cost depreciation} \times \frac{\text{average index of year}}{\text{index at acquisition}} = 50 \times \frac{96}{80} = 60$$

Less historical cost depreciation	50
Depreciation adjustment	10

Of course every debit has a credit. The credit side of this adjustment, and those that follow, will be considered together under current cost reserve.

The other type of price adjustment on the assets still held at the end of the year brings a revaluation of assets in the balance sheet. Here Bigshot's fixed assets at historical cost in Fig. 9.3 are £400m. net of depreciation, but the price index has risen from 80 at acquisition to *104 at the balance sheet date*. Unlike the charge against profit, where the average index related to use during the year, a new value is needed at the end of the year.

The amount of gross current replacement cost is given by:

$$\text{Gross historical cost} \times \frac{\text{index at balance sheet date}}{\text{index at acquisition}} = 500 \times \frac{104}{80} = 650$$

The simplest way of tackling the balance sheet depreciation is to consider that a certain proportion of asset life has expired: two-tenths in this case. Thus the expired value to be deducted is:

$$\text{Expired life} \times \text{gross current replacement cost} = \frac{2}{10} \times 650 = 130$$

Attempts to add up past depreciation provisions to arrive at a balance sheet figure are best avoided. They bring problems of 'backlogs' underprovided in earlier years. The method shown here sidesteps that issue.

The two major groups of fixed assets, plant and machinery and land and buildings, can bring different problems under CCA. The firm's partly used plant and machinery may be inferior to current replacements; here SSAP 16 says that existing assets should be valued at their (lower) service potential, and not by merely applying the price index for a new (improved) replacement.

As for land and buildings, where these are non-specialized they would be valued at the prices at which they could be bought in the open market. Independent valuations would normally be made every five years, with estimates in between. Many specialized buildings do not have a ready market; these would be treated like plant and machinery, with the underlying land at open market value.

2. Stock and the cost of sales adjustment (COSA)

The principles of adjusting for price changes in stock are the same as for fixed assets, but the methods used are different.

In most businesses stock is turned over frequently as goods are bought and sold. Accounting records which could produce price adjustments for each item are rare. Instead, a rough averaging formula, usually called the COSA formula[8], is normally used. This is best explained in two stages.

1. *Calculate the increase or decrease in stock, at historical cost, over the year.* Assuming for a moment that there had been no change in the *volume* of stock, an increase here would represent pure price change between the dates of the historical cost figures (ignoring problems like FIFO). So the next step is to adjust for the estimated volume change.

2. *Adjust for the estimated volume change, at average price of the period.* This is done by adding the opening stock and deducting the closing stock, both converted from historical cost to the average prices of the period. Applying the COSA formula to Bigshot gives:

Increase in historical cost of stock 40

$$\text{Add opening stock} \times \frac{\text{average price index for year}}{\text{opening price index}} = 156 \times \frac{130}{120} = 169$$

$$\text{Less closing stock} \times \frac{\text{average price index for year}}{\text{closing price index}} = 196 \times \frac{130}{140} = 182$$

−13

Cost of sales adjustment 27

Note that the opening stock was bought during November/December 19–1 at index 120 (*not* the 31 December 19–1 index of 123) and is updated to the average index for 19–2, i.e. 130. Similarly the closing stock was bought at the November/December index of 140. This is *brought back* to the average of the period price index of 130 for comparison with opening stock. The result is COSA of £27m. which reduces profit in Fig. 9.3.

The other aspect of stock, as with fixed assets, concerns revaluation in the balance sheet. The closing stock was bought when the November/December price index was 140, but at the balance sheet date the price index is 142. Consequently the historical cost figure can be updated:

$$\text{Historical cost of stock} \times \frac{\text{index at balance sheet date}}{\text{index at average date of acquisition of stock}} = 196 \times \frac{142}{140} = 199$$

3. Monetary working capital adjustment (MWCA)

The MWCA is a peculiarity of SSAP 16. It is based on the idea that a firm needs to deduct from profit any extra amount needed to finance increased prices affecting all working capital items. Just as COSA made an adjustment for price changes in stocks, so it is argued that an adjustment should be made for working capital fixed in money terms in the form of trade debtors minus trade creditors.

For this purpose the debtors minus creditors are treated as if they were part of stock. So the MWCA uses the same indices and formula as COSA.

The Bigshot example applies the formula again, except that there has been a decrease in the monetary working capital on this occasion:

		19–1	19–2	
Decrease in MWC	Debtors	151	160	−10
	Less creditors	117	136	
	MWC	34	24	

$$\text{Add opening MWC} \times \frac{\text{average price index for year}}{\text{opening price index}} = 34 \times \frac{130}{120} = 37$$

$$\textit{Less}\text{ closing MWC} \times \frac{\text{average price index for year}}{\text{closing price index}} = 24 \times \frac{130}{140} = 22$$

15

Monetary working capital adjustment 5

The similarity with stock does not extend to the balance sheet. Here debtors and creditors are fixed in money terms, so no revaluation can take place. It may seem illogical to treat debtors and creditors like stock for profit purposes but like money for balance sheet purposes – and it is. Whatever merits the MWCA may have, logic is not one of them.

SSAP 16 considers that 'a MWCA is equally necessary in a business which does not hold stocks'. In such cases, for example banks, an adjustment would normally be based on the retail price index. This comes to the same thing as the monetary borrowing gain/loss considered with 'real terms' in the previous section of this chapter, although with a more limited application.

4. The gearing adjustment

It was shown earlier than the gearing adjustment brings some borrowing benefits into profit when current costs have increased. This is done by adding back the gearing proportion of current cost adjustments into profit, where the gearing proportion is given by L/(L + S), and L is the average borrowing of the period and S is the average shareholder's equity of the period.

The calculation of the gearing proportion for Bigshot is shown in Fig. 9.4. The major points are:

1. All the items in the balance sheet which have not yet featured in the adjustment come into play now.
2. Among the net borrowing items are obvious ones like the debenture loan and bank overdraft (19–1) but also tax liabilities (financed by the tax man) and the deduction of money items like the bank balance in 19–2.
3. The shareholders' equity S has to come from the share capital and reserves in the *current cost balance sheets*. This may seem rather difficult when the gearing adjustment is being made in order to prepare the accounts! One way of finding the correct totals is by adding the asset revaluations (the familiar unrealized holding gains) to the historical cost balance sheet amounts. This method is shown in Fig. 9.4.

   Normally the opening current cost balance sheet would be available from the previous period. In that case shareholders' opening equity could be taken from that balance sheet.

Fig. 9.4 The gearing proportion calculation.

		19–1 £m.		19–2 £m.
Net borrowing				
Debenture loan		200		150
Deferred tax		45		45
Current tax		19		25
Bank overdraft (less balance 19–2)		12		(10)
L		276		210
Shareholders' equity				
Share capital and reserves from historical cost balance sheet		344		380
Proposed dividend		20		30
Add asset revaluations:				
Fixed assets	$\left[450 \times \frac{90-80}{80}\right]$	56	$\left[400 \times \frac{104-80}{80}\right]$	120
Stock	$\left[156 \times \frac{123-120}{120}\right]$	4	$\left[196 \times \frac{142-140}{140}\right]$	3
S		424		533
L + S		700		743

$$\text{Gearing proportion} = \frac{L}{L+S} = \frac{276+210}{700+743} = 33\% \text{ approx.}$$

4. Note that proposed dividends are added back to share capital and reserves. That is because these amounts are still part of shareholders' equity at the balance sheet date.

The gearing proportion of 33 per cent is then applied to the earlier current cost adjustments of £42m. In Fig. 9.3 the resulting amount of £14m. is grouped with interest on borrowing. That shows the gearing adjustments as a gain made with the lenders' money, which partly affects the interest cost. Some firms prefer to show the gearing adjustment after the tax charge.

5. The current cost reserve

The current cost reserve is the other (credit) side of the profit adjustments and asset revaluations. It can be found in two ways. The easiest, particularly when no opening current cost reserve figure is available, is to add together all the profit adjustments and asset revaluations. This has been done in the note to Fig. 9.3.

The amounts are really just like the familiar realized and unrealized holding gains. But SSAP 16 avoids the word gain, with some justification – because the MWCA is not a gain at all, but a financing adjustment.

The second way of arriving at the current cost reserve is to add current cost movements during the year to the opening balance of the reserve. This method is used in practice, and gives the movements that should be disclosed under the standard. The figures for Bigshot would be:

Retained current cost profit	8
Movements on current cost reserve	
[Closing 151 minus opening 60]	91
	99
Reserves at the beginning of the year	
[Historical cost 144 plus revaluations 60]	204
Reserves at the end of the year	303

As this was the first year of current cost accounts for Bigshot the opening current cost reserve equalled the opening asset revaluations.

9.4 Consequences

In its impact on the content of accounting statements, CCA is the most important development in recent years – because it goes to the root of the problem of valuation. However, accountants have handled the issues with very mixed success. SSAP 16 is the result of compromise, both in content and in its application only to large firms. The future acceptance of CCA will depend greatly on what happens to prices generally, because the limitations of conventional accounts are easier to overlook in periods of modest price changes.

Current cost profit, ignoring the peculiarities of MWCA, is a much more informative measure than conventional historical cost profit. It represents the return from operating activities after charging for the use of resources at estimated current prices. As such it is a useful indicator of operating viability, free from undisclosed elements of stock appreciation and less likely to suffer from the underdepreciation of fixed assets which bedevils conventional profit in times of rapidly rising prices.

The gearing adjustment gives a very rough indication of gains from borrowing. But it should be treated with particular caution if it is large in relation to the other amounts. It may arise from high borrowing combined with large price changes in the assets used up – not a joyful situation for the banker.

The holding gains of the period which go into current cost profit can help in the interpretation of accounts. In conjunction with current cost profit they give an overall picture of the increased or decreased command over resources which the firm has achieved in the year.

What a company may decide to do with its increased resources is another matter. The fact that amounts are set aside in the current cost reserve does not mean, eigher legally or in practice, that they are not available for dividends. Profits legally available for dividends under the Companies Act 1980 are *accumulated realized profits*, which means the profits shown in conventional historical cost accounts. In practice company dividends are influenced by a variety of factors, which include not only legal rules but also matters like financing needs and the confidence of investors.

For the banker, current valuations make the balance sheet a more consistently meaningful document, particularly where independent valuation of property is involved. But it must be remembered, as always, that the figures are estimates. Moreover they are estimates of value to the business *as a going concern*; if assets have to be sold off piecemeal the only certain thing is that the realizable total will be lower.

For the vast majority of companies profit measured on a current cost basis will be lower than conventional historical cost profit. That does not mean a change to current cost profit can make a financially sound company into a shaky enterprise overnight; the underlying economic facts, of course, are not altered at all. It means that gains have been treated differently and more informatively. It also means that for comparison purposes like must be compared with like; clearly this year's current cost profit cannot be compared meaningfully with last year's conventional accounting profit. It is equally dangerous to compare balance-sheet structures, since revaluations can have substantial impact in that respect.

The question of comparisons between years raises again the issue of *general* price changes. It is misleading to compare £s in one year with £s in another year if their purchasing power has changed at all significantly between the years. So if a company increases its *current cost* profit from £5m. a few years ago to £6m. this year, that would be discouraging if prices had generally doubled in the interval. The earlier profit in the hands of shareholders could have bought goods equivalent to some £10m. this year.

The same basic argument applies to the comparative figures for the previous year which appear in every company's accounts, and to the 10-year summaries which listed companies include with their annual reports. However, *ratio* comparisons are valid, because the amounts in each year's ratio calculation are in common £s. Unfortunately, ratios do not serve all comparison needs.

SSAP 16 carefully avoided general price changes, so that all the figures are measured in £s of a particular year and are not really comparable between years (unless adjusted). The ASC is moving on this issue[9] and the signs are that it will favour updating past figures for general price changes into £s of the latest year. The index chosen will probably be the retail price index.

Finally there is the question of whether companies should be taxed on current cost profits. The Sandilands Report hesitantly favoured the current cost basis for company tax, and there has been some support for the idea over the years. But the UK system of first-year capital allowances and stock relief gives most companies broadly similar benefits to current cost allowances, and government opinion has not favoured a current cost basis.

Notes and references

In the following ICAEW = Institute of Chartered Accountants in England and Wales.

1 *Provisional Statement of Standard Accounting Practice 7 (SSAP 7): Accounting for Changes in the Purchasing Power of Money*, ICAEW (1974).
2. *Inflation Accounting: Report of the Inflation Accounting Committee*, CMND 6225, HMSO (1975).
3. *Exposure Draft 18 (ED18): Current cost accounting*, ICAEW (1976).
4. *Statement of Standard Accounting Practice 16 (SSAP 16): Current cost accounting*, ICAEW (1980).
5. This example is adapted from material which appeared previously in D. A. Egginton, 'The inflation accounting bandwagon', *Journal of the Institute of Bankers* (Oct. 1974). As was stated on that occasion, the illustration and discussion borrow heavily from W. T. Baxter, 'General or special index', *Journal UEC* (1967), pp. 172–81 and E. O. Edwards and P. W. Bell, *The Theory and Measurement of Business Income*, University of California Press (1965).
6. *Price Index Numbers for Current Cost Accounting* (HMSO); also relevant is Current Cost Accounting – *Guide to price indices for Overseas Countries* (HMSO).

7. The figures used in this example have been loosely adapted from Question 7 of the Institute of Bankers Diploma examination (Stage 2) April 1981.
8. $$\text{COSA} = \left(\begin{matrix}\text{closing}\\ \text{stock}\end{matrix} - \begin{matrix}\text{opening}\\ \text{stock}\end{matrix}\right) + \left(\begin{matrix}\text{opening}\\ \text{stock}\end{matrix} \times \frac{\text{average index}}{\text{opening index}}\right) - \left(\begin{matrix}\text{closing}\\ \text{stock}\end{matrix} \times \frac{\text{average index}}{\text{closing stock}}\right)$$
where both opening and closing stocks are at historical cost.
9. *ASC Discussion paper: Corresponding amounts and ten year summaries in current cost accounting*, ICAEW (1982).

Chapter 10

Interpretation measures

This chapter will focus on certain measures used in the interpretation of accounts; broader aspects of financial assessment from the lending viewpoint will be the concern of Chapter 11. However, the emphasis throughout will be on the investigation of potential financial vulnerability rather than on, say, considerations of valuation for a potential investor.

10.1 Measures introduced

In the interpretation of accounts there are three fundamental ways in which figures may be viewed; these are listed below.

1. *As absolute amounts.* For example, the facts that *X* made a profit of £6,000 last year, that *Y* Ltd has a working capital of £240,000 or that *Z* Ltd has no long-term debt are all of potential interest in considering financial standing.
2. *As changes or differences.* For example, *X*'s profit last year may be £2,000 lower than the previous year's, or the working capital of *Y* Ltd may have increased by £40,000. Such changes in past figures suggest that the financial situation is 'worse' or 'better' than before, and in more elaborate forms the approach is often described as *trend* analysis. Whether such trends can be assumed to project into the future depends, of course, on considerations other than past results alone.

   In a sense profit statements and funds flow statements themselves represent changes in financial position, and the individual elements in these statements always deserve examination for their 'good' or 'bad' effects on the general financial condition of the firm.

   Accounts may also be examined for differences between actual results and expectations. This occurs frequently within the firm for management purposes, but the approach can also be applied by a lending banker who compares a customer's cash budget with actual monthly results. Such comparison is, however, more a method of controlling the progress of advance rather than a method of interpretation for lending.
3. *Relative to other figures.* Earlier examples were given of a £2,000 decline on *X*'s profit to £6,000 and an increase of £40,000 in the working capital of *Y* Ltd – to £240,000. Both these figures might be put in perspective if they were related to another figure from the accounts, such as total assets. *X*'s profit of £6,000 begins to look healthier if it was earned with total assets of £15,000. On the other hand the working capital of *Y* Ltd, despite its increase to £240,000, would look unimpressive against total assets of £50 m.

The message which comes through from the above comments is that figures rarely mean a great deal in isolation; they need to be compared in some way with something.

An experienced reader of accounts looking at a set of accounting figures will usually have certain, almost subconscious, presumptions about the relationships which might be plausible in the accounts. Consequently, it is often possible to look at absolute amounts and changes and reach a swift assessment. But for the novice (and others when difficult interpretation problems are involved) a more formal framework can be helpful.

Consequently, consideration will be given here to relationships between different accounting figures which can be expressed as *ratios.* The fact that they will be discussed in considerable detail in subsequent pages does *not* imply that they should all necessarily be calculated in all, or most, cases. Moreover, they are often better employed to 'trigger' points for investigation than to make final judgements. It is much more important for the user of accounts to concentrate on obtaining an overall view of a set of accounts than to become engrossed in minor changes in ratios.

A ratio is an expression of the relationship between two amounts, and it would be strictly accurate to write a ratio as £53,021:£9,468. But for comparison purposes with other ratios that would be useless, and the relationship between those two accounting figures may be expressed in any of the following ways:

$$\frac{53{,}021}{9{,}468} = 5{\cdot}6 \text{ or } 560 \text{ per cent}$$

$$\frac{9{,}468}{53{,}021} = 0{\cdot}18 \text{ or } 18 \text{ per cent}$$

The first method of expression in each case represents a ratio (implicitly 5·6:1 and 0·18:1) and the second method is, of course, a percentage. However, it is often convenient to talk sweepingly of 'accounting ratios' in the broad sense of any measure expressing a relationship between accounting figures; in what follows the adjective 'accounting' will indicate when the word 'ratios' is being used in that wider sense.

There are certain generally accepted methods of expressing relationships for particular purposes – for example, some indicators of solvency are normally stated as ratios, whereas profits are usually expressed as percentages of sales or capital. However, to avoid confusion in the presentation of examples later in Fig. 10.2 the measures are shown there as percentages; the discussion will explain how the different measures are normally shown.

Reasons for using ratios/percentages are diverse, and some reasons are better than others.

A fundamental argument for accounting ratios is that their use eliminates the effects of scale (size) so that comparison can be more readily made between different years and different firms. This is valid, *provided* the underlying figures are prepared on valuation bases which are consistent with each other. Current cost accounting provides substantial consistency, but historical cost does not. This reservation means that accounting ratios dependent on historical cost figures (particularly fixed assets) must be treated with caution.

An important use of ratios is in providing indicators of the financial capacity of a firm to meet its commitments. In this context one figure in the relationship represents particular resources (or the ability to generate resources) and the other element represents financial commitments. The higher is the former relative to the latter, the smaller is the implied risk. It will be seen later that, under certain circumstances, accounting figures have been shown to be effective in this role.

Accounting ratios can also be used to explore the ways in which the firm's operations are conducted, providing information for financial assessment, although to do this effectively often requires a finer breakdown of costs than is available in published accounting reports. For example, the trends in labour, materials and administrative costs relative to total costs may indicate changes in the firm's cost structure; such information can be obtained by bankers and used to test the expectations of the firm in the manner discussed in sections 4.4 and 4.5. The fact that these issues will not be examined again in this chapter does not mean they are unimportant; on the contrary they were considered earlier because they were fundamental. An analysis of a firm's cost structure and cash budgets explicitly recognizes the forward-looking assumptions which are so often hidden away when past results are 'interpreted'. Past figures are only of interest because they provide a starting-point for developing assumptions of some sort about the future.

Perhaps the most dangerous area in the use of accounting ratios is for the purpose of making judgements about 'efficiency' of activities. The outsider is usually in a poor position to judge on the accounts alone whether a particular change in the reported accounting figures represents a good or bad use of the opportunities available to the firm. For example, an increase in the average credit period taken by debtors could arise from inefficiency in the firm's collection procedures, it could arise from changes in the economic environment, or it could arise from a deliberate policy view that longer credit will produce more sales. Only after discussion with the firm's management and investigation into the background facts could any judgement be made. What is unambiguous is that longer credit allowances involve the firm in more risk in terms of having to wait longer for money to meet its financial commitments; that involves no 'efficiency' judgements.

A selection of accounting ratios will be briefly explained in this section. Subsequent sections will consider certain possible limitations, evidence on the effectiveness of accounting ratios, and trends in such ratios.

The examples in this section will use as a basis for calculation the summarized accounting figures for the British Leyland Motor Corporation Ltd (BLMC) for 1973 and 1974 appearing in Fig. 10.1. For readers unfamiliar with the history of BLMC it may help to know that the company's operations were taken over in 1975 by British Leyland Ltd (shortened later to BL), on the following grounds quoted from the 1975 report of that company:

The Ryder Report [sponsored by the UK government] concluded that in order to make BLMC a viable and fully competitive vehicle producer, a massive injection of new capital and other finance would be required. It recommended that as a preliminary step a reconstruction be effected by forming a new holding company to acquire the whole of the issued share capital of BLMC. . . .

The measures to be considered in turn will be summarized under five headings, and all the measures derived under these headings are reproduced in Fig. 10.2.

A mention must be made of those measures in Fig. 10.2 in which a figure representing 'flows' during the year (for example, sales, profit or funds generated) is related to a balance-sheet figure like total assets or debt. The view is often taken that in such cases the 'flow' figure should be related to the *average* of the figures from the opening and closing balance sheets for that year. In considering whether

Fig. 10.1 British Leyland Motor Corporation Ltd. Summary of results 1973 and 1974.*

		Year ended 30 Sept.		
		1973 £m.		1974 £m.
Sales		1,564		1,595
Excerpt from statement of source and application of funds				
Profit before taxation		51·3		2·3
Extraordinary items		0·6		(15·7)
		51·9		(13·4)
Adjustments for items not involving the movement of funds				
Depreciation and amortization		44·0		41·7
Tooling in Australia written off		–		6·1
Funds generated from operations		95·9		34·4
Profit and loss account				
Earnings before interest and taxation		58·2		19·4
Interest payable less interest receivable		(6·9)		(17·1)
Profit before taxation		51·3		2·3
Taxation		(23·4)		(9·0)
Profit after taxation		27·9		(6·7)
Minority interests in subsidiaries		(1·2)		(1·5)
Net income (before extraordinary items)		26·7		(8·2)
Extraordinary items (1974: loss on closure of overseas manufacturing division)		0·6		(15·7)
Dividends		(8·7)		(3·0)
Transfer to (from) reserves		18·6		(26·9)
Balance sheet				
Fixed assets, net of accumulated depreciation		203·2		239·9
Special tools, dies and jigs		31·7		45·8
Trade investments		11·5		10·7
Current assets:				
Stocks	354·4		472·5	
Debtors and bills receivable	188·7		180·9	
Amount receivable on asset sale	–		11·0	
Cash, short-term deposits, etc.	160·8		95·1	
		703·9		759·5
		950·3		1,055·9
Capital and reserves:				
Ordinary share capital	148·3		148·3	
Reserves	138·8		111·9	
		287·1		260·2
Minority interests in subsidiaries		9·8		11·2
Deferred taxation		10·2		22·4
Deferred currency exchange gains		9·5		6·4
Long-term debt:				
Convertible unsecured loan stock	26·8		26·8	
Debentures and long-term loans	71·2		73·3	
		98·0		100·1

Fig. 10.1 (cont.)

	Year ended 30 Sept.			
	£m.		£m.	
Current liabilities:				
Creditors and bills payable	362·6		478·9	
Bank and other short-term borrowing	110·1		130·3	
Corporation tax (due in 1 year or longer)	4·8		–	
Current taxation	11·3		6·1	
VAT and car tax	38·2		37·3	
Dividends	8·7		3·0	
		535·7		655·6
		950·3		1,055·9

* Adapted, with permission, for consistency with the presentation of accounting summaries earlier in this book.

Fig. 10.2 Accounting measures for interpretation (all expressed in percentages) (cont. p. 166)

Measures	Definitions	Example percentages based on Fig. 10.1 (for BLMC) 1973 £m.	%	1974 £m.	%
Earnings and funds generated					
EBIT/total assets	earnings before interest and tax / total assets	58·2 / 950·3	6	19·4 / 1,055·9	2
Net income/total assets	net profit after tax but before extraordinary items / total assets	26·7 / 950·3	3	(8·2) / 1,055·9	(1)
Return on equity	net income (as above) – preference dividends / ordinary capital + reserves	26·7 / 287·1	9	(8·2) / 260·2	(3)
Profit (before tax) on sales	profit before taxation / sales	51·3 / 1,564	3	2·3 / 1,595	0
Funds generated/ total debt	funds generated from operations / total debt	95·9 / 633·7	15	34·4 / 755·7	5
Interest cover	earnings before interest and tax / interest payable†	58·2 / 6·9	843	19·4 / 17·1	113
Asset and creditor levels					
Debtor/sales	debtors / sales	188·7 / 1,564	12	180·9 / 1,595	11
Creditors/sales	creditors / sales	362·6 / 1,564	23	478·9 / 1,595	30
Stocks/sales	stocks / sales	354·4 / 1,564	23	472·5 / 1,595	30
Sales/total assets	sales / total assets	1,564 / 950·3	165	1,595 / 1,055·9	151

Fig. 10.2 (cont.)

Measures	**Definitions**	**Example percentages based on Fig. 10.1 (for BLMC)** 1973 £m.	%	1974 £m.	%
Short-term liquidity					
Quick or liquid ratio	$\frac{\text{debtors + cash + near cash}}{\text{current liabilities}}$	$\frac{349{\cdot}5}{535{\cdot}7}$	65	$\frac{287{\cdot}0}{655{\cdot}6}$	44
Current ratio	$\frac{\text{current assets}}{\text{current liabilities}}$	$\frac{703{\cdot}9}{535{\cdot}7}$	131	$\frac{759{\cdot}5}{655{\cdot}6}$	116
Working capital/ total assets	$\frac{\text{current assets} - \text{current liabilities}}{\text{total assets}}$	$\frac{168{\cdot}2}{950{\cdot}3}$	18	$\frac{103{\cdot}9}{1{,}055{\cdot}9}$	10
Long-term financial stability					
Total debt/total assets	$\frac{\text{total debt}}{\text{total assets}}$	$\frac{633{\cdot}7}{950{\cdot}3}$	67	$\frac{755{\cdot}7}{1{,}055{\cdot}9}$	72
Total debt/equity	$\frac{\text{total debt}}{\text{ordinary capital + reserves}}$	$\frac{633{\cdot}7}{287{\cdot}1}$	221	$\frac{755{\cdot}7}{260{\cdot}2}$	290
Own funds/fixed assets	$\frac{\text{capital (incl. preference) + reserves}}{\text{fixed assets}}$	$\frac{287{\cdot}1}{203{\cdot}2}$	141	$\frac{260{\cdot}2}{239{\cdot}9}$	108
Short-term borrowing					
Bank and short borrowing/current assets	$\frac{\text{bank overdraft + short loans}}{\text{current assets}}$	$\frac{110{\cdot}1}{703{\cdot}9}$	16	$\frac{130{\cdot}3}{759{\cdot}5}$	17
Bank and short borrowing/working capital	$\frac{\text{bank overdraft + short loans}}{\text{current assets} - \text{current liabilities}}$	$\frac{110{\cdot}1}{168{\cdot}2}$	65	$\frac{130{\cdot}3}{103{\cdot}9}$	125

† In the example calculations the figures adopted from Fig. 10.1 represent interest payable *less interest receivable*. The latter amounts (which were very substantial) related mainly to 'bank and other short-term deposits' and seem appropriate for set-off against the short-term interest payable.

such averaging is necessary, two questions need to be asked: what is the purpose of the measure, and would averaging materially affect the result?

When the intention is to relate 'flow' figures to assess how well resources have been employed over the whole period, as in the first three measures in Fig. 10.2, averaging is legitimate. It is then a matter of deciding whether the balance-sheet changes are big enough to affect interpretation – bearing in mind that accounting ratios are more indicators of direction than precision instruments. In such cases averaging is occasionally worthwhile, but that is not so for BLMC.

However, when the intention is to explore the risk characteristics of the balance sheet by relating assets and liabilities to the level of trading operations it is the *closing* balance sheet which is of central interest. For example, the banker's interest would lie in the level of stock at the *end* of the year in relation to the volume of activity; it would be unhelpful to fudge the issue by averaging the opening and closing stock figures. Consequently, none of the measures in Fig. 10.2 relate to average balance-sheet figures.

1. Earnings and funds generated

The capacity to generate earnings is crucial to the survival of any business. A business which has, *and is expected to continue having,* a high level of profit relative to its financial commitments has good prospects of continuing. Even if the firm runs into short-term financing difficulties the chances of introducing new risk capital (or at least of disposing of the business as a going concern) are usually reasonably good for the profitable enterprise. On the other hand, no firm can indefinitely survive the depletion of resources through losses.

In employing *past* accounting results as an indicator of *future* earning capacity the user of accounts is, of course, in danger of making the assumption that what has happened in the past will necessarily continue in the future. Such a naïve view is not necessary; any sensible user must employ accounting measures in the context of economic developments effecting the firm and its industry.

The first three measures to be considered are different methods of expressing profit in relation to committed resources; there are other variations which could be used, but the results usually tend to point in the same direction. The fourth measure is concerned with profit in relation to the volume of business. The fifth and sixth are of particular interest in relating certain forms of earnings to the firm's financial commitments.

(a) *EBIT/total assets* shows earnings before interest and taxation as a percentage of total assets. This is a measure of overall earnings in relation to the total resources employed – before consideration is given to the division of earnings between different providers of finance.

(b) *Net income/total assets* takes the income which has been earned for shareholders (net profit after taxation but before extraordinary items) and relates that to total assets. The net income figure is, of course, after the deduction of interest and therefore reflects the impact of gearing. But financing by debt is not reflected in the asset base, and this accounting ratio is consequently not strictly consistent in its numerator and denominator. However, it is a widely used indicator of profitability.

Whether the income figure should be taken before or after extraordinary items is debatable. But extraordinary items are, by definition, outside the normal range of a firm's activities. Consequently the extraordinary loss has been omitted from the calculation in Fig. 10.2; even so, the result for BLMC shows a *negative* percentage (loss) in 1974.

(c) *Return on equity* is intended to represent the rate of return earned for ordinary shareholders, and this measure does fully reflect the impact of gearing. It relates net profit after charging interest, taxation and preference dividends (if any) to the ordinary shareholders' claim on the company (represented by ordinary share capital plus reserves).

(d) *Profit on sales* consists of net profit before taxation as a percentage of the year's sales. This measure is probably best used in combination with other information (particularly relating to costs) to explore developments in the firm's operations, perhaps linking back to earlier years in the manner of the budget projections examined in Chapter 4.

(e) *Funds generated/total debt* harks back to the discussion of working-capital funds generated by operations in Chapter 3. It may be remembered that working-capital funds generated from operations commonly masquerade under the title 'cash flow'; consequently the present measure is widely miscalled 'cash flow to debt'.

In this context total debt means all items on the claims side of the balance sheet except share capital and reserves and 'deferred' revenue (such as deferred tax). This is not one of the traditional accounting ratios but it represents an important indicator of the firm's capacity to earn funds to service its financial commitments; in this role it is more effective than more traditional measures of solvency, according to evidence to be mentioned later.

(f) *Interest cover* shows how many times the firm's earnings before interest and tax (EBIT) covers interest payable on all forms of borrowing by the firm. It has a similar function to the previous measure, except that on this occasion concern is confined to the servicing of those debts on which interest is charged[1].

Normally this measurę would be expressed strictly as a ratio rather than in percentage terms (cover is 8·43 and 1·13 times in Fig. 10.2). If the earnings do not cover the interest charges that does not, of course, mean that the firm cannot necessarily meet its current interest payments; provided the cash is there a firm need not make any earnings at all in order to meet its interest commitments in the short term. But failure to earn sufficient to cover interest cannot happen many times if the firm is to survive.

Of all the measures considered so far it can be said 'the higher the better', subject to the reservation that a high return on equity *accompanied by* exceptionally low measures elsewhere would suggest an adverse effect of gearing.

2. *Asset and creditor levels*

Measures of asset and creditor levels (sometimes termed 'turnover measures') need to be interpreted with care. They have certain uses, but their limitations are often overlooked.

In the final accounts of companies the only indicator of volume of activity which is always available is that for annual sales (normally labelled, confusingly, as 'turnover'). Consequently the sales figure tends to be adopted as a standard measure of volume instead of different measures like purchases, cost of goods sold and cost of goods purchased. The banker can insist on obtaining the full figures if necessary. However, it should be borne in mind that none of the figures can be relied upon to indicate changes in the *physical* volume of activity; cost and price changes are commonplace.

An important limitation of the annual sales figure (which would apply equally to any measure of annual activity) is that it can mask seasonal variations or trends within the year. To take an exaggerated example, if a company sold a full year's output on 1 month's credit at the end of its accounting year, the debtors in the balance sheet would equal sales; an outsider unaware of the underlying unevenness of sales activity might be tempted to assume that the firm's customers were being allowed a year's credit! However, it would remain true that money for a full year's sales is 'at risk' in the balance sheet, and any banker seeing the figures would want to know more about the nature of the risk.

Consequently the measures to be considered in this subsection must *not* be interpreted as definitive statements of how long particular items in the balance sheet have been held or left outstanding, but as signals of the levels of asset holding in relation to operating activity which may trigger further investigation.

(a) *Debtors/sales* represents that percentage of the year's sales which are still outstanding at the balance-sheet date. A decline in the percentage indicates a smaller proportion of debts 'at risk' relative to the volume of operations and vice versa. (However, such overall 'average' observations may mask the existence of long-standing, and implicitly doubtful debtors; consequently, bankers commonly obtain an age analysis of debtors from their customers.)

This accounting ratio is more often expressed the other way up, as are the next two measures. On that basis the figures in Fig. 10.2 would be stated as follows:

$$\frac{\text{sales}}{\text{debtors}} \qquad \frac{1{,}564}{188{\cdot}7} = 8{\cdot}29 \text{ times}; \qquad \frac{1{,}595}{180{\cdot}9} = 8{\cdot}82 \text{ times}$$

However, the latter approach appears to confuse many banking students, who are prone to believe that an increase in the measure suggests an increase in the relative level of debtors – whereas it really implies an increase in the *speed of payment* by debtors. The debtor/sales method adopted in Fig. 10.2 is rather less liable to be misinterpreted, and does have the merit of being consistent with other measures in putting the item of specific concern 'above the line' for comparison with the base figure.

The percentage in Fig. 10.2 could be expressed in credit periods of so many days by multiplying by 365:

12 per cent × 365 = 44 days; 11 per cent × 365 = 40 days

This is legitimate provided the results are not interpreted too literally. The earlier qualifications about seasonal fluctuations and trends must be borne in mind; moreover, if a firm has a substantial element of cash sales such a calculation based on total sales produces a notional 'average period' which really applies neither to cash nor to credit sales – and may therefore give a misleading impression of the speed of settlement for the latter.

(b) *Creditors/sales* shows the level of creditors relative to the volume of activity. If the purchases figure is available it would be strictly more consistent to adopt that instead of sales (since creditors largely relate to purchases of goods), and a cost of sales figure would also serve well. But the present measure gives an indicator of the relative level of creditors which is sufficient for broad interpretation purposes; a banker would seek an age analysis of creditors from the customer in cases of doubt.

(c) *Stocks/sales* performs a similar function as an indicator of the relative level of stockholding. A meticulous approach might relate raw materials stocks to purchases, finished goods to cost of goods sold and work-in-progress to goods purchased – but the result would rarely be more informative for the outside user of accounts than the measure shown here. Only if detailed internal cost and budget figures were available would a detailed analysis be likely to prove instructive. It may be noted that in Fig. 10.2 the stocks/sales percentage rose quite substantially in 1974, indicating relatively higher stocks – and creditors/sales changed similarly.

(d) *Sales/total assets* is a global indicator of total operating activity in relation to resources employed.

A high level of sales in relation to assets can be regarded as desirable, since sales generate funds for the firm – provided the sales are not unprofitable.

In an inflationary situation sales may increase in money terms more rapidly than assets, which include many items at historic cost. Consequently the sales/total assets ratio will tend to increase in inflation even if the firm's activity in physical terms is constant.

A further measure needs to be mentioned here: the ratio of debtors to creditors. This is favoured by some banking writers who suggest that debtors should normally exceed creditors – on the grounds that the viable firm will sell at a profit to its customers and will tend to give similar credit periods to its customers as it takes from its suppliers. But credit terms can rarely be assumed constant for all of a firm's suppliers and all of its customers, the fact that a firm may sell entirely or partly for cash (giving low debtors) is certainly no cause for alarm, and purchases and sales do not necessarily occur at constant rates throughout the year to give evenly matched creditors and debtors at the balance-sheet date.

Admittedly the interpretation of the debtors/creditors ratio is supposed to involve consideration of trends, but even here its meaning is obscure. For example, an increase in the ratio is supposed to be interpreted as 'favourable' if it arises from prompter payment of creditors, but as 'unfavourable' if it is caused by slower collection from debtors. It would seem a great deal easier and more informative to examine trends in debtor and creditor levels separately in the first place – in relation to sales volume and, where necessary, by way of age analyses.

3. Short-term liquidity

Measures of short-term liquidity relate working-capital items in some way to indicators of short-term financial commitments. Unlike the accounting ratios considered so far they are normally 'balance-sheet ratios' which are confined to different components of the balance sheet – as opposed to introducing the 'flow' figures relating to the year's operations which have been present in all the measures up to now.

The first two measures to be considered are the best-known traditional indicators of a firm's capacity to meet its current commitments. They are normally expressed in ratio rather than percentage terms.

(a) *The quick or liquid ratio,* which is also known as the 'acid test', relates liquid assets to current liabilities. Liquid assets are those which are either cash or can be regarded as being capable of swift conversion into cash; they would therefore include debtors and near-cash items like marketable securities. The major elements of current assets to be excluded are stocks of all kinds – finished goods, work-in-progress and raw materials.

There is a persistent myth that a financially sound firm must have liquid assets at least equal to its current liabilities, giving a liquid ratio of 1 (100 per cent in percentage terms). This blanket view is naïve. Consider a retail business which sells goods for cash and therefore has no debtors; with readily saleable stocks the firm cannot be regarded as financially unsound merely because it chooses not to hold cash permanently to cover all its creditors and tax liabilities. In practice, firms generally tend to have liquid ratios below 100 per cent.

Thus a liquid ratio (like any other) should be interpreted in the context of the firm's operating and general financial characteristics. Of course, the banker can always legitimately take the view that the higher the liquid ratio the more sound is the firm's short-term financial position – but firms which can maintain particularly high liquid ratios are unlikely to want to borrow money anyway.

(b) *The current ratio* relates current assets to current liabilities. Again a high value for this measure is taken as a favourable indicator of financial position – although an increase in current ratio which arises from increased stockholding is not an unmixed blessing. (Stocks can increase for good reasons, such as increased volume of activity, or for bad reasons like selling difficulties on finished goods or production delays on work-in-progress.)

The folklore in this case takes the line that a ratio of 2 (200 per cent) is the minimum acceptable level. In fact the average for large UK trading companies has been well below that level for many years. The current ratio will be largely dependent on the nature of the firm's operating cycle (as discussed in Chapter 2), although short-term borrowing is also clearly important in determining the current liability base.

However, it must be conceded that small firms tend to have higher current ratios than large companies. One of several reasons for this is that larger companies can generally indulge in relatively more short-term borrowing (on grounds of security and/or stability of earnings).

(c) *Working capital/total assets* measures net current assets as a percentage of total assets. It is an indicator of the adequacy of working capital in relation to the total resources of the firm. Although its use is not so popular as the two previous measures, it will be seen later that it is a rather more effective indicator of financial stability.

4. Long-term financial stability

Measures of long-term financial stability are concerned with the character of the overall financial structure. It will be evident that reliance on sources of finance other than shareholders' capital must increase financial risk, other things being equal.

Commonly, users of accounts concentrate on measures involving long-term debt when considering implications of long-term financial stability. That approach has not been adopted here. Two reasons are that the *overall* debt burden is of primary importance and that the distinction between long-term and short-term debt is already reflected in other measures (such as the current ratio and working capital/total assets).

(a) *Total debt/total assets* shows all non-shareholder claims as a proportion of the firm's total assets. It is therefore a measure of the firm's resources which are financed by 'outsiders'.

(b) *Total debt/equity* gives all non-shareholder claims as a percentage of the ordinary share capital plus reserves of the company. It is a measure of gearing which is rather better for the banker's purpose than concern merely with *long-term* debt, because the total debt approach accommodates debts of ambiguous duration (such as directors' temporary loans to some small companies). There is, of course, no reason why the banker should not *also* consider the relationship of long-term debt to equity if that aspect appears important in particular cases.

(c) *'Own funds'/fixed assets* represents the shareholders' funds (ordinary plus preference shares plus reserves) as a percentage of fixed assets. This shows the extent to which the shareholders are financing the long-term asset commitments of the company.

The view is often taken that 'own funds' should cover fixed assets, to provide a stable financial structure in which outsiders are financing only current assets. Although this is an understandable initial reference point, much depends on the nature of the assets and whether the accounting figures reflect current values. The argument is more appropriate for specialized machinery than, say, general purpose property.

5. Short-term borrowing

Bankers sometimes find it useful to look at bank advances in relation to certain items in the balance sheet, particularly with a view to assessing the proportion of short-term resources to be financed by the bank – an issue explained in section 11.1, subsection 7). Since short-term borrowing by firms can sometimes come from non-bank sources it is a sensible general practice to look at short-term borrowing as a whole. Consequently the measures in Fig. 10.2 relating to short-term borrowing have grouped bank and other short-term loans together. In this context 'borrowing' does *not* include trade creditors, bills payable or tax liabilities.

(a) *Bank and short borrowing/current assets* shows the proportion of current assets financed from short-term sources.
(b) *Bank and short borrowing/working capital* relates short-term borrowing to net current assets, and therefore shows the percentage of the working-capital value financed by temporary borrowing.

10.2 Averages, trends and cosmetic reporting

The primary concern of the lending banker with the measures discussed in section 10.1 can be summarized in a single phrase: would lending to the firm provide a 'fair risk'? It is too much to hope that the answer will be an unequivocal 'yes' or 'no'; accounting ratios, like other sources of information, can only contribute to an assessment of shades of risk.

Even so, before preparing to make his assessment the banker needs to have settled in his own mind his attitudes to certain preliminary questions. What is the 'benchmark' for judging accounting measures – how does a user decide whether a firm is good, bad or merely indifferent? Is it possible for firms to 'window-dress' their accounting results in ways which will make their accounting ratios give an erroneous impression of financial strength? Is there any evidence that accounting ratios are effective in predicting financial instability anyway? The first two questions will be considered in this section; the third will occupy section 10.3.

An obvious basis for a preliminary assessment of accounting ratios is a comparison with the corresponding ratios for the same firm in earlier years. The intention is to identify important movements which may indicate the direction of the firm's financial health. In an extreme case, if all the ratios are 'better' or as 'good' as those for the preceding year, there is at least a presumption that having survived so far the firm has improved its prospects of continuing. But in the more usual situations of mixed movements, comparison with earlier years provide 'signals' of aspects which deserve further consideration and, on occasion, investigation.

For the purpose of interpreting accounting ratios as signals of aspects for consideration, some additional notion of what is a reasonable ratio is needed. For example, few users of accounts would be perturbed by a decline in a current ratio from 5 (500 per cent) to 4 (400 per cent) because they would tend to make an implicit assumption that even the latter ratio is unduly high. Such assumptions are based on experience of ratios of similar firms, usually in the same industry.

Thus, industry ratios tend to provide some guidance for comparison of ratios; they can also help to puncture certain widespread misconceptions about acceptable ratios, such as that relating to the current ratio mentioned earlier. There are, however, important qualifications to be made about industry comparisons. The first is that it would be short-sighted to jump to the conclusion that a level of an accounting ratio which is commonplace in a particular industry must necessarily be right for an individual firm. The firm's conditions may be different in a variety of ways – even the choice of accounting date can affect comparisons in seasonal industries – and in any case general practice in an industry need not be best practice. Consequently a ratio which is 'out of line' should be used as a starting-point for understanding what the firm is doing, rather than as a basis for dogmatic conclusions.

The second point about industry ratios is that the information available is usually based on *averages* calculated by taking the total accounting figures for a sample of firms and dividing by the number of firms. It might be more fruitful to take the 'tail' of firms with the worst ratios (for example, the worst 10 per cent) and use their measures as a benchmark for risk assessment. But figures for such ranges are not readily available, nor is there any evidence on whether they would be more effective in indicating financial instability. Consequently a common approach of users is to look more closely at firms which display 'below-average' measures.

The use of industry averages suggests that acceptable levels for accounting ratios are determined by the economic and industrial environment in which the firms operate, and by the attitudes of creditors. There are often disparities between the average ratios in different countries with different financial practices. However, in recent years there has been a general downward trend in the ratios of large companies in industrial countries, influenced by low profits after tax and increased reliance on outside finance[2].

Small firms do not normally have the same access to outside funds. *On average* they tend to obtain less debt financing, particularly at the longer-term end of the borrowing scale.

Turning now to the second part of the questions raised at the beginning of this section, is it possible for firms to 'window-dress' their accounting results? The concern here is not with the possibility that the accounts may be *falsified* by the inclusion of spurious figures; the rare (and usually complex) frauds which do temporarily evade audit hardly cast serious doubt on the general usefulness of accounting information. The question really concerns whether accounts may be *'beautified'* by firms taking actions which, although quite legitimate in themselves, may be chosen or timed solely for their favourable effects on accounting reports – thus the term 'cosmetic reporting'.

The best-known possibility in this context is the window-dressing of the liquid or current ratios. In its simplest form (which was, incidentally, pioneered by banks to 'beautify' their balance sheets!) the firm would temporarily borrow money at the end of the year to provide an increase in cash on the assets side of the balance sheet. This would improve the liquid ratio *provided* the liquid assets were originally lower than the liabilities base against which they are to be compared. For example, a firm with liquid assets of £100 and current liabilities of £150 could raise its liquid ratio at the end of the year by borrowing £50:

$$\text{before } \frac{£100}{£150} = 66 \text{ per cent;} \qquad \text{after } \frac{£150}{£200} = 75 \text{ per cent}$$

A trading firm could obtain a similar effect by delaying its normal payments to creditors. But that would, of course, tend to show up elsewhere in the accounting ratios as a higher level of creditors relative to sales.

Any attempt to window-dress a liquid ratio of less than unity (100 per cent) would have an *opposite* effect on the firm's current ratio if that is over unity. Thus, if the firm considered above had stocks of £100, its total current assets before the window-dressing would have been £200; borrowing £50 would have the following effect on the current ratio:

$$\text{before } \frac{£200}{£150} = 133 \text{ per cent;} \qquad \text{after } \frac{£250}{£200} = 125 \text{ per cent}$$

In this case the firm effectively loses on the current ratio swings what it gained on the liquid ratio roundabouts. The window-dressing would have been fully effective only if *both* the liquid and current ratios had been below unity. Financial institutions like banks do not, of course, have stocks and therefore have no complicating current ratio.

An accounting standard includes certain checks against the window-dressing of balance sheets [3]. In particular, auditors should insist on the disclosure of material transactions which were reversed after the end of the year.

Where both ratios are already *above* unity they could both be increased by adopting the opposite tactics to that used above – by temporarily *reducing* borrowing or advancing the timing of payments. However, it is improbable that a firm would gain much from raising the ratios if the liquid ratio was already above unity.

Thus the scope for window-dressing the liquid and current ratio is limited for most firms. There have been suggestions for a class of substitute measures which would be invulnerable to manipulation, but one such measure performed no better than the current ratio in a test of prediction of company failure [4].

Another major aspect of potential cosmetic reporting concerns profit calculation. Accounting conventions give firms a certain amount of discretion in the choice of accounting procedures (e.g. in the treatment of overheads in stock valuation). Some North American studies have shown that when companies changed their accounting methods, in those cases which involved substantial sums the changes tended to make profit appear higher – and the changes also tended to be made in years in which profit would otherwise have been low [5]. In other words there was some statistical evidence of cosmetic reporting. The available evidence on UK companies is, however, inconclusive [6]. One of the intentions of the adoption of accounting standards by the professional accountancy bodies is the reduction of such choice in accounting procedures.

It must be appreciated that only in a very small minority of accounting changes is there likely to be any intention of cosmetic reporting by the firm, but users of accounts may be confused by an accounting change quite independently of any intention of the firm. A change in accounting procedures involving a material amount should be disclosed in the firm's annual accounts, and a sensible user should adjust for the accounting change in examining the profit trend. A similar approach will usually be appropriate for extraordinary items like profit or loss on the sale of part of the business: operating profit or loss exclusive of unusual items will normally provide the focus for the banker in assessing the financial viability of operations.

10.3 Accounting ratios and prediction of failure

Earlier the question was asked: is there any evidence that accounting ratios are effective in predicting financial instability? This section is concerned with providing an answer – which is a qualified 'yes', but some measures appear to be more effective than others.

Before proceeding it may be helpful to spell out what is being implicitly assumed when accounting ratios are used in assessing financial stability. The assumption might be stated as follows: given two firms which face an identical operating environment, the one with weaker ratios is more likely to become insolvent. That does not say a firm with weak ratios *will* fail, and it certainly does not suggest that a firm with strong ratios but poor operating prospects necessarily has a better chance of survival than another firm with weak ratios but good business opportunities. The accounting ratios are merely being used as indicators of financial risk, 'other things being equal'.

The two most interesting studies of the effectiveness of accounting ratios as predictors of financial failure were conducted in the USA. The first, by W. H. Beaver[7], examined a sample of seventy-nine publicly owned US corporations which failed in the period 1954–64. For each failed firm another matching, 'non-failed', firm of the same industry and asset size was selected. Thirty accounting ratios were then compared for the 'paired sample' companies.

In a test of the extent to which the ratios could classify correctly between 'failed' and 'non-failed' companies, the top five ratios in order of effectiveness were as follows:

Funds generated[8]/total debt
Net income/total assets
Total debt/total assets
Working capital/total assets
Current ratio

In this list low ratios are, of course, considered dangerous in all cases except the third (total debt/total assets) where a high ratio is considered unsafe.

Since the sample contained half failed and half non-failed firms any 'prediction' by a ratio had a 50 per cent chance of being right. So if a ratio classified correctly in 50 per cent of the cases, the result would be no better than random selection – or 'sticking in a pin'.

Funds generated/total debt in fact classified 87 per cent of the cases correctly 1 year before failure. Between 2 and 5 years before failure the proportion classified correctly ranged between 76 per cent and 79 per cent. The probability of getting these results by chance (a 'lucky fluke') was less than one in ten thousand.

The other ratios gave poorer results. The worst of the ratios being considered here, the current ratio, classified correctly in 80 per cent of the cases 1 year before failure, but only in 55 per cent of the cases 5 years before failure.

What are the implications? At first sight the best classification rate of 87 per cent in a rather contrived test seems unimpressive compared with the banker's required success rates of around 97–99 per cent which were implied by the interest-rate calculations considered earlier in Chapter 1. But given that past figures were being used to predict a future event, and that each ratio was being used in isolation, the success level may appear surprisingly high. The banker does not, of course, have to rely solely on a single ratio or even a group of ratios but can use accounting measures in the context of information on the plans and current activities of the firm.

The practical effect of the Beaver study for the banker is that it suggests certain ratios may be particularly worthy of consideration. The first two measures in the list are both 'mixed' ratios which relate figures for 'flows' (or, in the widest sense, earnings) to balance-sheet amounts. This contrasts with the traditional emphasis of many banking writers on static 'balance-sheet' relationships – and gives some support to the views of those bankers who give priority to the assessment of earning capacity in examining business lending.

The second study of business failure to be considered was conducted by E. I. Altmann[9]. This used a technique called 'multiple discriminant analysis' which is rather less formidable in operation than it sounds. The technique involves giving weights to different measures, to produce a score – for example:

Measure	Weight		Measure's value for company X		Score
This ratio	0·3	×	2·0	=	0·6
That ratio	0·1	×	0·5	=	0·05
etc.	etc.		etc.		etc.
					total score

Each total score is then compared with a predetermined acceptable score to divide the firms which are deemed 'safe' from those which are considered 'unsafe'. The technique has been widely used for consumer credit granting (using appropriate information about individuals) and has been employed in that role by one of the major credit card organizations in the UK.

The Altmann study examined a 'paired sample' of 33 failed and 33 non-failed US corporations between 1946 and 1965. Beaver's best ratio was not among the measures tested, but the results were better than Beaver's and correctly classified 95 per cent of the sample 1 year before failure. The ratios which were selected to make up the score were, in order of importance:

Sales/total assets;
Earnings before interest and taxes/total assets;
Retained earnings/total assets;
Working capital/total assets;
Market value of equity/book value of total debts.

In all cases a high ratio helped to produce a 'safe' score, and a low ratio was therefore considered dangerous. The weights attached to the ratios have been omitted here to avoid any suggestion that they could be used indiscriminately for company assessment. Whatever the advantages or disadvantages of the approach, weights derived in a distant period in the USA are unlikely to have global application. But the ratios themselves, which were shown to have a joint selective ability, are of general interest.

The sales/total assets ratio is notable because it was given much more weight in Altmann's scoring than all the other measures put together – yet on an *individual* basis it was the least significant ratio in predicting failure. Thus, its usefulness in other contexts is doubtful. However, in one important respect the Altmann results reinforce Beaver's findings: the top two ratios were again both 'mixed' measures which related 'flows' generated during the accounting period to committed resources.

The third measure, in using retained earnings, is concerned *not* with the year's retentions but with reserves in the balance sheet. Its use is as a very rough indicator of cumulative profitability. It discriminates against the young firm – and young firms are in general more vulnerable financially than longer established enterprises. The banker would tend to bear these issues in mind rather than attempt to incorporate them into a single measure.

Working capital/total assets appeared previously in Beaver's list of ratios. The final ratio is a measure of gearing, but in this form it would be applicable only to listed companies – since a calculation of the market value of the equity obviously requires a listed market price for shares.

Several versions of the Altmann approach have been employed for different purposes in the City of London in recent years, but in general the idea of attaching weights to ratios, even for preliminary 'screening', has found limited application.

The conclusion of this brief review of some of the evidence on accounting ratios as predictors of failure is that they can be effective. If relatively mechanical approaches to prediction can produce respectable results it would seem that the better measures have something to contribute to a balanced assessment of financial stability.

Notes and references

1. It was seen in sections 4.2 and 7.4 that the financial impact of fixed-interest commitments and fixed overhead cost commitments are very similar – indeed, borrowing to acquire assets is a straight alternative to leasing them. Consequently, it could be informative to consider earnings cover for all forms of fixed financial commitment. However, fixed overhead cost totals are not always available, even within firms, and the extent to which they represent continuing legal obligations varies. Therefore, such aspects are better considered in relation to information available on individual items than by any standardized measure.
2. Some trends in different countries are discussed by T. M. Rybczynski in 'Business finance in the EEC, USA and Japan', *The Three Banks Review* (Sept. 1974). The broad trends still apply in the early 1980s, only more so.
3. *Statement of Standard Accounting Practice 17: Accounting for post balance sheet events*, Institute of Chartered Accountants in England and Wales (1980).
4. W. H. Beaver, 'Financial ratios as predictors of failure', *Journal of Accounting Research – Empirical Research in Accounting: Selected Studies* (1966), pp. 71–111.
5. B. E. Cushing, 'An empirical study of changes in accounting policy', *Journal of Accounting Research* (Autumn 1969), pp. 196–203; E. Blaine, 'Reported accounting changes and financial statement manipulation: an empirical study', *Proceedings of the Canadian Branch of American Accounting Association* (1970), pp. 9–14.
6. R. C. Morris and G. H. Breakwell, 'Manipulation of earnings figures in the United Kingdom', *Accounting and Business Research* (Summer 1975). The relatively small number of companies involved in this study produced results which were consistent with the direction of the North American studies, but the effects were not statistically significant.

7. W. H. Beaver, op. cit.
8. Beaver uses the popular term 'cash flow' instead of the phrase 'funds generated' used here. Arguments for not adopting the term 'cash flow' when working-capital flow is really intended have been advanced in section 3.3.
9. E. I. Altmann, 'Financial ratios, discriminant analysis and the prediction of corporate bankruptcy', *Journal of Finance* (Sept. 1968), pp. 580–600.

Chapter 11

The lender's viewpoint

11.1 Considerations in financial assessment

Earlier chapters have been concerned with an understanding of accounting and related financial issues which are of potential interest to the lending banker. This chapter attempts to draw together some of the strands for an overall view of the contribution accounting information can make to financial assessment for lending. Naturally there is no suggestion that accounts can provide all the answers or that the non-accounting elements in lending will be adequately covered here. However, some mention has to be made of non-accounting aspects if the context is to be understood.

One well-known guideline in lending is that a borrower should satisfy the conditions of the 'three C's'. The letters stand for character, capability and capital – although different words with similar intentions are sometimes used. The methods by which bankers judge the character of their business customers might well make fascinating reading, but this is one aspect on which accounts can hardly be expected to help. Accounting information can, however, provide considerable guidance on the capabilities of a firm's management and on aspects of 'capital' – which in this context concerns the adequacy of the firm's financial structure.

The 'three C's' guideline may have the advantage of being pithy, but the student banker needs more extensive suggestions on the relevant aspects of financial assessment. For this purpose a 'checklist' is provided below; the list should be regarded as triggering points for consideration rather than as providing an exhaustive coverage. A danger of a list of headings is that it may give an artificial sense of compartmentalizing issues: it should be borne in mind that the interrelationships of different elements must be considered in forming an overall view – for example, minor shortcomings may be offset by strength in other directions.

1. Purpose

The purpose of borrowing is a convenient and important starting-point. It gives (or should give) an indication of the firm's intentions, and may shed some light on the ability of the management or proprietors. A proposal on which some 'homework' has been done should inspire rather more confidence than one which suggests a lax approach to financial matters.

Purpose has considerable bearing on risk, because of the effects of borrowing on financial structure. For example, if a firm proposed to borrow on overdraft solely for the acquisition of fixed assets, the balance sheet would swing towards 'borrowing short and investing long' (other things being equal). Since fixed assets are not usually saleable swiftly at a good price, the effect would be to make the firm's financial position riskier. For this sort of reason bankers tend to be more favourably disposed towards proposals involving the acquisition of current assets than those for fixed assets.

If the purpose of current asset financing is seasonal (say, financing Christmas stocks) the bank's risk is mitigated by the option to terminate lending at the end-of-season downswing in borrowing – if things go wrong the signal to consider cutting the bank's losses is at least unambiguous. Seasonality is also evident in the provision of temporary assistance towards 'lumpy' financial commitments like annual tax bills.

However, it is important to distinguish purpose from the repayment period. Acquisition of current assets need not involve any swifter prospects of repayment than the acquisition of fixed assets. For example, both may be needed for an expansion in trade, and the continuance of the expanded level would require both fixed assets and working-capital items.

In fact, for firms of any size it would often be quite arbitrary to identify bank advances with the acquisition of specific assets, because a large range of transactions take place in which bank finance is one component. Consequently, bank assistance is commonly an element in a 'package' of changes in the firm's finances. When the 'package' relates to a planned expansion of a range of assets, it would seem desirable that the bank should be satisfied on the overall viability of the planned transactions, in the light of considerations examined in Chapters 6 and 7.

2. Adequacy

The question of 'adequacy' is concerned with whether the purpose and amount of the requested advance appear consistent. For example, if an advance is requested to finance expanded stocks to support increased sales, have the consequent effects on debtors (less creditors) been adequately considered? Underestimation of the firm's needs may lead to difficult decisions on 'topping up' lending at a later stage; on the other hand the amount requested might be excessive, particularly in relation to the risk the bank is prepared to take. In appropriate cases the requested amount may be scaled up or down accordingly.

Judgement on whether the proposed level of borrowing is appropriate will depend on assessment of the anticipated cash flows. This may not necessarily be done by looking at explicit budgets but alternatively by a more 'intuitive' overall assessment of the firm's capacity to generate cash. However, *any* approval of lending implies that the advance has been pitched at a level at which the subsequent cash flows can satisfy the terms of the advance.

3. Repayment

In one sense repayment is *the* question in lending; the aim of financial assessment is to ensure that prospects of repayment are high. In a narrower sense the period and sources of repayment of a proposal need to be considered.

British bankers have a well-established preference for short repayment periods, but the increased willingness to contemplate medium-term loans has been mentioned before. Although in short-term lending the anticipated source of repayment may often be the disposal of specific assets (for example, in a bridging loan on property or in seasonal financing of working-capital items), in other proposals the cash surplus generated by operations will normally be the crucial source of repayment. Consequently the firm's past track record in 'cash creation' will be of particular interest to the banker. But readers should by now be well aware that accounts do not normally reveal the *cash* flow generated by operations; however, bankers can and do pay particular attention to the usual indicators of earnings capacity – profits and (working-capital) funds generated by operations.

Past indicators of earnings capacity are all very well, but history cannot be relied upon to repeat itself. Some explicit consideration of the firm's expected sources of repayment, of the sort which can be incorporated into a cash budget[1], would seem helpful in addition to an overall view of earnings capacity. In fact, although bankers commonly look at cash budgets they less frequently insist on them, and some bankers have a highly sceptical attitude to the usefulness of cash budgets anyway. The banker who accepts the figures in a cash budget without testing them, and expects the balances to be precisely achieved month by month would be naïve, to put it mildly. But as a means for pinning down the customer's intentions, as a basis for testing those intentions against past figures, and as a rough benchmark for observing the progress of an advance, the cash budget appears to be an under-utilized tool in banking.

4. Abilities

Incompetent management is a potent recipe for financial disaster, and bankers understandably give a high priority to satisfying themselves that the management of a borrowing firm appears reasonably competent. This issue is, of course, related to 'character and capability' which occupied two-thirds of the 'three C's'.

The experienced banker may form an opinion on the abilities of a firm's management by a subconscious process which absorbs a variety of pieces of information, often over a lengthy period of dealing with the firm. The fact that this process cannot be explained need not detract from the validity of the banker's conclusions – although there are always dangers of prejudice in inexplicable value judgements. For the young banker some specific aspects relating to management abilities are worth considering: the management's experience, qualifications, enthusiasm and apparent grasp of industrial and financial problems, with the related question of continuity raising the opposing dangers of a 'one-man band' or too frequent management changes.

For a firm of any size it would be short-sighted to confine a view of 'abilities' to board of director or owner level; a firm's corporate health is dependent on the efficiency and enthusiasm of all its employees. From a negative viewpoint it is obvious that bad industrial relations can prove disastrous for all concerned (including the banker), but no less important is the corresponding positive aspect that a capable and well-motivated organization can overcome the most daunting problems.

It is likely that information concerning employees will be included as a standard addition to the accounting reports of companies in the not-too-distant future. Some suggestions in this direction are ill-conceived, but figures for a few items like employee turnover and absenteeism could provide useful indicators of the well-being of an organization. However, the observant banker is in the privileged position of being able to glean a great deal on the attitudes of management and workers – just by arranging an innocent visit to the customer's premises.

Some aspects of orthodox accounting information which can assist in the judgement of management ability are the firm's earnings record (consistent performance implies some degree of competence) and the general approach to management control within the firm (involving issues touched upon in Chapter 4 – the existence of budgetary control, a coherent planning framework and so on).

5. *Stability*

Issues affecting a firm's stability which deserve consideration can relate to the national (or international) economy, to the industry or industries in which the firm operates and to the firm's own operating and financial structure. Some industries or firms are more vulnerable to economic fluctuations than others; for example, the building/construction industry is particularly volatile, but within that industry a firm which has a wide spread of interests (say house-building, repairs, public sector contracting and industrial construction) might well be more stable in the level of its operations than a firm in an exposed segment of a relatively stable industry.

It is worth noting that it is not the existence of fluctuations in the level of operations of a firm which need imply risk: it is uncertainty concerning the level and duration of those fluctuations[2]. Consequently, a firm which has 'seesaw' results might be a better risk than one which is stagnating – if the reasons for the seesawing are identifiable and the level of the results provide an appropriate safety margin.

An obvious way in which accounts can contribute to an assessment of a firm's stability of operations is by looking at fluctuations over a number of years' results. But how many years should be considered? Since the issues involved concern 'ups and downs' in trade, a study of successive accounts over a period of years covering the full business cycle would be appropriate.

Business cycles, whether of national economies or of individual industries, do not last obligingly for identical lengths of time. However, in recent decades a plausible working guideline would have been 4 years, which happens to be the normal period between general elections in some major trading nations. So if a rule of thumb is needed for how many years' figures should be examined, 4 years has some rational basis. Several banking writers recommend 3 years, but their reasons are not apparent.

Two aspects worth considering as relevant to the stability of a firm are its size and the length of time it has been established – since small and young firms have a relatively high mortality rate. One indicator of size favoured by bankers is the amount of the firm's 'own funds' or ownership stake (capital plus reserves), since this element also represents the lender's buffer against loss. The firm's own funds are also relevant to the accounting ratios of long-term financial stability, and all three of the long-term financial stability measures mentioned in section 10.1 are worth considering.

6. *Financial condition*

Consideration of financial condition is concerned with the firm's current state of financial health – a general view of the relationships between the firm's financing, its resources and its apparent earning capacity. For this purpose accounting information is indispensable.

The banker can look for danger signals among the measures considered in section 10.1: earnings and funds generated, asset and creditor levels, short-term liquidity and long-term financial stability. The first and last of these have already been included elsewhere in the present list.

Faced with a variety of measures, the banking student may well wonder where his priorities should lie in examining indicators of financial condition. It has already been seen in section 10.3 that the researches of Beaver and Altmann, particularly the former, provide some suggestions for priorities. Their results would seem to support some emphasis towards what might be called a 'going-concern' approach involving trading flows (funds generated, profits, sales) in relation to liabilities and resources.

In considering indicators of financial condition it is, of course, vital to consider not only the present situation but also the likely impact of the firm's proposed borrowing on those financial indicators. In looking at accounting ratios it is also important not to become so immersed in their analysis that the implications of the absolute figures in the accounts are ignored. To take a simple example, a return on equity of 50 per cent followed by 60 per cent in the succeeding year might sound prosperous, but for a sole trader whose equity in his firm was only £5,000 the calculation would hardly be significant to his financial standing.

7. Bank's share of financing

A banker will normally give some consideration to the relationship between the amount of a proposed advance to a firm and certain specific items in the firm's anticipated balance sheet (as it is expected to look after any package of financing and asset acquisition has been effected). This is partly a different way of looking at the likely impact of a proposal on the firm's financial condition from that discussed above, but it also provides a very rough check that the bank would not be shouldering an undue slice of the financial risk.

There are two suggested guidelines relating to working capital which deserve mention. One is that a bank might go as far as providing one-half of a firm's working-capital requirements where the firm was considered strong enough for unsecured business lending. The second is that as much as half the value of current assets might be lent with appropriately secured lending. A third, more general, rule of thumb is that 'for the bulk of businesses a proprietor's stake should be more than that of the banker'[3] – in other words 'own funds' or capital plus reserves ought to exceed the bank'ş advance.

Bankers use such tests as guidelines, not strait-jackets. One fairly obvious example of a situation in which the 'proprietor's stake' criterion might be ignored would occur when property assets were undervalued – giving rise to a corresponding understatement of the proprietor's stake on the claims side of the balance sheet.

8. Security

Security is the banker's safety net, which he requires unless he has very considerable confidence in the outcome of the lending. When there is such confidence, bankers often refer to the unsecured lending as 'balance-sheet lending'. That presumably refers to the fact that reliance is being placed on a sound financial structure in the balance sheet – but paradoxically in such circumstances the banker is normally relying on the strength of trading cash flows, and the last thing he wants is to have to rely on a 'break-up' of the balance sheet.

The complexities of security are not a matter for this book, but one aspect relating to accounts deserves mention here. In considering lending to one of a group of companies it is advisable to bear in mind the group relationship in examining accounts[4]. This is because although effective control rests with the parent company, each company is quite separate for legal purposes. As complex financial transactions take place between the companies of a group, often involving lending and the purchase and sale of goods at internally negotiated prices, the banker may find that lending to one company has the disadvantages of lending to the group – but without the corresponding advantages.

For example, assume that Prestige Ltd has two wholly owned subsidiaries: Quality Ltd and Rubbish Ltd. A banker trustingly lends unsecured to Quality Ltd on the strength of that company's accounts and general financial standing – a decision which is reinforced by the financial status of Prestige Ltd. The other subsidiary, Rubbish Ltd, gets into increasing financial difficulties and is temporarily supported by funds siphoned off from Quality Ltd. Both subsidiaries collapse and the bank is left with a claim against Quality Ltd (which in turn may have certain rights against Rubbish Ltd) – but without any legal rights against Prestige Ltd.

Concern over its own reputation *might* lead Prestige Ltd to mount a salvage operation, but that cannot be relied on in cases of this kind. Moreover, if the subsidiary were only partially owned, the holding company would be even less likely to recognize a moral obligation. Consequently, where groups are involved a banker will be inclined either to lend to the holding company, or alternatively to look for specific security when lending to a subsidiary – together with cross-guarantees from the other companies (including the parent) if feasible.

Broadly similar remarks could apply to associate companies, where although a shareholding may be under 50 per cent it may nevertheless be so substantial that significant influence can be exercised on company policy. The banker should normally be aware of the major shareholdings in a company, although publicly available information on shareholdings in excess of 5 per cent of a company's share capital must be maintained in a register held by the company, and the directors' annual report must disclose directors' personal interests (which have interlocking effects, particularly for smaller companies).

9. Control

After the approval of an advance, the banker has a traditional and very effective source of information on the firm's progress – the firm's bank account. The advantages of a good 'swing' in an overdraft intended to finance business fluctuations, and the dangers of 'hard-core' borrowing and persistent excesses over the agreed limit or failures to meet loan account reductions are all well known to bankers. The conduct of the advance also provides the banker with an accumulating record of the firm's reliability in adhering to its commitments, which can assist decisions on subsequent requests from the customer.

However, the bank account cannot provide anywhere near a complete picture of developments in a firm's financial affairs during the period of an advance – any more than it could provide all the information on which to make a lending decision in the first place. So, if the banker is anxious to ensure that the firm's finances are kept under control he will need accounting data more frequently than the annual accounts.

The banker could ask for unaudited balance sheets and profit and loss accounts to be submitted frequently, say monthly or quarterly; updated cash budgets might also be produced at intervals during the period of the advance. Much less onerous, because full final account preparation would not be involved, would be the submission of monthly or quarterly figures on debtors, creditors, stocks and sales. The latter group of figures would allow the banker to view the bank account in the context of working-capital developments; for example, what might at first sight appear to be a minor excess on the advance would deserve more serious consideration if accompanied by a growth in creditors and declining debtors, sales and stocks.

It appears that requirements for submission of more than annual accounting information during the period of an advance tend to be reserved for less 'straightforward' cases. Thus the customer might be asked to submit monthly or quarterly figures where the bank is providing an unusually high proportion of the firm's finance, where the period of lending is relatively long or where there have been signs of financial difficulties. It will be seen in section 11.2 that when such information is required it generally takes the second form mentioned above (debtors, creditors, etc.), whereas full accounting statements are more often annual requirements.

11.2 Information for company lending

The present section will consider some evidence on practices of bankers in examining information for lending purposes. Reasons for this approach are that it provides guidance on the sources of information available in lending (as opposed to those which may be thought desirable) and it indicates the extent to which customers are willing and able to supply certain types of information. It also provides a basis for questioning one or two popular generalizations on the topic.

A further reason is that the information priorities of experienced lending bankers may have elements worth imitating. But it must be borne in mind that information requirements will differ according to the needs of individual proposals. Moreover, the fact that a majority of a particular group of experienced bankers may adopt a certain approach does not prove that it is 'right' – any more than the views of the majority of experienced sailors in the fifteenth century proved the world was flat.

A basis for discussion is provided by the results of the survey reproduced in Appendix E. The survey, to which eighty-two bank managers responded in 1974, was confined to *company* lending; unincorporated businesses would tend to supply less information. The survey was supplemented by some interviews with lending bankers who were the source of quotations used in this section.

The major list of information sources is given under heading B of Appendix E. As was to be expected, bank managers made extensive use of the past record of lending to the company and of the audited accounts.

In view of the remarks made under item 5 of section 11.1 (that a business-cycle viewpoint suggested looking at 4 years' accounts, although the conventional wisdom among banking writers was 3 years) it is interesting that the number of years' accounts examined were almost equally divided between 3 and 4 years (31

Fig. 11.1 Example of customer's record sheet.

Balance Sheet of________________________________Ltd.

Accounts are Consolidated/Parent/Subsidiary (............% owned.) Delete as appropriate.

If a Subsidiary - name of Parent ________________________________Ltd.

Business________________________ Branch________________________

	Liabilities				
1	Capital - Preference				
	Ordinary				
2	Free Reserves				
3	Profit and Loss Account				
	Sub-Total 1 - 3 (Red)				
4	Less Intangible Assets (Red)				
5	Adverse Profit and Loss Account (Red)				
6	**Surplus Resources**				
7	Minority Interests				
8	Debentures 19........./........				
9	Mortgages and Secured Loans				
10	Directors Loans				
11	Loans from Parent/Subsidiaries/Associates				
12	Other Unsecured Loans				
13					
14	Sub-Total 8 - 13 (Red)				
15	Tax Equalisation Account				
16	Deferred Taxation				
17	Specific Provisions other than Tax				
18					
19	**Other Provisions** sub-total 15 - 18 (Red)				
20	Owing to Bank(s)				
21	Trade Creditors				
22	Corporation Tax (Current and Future)				
23	Hire Purchase				
24	Proposed Dividend				
25	Other Short Term Liabilities				
26	Due to Parent/Subsidiaries/Associates				
27					
28					
29	**Current Liabilities** - Sub-total 20 - 28 (Red)				
	Total Liabilities Total of 6, 7, 14, 19 & 29				
	Liquid Surplus Deficiency (Red) (difference of lines 29 & 36)				
	Assets				
30	Cash & Bank(s)				
31	Debtors				
32	Stock				
33	Work-in-Progress				
34	Quoted Investments				
35					
36	**Current Assets** Sub-total 30 - 35 (Red)				
37	Due by Parent/Subsidiaries/Associates				
38	Investments in Subsidiaries/Associates				
39	Other Investments				
40					
41	Sub-Total 37 - 40 (Red)				
42	Freehold Premises				
43	Leasehold Premises (Long)				
44	Fixed Plant & Machinery				
45	Loose Plant & Machinery				
46					
47					
48	**Fixed Assets** Sub-total 42 - 47 (Red)				
	Total Assets Total of 36, 41 & 48				
	Exports (Total shown in A/c's)				
	Capital Commitments				
	Contingent Liabilities				

Trading and P. & L. Accounts — Period covered				
Sales less returns				
Gross Profit				
Gross profit as percentage of sales				
Interest Paid				
Bad Debts written off or provided for				
Repairs and Renewals				
Depreciation				
Directors Withdrawals				
Net Profit				
Net profit as percentage of sales				
Non-recurring items (specify below)				
Corporation Tax (Current & Future)				
Deferred Taxation				
Minority Interests				
Preference Dividend				
Ordinary Dividend				
Specific Provisions				
Free Reserves				
Balance added to P. & L. A/c. (Reductions in Red) (see Retained Cash Flow)				
Date Balance Sheet received				
Auditors Report Dated (if qualified state below)				
Entered on Control and Information Card (initials)				
Name of Auditors and Qualifications				
Specification of Tabulated items requiring further information				

Comment on items in Balance Sheet (include comment on Hidden Reserves where applicable)

Period ended	
Period ended	
Period ended	
Period ended	

per cent and 28 per cent of the cases, respectively). When fewer years' figures were examined they were probably all that was available – because almost a quarter of the companies involved were young enterprises which had been established for less than 4 years.

It is, of course, commonplace for bankers to record the figures from their customers' audited accounts on a summary sheet which allows performance over a number of years to be seen at a glance – and the managers in the survey would in many cases have been relying on such summaries. An example of a record sheet is provided in Fig. 11.1.

It may be noticed that the bank form in Fig. 11.1 provides space under 'Trading and P & L a/cs' for some information which is not required to be disclosed under the Companies Acts: bad debts written off and repairs and renewals[5]. These items appear in fully detailed accounts which companies do not normally provide for shareholders. In the survey results in Appendix E (B3) it can be seen that fully detailed statements were commonly examined by bank managers, but their availability was much less than for audited accounts. Two of the possible reasons for this are that for very large companies such information was not produced in a compact form, and in other cases the bank managers simply accepted the accounts provided by customers. Without detailed accounts it would be exceedingly difficult to gauge the plausibility of customers' detailed expectations regarding cash flows (e.g. when it is desirable to test forecasts by referring to gross profit ratios and trends in costs).

In view of the care with which bankers collect audited accounts from their customers it is disconcerting to find that some consider the accounts they get are so outdated as to be useless. For example, one senior official said that the time audited accounts of customers took to prepare[6] was 'at least 9 months and on average 18 months – so the accounts serve no real purpose for future decisions'. This banker put heavy emphasis on the importance of future cash projections and the necessity for rigorous examination of detailed repayment arrangements.

The quotation is worth some detailed consideration. First, what delays in the preparation of audited accounts of customers were revealed by the survey? Under heading A of Appendix E it can be seen that the delay for the average (median) company customer was 5 months, although there was on average a further delay of 2 months before the accounts reached the bank. That is far from swift, but it does not bear out the interval of 9–18 months suggested in the earlier quotation. Admittedly, the banker concerned was referring to business lending generally, in relation to sums beyond branch managers' lending discretion. The audited accounts of some unincorporated businesses are particularly tardy in appearing, but average delays for sizeable businesses are unlikely to be greatly in excess of the survey figures. Laggards are another matter altogether: the slowest company reflected in the survey took 40 months to prepare its accounts[7], which must cause anyone to wonder what purpose such long-delayed accounts could serve.

Criticisms of delays in the availability of companies' annual accounts are implicit in the survey results under heading H of Appendix E. There the possibility of cutting delays in the availability of annual accounts was strongly favoured by bankers, from among seven possible changes affecting accounts.

Thus the timeliness of accounting information is considered by bankers to be very important – and rightly so. It is therefore rather surprising that the bank managers surveyed did not make more use of unaudited accounting results: only 16 per cent of the managers examined such figures for more than half of the borrowing requests they considered. Moreover, hardly any managers examined copies of quarterly VAT returns (Appendix E, B5) which would have given them up-to-date sales figures of similar status to those in the audited accounts – an issue mentioned earlier in Chapter 5.

One possible approach to the problem of laggardly accounts would be to impose and observe *punctuality* rules for the submission of accounts by borrowing customers – before and during an advance. At present such general application would presumably be thought to be asking too much of customers and their accountants, although it will be seen later that *regular* submission of accounting information is quite often a condition of an advance. Bankers might ponder two thoughts: one is that if a firm's management cannot produce up-to-date information for its bankers it is unlikely to be acting on up-to-date information for its own internal purposes; the other is the old adage 'bad figures take longer to add up than good ones'.

The other part of the quotation ('so the accounts serve no real purpose for decisions about the future') deserves separate consideration. Few people would be so foolhardy as to assume that *past* accounting results, whether or not punctually presented, provide the decision-maker with a crystal ball. However, some major ways in which past accounting results can help the lending banker, which by now should be evident to the reader, can be summarized in three broad groupings:

1. As a framework, either for injecting the banker's own assumptions about developments affecting the firm/industry/economy or for checking on the plausibility of the firm's own forecasts.
2. By providing indicators of financial health, of which some aspects were the particular concern of Chapter 10. In this respect it is the degree of resilience or leeway available to meet misfortune which is really being considered, rather than future events in themselves.
3. In giving danger signals about matters which may be getting out of control; this is particularly concerned with comparing accounting results with the assumptions on which the lending was approved. Here the information conveyed by the accounting results can be viewed as a matter of 'potential surprise' – the more surprising the results to the banker the more information they convey. It is in this function that timely (and therefore also frequent) information is particularly important.

Thus the dismissal of past accounts as serving 'no real purpose' was unduly sweeping. But it was accompanied by a logical recognition that the only alternative to using past data is to adopt assumptions about future figures – so that particular emphasis was placed on establishing and checking the customer's cash projections. In contrast, another banker produced the following gem on the usefulness of a cash budget: 'Pie in the sky, only useful as a minor tool to beat the customer with if the budget is not met.' This banker placed more emphasis on the customer's past borrowing record and accounts, and also on the safety factor of security. By now it should hardly be necessary to reiterate that past figures and future projections need to be used in conjunction with each other; they are not opposing alternatives.

The survey showed that cash budgets and profit forecasts were commonly, although by no means universally, examined in connection with company lending (Appendix E, B10, B11). Not entirely surprisingly the two tended to go together, so that companies commonly submitted both or neither. The most popular period for these projections was a year, although there were substantial numbers both for less than a year and for more than a year.

Other widely used sources of information shown under heading B in Appendix E included age analyses of debtors and creditors (B7). Such information would permit checks to be made on the 'stickiness' of debtors and on tendencies to 'stretch' credit periods obtained from suppliers. Searches of the Companies Register for charges over the customer's assets were also understandably common (B12); some respondents referred to a practice of updating searches about every 2 years. The final matter under heading B which deserves comment here concerns the use of funds flow statements (B6): at the time of the survey the inclusion of these statements with accounts was not a standard accounting practice, and their availability now should be broadly similar to that for audited balance sheets and profit and loss accounts (for firms with an annual turnover above £25,000).

Turning to conditions imposed on customers as a condition of an advance (Appendix E, heading D) it is to be expected that the more onerous requirements would apply to the riskier borrowers.

Requirements for regular submission of accounting information were imposed quite widely (D1). Figures for debtors, creditors, stocks and sales were required to be submitted in a little under one-fifth of cases. For those items the frequencies of submission were usually monthly or quarterly, in almost equal proportions.

However, for cash budgets, and balance sheet and profit and loss account figures most of the managers did not specify time periods, and by implication the periods were mainly annual. But there were instances of monthly requirements, and even one case of a fortnightly period, for cash budgets.

A bank debenture was required in about a third of the acceptable borrowing requests (D2). In 38 per cent of those cases a further condition was imposed that certain loans should not be withdrawn from the company during the period of the advance; these loans would normally be amounts owing to directors of director-controlled companies. Much less common was an explicit requirement that the company should maintain some relationship between its bank debt and current assets – of the sort discussed in 'guideline' terms under item 7 of section 11.1. In only 1 per cent of cases was such a requirement explicitly imposed; of these the most frequent was that bank debt should not exceed 50 per cent of current assets.

Understandably the imposition of the last two conditions was rarer in cases which did not involve debentures (Appendix E, D4). In only 12 per cent of those cases were conditions made regarding loans, and formal requirements regarding the relationship between borrowing and current assets were very rare indeed.

The survey provided some exceedingly approximate indications of the security obtained in company lending. Heading E shows that security on land and buildings and floating charges predominated, and that on average unsecured company lending provided a more modest proportion of the acceptable borrowing requests surveyed. As one banker put it: 'We don't lend on the balance sheet unless the message is loud and clear.'

The final part of the survey to be considered here appears under heading G; other aspects of the survey have either been discussed elsewhere or are self-explanatory.

The branch managers were asked to show the importance they assigned to a variety of financial indicators; they could also add their own suggestions. The full list and scores are not reproduced under heading G in Appendix E because the differences in average scores were often so small as to have little meaning. However, the top indicators in each group have been reproduced.

Among measures of 'earnings capacity' the most highly regarded were all absolute money amounts achieved (rather than, say, ratios or forecasts). Top of the list was 'net profit after tax plus depreciation' – which is essentially the measure of net funds generated (where funds = working capital) considered earlier in Chapter 3.

For indicators of 'stability' the amount of the company's capital plus reserves scored highly, followed by the nature of the product and industry. In the third category of 'financial condition' it was the traditional current ratio which came out well, together with the ratio of total debt to capital and reserves as a measure of gearing.

The indicators which were given good scores by the branch managers were all sensible. It may be tempting to debate their choice, particularly for the purpose of adding to the list – and by now the reader should be aware of some of the candidates. But it would be dangerous to attach too much importance to these expressions of priority. They offer indications of what branch managers regard as 'highlights' but they must be seen in the context of overall lending considerations discussed in section 11.1.

11.3 The onset of financial difficulties

In the discussion of the lender's assessment of financial health, no mention has so far been made of that malady of business borrowers from which all bankers are supposed to shrink: overtrading. Some comments on that and other facets of financial difficulties will provide an appropriately cautionary close to the present chapter.

'Overtrading' is a word more widely used by bankers than by accountants – and not always accurately by either. A basic definition would be that a firm is overtrading when it conducts a volume of trade far in excess of that justified by the proprietors' 'own funds', so that the substantial circulating (current) assets needed to support the high level of trade are unduly dependent on outside finance.

A variation on that definition would be that overtrading occurs when the volume of trade is far in excess of that justified by long-term finance (own funds plus long-term debt), so that current assets are excessively dependent on short-term finance. That is a plausible alternative, but the first (more traditional) definition will be adopted here.

The idea of overtrading can be explored by a simple example in which a firm expands its sales with a proportionate expansion in its acquisition of current assets. Such an example is provided in Fig. 11.2, where Wax Ltd had sales of £100,000 and purchases of £60,000 in the year 19–1. In the balance sheet the working capital (net current assets) supporting these transactions is £10,000, made up of stocks £5,000 and debtors £12,500, less creditors of £7,500. The stocks and debtors can be considered as 1 month's purchases and 1½ months' sales respectively, if transactions took place at an even rate throughout the year. Similarly, the creditors of £7,500 would be equivalent to 1½ months' purchases. Fixed assets of £2,500 complete the assets side of the balance sheet; long-term finance is provided by capital and reserves of £12,500.

Wax Ltd plans a 50 per cent increase in trading volume (with constant prices) in 19–2, so that sales become £150,000 and purchases increase to £90,000. The second column of Fig. 11.2 shows that a proportionate increase in working-capital

Fig. 11.2 Expansion of trade: Wax Ltd.

Trading volume	**Year 19–1**		**Planned for year 19–2**
	£		£
Sales	100,000		150,000
Purchases	60,000		90,000
Balance sheets			
	31 Dec. 19–1		**31 Dec. 19–2**
	£		£
Net current assets:			
Stocks	5,000		7,500
Trade debtors	12,500		18,750
	17,500		26,250
Less trade creditors	7,500		11,250
	10,000		15,000
Fixed assets	2,500		2,500
	£12,500		£17,500
Capital and reserves	12,500		12,500
		Finance needed →	5,000
	£12,500		£17,500

items would, not surprisingly, require a 50 per cent increase in working capital – to £15,000. If fixed assets remained constant at £2,500 (and whether that was plausible would depend on the facts of the case) then the £5,000 working-capital increase would represent the extra finance needed to support the new level of operations. Thus, on these assumptions, an increase in trading would involve a proportionately increased investment in working capital.

Where is the new finance to come from? If it comes from 'stretching' trade creditors and/or from borrowing, the firm's financial structure will be riskier than before. How far this process could go may be debatable, but it is clear that unsupported increases of this sort would set the firm along the overtrading path. Heavy dependence on short-term financing means that maintenance of a high level of sales becomes relatively more important in order to keep the finance 'turning over'.

Alternatively, if the finance comes from ownership finance, Wax's financial structure would be virtually maintained. The obvious potential source of ownership finance is retained profit, which has not been mentioned so far. If the firm can retain an amount of £5,000 or more from its profit in 19–2 the financing requirements would be met. However, if Wax Ltd expanded its level of business by 50 per cent virtually overnight (from 1 January 19–2, as is implied by the example) it would be exposed to the needs of short-term financing until sufficient earnings could be retained.

What is the moral? It is that, assuming the company starts from a 'satisfactory' position, the dangers of overtrading depend on two things: the size of the change in operating volume in a particular period and the profits which can be retained from operations. If the increase in working capital required by the growth in volume can be financed by retained profits (plus any injections of capital), the firm's financial stability is not threatened by expansion.

Of course, financing arguments of this sort can be applied not only to changes arising from a growth in physical volume but also to changes in money value of transactions through 'inflationary' price changes.

The importance of the size of changes mentioned above raises an interesting issue on the interpretation of financial reports. There is some evidence to suggest that large changes in balance-sheet *proportions* (relationships between items rather than changes in individual money amounts) may be associated with financial instability. In one study overall measures of these changes did better than ratios in 'predicting' financial failure[8]. Consequently, there is a case for viewing any sizeable shift in balance-sheet structure with a cautious eye.

A ratio which is often recommended in connection with the examination of accounts for overtrading is the sales/capital plus reserves ratio. The implication of this measure is that a high ratio (relative to similar firms, or previous results for this firm) would indicate overtrading.

In the case of Wax Ltd that view seems plausible. The ratio in 19–1 is 8 (or 800 per cent). In 19–2 there would be an increase to 12 if the additional finance were raised by some form of debt, but only to 8·57 if the increased finance were produced via retained profit.

However, when comparison with other firms is attempted, much more than the usual difficulties arise. Is another very similar firm with a ratio one-quarter of that of Wax Ltd any 'safer' financially? Probably not, if that firm had sales and purchases at a quarter of the volume of Wax Ltd, *but an identical balance sheet.* It would seem that sluggishness in stocks, debtors and creditors might indicate just as many financial dangers as Wax's ratio – in particular, inability to sell the firm's stocks.

Thus *undertrading* can be just as serious a problem as overtrading. The sales/capital plus reserves ratio is really so ambiguous that it is better ignored: low and high scores might well be both considered 'bad' but deciding where the 'middle' ends is likely to be unrewarding for risk assessment. The implications of what is happening to the capital structure can be more readily analysed by looking directly at such things as the relationships between working capital and total assets, debtors relative to sales and so on.

The idea of undertrading serves as a reminder that overambitious selling is by no means the only cause of financial difficulties. A struggling firm may have difficulty in reaching a sufficiently high volume of sales to make a decent profit. This is particularly applicable where there are large overheads and relatively fixed wage levels to meet, as in some parts of manufacturing industry. This condition is likely to leave the firm perenially vulnerable to a relatively small downturn in trade.

The latter situation would seem to present the more substantial problem for the banker. It may be possible to temper the overtrader's enthusiasm, but the undertrader may have inherent weaknesses in the quality of management, the nature of the firm's products, the siting of the firm's premises and so on. Perhaps that is why bankers rarely seem to refer to undertrading as such, but instead concentrate on such issues as quality of management.

Another potential source of financial difficulties might be called the 'domino effect'. The financial failure of the sizeable firm in an industry may have repercussions on other firms associated with the industry for two reasons. The first is simply that confidence is shaken; creditors suspect that other firms in the industry may also be vulnerable, and consequently attempt to get paid before the going gets too rough. The second is that the failed firm will have been a customer of other firms; if an amount due is large relative to the size of the supplier, that firm in turn may be unable to meet its financial obligations.

All that the banker can normally do about the first type of difficulty is to provide additional temporary assistance where the underlying financial situation of the customer is judged to be sound. (In fact, in recent years British banks have been involved in some rather elaborate operations of this kind.) For the second type of difficulty there is no cure, although there may be prevention: the lending banker would enquire into the pattern of the customer's trading and look particularly at any proportionately exceptional debtor. Regular reports on the level of the debtor's balance should provide an early warning of dangers.

When a firm does get into financial difficulties it is rarely an overnight occurrence (except occasionally when the domino effect applies). More often there is a gradual build-up of problems, often with a hardening of the level of borrowing. In this situation the banker is sometimes said to be 'locked in' – in the sense that there is no immediate prospect of repayment, but withdrawal of the existing advance would precipitate a financial crisis. Here the banker has perhaps the most difficult lending decision of all to make: when to stop.

Essentially, in making a 'stop' assessment the banker has to compare the probable amount which would be recouped from repayments against the estimated proceeds from calling in the advance, including realization of any security. The recall of an advance usually involves some uncertainties about the amount realizable, that amount itself may be small, and cases of this sort can create some 'badwill' among customers. Consequently, it may often be worth while to maintain the advance under conditions for which a new application would not be approved.

General issues of financial failure will be taken up in Chapter 12.

Notes and references

1. In connection with financial assessment for lending some bankers refer to cash budgets as 'cash-flow statements' – presumably on the grounds that three words sound more impressive than two. In view of the widespread misuse of 'cash flow' in relation to funds flow statements which relate to *past* transactions, the term 'cash-flow statements' raises such prospects of confusion that it should be avoided in all circumstances.
2. For example, a firm which has major but predictable trading fluctuations *during* the year (say, a diary manufacturer) can be more stable (reliable) in its operations than another which has less marked but unpredictable fluctuations (say, a restaurant).
3. All three suggestions are discussed in L. S. Dyer, *A Practical Approach to Bank Lending*, Institute of Bankers (1974), pp. 10–13.
4. Group relationships should be disclosed in the annual accounts, because a holding company must provide a statement with its accounts showing its subsidiaries and details of shareholdings, while a subsidiary must in turn disclose the name and place of incorporation of its ultimate holding company. Companies Act 1967, sections 3 and 5.
5. The word 'renewals' is potentially confusing in this context. It refers to expenditure to maintain the *status quo* and is normally associated with buildings (e.g. renewal of guttering on a building). Strictly, such sporadic outlays which bring benefits over many years should be treated as fixed assets and be depreciated over life – but that tends not to happen to small amounts. Note particularly that this very restricted use of the term 'renewals' does *not* suggest that replacements of fixed assets such as equipment get charged to profit and loss account on acquisition – that expenditure would only be written off as depreciation over the assets' lives.

6. Time elapsed between date of the balance sheet and the date of the audit report.
7. The survey was conducted before the Companies Act requirement for the presentation of accounts to shareholders within 10 months of the end of the accounting period by private companies, and within 7 months by public companies. However, it is still possible to come across companies that seem oblivious of this requirement.
8. The measures are not suitable for consideration here, but the interested reader is referred to B. Lev, 'Financial failure and informational decomposition measures', in R. R. Sterling and W. F. Bentz (eds.), *Accounting in Perspective: Contribution to Accounting Thoughts by Other Disciplines*, South-Western Publishing Co. (1971), pp. 102–11. See also B. Lev, *Financial Statement Analysis: A New Approach*, Prentice-Hall (1974).

Chapter 12

Financial failure

12.1 Default and dissolution

The risk inherent in bank lending makes it inevitable that business borrowers (among others) will on occasion fail to meet their financial obligations. When that happens all is rarely lost; the bank will normally be able to salvage a large part of its lending. The broad financial implications of such events will be considered in this chapter.

Actions of debtors and creditors in situations of financial crisis are closely regulated by statute and case law. The issues are comprehensively examined in legal texts[1], and many of the rules will be familiar to bankers through their legal studies. All that need be considered here are the major headings under which action may arise when a business customer defaults on debts – to provide the context for the banker's consideration of financial options.

The initiation of legal action on financial failure commonly does not come from the lending banker, at least in a formal sense, but from the action of other creditors or of the customer. However, bankers are well aware, in making day-to-day decisions on financially ailing customers, that unpaid cheques can provoke legal activity.

Major issues affecting defaulting customers will be considered under the headings of bankruptcy, liquidation and receivership.

1. Bankruptcy

Bankruptcy in the UK is concerned with the insolvency of individuals or partnerships of individuals. The major aspects of the law are contained in the Bankruptcy Act 1914 for England and Wales[2]. Proceedings may be commenced by presentation in the courts of a bankruptcy petition either by the debtor himself or by creditors where the debtor has committed an act of bankruptcy (for example, has failed to satisfy a High Court judgement).

If the court decides to make a *receiving order* the debtor's actions regarding his property become subject to the control of the Official Receiver. The investigation of the debtor's affairs then proceeds on the basis of a *statement of affairs*, prepared by the debtor, which sets out his assets and liabilities.

The debtor may propose a *composition with creditors* – some alternative financial arrangement which will avoid the creditor's being adjudicated bankrupt. The scheme must gain the court's approval before it can be adopted. Major requirements for approval by the court are that the scheme has the approval of a majority of creditors in number, and a majority three-fourths in value of proved debt; that it should benefit the general body of creditors, and that it should provide reasonable security for the payment of not less than 25p in the £ on the debtor's liabilities.

If a composition is not approved the debtor will normally be adjudicated bankrupt. After adjudication the creditors may appoint a trustee who is responsible for realizing the debtor's assets and paying appropriate dividends to the creditors.

2. Liquidation

Liquidation, or *winding-up*, marks the final phase of a company's life[3]. Liquidation need not, of course, mean that the company has difficulty in meeting its liabilities; many financially sound companies are wound up (e.g. on sale of the company's business).

The major forms of liquidation are as follows:

(a) *Compulsory winding-up* by the court. There are several grounds on which the court may impose a compulsory winding-up, a major one being that the company is considered to be unable to pay its debts.

(b) *Voluntary winding-up* can be commenced by a special resolution of the company's members (i.e. at a meeting of shareholders). If the directors make a declaration of solvency, stating that the company can pay its debts in full within 12 months, the liquidation becomes a *members' voluntary winding-up.* However, if no such declaration is made within 5 weeks of the resolution for winding up the process becomes a *creditors' voluntary winding-up.* The latter situation would imply that the members of a company chose to liquidate voluntarily when financial difficulties became unmanageable, rather than let matters drift until the creditors obtain a compulsory winding-up.

A principal distinction between the forms lies in the right to appoint the liquidator. In a compulsory winding-up this power lies with the court, but in a members' or creditors' winding-up the right rests with members or creditors respectively. In all liquidations there is the possibility of challenging the validity of the liquidator's acts in the courts.

In the case of a compulsory or creditors' winding-up the company's directors must prepare a statement of affairs of the company, setting out assets and liabilities, in a similar manner to that required for bankruptcy. However, only in the case of the compulsory winding-up does this statement have an official status which corresponds precisely to the bankruptcy case.

In a liquidation a variety of financial arrangements are possible which may be to the benefit of the parties involved. The major forms which these arrangements may take are as follows:

(a) *An arrangement out of court*, between the company and its creditors, can be sanctioned under section 306 of the Companies Act 1948. This has the onerous requirements that the arrangement must be sanctioned by three-quarters of the members attending a company meeting *and* by three-quarters of the creditors in number and value. Dissenters can appeal to the courts.

(b) *A scheme of arrangement with consent of the court* can be obtained under section 206 of the Companies Act 1948. This is rather less onerous and expensive in requiring approval at meetings of members and creditors by a *majority* in number representing three-quarters in value. Both this and the preceding type of arrangement would be binding on all members and creditors.

A liquidator can also reach compromises with individual creditors or a class of creditors willing to be bound by a compromise, subject to the sanction of the court or other creditors.

(c) *A reconstruction or amalgamation* can be effected when a liquidator is empowered to accept shares in another company in exchange for assets of the liquidating company. In the case of a reconstruction a purchasing company would be newly established for the purpose: for example, Aspen (19–1) Ltd might be established to acquire the assets of Aspen Ltd. In this way financing can be restructured and new funds are usually introduced.

The liquidator's powers in these cases would arise from section 287 of the Companies Act 1948 (for members' voluntary liquidation) or section 298 (for creditors' voluntary liquidation). Support of three-quarters of the members at a company meeting would be required, plus certain additional approval in the case of a creditors' winding-up.

There are no time limits for payments by liquidators as there are for the payment of dividends in bankruptcy.

3. Receivership

A receiver is some independent person (usually an accountant) appointed to take possession of assets and/or income in order to preserve or enforce certain legal rights. Receivers may be appointed by the court under the general law, but most commonly receivership arises from some legal instrument entered into by the contracting parties.

Receivership is of particular interest when a firm defaults on its secured debt obligations. In that case a receiver can be appointed under a mortgage or (for a company) under a debenture secured by either a fixed or a floating charge.

Most debentures do not rely on general legal powers for the appointment of receivers by the courts, but give power to debenture holders (usually trustees acting on their behalf) to appoint a receiver or a receiver and manager when the detailed obligations of the debenture are not met. The receiver *and manager* would have power not merely to realize assets over which lending is secured but would also have power to conduct the company's business. The object of the managing power would normally be to attempt to sell the business as a going concern – which should produce a higher value than breaking up the firm.

12.2 Realization of assets and ranking of claims

It was said earlier that a statement of affairs must be prepared in both bankruptcy proceedings and a compulsory or creditors' winding-up[4]. The form of the statement differs slightly between bankruptcy and liquidation, but the basic principles are the same (apart from a little more complexity in the liquidation case) and it will therefore be convenient to confine consideration to a company example.

In contrast with conventional accounting statements, a statement of affairs shows the assets of a company at their *realizable values.* As with all values, these must be estimated – and since the statement is prepared by the directors of the company the figures may be influenced by their attitudes. The manner of disposal will also affect value: if the liquidator can sell part or all of the business as a going concern the amount obtained will normally be much greater than if assets have to be sold individually.

Although it would perhaps be feasible to list the probabilities of obtaining different values, the amounts adopted in practice are intended to be relatively prudent estimates of the saleable values of assets as separate items. The figures will commonly be very much lower than value to an ongoing business, particularly for assets which are 'specific' to the business – such as equipment, fixtures and work-in-progress.

Fig. 12.1 Summarized statement of affairs.

Grain Ltd: statement of affairs at 31 May 19–1, showing assets at estimated realizable values and claims expected to rank*

				£000s	
Assets not specifically pledged					
Cash in hand				1	
Trade debtors				24	
Stocks				19	
Work-in-progress				7	
Plant and machinery				14	
Furniture and fittings				3	
					68
Assets specifically pledged					
	Estimated realizable value	Due to secured creditors	Deficiency, ranking as unsecured	Surplus, to last column	
Freehold property	32	25		7 →	7
Leasehold property	16	21	(5)		
					75
Preferential creditors					(27)
					48
10% debenture holders secured by floating charge					(42)
					6
Unsecured creditors					
Estimated unsecured balance of claims of secured creditors – see above				(5)	
Trade accounts and outstanding expenses				(41)	
Contingent liabilities				(4)	
					(50)
Estimated deficiency as regards creditors					(44)
Issued and called up capital					(55)
Estimated deficiency as regards members					(99)

Note: Estimates are subject to the costs of winding up and to any surplus or deficiency on trading pending realization of assets.

* 'Claims expected to rank' means those claims which is expected will need to be met (assets permitting). For example, the contingent liabilities should be included if there is a real prospect that they may give rise to a claim against the company.

A summarized version of a statement of affairs is shown in Fig. 12.1. It will be seen that the realizable values of all assets not specifically charged are listed first;

that applies even when the assets are subject to a floating charge. The assets specifically charged are then listed, and any surplus or deficiency affecting the general pool is estimated. As for the disposition of proceeds of assets for the general pool, the following order of priority is adopted:

(a) Costs of liquidation (these are not estimated in the statement of affairs);
(b) Preferential creditors;
(c) Creditors secured by floating charge;
(d) Unsecured creditors;
(e) Shareholders.

This ordering of claims on the liquidation of insolvent companies follows similar lines to the rules for individuals under the Bankruptcy Act 1914. Two items in the list deserve elaboration: secured creditors and preferential creditors.

1. Secured creditors

A creditor can obtain security over the assets of a company in a variety of ways. This is not the place to enter into the legal complexities of security, but some basic points are relevant.

Security over assets of a company would normally be obtained by way of legal charge – either 'fixed' on specific assets like freehold property or 'floating' over the company's assets in general. A company could also create an equitable charge over property; for example, by depositing property deeds with a lender. All charges should be registered with the Registrar of Companies, and appropriate disclosure must appear in annual accounts.

Much more difficult from a bank viewpoint is *reservation of title* to stocks. As was explained earlier[5], this can arise from a clause in the supplier's conditions of sale, which reserves ownership to the supplier until amounts due are paid. With valid wording this can result in such goods going to meet the supplier's claim on liquidation. Thus, although the claim is not secured in the formal sense, the financial effect is the same as if the supplier were a secured creditor.

Reservation of title, if material, should show up in a company's balance sheet (as in Appendix B, note 15). But a mere absence of warning notes in the accounts cannot be relied upon, if only because trading transactions and changes in stockholding occur all the time. Thus the terms on which a customer obtains goods from major suppliers is of great interest to the lending banker, particularly if the lending is unsecured or on a floating charge.

In liquidation a secured creditor has a choice of four options:

(a) Do nothing, if the creditor is fully secured. The onus is then upon the liquidator to decide whether to redeem the security or to allow the creditor to retain it in satisfaction of the debt.
(b) Surrender the security and prove for the full amount of the debt in winding-up – an improbable occurrence.
(c) Estimate the value of the security and prove in liquidation for the balance.
(d) Realize the security and prove for the balance, or hand any surplus to the liquidator.

In the event of a deficit under the last two headings, that amount ranks, of course, as an unsecured creditor (see Fig. 12.1).

2. Preferential creditors

Preferential creditors relate to two major categories:

(a) Taxes of any nature, including rates due to local authorities. However, preference is confined to 1 year's taxes.
(b) Payment due to employees, subject to certain limits, including not only wages and salaries but also a variety of other compensation (for example, accrued holiday remuneration) [6].

When money has been lent to the company for the payment of wages and salaries which would have been preferential in a winding-up, the lender is able to claim the same right of priority that would have been available to the employee (section 319(4), Companies Act 1948). This is, of course, an important consideration when a bank is faced with a decision on the payment of the wages cheque of a financially ailing customer.

In the liquidation of a company, interest in full is provable as part of the company's debt, provided the company agreed to a definitive rate of interest. In bankruptcy, however, not more than 5 per cent is provable as a debt even when there is an agreed contractual rate; the surplus can only rank as a *deferred* debt payable after all other debts have been met.

In both liquidation and bankruptcy the allowance of interest is, however, only made up to the date of commencement of the winding-up or of the receiving order. The lapse of time between that date and the distribution of proceeds to creditors can involve a material cost in lost interest on funds.

Returning to Fig. 12.1, estimated claims have been deducted in order of priority from the total realizable value of assets to produce an estimated deficiency (so far as creditors are concerned) of £44,000. Although that does not allow for liquidation costs, it does include liabilities which are only contingent but which are likely to become due – for example, on discounted bills of exchange. The result in the case of Grain Ltd is that £6,000 would be available to divide between claims of £50,000 – a payment of 12p in the £ if liquidation costs are ignored.

The final section of the statement of affairs would reconcile the estimated deficiency with the company's last balance sheet. That reconciliation has not been shown in Fig. 12.1 because it has no bearing on the central question of what can be salvaged from the company. It has more of a legal function relating to the past conduct of the company's affairs.

However, the current balance-sheet structure is of some importance in considering financial rescue operations for an ailing company. Consequently, it has been assumed for the purposes of exposition that Grain Ltd drew up a balance sheet on conventional lines on 31 May 19–1, as shown in Fig. 12.2. This permits a comparison of the approaches in the two documents and also provides a convenient starting-point for the consideration of alternatives in section 12.3.

12.3 Salvage operations

Financial failure rarely occurs without lengthy and serious attempts being made to mount salvage operations to enable the business to continue. From the strictly financial viewpoint the importance of such attempts lies in the fact that a business will often be worth more as an ongoing enterprise than if it is broken up. One exception would be where property assets are under-utilized in their present employment and their greater value in alternative use would outweigh losses on other assets; another exception occurs when there is plainly no prospect of making the business operate profitably under any circumstances.

Fig. 12.2 Conventional balance sheet at commencement of winding-up.

Grain Ltd: balance sheet at 31 May 19–1

	£000s			£000s	
Share capital and reserves			**Fixed assets**		
Share capital (£1 shares, fully paid)	55		Goodwill	15	
Reserves	4		Freehold property	30	
		59	Leasehold property	27	
			Plant and machinery	46	
Long-term debt			Furniture and fittings	10	
Mortgage loan, secured on freehold property	25				128
10% debentures, secured by floating charge	40		**Current assets**		
		65	Stocks	39	
Current liabilities			Work-in-progress	19	
Bank overdraft, secured on leasehold property	21		Trade debtors	28	
Sundry creditors*	70		Cash in hand	1	
					87
		91			
		215			215

* Sundry creditors of 70 have been distributed in the statement of affairs as follows:

Preferential creditors	27
Half-year's interest accrued on 10% debentures (added to debentures, giving 42, in statement of affairs)	2
Trade accounts and outstanding expenses	41
	70

There are other reasons why considerable efforts are made to ensure the continuance of a firm's activities. The most crucial is that the livelihood of many individuals may be at stake. However, the best prospects of continuance usually involve reducing the scale of activities and selling the slimmer business to an outside buyer. The creditors must then make do with the proceeds on liquidation.

Much more rarely, rescue operations may be attempted by introducing fresh finance on a permanent or at least medium-term basis. For such an injection to be viable requires that the firm's trading should either be profitable or have good prospects of becoming so. Potential sources of finance in such cases are often limited to those who have an existing financial interest and therefore significant amounts at stake (e.g. controlling shareholder or large suppliers) and those who expect to gain from financial control (such as a competitor).

A company's financial difficulties may be met by a wide variety of alternative arrangements, but there are three basic legal forms in which solutions can take place. The first involves share and loan capital reorganization within the existing company structure (which may involve a share capital 'takeover' by another company), the second involves setting up a new company for a reconstruction, and the third is the possibility of an amalgamation with another company.

Fig. 12.3 Options for Grain Ltd.

Claims	**Winding-up**	**Introduction of capital**	**Reconstruction**	**Amalgamation with Sand Ltd**
	£	£	£	£
Mortgage loan	25,000	25,000	25,000	25,000
Preferential creditors	27,000	27,000	27,000	27,000
Debenture holders	42,000	42,000	48,000	42,000
Unsecured creditors				
(excluding bank)	5,400	18,000	18,000	22,500
Bank (partially secured)	16,600	18,000	18,000	18,500
Shareholders' valuation	–	14,000	8,000	1,100

Each of the three possibilities will be briefly reviewed, with reference to Grain Ltd and the financial options shown in Fig. 12.3. The first column of Fig. 12.3 represents the amounts which different claimants would receive under the winding-up – if the figures in the earlier statement of affairs were precisely achieved and ignoring liquidation expenses.

1. Existing company structure: introduction of capital

Fresh funds may be introduced as share capital or as a loan of some sort, for the continuance of the business. The funds may come from existing or new participants: for example, an ailing company might be taken over as a subsidiary by another company, and the latter may provide new funds. In many situations, however, such an introduction may only be viable if a compromise is reached with existing creditors for some reduction in their claims. For their part creditors will require at least as much as they could obtain under liquidation.

In Fig. 12.3 it is assumed that existing shareholders are prepared to introduce £40,000 in cash, provided the unsecured creditors settle for a payment of 40p in the £ on their claims. That would mean the unsecured creditors for £45,000 (excluding the bank's £5,000) would obtain £18,000 compared with only £5,400 (12p in the £) under winding-up. It is assumed that the bank's claim is treated in the same way – so that £16,000 would be due in respect of the secured element of lending plus £2,000 on the unsecured part.

The other liabilities would remain to be met at their face values as they become due in the normal course of business. If the proposed injection of funds is considered to be sufficient to ensure the financial stability of Grain Ltd those claims would be worth their full amount, as shown in Fig. 12.3.

The shareholders would not usually be prepared to provide fresh funds for purely altruistic motives. The returns they anticipate depend on the expected earnings of Grain Ltd – and the value of those returns will depend upon the associated risk. The figure for the shareholders' valuation in the second column of the Grain example can be most conveniently considered with the financial arrangements of the following subsection.

2. Reconstruction

A reconstruction permits certain flexibility in dealing with the rights of existing claimants; for example, debenture holders may be given a choice between redemption and exchange for other forms of claims.

In the case of Grain Ltd it is assumed that a new company, Grain (19–1) Ltd, would take over the existing business; 80,000 shares of £1 would be issued: 40,000 for cash to existing shareholders and the remainder in exchange for the debentures. Assuming that the reconstructed company will be capable of earning £12,000 per year for the shareholders and that a 12½ per cent earnings yield (PE ratio of 8) is required on the shares, the value of the shares would total

$$£12{,}000 \times \frac{100}{12\tfrac{1}{2}} = £96{,}000$$

This value would be divided equally between the debenture holders and the existing shareholders (if they all subscribe). Thus there would be an element of benefit to both categories; in the case of the ordinary shareholders they would obtain shares worth £48,000 in exchange for introducing £40,000 – the difference of £8,000 represents the benefit from this option in Fig. 12.3. Some gain to the debenture holders would, of course, encourage their acceptance of the scheme.

The calculation also explains the shareholders' valuation for the 'introduction of capital' option in the second column of Fig. 12.3. Under that solution the £12,000 annual earnings would have been available for debenture holders and shareholders. If the value of those earnings is taken as £96,000, the deduction of £42,000 for the debenture holders would suggest a share valuation of £54,000 (adopting the valuation approach considered in section 7.4). Since the shareholders would be providing £40,000 the net value of the option to them would be £14,000.

For simplicity it has been assumed that the reconstruction would apply the same terms to other claimants as were mentioned for the previous option.

Although the timing of payments has not been specifically incorporated into Fig. 12.3, that is an aspect of some importance. For example, assume that the bank's funds can be employed at 10 per cent per year. If in liquidation the bank could realize its security in the leasehold property immediately, but would not receive its additional £600 payment as an unsecured creditor until a year later, the amounts could be discounted to a present value of

		£
Secured		16,000
Unsecured	£600 × 0·909	545
		£16,545

If, on the other hand, the proposed reconstruction involved a moratorium of 1 year on debts (during which time interest would not accrue) the value of the proposed £18,000 to the bank would be only

£18,000 × 0·909 = £16,362

In some circumstances the bank might be prepared to accept the lower-valued alternative, particularly if the difference involved is not large. To oppose a reconstruction on grounds of a small benefit to the bank would be harmful for the bank's goodwill, and in the Grain case the reconstruction might well prove acceptable to the bank if it were financially viable on general grounds. Another aspect is that the risk qualities of the alternatives need not be identical – although in this example it is likely that the lower amount would involve rather more risk.

3. Amalgamation

In an amalgamation another company would take over the assets and liabilities of the ailing company and incorporate them into its own business.

In the final column of Fig. 12.3 it is assumed that Sand Ltd is prepared to take over Grain's assets and liabilities, provided unsecured creditors will settle for a payment of 50p in the £. As a small inducement for the co-operation of the shareholders Sand Ltd would pay 2p for each £1 share in Grain Ltd. Other amounts would be settled in the ordinary course of business at their full values (but with the bank getting £16,000 secured plus £2,500 on the unsecured element).

The result is a solution which is better for unsecured creditors, less attractive for debenture holders and shareholders, and the same as before for the other claimants. However, much depends on Sand's financial standing; if that is undoubted, the values attached to its offer would be much less risky than, say, the reconstruction option. One way of making comparisons would be to weight alternatives for their probabilities of value being achieved – for example, 0·99 for each of Sand's offers, compared with lower factors for the individual amounts under reconstruction.

In the consideration of options there will often be conflicts of interest between different classes of claimant. It is to cater for such conflicts that the legal rules for acceptance of arrangements are established; in the last resort the courts can impose a decision.

In conclusion, it need hardly be said that the figures in these examples were oversimplified. But they demonstrate the point which is liable to get lost in the complexities of financial difficulties: valuation of all the known options can provide a useful framework for decisions by claimants, however rough those valuations may be.

Notes and references

1. Some texts in this area are: H. A. R. J. Wilson and R. D. Penfold, *The Rights and Duties of Liquidators, Trustees and Receivers*, HFL Publishers Ltd (various editions); G. H. L. Fridman, I. Hicks and E. C. Johnson, *Bankruptcy Law and Practice*, Butterworth (1970); P. Loose, *Loose on Liquidators*, Jordan (1972). An authoritative statement of the law of bankruptcy is provided in the bankruptcy section of Volume 3 of Halsbury's *Laws of England* (4th edition), Butterworth (1973).
2. The Bankruptcy Act 1913 applies to Scotland and Victorian legislation to Northern Ireland.
3. Most companies merely fade away; after failing to make returns to the Registrar of Companies they are 'struck off' as defunct under section 353 of the Companies Act 1948. But these would not be companies with ongoing financial difficulties.
4. A similar document is prepared for the declaration of solvency in a members' voluntary winding-up.
5. In section 2 of Chapter 8. For references to the legal background, see note 5 to Chapter 8. The earmarking of assets held by a company can take other forms; when a company in financial difficulties opened a separate bank account in which money received in advance from customers was held 'in trust' until the orders were filled, the trust was upheld – *Re Kayford Ltd*, (1975), 2 All E.R. 604.
6. These employee rights arise in bankruptcy from section 33 of the Bankruptcy Act 1914, and in liquidation from section 319 of the Companies Act 1948 as amended by section 63 of the Employment Protection Act 1975.

Appendix A

Interest tables

Future value of £1 n periods hence, interest rate r per period. $(1 + r)^n$

n \ r	2%	4%	6%	8%	10%	12%	14%	16%	18%	20%	22%	24%	26%	28%	30%
1	1·020	1·040	1·060	1·080	1·100	1·120	1·140	1·160	1·180	1·200	1·220	1·240	1·260	1·280	1·300
2	1·040	1·082	1·124	1·166	1·210	1·254	1·300	1·346	1·392	1·440	1·488	1·538	1·587	1·638	1·690
3	1·061	1·125	1·191	1·260	1·331	1·405	1·482	1·561	1·643	1·728	1·816	1·907	2·000	2·097	2·197
4	1·082	1·170	1·262	1·360	1·464	1·574	1·689	1·811	1·939	2·074	2·215	2·364	2·521	2·684	2·856
5	1·104	1·217	1·338	1·469	1·611	1·762	1·925	2·100	2·288	2·488	2·703	2·932	3·175	3·436	3·713
6	1·126	1·265	1·419	1·587	1·772	1·974	2·195	2·436	2·700	2·986	3·298	3·635	4·001	4·399	4·826
7	1·149	1·316	1·504	1·714	1·949	2·211	2·502	2·826	3·186	3·583	4·023	4·507	5·042	5·630	6·275
8	1·172	1·369	1·594	1·851	2·144	2·476	2·853	3·278	3·759	4·300	4·908	5·590	6·353	7·206	8·156
9	1·195	1·423	1·689	1·999	2·358	2·773	3·252	3·803	4·435	5·160	5·987	6·931	8·004	9·224	10·60
10	1·219	1·480	1·791	2·159	2·594	3·106	3·707	4·411	5·234	6·192	7·305	8·594	10·09	11·81	13·79
11	1·243	1·539	1·898	2·332	2·853	3·479	4·226	5·117	6·176	7·430	8·913	10·66	12·71	15·11	17·92
12	1·268	1·601	2·112	2·518	3·138	3·896	4·818	5·936	7·288	8·916	10·87	13·21	16·01	19·34	23·30
13	1·294	1·665	2·133	2·720	3·452	4·363	5·492	6·886	8·600	10·70	13·26	16·39	20·17	24·76	30·28
14	1·319	1·732	2·261	2·937	3·798	4·887	6·261	7·988	10·15	12·84	16·18	20·32	25·42	31·69	39·37
15	1·346	1·801	2·397	3·172	4·177	5·474	7·138	9·266	11·97	15·41	19·74	25·19	32·03	40·56	51·18
16	1·373	1·873	2·540	3·426	4·595	6·130	8·137	10·75	14·13	18·49	24·09	31·24	40·36	51·93	66·53
17	1·400	1·948	2·693	3·700	5·054	6·866	9·276	12·47	16·67	22·19	29·38	38·74	50·85	66·47	86·50
18	1·428	2·026	2·854	3·996	5·560	7·690	10·58	14·46	19·67	26·62	35·85	48·04	64·08	85·07	112·4
19	1·457	2·107	3·026	4·316	6·116	8·613	12·06	16·78	23·21	31·95	43·73	59·57	80·72	108·9	146·2
20	1·486	2·191	3·207	4·661	6·728	9·646	13·74	19·46	27·39	38·34	53·36	73·86	101·7	139·4	190·0
21	1·516	2·279	3·400	5·034	7·400	10·80	15·67	22·57	32·32	46·01	65·10	91·60	128·2	178·4	247·0
22	1·546	2·370	3·604	5·437	8·140	12·10	17·86	26·19	38·14	55·21	79·42	113·6	161·5	228·3	321·1
23	1·577	2·465	3·820	5·871	8·954	13·55	20·36	30·38	45·01	66·25	96·90	140·8	203·5	292·3	417·4
24	1·608	2·563	4·049	6·341	9·850	15·18	23·21	35·24	53·11	79·50	118·2	174·6	256·4	374·1	542·7
25	1·641	2·666	4·292	6·848	10·83	17·00	26·46	40·87	62·67	95·40	144·2	216·5	323·0	478·8	705·5
30	1·811	3·243	5·743	10·06	17·45	29·96	50·95	85·85	143·4	237·4	389·8	634·9	1,026	1,645	2,620
35	2·000	3·946	7·686	14·79	28·10	52·80	98·10	180·3	328·0	590·7	1,053	1,861	3,258	5,653	9,725
40	2·208	4·801	10·29	21·72	45·26	93·05	188·9	378·7	758·4	1,470	2,847	5,457	10,350	19,430	36,110
45	2·438	5·841	13·76	31·92	72·89	163·0	363·7	795·4	1,717	3,657	7,694	16,000	32,860	66,740	134,100
50	2·692	7·107	18·42	46·90	117·4	289·0	700·2	1,671	3,927	9,100	20,800	46,890	104,400	229,300	497,700

Present value of £1 to be received n periods hence, interest rate r per period. $v^n = (1+r)^{-n}$

n \ r	2%	4%	6%	8%	10%	12%	14%	16%	18%	20%	22%	24%	26%	28%	30%
1	0·980	0·962	0·943	0·926	0·909	0·893	0·877	0·862	0·847	0·833	0·820	0·806	0·794	0·781	0·769
2	0·961	0·925	0·890	0·857	0·826	0·797	0·769	0·743	0·718	0·694	0·672	0·650	0·630	0·610	0·592
3	0·942	0·889	0·840	0·794	0·751	0·712	0·675	0·641	0·609	0·579	0·551	0·524	0·500	0·477	0·455
4	0·924	0·855	0·792	0·735	0·683	0·636	0·592	0·552	0·518	0·482	0·451	0·423	0·397	0·373	0·350
5	0·906	0·822	0·747	0·681	0·621	0·567	0·519	0·476	0·437	0·402	0·370	0·341	0·315	0·291	0·269
6	0·888	0·790	0·705	0·630	0·564	0·507	0·456	0·410	0·370	0·335	0·303	0·275	0·250	0·227	0·207
7	0·871	0·760	0·665	0·584	0·513	0·452	0·400	0·354	0·314	0·279	0·249	0·222	0·198	0·178	0·159
8	0·853	0·731	0·627	0·540	0·467	0·404	0·351	0·305	0·266	0·233	0·204	0·179	0·157	0·139	0·123
9	0·837	0·703	0·592	0·500	0·424	0·361	0·308	0·263	0·225	0·194	0·167	0·144	0·125	0·108	0·094
10	0·820	0·676	0·558	0·463	0·386	0·322	0·270	0·227	0·191	0·162	0·137	0·116	0·099	0·085	0·073
11	0·804	0·650	0·527	0·429	0·350	0·287	0·237	0·195	0·162	0·135	0·112	0·094	0·079	0·066	0·056
12	0·788	0·625	0·497	0·397	0·319	0·257	0·208	0·168	0·137	0·112	0·092	0·076	0·062	0·052	0·043
13	0·773	0·601	0·469	0·368	0·290	0·229	0·182	0·145	0·116	0·093	0·075	0·061	0·050	0·040	0·033
14	0·758	0·577	0·442	0·340	0·263	0·205	0·160	0·125	0·099	0·078	0·062	0·049	0·039	0·032	0·025
15	0·743	0·555	0·417	0·315	0·240	0·183	0·140	0·108	0·084	0·065	0·051	0·040	0·031	0·025	0·020
16	0·728	0·534	0·394	0·292	0·218	0·163	0·123	0·093	0·071	0·054	0·042	0·032	0·025	0·019	0·015
17	0·714	0·513	0·371	0·270	0·198	0·146	0·108	0·080	0·060	0·045	0·034	0·026	0·020	0·015	0·012
18	0·700	0·494	0·350	0·250	0·180	0·130	0·095	0·069	0·051	0·038	0·028	0·021	0·016	0·012	0·009
19	0·686	0·475	0·331	0·232	0·164	0·116	0·083	0·060	0·043	0·031	0·023	0·017	0·012	0·009	0·007
20	0·673	0·456	0·312	0·215	0·149	0·104	0·073	0·051	0·037	0·026	0·019	0·014	0·010	0·007	0·005
21	0·660	0·439	0·294	0·199	0·135	0·093	0·064	0·044	0·031	0·022	0·015	0·011	0·008	0·006	0·004
22	0·647	0·422	0·278	0·184	0·123	0·083	0·056	0·038	0·026	0·018	0·013	0·009	0·006	0·004	0·003
23	0·634	0·406	0·262	0·170	0·112	0·074	0·049	0·033	0·022	0·015	0·010	0·007	0·005	0·003	0·002
24	0·622	0·390	0·247	0·158	0·102	0·066	0·043	0·028	0·019	0·013	0·008	0·006	0·004	0·003	0·002
25	0·610	0·375	0·233	0·146	0·092	0·059	0·038	0·024	0·016	0·010	0·007	0·005	0·003	0·002	0·001
30	0·552	0·308	0·174	0·099	0·057	0·033	0·020	0·012	0·007	0·004	0·003	0·002	0·001	0·001	*
35	0·500	0·253	0·130	0·068	0·036	0·019	0·010	0·006	0·003	0·002	0·001	0·001	*	*	*
40	0·453	0·208	0·097	0·046	0·022	0·011	0·005	0·003	0·001	0·001	*	*	*	*	*
45	0·410	0·171	0·073	0·031	0·014	0·006	0·003	0·001	0·001	*	*	*	*	*	*
50	0·372	0·141	0·054	0·021	0·009	0·003	0·001	0·001	*	*	*	*	*	*	*

* Less than 0·001.

Present value of an annuity of £1 for n periods, interest rate r per period. $a_{\overline{n}|} = \frac{1-(1+r)^{-n}}{r}$

n \ r	2%	4%	6%	8%	10%	12%	14%	16%	18%	20%	22%	24%	26%	28%	30%
1	0·980	0·962	0·943	0·926	0·909	0·893	0·877	0·862	0·847	0·833	0·820	0·806	0·794	0·781	0·769
2	1·942	1·886	1·833	1·783	1·736	1·690	1·647	1·605	1·566	1·528	1·492	1·457	1·424	1·392	1·361
3	2·884	2·775	2·673	2·577	2·487	2·402	2·322	2·246	2·174	2·106	2·042	1·981	1·923	1·868	1·816
4	3·808	3·630	3·465	3·312	3·170	3·037	2·914	2·798	2·690	2·589	2·494	2·404	2·320	2·241	2·166
5	4·713	4·452	4·212	3·993	3·791	3·605	3·433	3·274	3·127	2·991	2·864	2·745	2·635	2·532	2·436
6	5·601	5·242	4·917	4·623	4·355	4·111	3·889	3·685	3·498	3·326	3·167	3·020	2·885	2·759	2·643
7	6·472	6·002	5·582	5·206	4·868	4·564	4·288	4·039	3·812	3·605	3·416	3·242	3·083	2·937	2·802
8	7·325	6·733	6·210	5·747	5·335	4·968	4·639	4·344	4·078	3·837	3·619	3·421	3·241	3·076	2·925
9	8·162	7·435	6·802	6·247	5·759	5·328	4·946	4·607	4·303	4·031	3·786	3·565	3·366	3·184	3·019
10	8·983	8·111	7·360	6·710	6·145	5·650	5·216	4·833	4·494	4·192	3·923	3·682	3·465	3·269	3·091
11	9·787	8·760	7·887	7·139	6·495	5·938	5·453	5·029	4·656	4·327	4·035	3·776	3·544	3·335	3·147
12	10·57	9·385	8·384	7·536	6·814	6·194	5·660	5·197	4·793	4·439	4·127	3·851	3·606	3·387	3·190
13	11·35	9·986	8·853	7·904	7·103	6·424	5·842	5·342	4·910	4·533	4·203	3·912	3·656	3·427	3·223
14	12·11	10·56	9·295	8·244	7·367	6·628	6·002	5·468	5·008	4·611	4·265	3·962	3·695	3·459	3·249
15	12·85	11·12	9·712	8·559	7·606	6·811	6·142	5·575	5·092	4·675	4·315	4·001	3·726	3·483	3·268
16	13·58	11·65	10·11	8·851	7·824	6·974	6·265	5·669	5·162	4·730	4·357	4·033	3·751	3·503	3·283
17	14·29	12·17	10·48	9·122	8·022	7·120	6·373	5·749	5·222	4·775	4·391	4·059	3·771	3·518	3·295
18	14·99	12·66	10·83	9·372	8·201	7·250	6·467	5·818	5·273	4·812	4·419	4·080	3·786	3·529	3·304
19	15·68	13·13	11·16	9·604	8·365	7·366	6·550	5·877	5·316	4·844	4·442	4·097	3·799	3·539	3·311
20	16·35	13·59	11·47	9·818	8·514	7·470	6·623	5·929	5·353	4·870	4·460	4·110	3·808	3·546	3·316
21	17·01	14·03	11·76	10·02	8·649	7·562	6·687	5·973	5·384	4·891	4·476	4·121	3·816	3·551	3·320
22	17·66	14·45	12·04	10·20	8·772	7·645	6·743	6·011	5·410	4·909	4·488	4·130	3·822	3·556	3·323
23	18·29	14·86	12·30	10·37	8·883	7·718	6·792	6·044	5·432	4·925	4·499	4·137	3·827	3·560	3·325
24	18·91	15·25	12·55	10·53	8·985	7·784	6·835	6·073	5·451	4·937	4·507	4·143	3·831	3·562	3·327
25	19·52	15·62	12·78	10·67	9·077	7·843	6·873	6·097	5·467	4·948	4·514	4·147	3·834	3·564	3·329
30	22·40	17·29	13·76	11·26	9·427	8·055	7·003	6·177	5·517	4·979	4·534	4·160	3·842	3·569	3·332
35	25·00	18·66	14·50	11·65	9·644	8·176	7·070	6·215	5·539	4·992	4·541	4·164	3·845	3·571	3·332
40	27·36	19·79	15·05	11·92	9·779	8·244	7·105	6·234	5·548	4·997	4·544	4·166	3·846	3·571	3·333
45	29·49	20·72	15·46	12·11	9·863	8·283	7·123	6·242	5·552	4·999	4·545	4·166	3·846	3·571	3·333
50	31·42	21·48	15·76	12·23	9·915	8·305	7·133	6·246	5·554	4·999	4·545	4·167	3·846	3·571	3·333

Appendix B

Abbreviations

CA48, CA67, etc. or 1948 Act, etc.	Companies Act 1948, 1967, etc.
Schedule 1	Schedule 1 to Companies Act 1981 (which is the new Schedule 8 to Companies Act 1948).
Sch. 39	Paragraph 39 of Schedule 1 to Companies Act 1981 (which is the new Schedule 8 to Companies Act 1948).
Sch. 2 para 2	Paragraph 2 of Schedule 2 to Companies Act 1981.
CA81 S. 13	Section 13 of Companies Act 1981.
CA67 S. 16 (CA81 S. 13)	Section 16 of Companies Act 1967 as amended by Section 13 of Companies Act 1981.
SI 1980 No. 1055	Statutory Instrument No. 1055 1980.
ICAS 7.102	Institute of Chartered Accountants of Scotland Statement 7.102.
ICAEW 3.102	Institute of Chartered Accountants in England and Wales Statement 3.102.
SSAP	Statement of Standard Accounting Practice.

A number of words and phrases are given statutory meaning; the principal ones are marked in the text with an asterisk (*)

Note: **Some of the comments alongside the accounts refer to Good Group P.L.C., which is a further sample set of accounts prepared by Arthur Young McClelland Moores & Co. Those accounts are not reproduced in this Appendix.**

Good Practice Limited
Report and Accounts
December 31, 19X1

The model accounts are only illustrative and they do not attempt to show all the disclosure requirements. In any case of doubt as to the legal requirements, it is essential to refer to the actual legislation and, where necessary, to seek appropriate professional advice. Although the model accounts attempt to illustrate the most likely requirements of manufacturing companies, they should not be regarded as a comprehensive checklist of statutory and accounting requirements. They comply with the Companies Acts 1948 to 1981 and with other requirements in force at September 30, 1981.

Arthur Young McClelland Moores & Co.

Chartered Accountants

Source	*Comments*
General comments on the statutory formats	
Sch. 1	Every balance sheet and profit and loss account must show the items denoted by the letters or Roman numerals in any of the given formats in the order and under the headings and sub-headings shown (unless the amounts are nil in both years).
CA81 S.1 Sch. 15	The requirement to show a true and fair view overrides all other accounting requirements* of the Companies Acts. For any departure from these requirements in order to give a true and fair view the particulars and reasons for departure and its effect must be disclosed in a note.
Sch. 3(1)	Greater detail is allowed than is given in the formats.
Sch. 3(4)	Items denoted by Arabic numbers may be combined on the face of the accounts but must be disclosed in the notes unless they are immaterial.
Sch. 2	The format chosen may not be changed from year to year unless, in the directors' opinion, there are special reasons for change. Disclose particulars of any change in the format used and the reasons for the change in a note.
Sch. 3(3)	The arrangement of items denoted by an Arabic number should be adapted to suit the special nature of the company's business.
Sch. 4(1)	Corresponding amounts for the preceding financial year must be shown.
Sch. 4(2)	Where the corresponding amount is not comparable it should be adjusted and particulars and reasons given in a note.
Sch. 5	Items representing income or assets may not be offset against items representing expenditure or liabilities.

Good Practice Limited

Directors
J.N. Smith (Chairman)
F.R. Brown
J. Archer
P.A. MacBryde

Secretary
J. Harris

Auditors
Chartered Accountants & Co.,
7 Moor Street, Edinburgh

Bankers
Bank Limited
George Street, Glasgow

Solicitors
Solicitors & Co.
7 Waverley, Edinburgh

Registered Office
11 Smithdown Lane, Edinburgh

Source	*Comments*
General	
CA48 S. 157 CA76 S. 1(5)	Directors' report to be attached to every set of accounts prepared for every accounting reference period.
Results and dividends	
CA48 S. 157	State amount of dividend recommended (if any) and amount proposed to be carried to reserves.
CA80 S. 39	A company shall not make a distribution except out of profits available for the purpose.
Review of business	
CA67 S. 16(1)	Disclose principal activities and any significant change.
CA48 S. 157(1) (CA81 S. 13)	Fair review of the development of the business of the company during the year and the position at the end of it.
Share capital	
CA67 S. 16A(2) (CA81 S. 14)	For further details refer to Appendix 2.
Sch. 39	The information relating to issues during the year must be given in the notes but is not specifically required in the directors' report.
CA80 S. 14	The directors must have authority to allot shares, although this does not have to be stated in the directors' report.
Market value of land and buildings	
CA67 S. 16(1)(*a*)	The amount of difference between market value and book value should be disclosed where it is substantial and the directors think it is of significance to members.
Fixed assets	
CA67 S. 16(1)(*a*)	Give details of significant changes in fixed assets.*
Research and development	
CA67 S. 16(1)(*f*) (CA81 S. 13)	Give an indication of activities (if any) in the field of research and development.
Future developments	
CA67 S. 16(1)(*f*) (CA81 S. 13)	Give an indication of likely future developments in the business of the company.

Good Practice Limited

Directors' Report

The directors submit their report and accounts for the year ended December 31, 19X1.

Results and dividends

The trading profit for the year, after taxation, was £18,760 before charging an extraordinary loss of £2,250 incurred when a factory building subsided as a result of uncharted mine works.

The directors recommend a final ordinary dividend amounting to £1,500 making a total of £3,060 for the year, which, with preference dividends of £875, leaves a profit of £12,575 to be retained.

Review of the business

The company's principal activity during the year was the manufacture and installation of fire-prevention equipment.

Turnover has increased by 21% to £395,750 during the year and the directors believe that the trend will continue. However the costs of materials, labour and other overheads have also increased substantially. The market for equipment has improved to some extent since the middle of the year and the company is in a good position to take advantage of any opportunities which may arise in the future.

Share capital

The authorised ordinary share capital of the company was increased during the year to 50,000 ordinary shares of £1 each. 6,250 ordinary shares of £1, credited as fully paid, were issued for cash of £8,750 on July 1, 19X1 to help finance the purchase of plant and machinery. The articles of the company exclude the requirements under Section 17(1) of the Companies Act 1980 relating to pre-emption rights and give the directors general authority to allot shares.

Market value of land and buildings

The freehold properties were revalued at December 31, 19X1. The valuation of £55,000, which was £12,500 higher than the former net book value, has been incorporated in these accounts.

The market value of the short leasehold properties is higher than the book value. They have been sold since the end of the year and details of the sale are given in the paragraph relating to events since the end of the year.

Fixed assets

The company has continued to improve plant and machinery during the year, involving expenditure of £27,525 (after government grants of £4,000).

Research and development

The company has increased its commitment in the area of research and development. There is now one employee working solely on research and development activities. Continuity of investment in this area is essential if the company is to retain a competitive position in the market.

Future developments

The directors consider that 19X2 will be another year of difficult trading conditions both in this country and abroad. Their aim is to maintain the management policies which have strengthened the company in recent years and assisted in successfully overcoming the difficulties and uncertainties in the market place in 19X1. The success of the efforts last year is encouraging and the directors expect there will be an effective response to the challenges of 19X2.

Source	*Comments*
Events since the end of the year	
CA67 S. 16(1)(*f*) (CA81 S. 13)	Give particulars of any important events affecting the company which have occurred since the end of the year.
Directors and their interests	
CA67 S. 16(1)	Disclose names of persons who were directors at any time during the financial year. Also, it is preferable to show any changes between the year end and the date of the report.
CA67 S. 16(1)(*e*) CA67 S. 27 SI 1968 No. 864, 865, 1533	Give details for directors at the year end of interests in share and loan capital at the year-end and at the beginning of the year or subsequent date of appointment. Where no interest requires to be disclosed state, for example, 'There are no directors' interests requiring disclosure under the Companies Act 1967'. The distinction between beneficial and non-beneficial holdings should normally be made, but is only required for listed companies.
CA67 S. 16(4A) (CA81 S. 13(4))	The particulars required on directors' interests may alternatively be given in a note.
Directors retiring	
CA48 S. 185	All directors aged 70 or over must, subject to the Articles, be reappointed annually if the company is a public company or the subsidiary of a UK public company.
Political and charitable donations	
CA67 S. 19 SI 1980 No. 1055	Exemption if: (*a*) Total less than £200 (*b*) Wholly owned subsidiary of a GB company. Name recipient of each political contribution over £200.
Close company	
	Disclosure of close company status may be made, but is only required for listed companies.
Auditors	
CA76 S. 14	Auditors are required to be reappointed annually by the shareholders (unless company is dormant – CA81 S. 12)
Authorisation or signature	
	Change to 'On behalf of the board' if signed by a director or chairman, other than as secretary.
Disabled persons	
SI 1980 No. 1160	See Good Group P.L.C.

Good Practice Limited
Directors' Report

Events since the end of the year
The company completed the sale of its leasehold property in Berwick-upon-Tweed on March 10, 19X2 realising a gain after tax on disposal of £7,750.

An export contract to the U.S.A. worth £80,000 has been won against substantial competition. The contract is due for delivery in September 19X2.

Directors and their interests
The directors at December 31, 19X1 and their interests in the share capital of the company (all beneficially held except those marked with an asterisk which are held as trustee) were as follows:

	At December 31, 19X1	At January 1, 19X1 or subsequent date of appointment
	Ordinary shares	*Ordinary shares*
J.N. Smith (Chairman)	1,000	1,000
F.R. Brown	625	625
	2,500*	2,500*
J. Archer	—	—
P.A. MacBryde (Appointed July 1, 19X1)	250	125

No director was interested in the preference shares at either date.

In addition R.D. Dixon served as a director until June 30, 19X1 when he resigned.

P.A. MacBryde retires from the board at the Annual General Meeting and, being eligible, offers himself for re-election. J. Archer retires by rotation and, being eligible, offers himself for re-election.

Political and charitable contributions
During the year the company made a political contribution of £250 to the Conservative Party and various charitable contributions totalling £1,000.

Auditors
A resolution to reappoint as auditors Chartered Accountants & Co. will be put to the members at the Annual General Meeting.

By order of the Board

J. Harris
Secretary.
June 25, 19X2

Source	*Comments*
General	
CA48 S. 156 CA67 S. 14 CA76 S. 1(5)	An audit report is required to be attached to every set of accounts prepared for every accounting reference period (except dormant companies CA81 S. 12).
ICAS 7.102 ICAEW 3.102	The audit report should state whether in the opinion of the auditors the balance sheet and profit and loss account comply with the Companies Acts and give a 'true and fair view'. The scope of the report may be restricted for certain types of company, e.g. banks and insurance companies.
SSAP 10	Reference should also be made to the source and application of funds in the opinion paragraph of the report.
CA67 S.14	If applicable state that: (*a*) proper accounting records have *not* been kept (*b*) proper returns have *not* been obtained from branches *not* visited by the auditor (*c*) the accounts are *not* in agreement with the accounting records and returns (*d*) all information and explanations considered necessary for the audit have *not* been obtained.
CA76 S. 12	Accounting records shall be sufficient to show and explain the company's transactions and to ensure that the accounts give a true and fair view.
ICAS 7.102 ICAEW 3.102	Refer to the accounting convention under which the accounts have been prepared.
ICAS 7.103 ICAEW 3.103	Refer to significant departures from SSAPs where: (*a*) they are not explained in the accounts; or (*b*) they are explained in the accounts but the auditor does not concur.
	The date on the audit report should be the date on which the auditors agreed to sign the report which should be on or after the date of board approval of the financial statements.
CA48 S. 196 (8) CA67 S. 6(4) CA80 S. 59	If the information required on directors' emoluments, loans and material interests in contracts is not given the auditors must disclose it in their report.
CA67 S. 23A (CA81 S. 15)	If the information in the directors' report is *not* consistent with the accounts the auditors must disclose the fact in their report.

Report of the Auditors

to the members of Good Practice Limited

We have audited the accounts on pages 21 to 39 in accordance with approved auditing standards.

In our opinion the accounts, which have been prepared under the historical cost convention modified to include the revaluation of freehold land and buildings, give a true and fair view of the state of the company's affairs at December 31, 19X1 and of its profit and source and application of funds for the year then ended and comply with the Companies Acts 1948 to 1981.

Chartered Accountants & Co.
June 25, 19X2.

Source	*Comments*
General	
CA76 S. 1 CA48 S. 149 (CA81 S. 1)	Profit and loss account (with comparative figures) to be drawn up for the defined accounting reference period and in one of the required formats. For an example of another format see Good Group P.L.C.
	Profit and loss account to give a true and fair view of profit or loss for the period. This is an overriding requirement.
Sch. 12 Sch. 90	Only realised profits* may be included in the profit and loss account.
Interest payable	
Sch. 53	Disclose interest or similar charges on: (*a*) all bank loans and overdrafts, and other loans wholly repayable within five years (either by instalments or otherwise); and (*b*) all other loans.
Profit on ordinary activities before taxation	
Sch. 3(6)	This amount must be shown.
Dividends	
Sch. 3(7)	The aggregate of dividends paid or proposed must be separately disclosed on the face of the profit and loss account.
Retained profit brought forward	
	For an example of prior year adjustment see Good Group P.L.C.
Reserves	
Sch. 3(7)	Transfers to and from reserves must be disclosed on the face of the profit and loss account.

Good Practice Limited

Profit and loss account

for the year ended December 31, 19X1

	Notes		19X1	19X0
		£	£	£
Turnover	2		395,750	326,750
Change in stocks of finished goods and work in progress			1,500	(2,745)
			397,250	324,005
Other operating income	3		3,125	3,250
			400,375	327,255
Raw materials and consumables		149,600		117,905
Other external charges		14,600		3,420
			164,200	121,325
			236,175	205,930
Staff costs	4	134,375		121,000
Depreciation		11,125		9,750
Other operating charges		64,750		64,780
			210,250	195,530
Operating profit	5		25,925	10,400
Income from investments	6		1,250	1,000
Interest payable on loan not wholly repayable within five years			(1,400)	(1,400)
Profit on ordinary activities before taxation			25,775	10,000
Tax on profit on ordinary activities	7		7,015	4,000
Profit on ordinary activities after taxation			18,760	6,000
Extraordinary charge after taxation	8		2,250	—
Profit for the financial year			16,510	6,000
Dividends	9		3,935	3,685
			12,575	2,315
Retained profit brought forward			35,740	33,425
Retained profit carried forward			£48,315	£35,740

The notes on pages 27 to 39 form part of these accounts

Source	*Comments*
General	
CA76 S. 1 CA48 S. 149 (CA81 S. 1)	Balance sheet (with comparative figures) to be drawn up in one of the required formats at the date to which the profit and loss account is drawn up. It must give a true and fair view of the state of affairs of the company. This is an overriding requirement.
Intangible fixed assets	
Sch. formats	Must be separately disclosed on the face of the balance sheet.
Sch. Note 2 to the formats	Concessions, patents, licences, trade marks and similar items may only be shown as assets if they were acquired for a valuable consideration or the asset was created by the company itself.
Sch. Note 3 to the formats	Goodwill may only be included to the extent that it was acquired for valuable consideration.
Sch. 3(2)	Preliminary expenses, share or debenture issue expenses and commission, and costs of research may not be shown as an asset.
Investments	
Sch. formats	Disclose interests in and indebtedness with related companies* defined in Sch. 91 similarly to associated companies in SSAP 1 and ED 25.
Sch. formats	Disclose investments held as current assets.*
Creditors	
Sch. formats	Exclude non-current amounts from current liabilities.
Sch. 47	Disclose provisions for taxation.
Loan instalment/bank loan	
Sch. formats SSAP 10	Classify as a current liability any balance or part thereof due to be extinguished within one year from the balance sheet date. These amounts should also be treated as part of net liquid funds in the statement of source and application of funds.
Called up share capital	
Sch. Note 11 to the formats	The amount of allotted and the amount of called up share capital which has been paid up must be shown separately.
Signatures	
CA48 S. 155	Every balance sheet of a company to be signed on behalf of the board by two directors or, if only one director, by that director. The directors may date their signature to indicate the date on which the accounts were formally considered and approved in accordance with SSAP 17. For alternative presentation see Good Group P.L.C. page 63.

Good Practice Limited

Balance sheet

at December 31, 19X1

	Notes	£	19X1 £	19X0 £
Fixed assets				
Tangible assets:	10			
Land and buildings			63,000	51,400
Plant and machinery			33,510	21,710
			96,510	73,110
Investments	11		11,250	13,625
			107,760	86,735
Current assets				
Stocks	12	34,000		35,000
Long term contracts	13	12,250		10,000
Debtors	14	62,500		52,500
Cash at bank and in hand		17,887		12,012
		126,637		109,512
Creditors: amounts falling due within one year				
Current instalment due on bank loan	16	2,500		—
Loan from a former director	17	8,250		5,750
Payments received on account	13	9,500		7,500
Trade creditors	15	64,112		69,757
Current corporation tax		3,925		2,910
Other taxes and social security costs		3,100		2,400
Proposed dividend		1,500		1,250
Other creditors		6,300		6,180
Accruals		2,600		1,920
		101,787		97,667
Net current assets			24,850	11,845
Total assets less current liabilities			132,610	98,580
Creditors: amounts falling due after more than one year				
Bank loan	16		(15,000)	(17,500)
Provision for liabilities and charges				
Deferred taxation	18		(1,045)	(1,340)
Accruals and deferred income				
Deferred government grants			(7,000)	(4,000)
			£109,565	£75,740
Capital and reserves				
Called up share capital	19		43,750	37,500
Share premium account	20		5,000	2,500
Revaluation reserve	21		12,500	—
Profit and loss account			48,315	35,740
			£109,565	£75,740

J.N. Smith *Director*
J. Archer *Director*
June 25, 19X2

The notes on pages 27 to 39 form part of these accounts

23

Source	*Comments*
General	
SSAP 10	A statement of source and application of funds (with comparative figures) is required in all financial accounts intended to give a true and fair view of financial position and profit or loss.
	Exemption for any enterprise with turnover or gross income of less than £25,000 per annum.
	A minimum of 'netting-off' should take place i.e. only immaterial items should be netted.
	All borrowings repayable within one year of the accounting date should be included as part of net liquid funds.
	Alternative presentation where there is a loss on operations after adding back items not involving the movement of funds:

		19X1	19X0
	£	£	£
Source of funds:			
Total generated from operations†		—	13,500
Proceeds of share issue		8,750	—
		8,750	13,500
Application of funds:			
Funds absorbed by operations†	(16,625)		—
Purchase of fixed assets	(1,250)		(1,000)
		(17,875)	(1,000)
Working capital – (decrease)/increase		£(9,125)	£12,500

	19X1	19X0
	£	£
†Total (absorbed)/generated by operations:		
(Loss)/profit after taxation	(25,000)	6,000
Adjustment for item not involving the movement of funds:		
Depreciation	8,375	7,500
	£(16,625)	£13,500

Good Practice Limited

Statement of source and application of funds

for the year ended December 31, 19X1

		19X1	19X0
	£	£	£
Source of funds			
Profit on ordinary activities before taxation		25,775	10,000
Adjustment for items not involving the movement of working capital:			
Depreciation		11,125	9,750
Loss/(profit) on disposal of tangible fixed assets		250	(375)
Release from deferred government grants		(1,000)	(750)
Profit on disposal of investments		(500)	—
Total generated from operations		35,650	18,625
Funds from other sources			
Proceeds of share issue		8,750	—
Increase in loan from former director		2,500	(1,250)
Proceeds of disposal of tangible fixed assets		9,625	6,225
Proceeds of sale of investments		8,995	—
Government grants received		4,000	2,500
		69,520	26,100
Application of funds			
Dividends paid	(3,685)		(3,438)
Extraordinary expenses (before taxation)	(3,750)		—
Purchase of tangible fixed assets	(31,900)		(17,500)
Purchase of investments	(6,120)		(3,000)
Current instalment due on loan	(2,500)		—
Tax paid	(4,795)		(1,112)
		(52,750)	(25,050)
Working capital – increase/(decrease)		£16,770	£1,050
Components of increase/(decrease) in working capital			
Stocks		(1,000)	2,245
Long term contracts		2,250	(800)
Debtors and prepayments		10,000	2,062
Payments received on account		(2,000)	(1,500)
Creditors		4,145	(2,207)
		13,395	(200)
Movement in net liquid funds			
Bank and cash	5,875		1,250
Current instalment due on loan	(2,500)		—
		3,375	1,250
		£16,770	£1,050

The notes on pages 27 to 39 form part of these accounts

25

Source	*Comments*
Depreciation	
Sch. 18 SSAP 12	The depreciable amount of a depreciating asset should be allocated on a systematic basis to each accounting period during the useful life of the asset.
	Freehold land should not be depreciated, unless its expected residual value is less than book value.
Sch. 32 and 34 SSAP 12	On revaluation the revalued amount less any residual value should be depreciated over the remaining useful life. The revaluation reserve arising may be written off under certain circumstances.
Deferred government grants	
SSAP 4	Capital grants may alternatively be deducted from the cost of the relevant asset.
Stocks	
SSAP 9 Sch. 23	Stocks and work-in-progress other than long term contracts should be valued at the lower of cost and net realisable value.
Sch. 27	The Act allows the use of FIFO, LIFO, weighted average price, and other similar methods for valuing stocks and fungible assets* but the method chosen must appear to the directors to be appropriate. Thus SSAP 9 should normally be followed.
Long term contracts	
SSAP 9	Long term contract work should be valued at cost plus attributable profit, less foreseeable losses and progress payments received and receivable.
Research and development	
Sch. 20 SSAP 13	Under certain circumstances development expenditure may be deferred. See Good Group P.L.C.
Sch. 3(2) SSAP 13	Research costs must be written off.
Deferred taxation	
SSAP 15	Where material, deferred taxation should be accounted for, using either the deferral or liability method, on all short term timing differences and, in the case of all other timing differences, on the full amount of such differences other than any whose effect is expected to continue.
SSAP 8	ACT can be shown as deferred tax asset if recovery is reasonably certain and foreseeable – see Good Group P.L.C.
Foreign currencies	
Sch. 58(1)	Disclose the basis of translation of foreign currencies. A SSAP dealing with foreign currency translations is expected to be published in 1982; the accounting policy illustrated here may have to be amended for subsequent accounting periods in the light of that SSAP.
General	
Sch. 10 to 13	Fundamental accounting concepts should be followed – going concern, consistency, prudence and accruals.
Sch. 15 SSAP 2	Disclose if any fundamental accounting concept has not been observed giving particulars of the departure, the reasons and the effect.
Sch. 36 and 58(1) SSAP 2	Disclose all material accounting policies including policies for translating foreign currencies and depreciation.

Good Practice Limited

Notes to the accounts

at December 31, 19X1

1. Accounting policies

Accounting convention

The accounts are prepared under the historical cost convention, modified to include the revaluation of freehold land and buildings.

Depreciation

Depreciation is provided on all tangible fixed assets, other than freehold land, at rates calculated to write off the cost or valuation, less estimated residual value, of each asset evenly over its expected useful life, as follows:

Freehold buildings	– over 50 years
Leasehold land and buildings	– over the lease term
Plant and machinery	– over 5 to 15 years

Deferred government grants

Government grants on capital expenditure are credited to a deferral account and are released to revenue over the expected useful life of the relevant asset by equal annual amounts.

Grants of a revenue nature are credited to income in the period to which they relate.

Stocks

Stocks are stated at the lower of cost and net realisable value as follows:

Cost incurred in bringing each product to its present location and condition:

Raw materials	– purchase cost on a first-in, first-out basis
Work-in-progress and finished goods	– cost of direct materials and labour plus attributable overheads based on the normal level of activity

Net realisable value is based on estimated selling price less further costs expected to be incurred to completion and disposal.

Long term contracts

Long term contract work-in-progress is stated at cost (as defined in Stocks above) plus attributable profits, estimated to be earned to date based on the stage of completion, less provision for any known or anticipated losses and payments on account received or receivable.

Research and development

Research and development expenditure is written off as incurred.

Deferred taxation

Deferred taxation is provided on the liability method on all short term timing differences. Provision is also made for long term timing differences, except for those which are not expected to reverse in the future.

Foreign currencies

Assets and liabilities denominated in foreign currencies are translated at the rate of exchange ruling at the balance sheet date.

Transactions in foreign currencies are recorded at the rate ruling at the date of the transaction.

All differences are taken to the profit and loss account.

Source	*Comments*
Turnover	
Sch. 94	Turnover must be net of trade discounts, VAT and similar taxes and derives from the provision of goods and services falling within the company's ordinary activities.
Sch. 55	Disclosure must be given in respect of each class of business and each geographical market unless the directors believe it would be seriously prejudicial to the interests of the company. The fact that the information is omitted must be stated.
	Where turnover is given for more than one class of business, profit before taxation must be similarly analysed.
Profit	
Sch. 53(3)	Disclose any amounts respectively set aside for redemption of share capital and loans.
Sch. 57(3) SSAP 6	Disclose exceptional items.
Sch. 53(4) to (7)	Disclose hire of plant, auditors remuneration, rental income if material, and income from listed investments.
Employees' share schemes	
Sch. 51(2)	The aggregate amount of financial assistance provided under CA81 S. 42(6) for employees' share schemes or direct to employees for the purchase of shares in the company or its holding company shall be disclosed for each item in question.
Particulars of staff	
Sch. 56	The average number of employees to be analysed into categories determined by directors.
	Staff costs* must be analysed into wages and salaries, social security costs*, and other pension costs.
Sch. 93	Social security costs* defined as contributions to State Scheme made by the company.
	Staff include the directors.
Directors' remuneration	
CA48 S. 196	Disclose fees, other emoluments, pensions and compensation for loss of office.
	Include amounts paid by any person.
	For compensation for loss of office distinguish by whom the payments are made.
CA67 S. 6 SI 1979 No. 1618	Disclose emoluments of chairman, highest paid director (if more than the chairman) and other directors (within rising bands of £5,000) excluding pension contributions. Not required in respect of:
	(*a*) non-group companies with total directors' emoluments (including pension contributions) under £40,000; or
	(*b*) emoluments of directors whose duties are mainly discharged outside the UK.
CA67 S. 7	Disclose number of directors waiving emoluments and aggregate amount thereof.
CA67 S. 8 SI 1979 No. 1618	Show the number of employees (excluding directors and persons working mainly outside the UK) in rising bands of £5,000 with emoluments over £20,000 a year.

Good Practice Limited
Notes to the accounts
at December 31, 19X1

2. Turnover

Turnover represents the invoiced amount of goods sold and services provided stated net of value added tax and, in the case of long term contracts, the value of work done during the year.

The turnover and pre-tax profit is attributable to one activity, the manufacture and installation of fire-prevention equipment. An analysis of turnover by market is given below:

	19X1	19X0
	£	£
United Kingdom	330,750	294,750
U.S.A.	65,000	32,000
	£395,750	£326,750

3. Other operating income

	19X1	19X0
	£	£
Rental income	£3,125	£3,250

4. Staff costs

	19X1	19X0
	£	£
Wages and salaries	109,355	98,670
Social security costs	21,520	19,230
Other pension costs	3,500	3,100
	£134,375	£121,000

The average weekly number of employees during the year was 34 made up as follows:

	No.	No.
Office and management	12	11
Manufacturing and installation	22	20
	34	31

5. Operating profit

	19X1	19X0
	£	£
This is stated after charging:		
Directors' remuneration (see below)	34,000	28,000
Hire of plant and machinery	3,750	3,375
Auditors' remuneration	1,565	1,435

	£	£
Directors' remuneration consists of:		
Fees	500	—
Other emoluments (including pension contributions)	30,000	25,500
Pensions to former directors	3,500	2,500
	£34,000	£28,000

Source	*Comments*
Taxation	
Sch. 54	Basis for computing UK corporation and income tax to be stated.
SSAP 8	Any special circumstances affecting the liability in respect of taxation on profits, income or capital gains for the current financial year or succeeding financial years should be explained.
	Any oversea tax to be separately disclosed and the corporation tax charge shown gross of any double tax relief.
SSAP 15	If advance corporation tax cannot be set against the balance on the deferred taxation account and recovery cannot be foreseen with reasonable certainty, the balance must be written off and separately disclosed.
Extraordinary items	
Sch. 57(2)	Disclose particulars of extraordinary items.
SSAP 6	Extraordinary items are defined as items which derive from events or transactions outside the ordinary activities of the business and which are both material and expected not to recur frequently or regularly.
Sch. format	Extraordinary income, charges, the net of these two and tax on the net amount must be shown separately on the face of the profit and loss account or in a note.
Dividends	
Sch. 49	Disclose the amount and period for which each class of dividend is in arrears.
Sch. 51(3)	Disclose recommended dividends.

Good Practice Limited
Notes to the accounts
at December 31, 19X1

6. Income from investments

	19X1 £	19X0 £
Listed	750	500
Unlisted	500	500
	£1,250	£1,000

7. Tax on profit on ordinary activities

	19X1 £	19X0 £
Based on the profit for the year:		
Corporation tax at 40% (19X0 – 40%)	6,887	3,575
Tax credits attributable to dividends received	375	300
Deferred taxation	(187)	250
	7,075	4,125
Taxation overprovided in previous years	(60)	(125)
	£7,015	£4,000

If full provision had been made for the potential amount of deferred tax, the tax charge for the year would have been increased by £2,975 (19X0 – £1,105).

8. Extraordinary charge

	19X1 £	19X0 £
Expenses connected with factory subsidence due to uncharted mine workings	3,750	—
Corporation tax relief on extraordinary charge	(1,500)	—
	£2,250	£—

9. Dividends

	19X1 £	19X0 £
Preference – paid	875	875
Ordinary – interim paid	1,560	1,560
– final proposed	1,500	1,250
	£3,935	£3,685

Source	*Comments*
Fixed assets* (intangible, tangible and investments)	
Sch. 42	State the method of arriving at the value of fixed assets (e.g. 'cost' or 'cost or valuation'). Disclose aggregate additions, disposals, revaluations and transfers.
Sch. 33	For each balance sheet item revalued (except stocks) give comparable amounts under the historical cost convention or the differences between revaluation and cost. 'Comparable amounts' covers aggregate cost and aggregate depreciation.
Sch. 34(4) CA80 S. 39(5)	Release to distributable reserves any revaluation surplus relating to assets which have been sold, or, in the case of depreciating assets, that proportion which has been depreciated. Disclose amount released during the year.
Tangible fixed assets	
ED 26	Contains special provisions for investment properties.
Sch. 44	Distinguish between freeholds, long leaseholds and short leaseholds. Short leaseholds are defined as those with less that 50 years *to run.* (Sch. 82).
Sch. 43 SSAP 12	For assets shown at valuation, disclose the years and amounts of valuation. If the current year, also disclose names or qualification of valuers, basis of valuation and the effect on depreciation (if material).
Sch. 19 SSAP 12	Disclose details of any provision for diminution in value in addition to the normal depreciation charge and also any provisions written back.
	A change in depreciation method, e.g. from reducing balance to straight line, or in depreciation rate should be accounted for by writing off the remaining balance on the new basis over the remaining life. Disclose effect in year of change, if material.
	Gross amount and accumulated depreciation of *all* depreciable assets to be disclosed.
SSAP 12	Where stated at valuation, depreciation should be charged on the revalued amount disclosing effect on the depreciation charge, if material, in the year of change.
SSAP 15	Recognition of the tax on the potential capital gain on disposal at valuation does not have to be made in the accounts, other than by way of note, where it can be demonstrated that no liability is expected to arise in the foreseeable future.

Good Practice Limited
Notes to the accounts
at December 31, 19X1

10. Tangible fixed assets

	Land and buildings Freehold	Short leasehold	Plant and machinery	Total
	£	£	£	£
Cost or valuation:				
At January 1, 19X1	45,000	9,875	58,250	113,125
Additions	—	375	31,525	31,900
Surplus on revaluation	10,000	—	—	10,000
Disposals	—	(1,000)	(22,000)	(23,000)
At December 31, 19X1	55,000	9,250	67,775	132,025
Depreciation:				
At January 1, 19X1	2,000	1,475	36,540	40,015
Provided during the year	500	400	10,225	11,125
Surplus on revaluation	(2,500)	—	—	(2,500)
Disposals	—	(625)	(12,500)	(13,125)
At December 31, 19X1	—	1,250	34,265	35,515
Net book amounts at December 31, 19X1	£55,000	£8,000	£33,510	£96,510
Net book amounts at January 1, 19X1	£43,000	£8,400	£21,710	£73,110

For the freehold land and buildings included at valuation:

	£
Historical cost:	
At January 1, 19X1 and December 31, 19X1	£45,000
Depreciation based on cost:	
At January 1, 19X1	2,000
Charge for the year	500
At December 31, 19X1	£2,500
Net historical cost value:	
At December 31, 19X1	£42,500
At January 1, 19X1	£43,000

The freehold properties were valued at December 31, 19X1, by Estate Valuers & Co. Chartered Surveyors, on an open market basis at an amount of £55,000 including £23,000 in respect of land. The surplus of £12,500 has been credited to revaluation reserve. The depreciation charge in the future will be increased by £140 per annum.

Source	*Comments*
Investments	
Sch. 45	Divide listed investments between those with permission to deal on a recognised stock exchange and others for both fixed and current asset investments.
	Give market value and if stock exchange value is less than market value disclose both.
CA67 S. 4(1A) (CA81 S. 3) CA81 S. 4	For all investments in which the investor holds more than 10% of any class of equity share capital, or more than 10% of all allotted share capital, and for all investments having a book value in excess of 10% of the investor's own assets, give additional disclosure. See Appendix 2.
	When the number of bodies is large only those principally affecting the profit or assets need to be given but see CA67 S. 4(5).
SSAP 15	The amount of tax payable if the investments were sold at valuation should be disclosed.
	Directors' valuation for unlisted investments is no longer required.
Stocks	
Sch. format SSAP 9	Show separate amounts for all significant stock categories.
Sch. 26(3)	Disclose any interest included in the production cost* of any asset.
Sch. 27(3) to (5)	Disclose difference, if material, for each category of stock between carrying value and replacement cost. The most recent purchase price* or production cost* may be used but only if it constitutes a more appropriate standard of comparison than does replacement cost.
Long term contracts	
SSAP 9	Disclose total of work-in-progress at cost plus attributable profit, less foreseeable losses, less total of progress payments received and receivable.
Sch. Note 8 to the formats	Show payments received on account of orders separately under creditors except where they are shown as deductions from stocks.
CA48 S. 149 (CA81 S. 1)	The inclusion of profit on long term contracts is a departure from the valuation rules for current assets (Sch. 22 and 23) to enable the accounts to give a true and fair view. It is therefore necessary to give additional particulars.
Creditors	
ICAS 4.5 ICAEW 2.207	Goods sold subject to reservation of title should be mentioned if material.

Good Practice Limited
Notes to the accounts
at December 31, 19X1

11. Investments

		£
Cost:		
At January 1, 19X1		13,625
Additions		6,120
Disposals		(8,495)
At December 31, 19X1		£11,250

	19X1	19X0
	£	£
Listed investments	3,875	3,875
Unlisted investments	7,375	9,750
	£11,250	£13,625
Valuation:		
Listed investments – market value	£30,000	£25,000
Taxation on potential capital gain if sold at valuation	£7,800	£6,300

The listed investments are dealt on a recognised stock exchange.
The company owns 15% of the issued ordinary share capital of Southlands Limited, an unlisted company registered in England.

12. Stocks

	19X1	19X0
	£	£
Raw materials	11,500	14,000
Work-in-progress	14,750	11,250
Finished goods	7,750	9,750
	£34,000	£35,000

Finished goods would amount to £10,650 (19X0 – £11,920) if valued at replacement cost at December 31, 19X1.

13. Long term contracts

	19X1	19X0
	£	£
Cost to date plus attributable profit less provision for losses	44,000	38,250
Payments received on account	31,750	28,250
	£12,250	£10,000

Profit is included on long term contracts in accordance with Statement of Standard Accounting Practice No. 9 and amounts to £3,000 (19X0 – £2,000). The inclusion of such profit is a departure from the statutory valuation rules for current assets and is required by S. 149 (3) of the Companies Act 1948 to enable the accounts to give a true and fair view. Progress payments received in excess of the value of work done on individual contracts are shown separately under current liabilities in the balance sheet.

14. Debtors

	19X1	19X0
	£	£
Trade debtors	56,250	47,340
Other debtors (Note 26)	4,000	3,200
Prepayments	2,250	1,960
	£62,500	£52,500

15. Trade creditors

Included in trade creditors are amounts totalling £9,750 (19X0 – £6,875) due in respect of goods for which title does not pass until payment is made.

Source	*Comments*
Loans	
Sch. 48	For each item shown under creditors disclose aggregate amount of debts not wholly payable or repayable within five years (*a*) by instalments and (*b*) otherwise. Also disclose aggregate amount of instalments due after five years.
	Repayment terms and rates of interest must be given for each debt not wholly repayable within five years. Where a statement would be of excessive length only a general indication is required.
	For each item also disclose the aggregate amount of secured liabilities and give an indication of the nature of the securities.
Loan	
Sch. 84	Loans without fixed repayment terms should be treated as falling due on the earliest date on which the lender could require payment if he exercises all the options and rights available to him.
Deferred taxation	
SSAP 15	Give amounts for each material timing difference both provided and potential.
SSAP 8	The amount of ACT that can be set off against deferred taxation is subject to the same limit as applies in computing the amount of reduction in the corporation tax liability as a result of ACT.
Sch. 34(5)	Explain taxation implications of amounts included in revaluation reserve.
Share capital	
Sch. 38(1)	Give number and aggregate nominal value of authorised and allotted shares of each class.
Sch. 38(2)	Give details of redeemable shares.
Sch. 39	For all shares allotted during the year give, class by class, reasons, classes of shares, number, nominal value and consideration received.
Sch. 40	Give details for any contingent right to allotment of shares.
Debentures	
Sch. 41	Give details of debentures issued, redeemed and held by trust or nominee.
Share premium account	
Sch. 46	Disclose movements.

Good Practice Limited
Notes to the accounts
at December 31, 19X1

16. Bank loan

The long term bank loan bears interest at 8% per annum and is repayable in annual instalments of £2,500 commencing October 31, 19X2.

	19X1	19X0
	£	£
Amounts repayable within five years	12,500	10,000
Amounts repayable after five years	5,000	7,500
	£17,500	£17,500

The current portion of the loan amounting to £2,500 (19X0 – £Nil) is shown in current liabilities. The loan is secured on the freehold property.

17. Loan

The loan from a former director is interest free and there is no fixed date for repayment.

18. Deferred taxation

Deferred taxation provided in the accounts and the potential amounts, including the amounts for which provision has been made, are as follows:

	Provision		Potential	
	19X1	19X0	19X1	19X0
	£	£	£	£
Capital allowances in advance of depreciation and amortisation	—	—	9,662	6,687
Other differences in recognising revenue and expense items in other periods for taxation purposes	1,688	1,875	1,688	1,875
	1,688	1,875	11,350	8,562
Less: Advance corporation tax on proposed dividend	643	535	643	535
	1,045	1,340	10,707	8,027
Taxation on valuation surplus	—	—	3,650	—
	£1,045	£1,340	£14,357	£8,027

19. Share capital

	Authorised		Allotted, issued and fully paid	
	19X1	19X0	19X1	19X0
	No.	No.	£	£
Ordinary shares of £1 each	50,000	37,500	31,250	25,000
10% (now 7% plus tax credit) preference shares of £1 each	12,500	12,500	12,500	12,500
	62,500	50,000	£43,750	£37,500

During the year 6,250 ordinary shares of £1 each with an aggregate nominal value of £6,250, were issued fully paid for cash of £8,750 to help finance the purchase of plant and machinery.

20. Share premium account

	19X1	19X0
	£	£
At January 1, 19X1	2,500	2,500
On issue of shares during the year	2,500	—
At December 31, 19X1	£5,000	£2,500

Source	*Comments*
Revaluation reserve	
Sch. 46	Disclose movements.
Post balance sheet events	
Sch. 12(*b*) SSAP 17	Include all material adjusting events up to the date that the accounts are formally approved by the directors. Disclose nature of event and an estimate of the financial effect for non-adjusting events. The tax implications of the event should be disclosed where necessary for a proper understanding of the financial position.
Guarantees and financial commitments	
Sch. 50	Give particulars (including amount where practicable) of any charge on the assets of the company to secure the liabilities of any other person or details of any other restrictions on the title to assets. Give details of pension commitments including any provisions in the balance sheet, giving separate details for past directors. Give any other financial commitments relevant to assessing the company's affairs. Give capital commitments analysed as shown in note 23.
Sch. 50 SSAP 18	All material contingencies (gains and losses) should be disclosed with an estimate of the financial effect before tax where this is possible. Give the legal nature and details of any security. The tax implications of the contingency crystallising should be explained where necessary for a proper understanding of the financial position.
Directors' loans	
CA80 S. 54 and 55	Disclose details of loans to directors of the company, or the persons connected* with such directors, made by the company subsisting at any time during the year. Loans include quasi-loans* and credit transactions.* Disclose details of any other transaction or arrangement with the company in which a director of the company has (or had) a material interest (either directly or through connected* persons).
Loans to officers	
CA80 S. 56	Give number of officers and aggregate amount at the year end for each of loans, quasi-loans* and credit transactions.*

Good Practice Limited
Notes to the accounts
at December 31, 19X1

21. Revaluation reserve

	19X1	19X0
	£	£
Arising on revaluation during the year (Note 10)	12,500	—
Amortisation for the year	—	—
At December 31, 19X1	£12,500	£--

22. Sale of property subsequent to year end

The company completed the sale of its leasehold property in Berwick-upon-Tweed on March 10, 19X2 and realised a gain on disposal of £7,750 (after providing for taxation of £2,902) which will be credited to the profit and loss account in 19X2.

23. Capital commitments

	19X1	19X0
Contracted	£33,500	£16,250
Authorised but not contracted	£6,125	£3,000

In arriving at the above amounts government grants have not been taken into account.

24. Contingent liabilities

	19X1	19X0
Guarantee of the bank overdraft of a supplier	£10,000	£10,000
Bills discounted	£1,250	£1,000

25. Pension commitments

The company has pension commitments to past directors amounting to £3,500 (19X0 – £2,500) per annum at December 31, 19X1 consisting of premiums payable under annuity policies. The company has no such commitments to the present directors at December 31, 19X1.

26. Other debtors

Included in other debtors is a quasi-loan to a director, J. Archer. It is an interest free season-ticket loan repayable in monthly instalments.

	19X1	19X0
Amount outstanding at end of the year	£650	£820
Maximum outstanding during the year	£910	£860

Appendix C

Companies Act 1981

SCHEDULE 1

(SCHEDULE TO BE INSERTED IN THE 1948 ACT AS SCHEDULE 8)

ACCOUNTS

PART I

BASIC REQUIREMENTS WITH RESPECT TO THE FORM AND CONTENT OF A COMPANY'S ACCOUNTS

SECTION A

GENERAL RULES WITH RESPECT TO THE FORM AND CONTENT OF ACCOUNTS

1.–(1) Subject to the following provisions of this Schedule–

(*a*) every balance sheet of a company shall show the items listed in either of the balance sheet formats set out below in section B of this Part; and

(*b*) every profit and loss account of a company shall show the items listed in any one of the profit and loss account formats so set out;

in either case in the order and under the headings and sub-headings given in the format adopted.

(2) Sub-paragraph (1) above shall not be read as requiring the heading or sub-heading for any item to be distinguished by any letter or number assigned to that item in the format adopted.

2.–(1) Where in accordance with paragraph 1 above a company's balance sheet or profit and loss account for any financial year has been prepared by reference to one of the formats set out in section B below, the directors of the company shall adopt the same format in preparing the accounts for subsequent financial years of the company unless in their opinion there are special reasons for a change.

(2) Particulars of any change in the format adopted in preparing a company's balance sheet or profit and loss account in accordance with paragraph 1 above shall be disclosed, and the reasons for the change shall be explained, in a note to the accounts in which the new format is first adopted.

3.–(1) Any item required in accordance with paragraph 1 above to be shown in a company's balance sheet or profit and loss account may be shown in greater detail than required by the format adopted.

(2) A company's balance sheet or profit and loss account may include an item representing or covering the amount of any asset or liability, income or expenditure not otherwise covered by any of the items listed in the format adopted, but the following shall not be treated as assets in any company's balance sheet–

(*a*) preliminary expenses;

(*b*) expenses of and commission on any issue of shares or debentures; and

(*c*) costs of research.

(3) In preparing a company's balance sheet or profit and loss account the directors of the company shall adapt the arrangement and headings and sub-headings otherwise required by paragraph 1 above in respect of items to which an Arabic number is assigned in the format adopted, in any case where the special nature of the company's business requires such adaptation.

(4) Items to which Arabic numbers are assigned in any of the formats set out in section B below may be combined in a company's accounts for any financial year if either–

(*a*) their individual amounts are not material to assessing the state of affairs or profit or loss of the company for that year; or

(*b*) the combination facilitates that assessment;

but in a case within paragraph (*b*) above the individual amounts of any items so combined shall be disclosed in a note to the accounts.

(5) Subject to paragraph 4(3) below, a heading or sub-heading corresponding to an item listed in the format adopted in preparing a company's balance sheet or profit and loss account shall not be included if there is no amount to be shown for that item in respect of the financial year to which the balance sheet or profit and loss account relates.

(6) Every profit and loss account of a company shall show the amount of the company's profit or loss on ordinary activities before taxation.

(7) Every profit and loss account of a company shall show separately as additional items–

(*a*) any amount set aside or proposed to be set aside to, or withdrawn or proposed to be withdrawn from, reserves; and

(*b*) the aggregate amount of any dividends paid and proposed.

4.–(1) In respect of every item shown in a company's balance sheet or profit and loss account the corresponding amount for the financial year immediately preceding that to which the balance sheet or profit and loss account relates shall also be shown.

(2) Where that corresponding amount is not comparable with the amount to be shown for the item in question in respect of the financial year to which the balance sheet or profit and loss account relates, the former amount shall be adjusted and particulars of the adjustment and the reasons for it shall be disclosed in a note to the accounts.

(3) Paragraph 3(5) above shall not apply in any case where an amount can be shown for the item in question in respect of the financial year immediately preceding that to which the balance sheet or profit and loss account relates, and that amount shall be shown under the heading or sub-heading required by paragraph 1 above for that item.

5. Amounts in respect of items representing assets or income may not be set off against amounts in respect of items representing liabilities or expenditure (as the case may be), or vice versa.

SECTION B

THE REQUIRED FORMATS FOR ACCOUNTS

Preliminary

6. References in this Part of this Schedule to the items listed in any of the formats set out below are references to those items read together with any of the notes following the formats which apply to any of those items, and the requirement imposed by paragraph 1 above to show the items listed in any such format in the order adopted in the format is subject to any provision in those notes for alternative positions for any particular items.

7. A number in brackets following any item in any of the formats set out below is a reference to the note of that number in the notes following the formats.

8. In the notes following the formats–

(*a*) the heading of each note gives the required heading or sub-heading for the item to which it applies and a reference to any letters and numbers assigned to that item in the formats set out below (taking a reference in the case of Format 2 of the balance sheet formats to the item listed under "Assets" or under "Liabilities" as the case may require); and

(*b*) references to a numbered format are references to the balance sheet format or (as the case may require) to the profit and loss account format of that number set out below.

Balance Sheet Formats

Format 1

A. Called up share capital not paid (*1*)

B. Fixed assets

I Intangible assets
1. Development costs
2. Concessions, patents, licences, trade marks and similar rights and assets (*2*)
3. Goodwill (*3*)
4. Payments on account

II Tangible assets
1. Land and buildings
2. Plant and machinery
3. Fixtures, fittings, tools and equipment
4. Payments on account and assets in course of construction

III Investments
1. Shares in group companies
2. Loans to group companies
3. Shares in related companies
4. Loans to related companies
5. Other investments other than loans
6. Other loans
7. Own shares (*4*)

C. Current assets

I Stocks
1. Raw materials and consumables
2. Work in progress
3. Finished goods and goods for resale
4. Payments on account

II Debtors (*5*)
1. Trade debtors
2. Amounts owed by group companies
3. Amounts owed by related companies
4. Other debtors
5. Called up share capital not paid (*1*)
6. Prepayments and accrued income (*6*)

III Investments
1. Shares in group companies
2. Own shares (*4*)
3. Other investments

IV Cash at bank and in hand

D. Prepayments and accrued income (*6*)

E. Creditors: amounts falling due within one year
1. Debenture loans (*7*)
2. Bank loans and overdrafts
3. Payments received on account (*8*)
4. Trade creditors
5. Bills of exchange payable
6. Amounts owed to group companies
7. Amounts owed to related companies
8. Other creditors including taxation and social security (*9*)
9. Accruals and deferred income (*10*)

F. Net current assets (liabilities) (*11*)

G. Total assets less current liabilities

H. Creditors: amounts falling due after more than one year
   1. Debenture loans (7)
   2. Bank loans and overdrafts
   3. Payments received on account (*8*)
   4. Trade creditors
   5. Bills of exchange payable
   6. Amounts owed to group companies
   7. Amounts owed to related companies
   8. Other creditors including taxation and social security (*9*)
   9. Accruals and deferred income (*10*)

I. Provisions for liabilities and charges
   1. Pensions and similar obligations
   2. Taxation, including deferred taxation
   3. Other provisions

J. Accruals and deferred income (*10*)

K. Capital and reserves
   I Called up share capital (*12*)
   II Share premium account
   III Revaluation reserve
   IV Other reserves
      1. Capital redemption reserve
      2. Reserve for own shares
      3. Reserves provided for by the articles of association
      4. Other reserves
   V Profit and loss account.

Balance Sheet Formats

Format 2

ASSETS

A. Called up share capital not paid (*1*)

B. Fixed assets
   I Intangible assets
      1. Development costs
      2. Concessions, patents, licences trade marks and similar rights and assets (*2*)
      3. Goodwill (*3*)
      4. Payments on account
   II Tangible assets
      1. Land and buildings
      2. Plant and machinery
      3. Fixtures, fittings, tools and equipment
      4. Payments on account and assets in course of construction
   III Investments
      1. Shares in group companies
      2. Loans to group companies
      3. Shares in related companies
      4. Loans to related companies
      5. Other investments other than loans
      6. Other loans
      7. Own shares (*4*)

C. Current assets

I Stocks
1. Raw materials and consumables
2. Work in progress
3. Finished goods and goods for resale
4. Payments on account

II Debtors (*5*)
1. Trade debtors
2. Amounts owed by group companies
3. Amounts owed by related companies
4. Other debtors
5. Called up share capital not paid (*1*)
6. Prepayments and accrued income (*6*)

III Investments
1. Shares in group companies
2. Own shares (*4*)
3. Other investments

IV Cash at bank and in hand

D. Prepayments and accrued income (*6*)

LIABILITIES

A. Capital and reserves

I Called up share capital (*12*)

II Share premium account

III Revaluation reserve

IV Other reserves
1. Capital redemption reserve
2. Reserve for own shares
3. Reserves provided for by the articles of association
4. Other reserves

V Profit and loss account

B. Provisions for liabilities and charges
1. Pensions and similar obligations
2. Taxation including deferred taxation
3. Other provisions

C. Creditors (*13*)
1. Debenture loans (*7*)
2. Bank loans and overdrafts
3. Payments received on account (*8*)
4. Trade creditors
5. Bills of exchange payable
6. Amounts owed to group companies
7. Amounts owed to related companies
8. Other creditors including taxation and social security (*9*)
9. Accruals and deferred income (*10*)

D. Accruals and deferred income (*10*)

Notes on the balance sheet formats

(1) *Called up share capital not paid*
(Formats 1 and 2, items A and C.II.5.)
This item may be shown in either of the two positions given in Formats 1 and 2.

(2) *Concessions, patents, licences, trade marks and similar rights and assets*
(Formats 1 and 2, item B.I.2.)
Amounts in respect of assets shall only be included in a company's balance sheet under this item if either—
(a) the assets were acquired for valuable consideration and are not required to be shown under goodwill, or
(b) the assets in question were created by the company itself.

(3) *Goodwill*
(Formats 1 and 2, item B.I.3.)
Amounts representing goodwill shall only be included to the extent that the goodwill was acquired for valuable consideration.

(4) *Own shares*
(Formats 1 and 2, items B.III.7 and C.III.2.)
The nominal value of the shares held shall be shown separately.

(5) *Debtors*
(Formats 1 and 2, items C.II.1 to 6.)
The amount falling due after more than one year shall be shown separately for each item included under debtors.

(6) *Prepayments and accrued income*
(Formats 1 and 2, items C.II.6 and D.)
This item may be shown in either of the two positions given in Formats 1 and 2.

(7) *Debenture loans*
(Format 1, items E.1 and H.1 and Format 2, item C.1.)
The amount of any covertible loans shall be shown separately.

(8) *Payments received on account*
(Format 1, items E.3 and H.3 and Format 2, item C.3.)
Payments received on account of orders shall be shown for each of these items in so far as they are not shown as deductions from stocks.

(9) *Other creditors including taxation and social security*
(Format 1, items E.8 and H.8 and Format 2, item C.8.)
The amount for creditors in respect of taxation and social security shall be shown separately from the amount for other creditors.

(10) *Accruals and deferred income*
(Format 1, items E.9, H.9 and J and Format 2, items C.9 and D.)
The two positions given for this item in Format 1 at E.9 and H.9 are an alternative to the position at J, but if the item is not shown in a position corresponding to that at J it may be shown in either or both of the other two positions (as the case may require).

The two positions given for this item in Format 2 are alternatives.

(11) *Net current assets (liabilities)*
(Format 1, item F.)
In determining the amount to be shown for this item any amounts shown under "prepayments and accrued income" shall be taken into account wherever shown.

(12) *Called up share capital*
(Format 1, item K.1 and Format 2, item A.I.)
The amount of allotted share capital and the amount of called up share capital which has been paid up shall be shown separately.

(13) *Creditors*
(Format 2, items C.1 to 9.)
Amounts falling due within one year and after one year shall be shown separately for each of these items and their aggregate shall be shown separately for all of these items.

Profit and loss account formats

Format 1
(see note (*17*) below)

1. Turnover
2. Cost of sales (*14*)
3. Gross profit or loss
4. Distribution costs (*14*)
5. Administrative expenses (*14*)
6. Other operating income
7. Income from shares in group companies
8. Income from shares in related companies
9. Income from other fixed asset investments (*15*)
10. Other interest receivable and similar income (*15*)
11. Amounts written off investments
12. Interest payable and similar charges (*16*)
13. Tax on profit or loss on ordinary activities
14. Profit or loss on ordinary activities after taxation
15. Extraordinary income
16. Extraordinary charges
17. Extraordinary profit or loss
18. Tax on extraordinary profit or loss
19. Other taxes not shown under the above items
20. Profit or loss for the financial year

Profit and loss account formats

Format 2

1. Turnover
2. Change in stocks of finished goods and in work progress
3. Own work capitalised
4. Other operating income
5. (*a*) Raw materials and consumables
   (*b*) Other external charges
6. Staff costs:
   (*a*) wages and salaries
   (*b*) social security costs
   (*c*) other pension costs
7. (*a*) Depreciation and other amounts written off tangible and intangible fixed assets
   (*b*) Exceptional amounts written off current assets
8. Other operating charges
9. Income from shares in group companies
10. Income from shares in related companies
11. Income from other fixed asset investments (*15*)
12. Other interest receivable and similar income (*15*)
13. Amounts written off investments
14. Interest payable and similar charges (*16*)
15. Tax on profit or loss on ordinary activities
16. Profit or loss on ordinary activities after taxation
17. Extraordinary income
18. Extraordinary charges
19. Extraordinary profit or loss
20. Tax on extraordinary profit or loss
21. Other taxes not shown under the above items
22. Profit or loss for the financial year

Profit and loss account formats

Format 3
(see note (*17*) below)

A. Charges
1. Cost of sales (*14*)
2. Distribution costs (*14*)
3. Administrative expenses (*14*)
4. Amounts written off investments
5. Interest payable and similar charges (*16*)
6. Tax on profit or loss on ordinary activities
7. Profit or loss on ordinary activities after taxation
8. Extraordinary charges
9. Tax on extraordinary profit or loss
10. Other taxes not shown under the above items
11. Profit or loss for the financial year

B. Income
1. Turnover
2. Other operating income
3. Income from shares in group companies
4. Income from shares in related companies
5. Income from other fixed asset investments (*15*)
6. Other interest receivable and similar income (*15*)
7. Profit or loss on ordinary activities after taxation
8. Extraordinary income
9. Profit or loss for the financial year

Profit and loss account formats

Format 4

A. Charges
1. Reduction in stocks of finished goods and in work in progress
2. (*a*) Raw materials and consumables
   (*b*) Other external charges
3. Staff costs:
   (*a*) wages and salaries
   (*b*) social security costs
   (*c*) other pension costs
4. (*a*) Depreciation and other amounts written off tangible and intangible fixed assets
   (*b*) Exceptional amounts written off current assets
5. Other operating charges
6. Amounts written off investments
7. Interest payable and similar charges (*16*)
8. Tax on profit or loss on ordinary activities
9. Profit or loss on ordinary activities after taxation
10. Extraordinary charges
11. Tax on extraordinary profit or loss
12. Other taxes not shown under the above items
13. Profit or loss for the financial year

B. Income
1. Turnover
2. Increase in stocks of finished goods and in work in progress
3. Own work capitalised
4. Other operating income
5. Income from shares in group companies
6. Income from shares in related companies
7. Income from other fixed asset investments (*15*)
8. Other interest receivable and similar income (*15*)
9. Profit or loss on ordinary activities after taxation
10. Extraordinary income
11. Profit or loss for the financial year

Notes on the profit and loss account formats

(14) *Cost of sales: distribution costs: administrative expenses*
(Format 1, items 2, 4 and 5 and Format 3, items A.1, 2 and 3.)

These items shall be stated after taking into account any necessary provisions for depreciation or diminution in value of assets.

(15) *Income from other fixed asset investments: other interest receivable and similar income*
(Format 1, items 9 and 10: Format 2, items 11 and 12: Format 3, items B.5 and 6: Format 4, items B.7 and 8.)

Income and interest derived from group companies shall be shown separately from income and interest derived from other sources.

(16) *Interest payable and similar charges*
(Format 1, item 12: Format 2, item 14: Format 3, item A.5: Format 4, item A.7.)

The amount payable to group companies shall be shown separately.

(17) *Formats 1 and 3*

The amount of any provisions for depreciation and diminution in value of tangible and intangible fixed assets falling to be shown under items 7(*a*) and A.4(*a*) respectively in Formats 2 and 4 shall be disclosed in a note to the accounts in any case where the profit and loss account is prepared by reference to Format 1 or Format 3.

PART II

ACCOUNTING PRINCIPLES AND RULES

SECTION A

ACCOUNTING PRINCIPLES

Preliminary

9. Subject to paragraph 15 below, the amounts to be included in respect of all items shown in a company's accounts shall be determined in accordance with the principles set out in paragraphs 10 to 14 below.

Accounting principles

10. The company shall be presumed to be carrying on business as a going concern.

11. Accounting policies shall be applied consistently from one financial year to the next.

12. The amount of any item shall be determined on a prudent basis, and in particular—

(*a*) only profits realised at the balance sheet date shall be included in the profit and loss account; and

(*b*) all liabilities and losses which have arisen or are likely to arise in respect of the financial year to which the accounts relate or a previous financial year shall be taken into account, including those which only became apparent between the balance sheet date and the date on which it is signed on behalf of the board of directors in pursuance of section 155 of this Act.

13. All income and charges relating to the financial year to which the accounts relate shall be taken into account, without regard to the date of receipt or payment.

14. In determining the aggregate amount of any item the amount of each individual asset or liability that falls to be taken into account shall be determined separately.

Departure from the accounting principles

15. If it appears to the directors of a company that there are special reasons for departing from any of the principles stated above in preparing the company's accounts in respect of any financial year they may do so, but particulars of the departure, the reasons for it and its effect shall be given in a note to the accounts.

SECTION B

HISTORICAL COST ACCOUNTING RULES

Preliminary

16. Subject to section C of this Part of this Schedule, the amounts to be included in respect of all items shown in a company's accounts shall be determined in accordance with the rules set out in paragraphs 17 to 28 below.

Fixed assets

General rules

17. Subject to any provision for depreciation or diminution in value made in accordance with paragraph 18 or 19 below, the amount to be included in respect of any fixed asset shall be its purchase price or production cost.

18. In the case of any fixed asset which has a limited useful economic life, the amount of–

(*a*) its purchase price or production cost; or

(*b*) where it is estimated that any such asset will have a residual value at the end of the period of its useful economic life, its purchase price or production cost less that estimated residual value;

shall be reduced by provisions for depreciation calculated to write off that amount systematically over the period of the asset's useful economic life.

19.–(1) Where a fixed asset investment of a description falling to be included under item B.III of either of the balance sheet formats set out in Part I of this Schedule has diminished in value provisions for diminution in value may be made in respect of it and the amount to be included in respect of it may be reduced accordingly; and any such provisions which are not shown in the profit and loss account shall be disclosed (either separately or in aggregate) in a note to the accounts.

(2) Provisions for diminution in value shall be made in respect of any fixed asset which has diminished in value if the reduction in its value is expected to be permanent (whether its useful economic life is limited or not), and the amount to be included in respect of it shall be reduced accordingly; and any such provisions which are not shown in the profit and loss account shall be disclosed (either separately or in aggregate) in a note to the accounts.

(3) Where the reasons for which any provision was made in accordance with sub-paragraph (1) or (2) above have ceased to apply to any extent, that provision shall be written back to the extent that it is no longer necessary; and any amounts written back in accordance with this sub-paragraph which are not shown in the profit and loss account shall be disclosed (either separately or in aggregate) in a note to the accounts.

Rules for determining particular fixed asset items

20.–(1) Notwithstanding that an item in respect of "development costs" is included under "fixed assets" in the balance sheet formats set out in Part I of this Schedule, an amount may only be included in a company's balance sheet in respect of development costs in special circumstances.

(2) If any amount is included in a company's balance sheet in respect of development costs the following information shall be given in a note to the accounts–

(*a*) the period over which the amount of those costs originally capitalised is being or is to be written off; and

(*b*) the reasons for capitalising the development costs in question.

21.–(1) The application of paragraphs 17 to 19 above in relation to goodwill (in any case where goodwill is treated as an asset) is subject to the following provisions of this paragraph.

(2) Subject to sub-paragraph (3) below, the amount of the consideration for any goodwill acquired by a company shall be reduced by provisions for depreciation calculated to write off that amount systematically over a period chosen by the directors of the company.

(3) The period chosen shall not exceed the useful economic life of the goodwill in question.

(4) In any case where any goodwill acquired by a company is shown or included as an asset in a company's balance sheet the period chosen for writing off the consideration for that goodwill and the reasons for choosing that period shall be disclosed in a note to the accounts.

Current assets

22. Subject to paragraph 23 below, the amount to be included in respect of any current asset shall be its purchase price or production cost.

23.–(1) If the net realisable value of any current asset is lower than its purchase price or production cost the amount to be included in respect of that asset shall be the net realisable value.

(2) Where the reasons for which any provision for diminution in value was made in accordance with sub-paragraph (1) above have ceased to apply to any extent, that provision shall be written back to the extent that it is no longer necessary.

Miscellaneous and supplementary provisions

Excess of money owed over value received as an asset item

24.–(1) Where the amount repayable on any debt owed by a company is greater than the value of the consideration received in the transaction giving rise to the debt, the amount of the difference may be treated as an asset.

(2) Where any such amount is so treated–

(*a*) it shall be written off by reasonable amounts each year and must be completely written off before repayment of the debt; and

(*b*) if the current amount is not shown as a separate item in the company's balance sheet it must be disclosed in a note to the accounts.

Assets included at a fixed amount

25.–(1) Subject to sub-paragraph (2) below, assets which fall to be included–

(*a*) amongst the fixed assets of a company under the item "tangible assets"; or

(*b*) amongst the current assets of a company under the item "raw materials and consumables";

may be included at a fixed quantity and value.

(2) Sub-paragraph (1) above applies to assets of a kind which are constantly being replaced, where–

(*a*) their overall value is not material to assessing the company's state of affairs; and

(*b*) their quantity, value and composition are not subject to material variation.

Determination of purchase price or production cost

26.–(1) The purchase price of an asset shall be determined by adding to the actual price paid any expenses incidental to its acquisition.

(2) The production cost of an asset shall be determined by adding to the purchase price of the raw materials and consumables used the amount of the costs incurred by the company which are directly attributable to the production of that asset.

(3) In addition, there may be included in the production cost of an asset–

(*a*) a reasonable proportion of the costs incurred by the company which are only indirectly attributable to the production of that asset, but only to the extent that they relate to the period of production; and

(*b*) interest on capital borrowed to finance the production of that asset, to the extent that it accrues in respect of the period of production;

provided, however, in a case within paragraph (*b*) above, that the inclusion of the interest in determining the cost of that asset and the amount of interest so included is disclosed in a note to the accounts.

(4) In the case of current assets distribution costs may not be included in production costs.

27.–(1) Subject to the qualification mentioned below, the purchase price or production cost of–

(*a*) any assets which fall to be included under any item shown in a company's balance sheet under the general item "stocks"; and

(*b*) any assets which are fungible assets (including investments);

may be determined by the application of any of the methods mentioned in sub-paragraph (2) below in relation to any such assets of the same class.

The method chosen must be one which appears to the directors to be appropriate in the circumstances of the company.

(2) Those methods are–

(*a*) the method known as "first in, first out" (FIFO);

(*b*) the method known as "last in, first out" (LIFO);

(*c*) a weighted average price; and

(*d*) any other method similar to any of the methods mentioned above.

(3) Where in the case of any company–

(*a*) the purchase price or production cost of assets falling to be included under any item shown in the company's balance sheet has been determined by the application of any method permitted by this paragraph; and

(*b*) the amount shown in respect of that item differs materially from the relevant alternative amount given below in this paragraph;

the amount of that difference shall be disclosed in a note to the accounts.

(4) Subject to sub-paragraph (5) below, for the purposes of sub-paragraph (3)(*b*) above the relevant alternative amount, in relation to any item shown in a company's balance sheet, is the amount which would have been shown in respect of that item if assets of any class included under that item at an amount determined by any method permitted by this paragraph had instead been included at their replacement cost as at the balance sheet date.

(5) The relevant alternative amount may be determined by reference to the most recent actual purchase price or production cost before the balance sheet date of assets of any class included under the item in question instead of by reference to their replacement cost as at that date, but only if the former appears to the directors of the company to constitute the more appropriate standard of comparison in the case of assets of that class.

(6) For the purposes of this paragraph, assets of any description shall be regarded as fungible if assets of that description are substantially indistinguishable one from another.

Substitution of original stated amount where price or cost unknown

28. Where there is no record of the purchase price or production cost of any asset of a company or of any price, expenses or costs relevant for determining its purchase price or production cost in accordance with paragraph 26 above, or any such record cannot be obtained without unreasonable expense or delay, its purchase price or production cost shall be taken for the purposes of paragraphs 17 to 23 above to be the value ascribed to it in the earliest available record of its value made on or after its acquisition or production by the company.

SECTION C

ALTERNATIVE ACCOUNTING RULES

Preliminary

29.–(1) The rules set out in section B above are referred to below in this Schedule as the historical cost accounting rules.

(2) Those rules, with the omission of paragraphs 16, 21 and 25 to 28, are referred to below in this Part of this Schedule as the depreciation rules; and references below in this Schedule to the historical cost accounting rules do not include the depreciation rules as they apply by virtue of paragraph 32 below.

30. Subject to paragraphs 32 to 34 below, the amounts to be included in respect of assets

of any description mentioned in paragraph 31 below may be determined on any basis so mentioned.

Alternative accounting rules

31.—(1) Intangible fixed assets, other than goodwill, may be included at their current cost.

(2) Tangible fixed assets may be included at a market value determined as at the date of their last valuation or at their current cost.

(3) Investments of any description falling to be included under item B.III of either of the balance sheet formats set out in Part I of this Schedule may be included either—

(*a*) at a market value determined as at the date of their last valuation; or

(*b*) at a value determined on any basis which appears to the directors to be appropriate in the circumstances of the company;

but in the latter case particulars of the method of valuation adopted and of the reasons for adopting it shall be disclosed in a note to the accounts.

(4) Investments of any description falling to be included under item C.III of either of the balance sheet formats set out in Part I of this Schedule may be included at their current cost.

(5) Stocks may be included at their current cost.

Application of the depreciation rules

32.—(1) Where the value of any asset of a company is determined on any basis mentioned in paragraph 31 above, that value shall be or (as the case may require) be the starting point for determining the amount to be included in respect of that asset in the company's accounts, instead of its purchase price or production cost or any value previously so determined for that asset; and the depreciation rules shall apply accordingly in relation to any such asset with the substitution for any reference to its purchase price or production cost of a reference to the value most recently determined for that asset on any basis mentioned in paragraph 31.

(2) The amount of any provision for depreciation required in the case of any fixed asset by paragraph 18 or 19 above as it applies by virtue of sub-paragraph (1) above is referred to below in this paragraph as the adjusted amount, and the amount of any provision which would be required by that paragraph in the case of that asset according to the historical cost accounting rules as the historical cost amount.

(3) Where sub-paragraph (1) above applies in the case of any fixed asset the amount of any provision for depreciation in respect of that asset—

(*a*) included in any item shown in the profit and loss account in respect of amounts written off assets of the description in question; or

(*b*) taken into account in stating any item so shown which is required by note (*14*) of the notes on the profit and loss account formats set out in Part I of this Schedule to be stated after taking into account any necessary provisions for depreciation or diminution in value of assets included under it;

may be the historical cost amount instead of the adjusted amount, provided that the amount of any difference between the two is shown separately in the profit and loss account or in a note to the accounts.

Additional information to be provided in case of departure from historical cost accounting rules

33.—(1) This paragraph applies where the amounts to be included in respect of assets covered by any items shown in a company's accounts have been determined on any basis mentioned in paragraph 31 above.

(2) The items affected and the basis of valuation adopted in determining the amounts of the assets in question in the case of each such item shall be disclosed in a note to the accounts.

(3) In the case of each balance sheet item affected (except stocks) either—

(*a*) the comparable amounts determined according to the historical cost accounting rules; or

(*b*) the differences between those amounts and the corresponding amounts actually shown in the balance sheet in respect of that item;

shall be shown separately in the balance sheet or in a note to the accounts.

(4) In sub-paragraph (3) above, references in relation to any item to the comparable amounts determined as there mentioned are references to—

(*a*) the aggregate amount which would be required to be shown in respect of that item if the amounts to be included in respect of all the assets covered by that item were determined according to the historical cost accounting rules; and

(*b*) the aggregate amount of the cumulative provisions for depreciation or diminution in value which would be permitted or required in determining those amounts according to those rules.

Revaluation reserve

34.—(1) With respect to any determination of the value of an asset of a company on any basis mentioned in paragraph 31 above, the amount of any profit or loss arising from that determination (after allowing, where appropriate, for any provisions for depreciation or diminution in value made otherwise than by reference to the value so determined and any adjustments of any such provisions made in the light of that determination) shall be credited or (as the case may be) debited to a separate reserve ("the revaluation reserve").

(2) Sub-paragraph (1) above applies in relation to any determination of the value of an asset of a company which takes place before the appointed day as it applies to any such determination taking place on or after that day.

(3) The amount of the revaluation reserve shall be shown in the company's balance sheet under a separate sub-heading in the position given for the item "revaluation reserve" in Format 1 or 2 of the balance sheet formats set out in Part I of this Schedule, but need not be shown under that name.

(4) The revaluation reserve shall be reduced to the extent that the amounts standing to the credit of the reserve are in the opinion of the directors of the company no longer necessary for the purpose of the accounting policies adopted by the company; but an amount may only be transferred from the reserve to the profit and loss account if either—

(*a*) the amount in question was previously charged to that account; or

(*b*) it represents realised profit.

(5) The treatment for taxation purposes of amounts credited or debited to the revaluation reserve shall be disclosed in a note to the accounts.

PART III

NOTES TO THE ACCOUNTS

Preliminary

35. Any information required in the case of any company by the following provisions of this Part of this Schedule shall (if not given in the company's accounts) be given by way of a note to those accounts.

Disclosure of accounting policies

36. The accounting policies adopted by the company in determining the amounts to be included in respect of items shown in the balance sheet and in determining the profit or loss of the company shall be stated (including such policies with respect to the depreciation and diminution in value of assets).

Information supplementing the balance sheet

37. Paragraphs 38 to 51 below require information which either supplements the information given with respect to any particular items shown in the balance sheet or is otherwise relevant to assessing the company's state of affairs in the light of the information so given.

Share capital and debentures

38.—(1) The following information shall be given with respect to the company's share capital—

(*a*) the authorised share capital; and

(*b*) where shares of more than one class have been allotted, the number and aggregate nominal value of shares of each class allotted.

(2) In the case of any part of the allotted share capital that consists of redeemable shares, the following information shall be given–

(*a*) the earliest and latest dates on which the company has power to redeem those shares;

(*b*) whether those shares must be redeemed in any event or are liable to be redeemed at the option of the company; and

(*c*) whether any (and, if so, what) premium is payable on redemption.

39. If the company has allotted any shares during the financial year, the following information shall be given–

(*a*) the reason for making the allotment;

(*b*) the classes of shares allotted; and

(*c*) as respects each class of shares, the number allotted, their aggregate nominal value, and the consideration received by the company for the allotment.

40.–(1) With respect to any contingent right to the allotment of shares in the company the following particulars shall be given–

(*a*) the number, description and amount of the shares in relation to which the right is exercisable;

(*b*) the period during which it is exercisable; and

(*c*) the price to be paid for the shares allotted.

(2) In sub-paragraph (1) above "contingent right to the allotment of shares" means any option to subscribe for shares and any other right to require the allotment of shares to any person whether arising on the conversion into shares of securities of any other description or otherwise.

41.–(1) If the company has issued any debentures during the financial year to which the accounts relate, the following information shall be given–

(*a*) the reason for making the issue;

(*b*) the classes of debentures issued; and

(*c*) as respects each class of debentures, the amount issued and the consideration received by the company for the issue.

(2) Particulars of any redeemed debentures which the company has power to reissue shall also be given.

(3) Where any of the company's debentures are held by a nominee of or trustee for the company, the nominal amount of the debentures and the amount at which they are stated in the accounting records kept by the company in accordance with section 12 of the Companies Act 1976 shall be stated.

Fixed assets

42.–(1) In respect of each item which is or would but for paragraph 3(4)(*b*) above be shown under the general item "fixed assets" in the company's balance sheet the following information shall be given–

(*a*) the appropriate amounts in respect of that item as at the date of the beginning of the financial year and as at the balance sheet date respectively;

(*b*) the effect on any amount shown in the balance sheet in respect of that item of–

(i) any revision of the amount in respect of any assets included under that item made during that year on any basis mentioned in paragraph 31 above;

(ii) acquisitions during that year of any assets;

(iii) disposals during that year of any assets; and

(iv) any transfers of assets of the company to and from that item during that year.

(2) The reference in sub-paragraph (1)(*a*) above to the appropriate amounts in respect of any item as at any date there mentioned is a reference to amounts representing the aggregate amounts determined, as at that date, in respect of assets falling to be included under that item either–

(*a*) on the basis of purchase price or production cost (determined in accordance with paragraphs 26 and 27 above); or

(*b*) on any basis mentioned in paragraph 31 above;

(leaving out of account in either case any provisions for depreciation or diminution in value).

(3) In respect of each item within sub-paragraph (1) above–

(*a*) the cumulative amount of provisions for depreciation or diminution in value of assets included under that item as at each date mentioned in sub-paragraph (1)(*a*);

(*b*) the amount of any such provisions made in respect of the financial year;

(*c*) the amount of any adjustments made in respect of any such provisions during that year in consequence of the disposal of any assets; and

(*d*) the amount of any other adjustments made in respect of any such provisions during that year;

shall also be stated.

43. Where any fixed assets of the company (other than listed investments) are included under any item shown in the company's balance sheet at an amount determined on any basis mentioned in paragraph 31 above, the following information shall be given–

(*a*) the years (so far as they are known to the directors) in which the assets were severally valued and the several values; and

(*b*) in the case of assets that have been valued during the financial year, the names of the persons who valued them or particulars of their qualifications for doing so and (whichever is stated) the bases of valuation used by them.

44. In relation to any amount which is or would but for paragraph 3(4)(*b*) above be shown in respect of the item "land and buildings" in the company's balance sheet there shall be stated–

(*a*) how much of that amount is ascribable to land of freehold tenure and how much to land of leasehold tenure; and

(*b*) how much of the amount ascribable to land of leasehold tenure is ascribable to land held on long lease and how much to land held on short lease.

Investments

45.–(1) In respect of the amount of each item which is or would but for paragraph 3(4)(*b*) above be shown in the company's balance sheet under the general item "investments" (whether as fixed assets or as current assets) there shall be stated–

(*a*) how much of that amount is ascribable to listed investments; and

(*b*) how much of any amount so ascribable is ascribable to investments as respects which there has been granted a listing on a recognised stock exchange and how much to other listed investments.

(2) Where the amount of any listed investments is stated for any item in accordance with sub-paragraph (1)(*a*) above, the following amounts shall also be stated–

(*a*) the aggregate market value of those investments where it differs from the amount so stated; and

(*b*) both the market value and the stock exchange value of any investments of which the former value is, for the purposes of the accounts, taken as being higher than the latter.

Reserves and provisions

46.–(1) Where any amount is transferred–

(*a*) to or from any reserves; or

(*b*) to any provisions for liabilities and charges; or

(*c*) from any provision for liabilities and charges otherwise than for the purpose for which the provision was established;

and the reserves or provisions are or would but for paragraph 3(4)(*b*) above be shown as separate items in the company's balance sheet, the information mentioned in sub-paragraph (2) below shall be given in respect of the aggregate of reserves or provisions included in the same item.

(2) That information is—

(*a*) the amount of the reserves or provisions as at the date of the beginning of the financial year and as at the balance sheet date respectively;

(*b*) any amounts transferred to or from the reserves or provisions during that year; and

(*c*) the source and application respectively of any amounts so transferred.

(3) Particulars shall be given of each provision included in the item "other provisions" in the company's balance sheet in any case where the amount of that provision is material.

Provision for taxation

47. The amount of any provisions for taxation other than deferred taxation shall be stated.

Details of indebtedness

48.—(1) In respect of each item shown under "creditors" in the company's balance sheet there shall be stated—

(*a*) the aggregate amount of any debts included under that item which are payable or repayable otherwise than by instalments and fall due for payment or repayment after the end of the period of five years beginning with the day next following the end of the financial year; and

(*b*) the aggregate amount of any debts so included which are payable or repayable by instalments any of which fall due for payment after the end of that period;

and in the case of debts within paragraph (*b*) above the aggregate amount of instalments falling due after the end of that period shall also be disclosed for each such item.

(2) Subject to sub-paragraph (3) below, in relation to each debt falling to be taken into account under sub-paragraph (1) above, the terms of payment or repayment and the rate of any interest payable on the debt shall be stated.

(3) If the number of debts is such that, in the opinion of the directors, compliance with sub-paragraph (2) above would result in a statement of excessive length, it shall be sufficient to give a general indication of the terms of payment or repayment and the rates of any interest payable on the debts.

(4) In respect of each item shown under "creditors" in the company's balance sheet there shall be stated—

(*a*) the aggregate amount of any debts included under that item in respect of which any security has been given; and

(*b*) an indication of the nature of the securities so given.

(5) References above in this paragraph to an item shown under "creditors" in the company's balance sheet include references, where amounts falling due to creditors within one year and after more than one year are distinguished in the balance sheet—

(*a*) in a case within sub-paragraph (1) above, to an item shown under the latter of those categories; and

(*b*) in a case within sub-paragraph (4) above, to an item shown under either of those categories;

and references to items shown under "creditors" include references to items which would but for paragraph 3(4)(*b*) above be shown under that heading.

49. If any fixed cumulative dividends on the company's shares are in arrear, there shall be stated—

(*a*) the amount of the arrears; and

(*b*) the period for which the dividends or, if there is more than one class, each class of them are in arrear.

Guarantees and other financial commitments

50.–(1) Particulars shall be given of any charge on the assets of the company to secure the liabilities of any other person, including, where practicable, the amount secured.

(2) The following information shall be given with respect to any other contingent liability not provided for–

(*a*) the amount or estimated amount of that liability;

(*b*) its legal nature; and

(*c*) whether any valuable security has been provided by the company in connection with that liability and if so, what.

(3) There shall be stated, where practicable–

(*a*) the aggregate amount or estimated amount of contracts for capital expenditure, so far as not provided for; and

(*b*) the aggregate amount or estimated amount of capital expenditure authorised by the directors which has not been contracted for.

(4) Particulars shall be given of–

(*a*) any pension commitments included under any provision shown in the company's balance sheet; and

(*b*) any such commitments for which no provision has been made;

and where any such commitment relates wholly or partly to pensions payable to past directors of the company separate particulars shall be given of that commitment so far as it relates to such pensions.

(5) Particulars shall also be given of any other financial commitments which–

(*a*) have not been provided for; and

(*b*) are relevant to assessing the company's state of affairs.

(6) Commitments within any of the preceding sub-paragraphs undertaken on behalf of or for the benefit of–

(*a*) any holding company or fellow subsidiary of the company; or

(*b*) any subsidiary of the company;

shall be stated separately from the other commitments within that sub-paragraph (and commitments within paragraph (*a*) above shall also be stated separately from those within paragraph (*b*) above).

Miscellaneous matters

51.–(1) Particulars shall be given of any case where the purchase price or production cost of any asset is for the first time determined under paragraph 28 above.

(2) Where any outstanding loans made under the authority of section 42(6)(*b*) or (*c*) or 43 of the Companies Act 1981 are included under any item shown in the company's balance sheet, the aggregate amount of those loans shall be disclosed for each item in question.

(3) The aggregate amount which is recommended for distribution by way of dividend shall be stated.

Information supplementing the profit and loss account

52. Paragraphs 53 to 57 below require information which either supplements the information given with respect to any particular items shown in the profit and loss account or otherwise provides particulars of income or expenditure of the company or of circumstances affecting the items shown in the profit and loss account.

Separate statement of certain items of income and expenditure

53.–(1) Subject to the following provisions of this paragraph, each of the amounts mentioned below shall be stated.

(2) The amount of the interest on or any similar charges in respect of–

(*a*) bank loans and overdrafts, and loans made to the company (other than bank loans and overdrafts) which–

(i) are repayable otherwise than by instalments and fall due for repayment before the end of the period of five years beginning with the day next following the end of the financial year; or

(ii) are repayable by instalments the last of which falls due for payment before the end of that period; and

(*b*) loans of any other kind made to the company.

This sub-paragraph does not apply to interest or charges on loans to the company from group companies, but, with that exception, it applies to interest or charges on all loans, whether made on the security of debentures or not.

(3) The amounts respectively set aside for redemption of share capital and for redemption of loans.

(4) The amount of income from listed investments.

(5) The amount of rents from land (after deduction of ground rents, rates and other outgoings).

This amount need only be stated if a substantial part of the company's revenue for the financial year consists of rents from land.

(6) The amount charged to revenue in respect of sums payable in respect of the hire of plant and machinery.

(7) The amount of the remuneration of the auditors (taking "remuneration", for the purposes of this sub-paragraph, as including any sums paid by the company in respect of the auditors' expenses).

Particulars of tax

54.–(1) The basis on which the charge for United Kingdom corporation tax and United Kingdom income tax is computed shall be stated.

(2) Particulars shall be given of any special circumstances which affect liability in respect of taxation of profits, income or capital gains for the financial year or liability in respect of taxation of profits, income or capital gains for succeeding financial years.

(3) The following amounts shall be stated–

(*a*) the amount of the charge for United Kingdom corporation tax;

(*b*) if that amount would have been greater but for relief from double taxation, the amount which it would have been but for such relief;

(*c*) the amount of the charge for United Kingdom income tax; and

(*d*) the amount of the charge for taxation imposed outside the United Kingdom of profits, income and (so far as charged to revenue) capital gains.

These amounts shall be stated separately in respect of each of the amounts which is or would but for paragraph 3(4)(*b*) above be shown under the following items in the profit and loss account, that is to say "tax on profit or loss on ordinary activities" and "tax on extraordinary profit or loss".

Particulars of turnover

55.–(1) If in the course of the financial year the company has carried on business of two or more classes that, in the opinion of the directors, differ substantially from each other, there shall be stated in respect of each class (describing it)–

(*a*) the amount of the turnover attributable to that class; and

(*b*) the amount of the profit or loss of the company before taxation which is in the opinion of the directors attributable to that class.

(2) If in the course of the financial year the company has supplied markets that, in the opinion of the directors, differ substantially from each other, the amount of the turnover attributable to each such market shall also be stated.

In this paragraph "market" means a market delimited by geographical bounds.

(3) In analysing for the purposes of this paragraph the source (in terms of business or in terms of market) of turnover or (as the case may be) of profit or loss, the directors of the company shall have regard to the manner in which the company's activities are organised.

(4) For the purposes of this paragraph—

(*a*) classes of business which, in the opinion of the directors, do not differ substantially from each other shall be treated as one class; and

(*b*) markets which, in the opinion of the directors, do not differ substantially from each other shall be treated as one market;

and any amounts properly attributable to one class of business or (as the case may be) to one market which are not material may be included in the amount stated in respect of another.

(5) Where in the opinion of the directors the disclosure of any information required by this paragraph would be seriously prejudicial to the interests of the company, that information need not be disclosed, but the fact that any such information has not been disclosed must be stated.

Particulars of staff

56.—(1) The following information shall be given with respect to the employees of the company—

(*a*) the average number of persons employed by the company in the financial year; and

(*b*) the average number of persons so employed within each category of persons employed by the company.

(2) The average number required by sub-paragraph (1)(*a*) or (*b*) above shall be determined by dividing the relevant annual number by the number of weeks in the financial year.

(3) The relevant annual number shall be determined by ascertaining for each week in the financial year—

(*a*) for the purposes of sub-paragraph (1)(*a*) above, the number of persons employed under contracts of service by the company in that week (whether throughout the week or not);

(*b*) for the purposes of sub-paragraph (1)(*b*) above, the number of persons in the category in question of persons so employed;

and, in either case, adding together all the weekly numbers.

(4) In respect of all persons employed by the company during the financial year who are taken into account in determining the relevant annual number for the purposes of sub-paragraph (1)(*a*) above there shall also be stated the aggregate amounts respectively of—

(*a*) wages and salaries paid or payable in respect of that year to those persons;

(*b*) social security costs incurred by the company on their behalf; and

(*c*) other pension costs so incurred;

save in so far as those amounts or any of them are stated in the profit and loss account.

(5) The categories of persons employed by the company by reference to which the number required to be disclosed by sub-paragraph (1)(*b*) above is to be determined shall be such as the directors may select, having regard to the manner in which the company's activities are organised.

Miscellaneous matters

57.—(1) Where any amount relating to any preceding financial year is included in any item in the profit and loss account, the effect shall be stated.

(2) Particulars shall be given of any extraordinary income or charges arising in the financial year.

(3) The effect shall be stated of any transactions that are exceptional by virtue of size or incidence though they fall within the ordinary activities of the company.

General

58.—(1) Where sums originally denominated in foreign currencies have been brought into account under any items shown in the balance sheet or profit and loss account, the basis on which those sums have been translated into sterling shall be stated.

(2) Subject to sub-paragraph (3) below, in respect of every item stated in a note to the accounts the corresponding amount for the financial year immediately preceding that to which the accounts relate shall also be stated and where the corresponding amount is not comparable, it shall be adjusted and particulars of the adjustment and the reasons for it shall be given.

(3) Sub-paragraph (2) above does not apply in relation to any amounts stated by virtue of any of the following provisions, that is to say—

(*a*) sections 3 and 4 of the Companies Act 1967 (statement in notes to a company's accounts of proportion of share capital of subsidiaries or certain other bodies corporate held by that company, etc.);

(*b*) sections 54 and 56 of the Companies Act 1980 (particulars of certain loans etc. to directors and others to be disclosed in notes to a company's accounts); and

(*c*) paragraphs 42 and 46 above.

PART IV

SPECIAL PROVISIONS WHERE THE COMPANY IS A HOLDING OR SUBSIDIARY COMPANY

[Not provided in this Appendix]

PART V

SPECIAL PROVISIONS WHERE THE COMPANY IS AN INVESTMENT COMPANY

[Not provided in this Appendix]

PART VI

INTERPRETATION OF SCHEDULE

Assets: fixed or current

75. For the purposes of this Schedule, assets of a company shall be taken to be fixed assets if they are intended for use on a continuing basis in the company's activities, and any assets not intended for such use shall be taken to be current assets.

Balance sheet date

76. For the purposes of this Schedule, "balance sheet date", in relation to a balance sheet, means the date as at which the balance sheet was prepared.

Called-up share capital

77. For the purposes of this Schedule, "called-up share capital" has the meaning given by section 87(1) of the Companies Act 1980.

Capitalisation

78. References in this Schedule to capitalising any work or costs are references to treating that work or those costs as a fixed asset.

Fellow subsidiary

79. For the purposes of this Schedule, a body corporate shall be treated as a fellow subsidiary of another body corporate if both are subsidiaries of the same body corporate but neither is the other's.

Group companies

80. For the purposes of this Schedule, "group company", in relation to any company, means any body corporate which is that company's subsidiary or holding company, or a subsidiary of that company's holding company.

Historical cost accounting rules

81. References in this Schedule to the historical cost accounting rules shall be read in accordance with paragraph 29 above.

Leases

82. In this Schedule–

"long lease" means a lease in the case of which the portion of the term for which it was granted remaining unexpired at the end of the financial year is not less than fifty years;

"short lease" means a lease which is not a long lease; and

"lease" includes an agreement for a lease.

Listed investments

83. In this Schedule, "listed investment" means an investment as respects which there has been granted a listing on a recognised stock exchange, or on any stock exchange of repute (other than a recognised stock exchange) outside Great Britain.

Loans

84. For the purposes of this Schedule, a loan shall be treated as falling due for repayment, and an instalment of a loan shall be treated as falling due for payment, on the earliest date on which the lender could require repayment or (as the case may be) payment, if he exercised all options and rights available to him.

Materiality

85. Amounts which in the particular context of any provision of this Schedule are not material may be disregarded for the purposes of that provision.

Notes to the accounts

86. Notes to a company's accounts may be contained in the accounts or in a separate document annexed to the accounts.

Provisions

87.–(1) References in this Schedule to provisions for depreciation or diminution in value of assets are references to any amount written off by way of providing for depreciation or diminution in value of assets.

(2) Any reference in the profit and loss account formats set out in Part I of this Schedule to the depreciation of, or amounts written off, assets of any description is a reference to any provision for depreciation or diminution in value of assets of that description.

88. References in this Schedule to provisions for liabilities or charges are references to any amount retained as reasonably necessary for the purpose of providing for any liability or loss which is either likely to be incurred, or certain to be incurred but uncertain as to amount or as to the date on which it will arise.

Purchase price

89. References in this Schedule (however expressed) to the purchase price of any asset of a company or of any raw materials or consumables used in the production of any such asset shall be read as including references to any consideration (whether in cash or otherwise) given by the company in respect of that asset or in respect of those materials or consumables (as the case may require).

Realised profits

90. Without prejudice to–

(*a*) the construction of any other expression (where appropriate) by reference to accepted accounting principles or practice; or

(*b*) any specific provision for the treatment of profits of any description as realised;

it is hereby declared for the avoidance of doubt that references in this Schedule to realised profits, in relation to a company's accounts, are references to such profits of the company as fall to be treated as realised profits for the purposes of those accounts in accordance with principles generally accepted with respect to the determination for accounting purposes of realised profits at the time when those accounts are prepared.

Related companies

91.–(1) For the purposes of this Schedule, "related company", in relation to any company, means any body corporate (other than one which is a group company in relation to that company) in which that company holds on a long-term basis a qualifying capital interest for the purpose of securing a contribution to that company's own activities by the exercise of any control or influence arising from that interest.

(2) In this paragraph "qualifying capital interest" means, in relation to any body corporate, an interest in shares comprised in the equity share capital of that body corporate of a class carrying rights to vote in all circumstances at general meetings of that body corporate, and "equity share capital" has the meaning given by section 154(5) of this Act.

(3) Where–

(*a*) a company holds a qualifying capital interest in a body corporate; and

(*b*) the nominal value of any relevant shares in that body corporate held by that company is equal to twenty per cent or more of the nominal value of all relevant shares in that body corporate;

it shall be presumed to hold that interest on the basis and for the purpose mentioned in sub-paragraph (1) above, unless the contrary is shown.

In this sub-paragraph "relevant shares" means, in relation to any body corporate, any such shares in that body corporate as are mentioned in sub-paragraph (2) above.

Scottish land tenure

92. In the application of this Schedule to Scotland, "land of freehold tenure" means land in respect of which the company is the proprietor of the *dominium utile* or, in the case of land not held on feudal tenure, is the owner; "land of leasehold tenure" means land of which the company is the tenant under a lease; and the reference to ground-rents, rates and other outgoings includes a reference to feu-duty and ground annual.

Staff costs

93. In this Schedule–

"social security costs" means any contribution by the company to any state social security or pension scheme, fund or arrangement; and

"pension costs" includes any other contributions by the company for the purposes of any pension scheme established for the purpose of providing pensions for persons employed by the company, any sums set aside for that purpose and any amounts paid by the company in respect of pensions without first being so set aside;

and any amount stated in respect of either of the above items or in respect of the item "wages and salaries" in the company's profit and loss account shall be determined by reference to payments made or costs incurred in respect of all persons employed by the company during the financial year who are taken into account in determining the relevant annual number for the purposes of paragraph 56(1)(*a*) above.

Turnover

94. For the purposes of this Schedule "turnover", in relation to any company, means the amounts derived from the provision of goods and services falling within the company's ordinary activities, after deduction of–

(*a*) trade discounts;

(*b*) value added tax; and

(*c*) any other taxes based on the amounts so derived.

Wholly owned subsidiaries

95. In this Schedule, "wholly owned subsidiary" has the same meaning as it has for the purposes of section 150 of this Act.

Appendix D

Preparation of group accounts

An introduction to group accounts (consolidated accounts) was provided in section 8.3. The purpose of this appendix is to explain certain fundamentals in the preparation of group accounts, commonly termed 'consolidation'.

An appendix of this length cannot be expected to provide a comprehensive coverage of all the intricacies of group accounts; readers who wish to go further should consult the material given in reference note 5 of Chapter 8. Moreover, although some conventions in the consolidation of accounts are well established there are other aspects which are subject to varying degrees of controversy; serious discussion of the issues cannot be attempted here. As far as possible the most common practice will be adopted (which is not necessarily the 'best'), but where there are different views and practices some indication of their existence will be given.

Throughout consolidation however, the one basic guideline suggested in Chapter 8 remains helpful: eliminate those amounts in the separate company summaries which arise from inter-company transactions, and total the results. That guideline sometimes has to be qualified, but it holds broadly true.

The selected issues, with examples, will now be considered in turn; the emphasis throughout will, for simplicity, be on the balance sheet.

1. Pre-acquisition profits

When a company acquires a controlling interest in a subsidiary the latter will normally have reserves, made up of retained profits, revaluation reserves, etc. built up before the purchase (unless, of course, the subsidiary is set up as a newly established company). If the reserves were added to the parent's on consolidation, there would be an instant increase in the group's reserves available for dividend. This is usually considered undesirable, so these *pre-acquisition profits* are eliminated on consolidation.

The elimination is achieved for consolidation purposes by offsetting the parent's interests in the subsidiary's capital plus reserves at acquisition against the cost at which the parent acquired its shares in the subsidiary. The difference gives goodwill for the group balance sheet if, as is most commonly the case, the cost exceeds the relevant amount of the subsidiary's capital plus reserves.

An example is provided in Fig. D1, where *A* Ltd acquired for £55,000 all the share capital of *B* Ltd, when the latter company had capital and reserves totalling £49,000 (£40,000 + £9,000). Clearly *A* Ltd paid £6,000 more than the £49,000 'book value' of the subsidiary, and that £6,000 represents goodwill which can appear as an asset to balance the group's balance sheet when the inter-company 'shareholding' elements are eliminated.

Figure D1 gives calculations for the group balance sheet using a double-entry worksheet approach. This shows what really goes on when consolidation occurs in practice, and the method can be expanded to deal with very complex consolidations. But for dealing with less difficult problems which the banking student is likely to meet, a simpler approach will be explained later.

In the worksheet the first two double columns show the original balance sheets of *A* Ltd and *B* Ltd. In the third double column the investment of £55,000 in *A*'s books is set against the ownership claims totalling £49,000 in *B*'s balance sheet, leaving only the difference of £6,000 goodwill to go forward into the group balance sheet.

Fig. D1 Goodwill.

A Ltd acquired all shares of *B* Ltd on 31 Dec. 19–0. No dividends were proposed or paid in the relevant periods.

£000s throughout

Balance sheets at 31 Dec. 19–1

	A Ltd	*B* Ltd		*A* Ltd	*B* Ltd
Capital (£1 shares)	100	40	Assets	145	90
Reserves at 31 Dec. 19–0	30	9	40,000 shares in *B*, at cost	55	
Profit 19–1	10	12			
Liabilities	60	29			
	200	90		200	90

Double-entry worksheet

	A Ltd		*B* Ltd		Elimination		Group balance sheet	
	Dr	Cr	Dr	Cr	Dr	Cr	Dr	Cr
Share capital		100		40	40			100
Reserves		30		9	9			} 52
Profit 19–1		10		12				
Liabilities		60		29				89
Assets	145		90				235	
Shares in *B*	55					55		
Goodwill					6		6	
	200	200	90	90	55	55	241	241

***A* Ltd and subsidiary**

Group balance sheet at 31 Dec. 19–1

Share capital	100	Sundry assets	235
Reserves	52	Goodwill	6
Liabilities	89		
	241		241

The final double column of the worksheet shows the group balance sheet after the elimination entries have been effected. The amounts are derived by adding the amounts for each item horizontally, setting debits and credits against each other as necessary.

The last section of Fig. D1 sets out the resulting group balance sheet.

What would have happened if the cost of shares acquired in *B* Ltd had been *less* than the company's capital plus reserves? The difference would have been a credit balance, appearing in the group balance sheet as an undistributable or 'capital' reserve. An illustration will be provided in the next subsection.

Shares in subsidiaries are commonly acquired *in exchange* for shares issued by the parent; cost will then be whatever value is assigned to the parent's shares issued. For example, if *B*'s shares had been acquired on 31 December 19–0 in exchange for 44,000 shares of £1 each in *A* Ltd, and each of *A*'s shares had a market price of £1·25, the entries in the books of *A* Ltd at 31 December 19–0 would have been as follows:

	£ Dr	£ Cr
Investment in 40,000 shares in *B* Ltd at cost	55,000	
Issued share capital, 44,000 shares of £1 each		44,000
Share premium (44,000 at 25p)		11,000

Thus, in the balance sheet for *A* Ltd shown earlier, the above £44,000 would be included in the share capital of £100,000 and the £11,000 share premium would form part of *A*'s reserves of £30,000.

When unquoted shares are issued for an acquisition their value will be a matter of judgement, and even for quoted shares the Stock Exchange prices may fluctuate substantially around the time of the acquisition. In any case the past cost of an acquisition will have decreasing relevance as time passes. Consequently the goodwill or capital reserve derived from acquisition cost is more a convenient means of linking the component balance sheets together than a figure of significance for interpretation.

The method demonstrated in Fig. D1 for dealing with the *cost* of an investment in a subsidiary is termed the *acquisition method* in the UK, where it is by far the most common approach to consolidation. A much rarer approach may be adopted when two companies of roughly similar status 'merge' with each other. In that case, instead of using market value for 'cost', the lower par (nominal) value may be adopted – which normally leaves uneliminated reserves of the subsidiary to go into the group balance sheet. These amounts would be regarded as available for dividend distributions, unlike a capital reserve derived under the acquisition method. However, legal complications over the *merger method* in the UK makes its use exceptional, and all subsequent discussion in this appendix will assume adoption of the acquisition method.

2. Minority interests

Figure D2 demonstrates a consolidation involving minority interests, where the parent *C* Ltd owns only a 60 per cent majority of the share capital of *D* Ltd.

At acquisition on 31 December 19–0 the capital plus reserves of the subsidiary totalled £150,000, made up of capital, share premium and retained profits. A dotted line has been put under the third item in *D*'s balance sheet to mark the division between the company's equity at acquisition and the post-acquired profit.

The abbreviated worksheet in the middle section of Fig. D2 concentrates on the ownership interests in the subsidiary. The results could be put into the full double-entry form shown previously in Fig. D1, but for relatively simple problems it is usually quickest to employ the abbreviated calculations alone.

The worksheet shows the division of the capital plus reserves total between the group's majority interest of 60 per cent (£90,000) and the minority of 40 per cent (£60,000). The post-acquisition figures are divided likewise – but the majority's £12,000 must be kept separate because it is to be added to the distributable profit of the group.

The final calculation of the worksheet offsets the cost of £77,000 investment in the subsidiary against the group's £90,000 slice of the subsidiary's equity. This time a capital reserve of £13,000 is produced for the group balance sheet – a notional gain because the book value of equity acquired is greater than its cost of acquisition.

These calculations give figures which are to be substituted for items appearing in the subsidiary's balance sheet. The amounts eliminated in this way are indicated by the letter 'e' in the balance sheet of *D* Ltd. The only items to be eliminated which do not appear in the

Fig. D2 Minority interests.

C Ltd acquired 60,000 £1 shares and £50,000 debenture stock in D Ltd on 31 Dec. 19–0.

£000s throughout

Balance sheets at 31 Dec. 19–1

	C Ltd	D Ltd		C Ltd	D Ltd
Capital (£1 shares)	200	100 e	Fixed assets	180	150
Share premium a/c	20	15 e	Investments in D Ltd, at cost:		
Retained profits at 31 Dec. 19–0	65	35 e	60,000 shares	77 e	–
Profit 19–1	15	20	£50,000 debenture stock	50 e	–
	300	170	Net current assets	93	70
Debenture stock	100	50 e			
	400	220		400	220

e = eliminated (wholly or partially) on consolidation.

Abbreviated worksheet

Interests in D Ltd	Total	Majority interest 60%		Minority interest 40%
		Acquisition	Post-acquisition	
Share capital	100			
Share premium	15			
Retained profits 31 Dec. 19–0	35			
Capital plus reserves at acquisition	150	90	–	60
Post-acquisition profit	20	–	12	8
	170	90	12	68
Less cost		77		
Capital reserve		13		

C Ltd and subsidiary

Group balance sheet at 31 Dec. 19–1

Share capital	200	Fixed assets [180 + 150]	330
Share premium	20	Net current assets [93 + 70]	163
Capital reserve on consolidation	13		
Retained profits [65 + 15 + 12]	92		
	325		
Minority interests in subsidiary	68		
Debenture stock	100		
	493		493

worksheet are the two relating to the £50,000 debenture stock acquired at par by *C* Ltd; they cancel out as internal transactions which have no bearing on the group's external financial position. Nor does the £50,000 debenture stock affect the calculation of capital reserve or goodwill – because it is a loan which does not affect ownership control.

The group balance sheet, shown in the final section of Fig. D2, can now be prepared by totalling amounts which have not been eliminated from the original balance sheets, and by slotting in the results from the worksheet as required. Share capital and share premium are the holding company's alone (as must always be the case). The capital reserve of £13,000 is derived from the worksheet, and retained profits of £9,000 represent amounts from *C* Ltd plus the group's £12,000 share in the post-acquisition profit of the subsidiary (from the worksheet). Minority interests of £68,000 were derived from the worksheet and the £100,000 debenture stock represents all that is left after eliminating the £50,000 stock of *D* Ltd held within the group.

When a subsidiary with preference share capital is involved in a consolidation, those shares can be treated simply as capital which does not affect control or carry a right to a slice of past retained profits (provided preference dividends are not in arrears). Thus, if the preference shares are owned by outsiders, as would usually be the case, the nominal amount of the shares would be added to minority interests. If the preference shares were held by the group, their nominal values (but *without* any corresponding slice of reserves) could be set off against cost in a similar manner to that for ordinary shares.

3. Inter-company transactions

Figure D3 concerns *E* Ltd and its 75 per cent owned subsidiary *F* Ltd. The example deals with three aspects of inter-company transactions not considered so far in this appendix: dividends paid from pre-acquisition profits, unrealized profit on goods transferred within the group, and money in transit at the balance-sheet date.

A dividend received by a parent company from the *pre*-acquisition profits of a subsidiary is effectively a partial disinvestment of the original outlay on acquiring control of the subsidiary. Consequently the £9,000 dividend received by *E* Ltd (75 per cent of the £12,000 paid by *F* Ltd) has been deducted in *E*'s accounts from the cost of investment in the subsidiary. The resulting balance of £127,000 goes into the worksheet – to be set off against the majority's £120,000 slice remaining from the capital and reserves originally acquired. The difference between the two figures yields a goodwill figure of £7,000.

Of course, the £7,000 goodwill could have been calculated by offsetting the original cost of £136,000 against £129,000, representing 75 per cent of the originally acquired capital and reserves of £172,000. The £9,000 dividend transfer between the group could then be cancelled out. So what purpose is served by the usual practice of deducting a dividend paid out of pre-acquisition profits from cost of investment, as shown in Fig. D3? That practice ensures that the £9,000 does get offset, and is not swallowed up in the retained profits on the other side of the parent's balance sheet.

The other ownership interest calculations follow the pattern discussed in the previous example; the results can then be transferred to the group balance sheet. As a consequence these figures can go into the group's retained profits: £162,000 and £33,000 from *E*'s balance sheet, less the group's £6,000 share of *F*'s loss from the worksheet.

The fourth element affecting retained profits in the group balance sheet is the last deduction shown in brackets, for £1,000. This is the profit on goods bought by *F* for £9,000 and sold to *E* for £10,000. The profit is eliminated because the goods are still held within the group – the profit is *unrealized.* Profits are not usually recognized in accounts until they have been realized by sale to outsiders, and in any case inter-company dealings may be susceptible to profit manipulation. Whether the whole amount of unrealized profit, or some slice relating to the majority only, should be eliminated is a matter of controversy and varying practice. But the approach of writing off all unrealized profit, irrespective of the interests involved, is commonplace and has the merit of simplicity in the present context.

When unrealized profit is eliminated it does, of course, require a corresponding reduction in stock values. In the group balance sheet of Fig. D3 the £1,000 has accordingly been deducted in deriving the total for sundry assets.

Finally, for the purposes of consolidation the cheque in transit can be entered into *F*'s balance sheet as if it had been received by the accounting date. The amount due from *E* Ltd is *reduced* by £5,000 and 'other net assets' are *increased* by £5,000. Thus, for the group balance sheet the remaining amounts still outstanding between the companies cancel out, but the £5,000 cheque in transit is added to sundry assets to give the total of £519,000.

Fig. D3 Inter-company transactions.

E Ltd acquired 75,000 £1 shares in *F* Ltd at 31 Dec. 19–0.

F Ltd made a loss in 19–1 and paid a dividend of £12,000 out of pre-acquisition profits.

Included in the current assets of *E* Ltd at 31 Dec. 19–1 were goods purchased from *F* Ltd for £10,000. These goods had cost *F* Ltd £9,000.

Towards the end of Dec. 19–1 *E* Ltd sent a cheque for £5,000 to *F* Ltd in part payment for the goods mentioned above. This amount was recorded in the accounts of *E* Ltd but the cheque was not received by *F* Ltd until Jan. 19–2, when it was duly recorded in that company's books.

£000s throughout

Balance sheets at 31 Dec. 19–1

	E Ltd		*F* Ltd		*E* Ltd	*F* Ltd
Capital (£1 shares)	300		100 e	Investment in *F* Ltd		
Retained profits at				(75,000 shares)		
31 Dec. 19–0	162	72		at cost	136 e	–
Dividend paid 19–1		(12)		Less *E*'s share of		
				19–1 dividend	(9)e	–
			60 e			
Profit (loss) 19–1	33		(8)		127 e	
	495		152	Due from *E* Ltd	–	10 e
Due to *F* Ltd	5 e		–	Other net assets	373	142
	500		152		500	152

e = eliminated (wholly or partially) on consolidation.

Abbreviated worksheet

Interests in *F* Ltd		Total	Majority interest 75%		Minority interest 25%
			Acquisition	Post-acquisition	
Share capital		100			
Pre-acquisition profits	72				
Dividend from pre-acquisition profits	(12)				
		60			
		160	120		40
Post-acquisition loss		(8)		(6)	(2)
		152	120	(6)	38
Less cost			127		
Goodwill			7		

***E* Ltd and subsidiary**

Group balance sheet at 31 Dec. 19–1

Share capital	300	Sundry assets	519
Retained profits	188	[373 + 142 + 5 – 1]	
[162 + 33 – 6 – 1]		Goodwill	7
Minority interests in subsidiary	38		
	526		526

Fig. D4 Sub-subsidiary

G Ltd acquired 150,000 £1 shares in *H* Ltd at 31 Dec. 19–0. *H* Ltd in turn acquired 80,000 £1 shares in *I* Ltd at 31 Dec. 19–1.

£000s throughout

Balance sheets at 31 Dec. 19–2

	G Ltd	*H* Ltd	*I* Ltd		*G* Ltd	*H* Ltd	*I* Ltd
Capital (£1 shares)	400	200 e	100 e	Investment in *H* Ltd (150,000 shares) at cost	234 e	–	–
Retained profits at 31 Dec. 19–0	49	80 e	57 e				
Retained profit 19–1	26	10	13 e	Investment in *I* Ltd (80,000 shares) at cost	–	140 e	–
Retained profit 19–2	33	6	10				
Proposed dividends	22	20	5				
	530	316	185	Other assets	716	376	300
Debentures	300	150	75				
Current liabilities	120	50	40				
	950	516	300		950	516	300

e = eliminated (wholly or partially) on consolidation.

Abbreviated worksheets

Interests in *H* Ltd	Total	Majority interests 75% Acquisition	Majority interests 75% Post-acquisition	Minority interests 25% In capital + reserves	Minority interests 25% Proposed dividend
Share capital	200				
Retained profits 31 Dec. 19–0	80				
Capital plus reserves at acquisition	280	210		70	
Post-acquisition profits [10 + 6]	16		12	4	
Proposed dividend	20		15		5
	316	210	27	74	5
Less cost		234			
Goodwill		24			
H's interest in *I* Ltd (transferred from calculations for *I* Ltd)	12		9	3	

Interests in *I* Ltd	Total	Majority interests 80% Acquisition	Majority interests 80% Post-acquisition	Minority interests 20% In capital + reserves	Minority interests 20% Proposed dividend
Share capital	100				
Retained profits [57 + 13]	70				
Capital plus reserves at acquisition	170	136		34	
Post-acquisition profit 19–2	10		8	2	
Proposed dividend	5		4		1
	185	136	12	36	1
Less cost		140	↓		
Goodwill		4	transferred to calculations for *H* Ltd		

Fig. D4 (cont.)

G Ltd and subsidiaries

Group balance sheet at 31 Dec. 19–2

Share capital		400	Sundry assets [716 + 376 + 300]	1,392
Retained profits:			Goodwill [24 + 4]	28
G [49 + 26 + 33]	108			
H	27			
H in *I*	9			
		144		
		544		
Minority interests in subsidiaries:				
H	74			
H in *I*	3			
I	36			
		113		
Debentures [300 + 150 + 75]		525		
Current liabilities [120 + 50 + 40]		210		
Proposed dividends:				
G Ltd		22		
minority interests [5 + 1]		6		
		1,420		1,420

4. Sub-subsidiary

Figure D4 shows a balance sheet for a 'chain' of three companies in which *G* Ltd owns 75 per cent of *H* Ltd, which in turn owns 80 per cent of *I* Ltd. The subsidiaries are consolidated in turn.

The worksheets in Fig. D4 differ from those shown earlier in two respects. One is in the additional column for proposed dividends to minority shareholders, the other is in the additional section underneath the worksheet for *H* Ltd. These represent the two new aspects to be considered here.

The calculations of the interests in *H* Ltd follow a largely familiar pattern in the upper section of the worksheet – apart from the line relating to *H*'s proposed dividend of £20,000. That dividend clearly arises from post-acquisition earnings, because there are unutilized retained profits for both 19–1 and 19–2. Here, 75 per cent will go to the holding company, *G* Ltd, so £15,000 is added to the post-acquisition column to produce a total of £27,000.

But the 25 per cent relating to the minority shareholders will involve a *current* liability for a cash payment outside the company. Consequently the £5,000 proposed minority dividend has been entered separately in the worksheet.

The line '*H*'s interest in *I* Ltd' starts with a total of £12,000 transferred from the worksheet for *I* Ltd. That worksheet is calculated in the usual way, but so far as the post-acquisition profits of *I* Ltd are concerned they belong to *H* Ltd – which in turn is 75 per cent owned by the group. Thus 75 per cent of the £12,000 has been allocated to the group, and the remaining £3,000 to the 25 per cent minority interest in *H* Ltd.

Totals are then transferred from the worksheet and original balance sheets to the group balance sheet in the usual way. All the items in the individual balance sheet of *G* Ltd go into the group accounts, including the £22,000 proposed dividend payable to the holding company's shareholders. The £6,000 proposed dividends for minorities appear similarly; it would have been legitimate, but less desirable, to have dispensed with the separate columns for minority dividends and to have grouped proposed dividends with other minority interests.

The two amounts for goodwill on acquisition of the two subsidiaries have been added together for the group balance sheet.

In all the examples in this appendix, the calculations of goodwill or capital reserve have related only to the purchased majority interest. For example, there has been no suggestion that because the 75 per cent majority interest in *H* Ltd had a calculated goodwill of £24,000 there is any case for recognizing a corresponding £8,000 for the 25 per cent minority. That is because the market price which applied for the actual purchase of the majority holding cannot be applied to a hypothetical minority transaction.

Some accountants would carry the argument further still, and recognize only the group's proportion of goodwill in a partly owned *sub*-subsidiary. For example, instead of including £4,000 goodwill in the calculations for *I* Ltd, only £3,000, representing *G*'s 75 per cent majority interest in the acquiring company, would be recorded. Thus the minority interest would be £1,000 lower in the group balance sheet. That practice would seem dubious, because on this occasion the minority's interest in the purchased goodwill is not hypothetical – control of *I* Ltd was acquired on behalf of all the shareholders of *H*.

Appendix E

Survey of information for company lending

This appendix provides a selective summary of responses to a survey conducted by the author in 1974 with the co-operation of five banks: the Bank of Ireland, Barclays Bank, the Midland Bank, the National Westminster Bank and the Northern Bank.

Ninety-one questionnaires on information used in company lending were despatched to branch managers (mainly in medium- to large-sized branches) in the UK and Ireland. Eighty-two questionnaires were completed, a response rate of 90 per cent.

A. Timeliness of audited accounts received from company customers *

	Fastest 25%	**Average (median†)**	**Slowest 25%**
Time elapsed between balance-sheet date and audit report	4 months or less	5 months	5½ months or more
Time elapsed between audit report and receipt of accounts by bank	1 month or less	2 months	4 months or more

* These figures were derived from the responses of eighty managers for the set of audited accounts they had most recently received from a company customer.

† *Median* is the middle value of a range of values arranged in order of size.

B. Information examined, however cursorily, in considering company requests for borrowing facilities

	Percentage of managers who, in considering ten requests for borrowing facilities, examined information from the listed sources:		
	in at least one case	in more than half the cases	in all cases
	%	%	%
1. Record of past lending to company	100	98	56
2. Audited balance sheets and profit and loss accounts [For the total of 820 borrowing requests, the number of years accounts examined were: 1 year 2%; 2 years 22%; 3 years 31%; 4 years 28%; more than 4 years 5%. The percentage of companies involved which had been established for less than 4 years was 22%.]	100	98	49

B. Information examined, however cursorily, in considering company requests for borrowing facilities (cont.)

	Percentage of managers who, in considering ten requests for borrowing facilities, examined information from the listed sources:		
	in at least one case	in more than half the cases	in all cases
	%	%	%
3. 'Full' audited profit statements which included cost figures not required by the Companies Acts (e.g. cost of goods sold, bad debts written off, advertising, etc.)	77	45	17
4. Unaudited accounting results for a period subsequent to the last audited accounts	91	16	0
5. Copies of quarterly VAT (value added tax) returns	6	0	0
6. Funds flow statements (statements of source and application of funds)	80	16	5
7. Age analysis of: debtors	73	29	9
creditors	68	28	7
8. Conversations with company auditors, including telephone	79	6	1
9. Professional valuations of company assets	78	6	0
10. Cash budgets	91	26	4
11. Profit forecasts	91	28	11
12. Search of Companies Register at Companies House	51	28	16

C. Responses to borrowing requests

Of the 820 borrowing requests (ten per manager) which were considered in the survey 12 per cent were rejected, 16 per cent were scaled down and 4 per cent were scaled up.

D. Conditions imposed on company borrowers

The following list shows the requirements specified or likely to be specified, as conditions of an advance for those (720) borrowing requests not rejected in C above.

	Percentage of eligible borrowing requests to which requirements were applied
	%
1. Regular* submission of:	
(a) debtors' figures	19
(b) creditors' figures	19
(c) stocks figures	19
(d) sales figures	16
(e) cash budgets	17
(f) balance sheet and profit and loss account	84
2. A bank debenture	34

D. Conditions imposed on company borrowers (cont.)

	Percentage of eligible borrowing requests to which requirements were applied
	%
3. Conditions in cases involving debentures:	
(a) certain loans not to be withdrawn	38
(b) bank debt to be maintained at some specified proportion of current assets	1
[Percentages here relate only to the 246 cases which involved debentures.]	
4. Conditions in cases not involving debentures:	
(a) certain loans not to be withdrawn	12
(b) bank debt to be maintained at some specified proportion of current assets	1
[Percentages here relate only to the 474 cases which did not involve debentures.]	

* Required frequencies for the first four items were usually monthly or quarterly; frequencies for cash budgets, balance sheet and profit and loss accounts were mainly left unstated in questionnaire responses – and were by implication annual.

E. Security

Percentages of total monetary amounts secured and unsecured, for each branch's lending to the accepted borrowing requests considered in D above.

	Average (median) branch percentage
(a) Secured on land and buildings	38
(b) Secured on floating charges	25
(c) Secured on directors' guarantees	11
(d) Secured on other collateral	4
(e) Unsecured	16

[Percentages do not sum to 100 because the middle of each range has been calculated for categories separately. The values of security for many branches exceeded lending.]

F. Estimated uncollectable company lending, as percentage of total company lending

	Average (median) branch	Highest 25% of branches
	%	%
1973	0	0·01 upwards
Average for 5 years to 1973	0	0·1 upwards

When all branch percentages for the 5 years to 1973 were totalled, and divided by the number of branches responding to this question, the result was an average of *0·1 per cent.* That would represent the overall uncollectable company lending percentage *if all branches lent identical amounts* – obviously an arbitrary assumption, but the result is broadly consistent with the disclosed bad debt experience of clearing banks in later years.

G. Financial indicators

Branch managers were asked to give scores for the relative importance, in company lending, of a variety of indicators (largely accounting measures). The indicators were grouped under three headings, and those which obtained the best scores (based on the median score of each indicator) are shown below. The closeness of the scores on many of the other indicators makes full listing inappropriate for present purposes.

1. 'Earnings capacity'
(a) Amount of net profit after tax, plus depreciation;
(b) Amount of net profit after tax;
(c) Amount of net profit before tax and before extraordinary items.
[Measures of profit in relation to balance-sheet figures and to sales, and the company's profit and cash forecasts were given lower scores.]

2. 'Stability'
(a) Size of company, indicated by capital and reserves;
(b) Nature of product/industry.
[Other size measures and diversification of debtors and creditors earned lower median scores. Some managers volunteered 'quality of management' and 'profit retention record'.]

3. 'Financial condition'
(a) Current ratio (ratio of current assets to current liabilities);
(b) Total debt to capital plus reserves.
[Indicators which earned lower median scores included liquid ratio; ratios relating to 'turnover' of debtors, creditors and stocks; funds generated/total debt; working capital/total assets.]

H. Changes in accounting information

Branch managers were asked to give their opinion of the relative importance to a lending banker of the possible changes in accounts listed below, by allocating 100 points among them.

	Average (median) scores
1. 'Inflation accounts' adjusted for general price level changes*	10
2. Accounts disclosing estimated replacement costs of assets*	10
3. Accounts disclosing estimated net realizable values of assets*	11½
4. Inclusion of funds flow statements in annual accounts*	15
5. Shorter delays in the availability of annual accounts	30
6. Fuller disclosure of accounting policies	10
7. Greater standardization of accounting policies	10

* Supplements to annual accounts.

Since the survey some progress has been made by accounting standards on items 2, 4, 6 and 7, and by legislation on item 5.

Index